# INDUSTRIAL FARM ANIMAL PRODUCTION, THE ENVIRONMENT, AND PUBLIC HEALTH

# Industrial Farm Animal Production, the Environment, and Public Health

EDITED BY
## JAMES MERCHANT
## ROBERT MARTIN

JOHNS HOPKINS UNIVERSITY PRESS | *Baltimore*

Johns Hopkins University Press
2715 North Charles Street
Baltimore, Maryland 21218
www.press.jhu.edu

Library of Congress Cataloging-in-Publication Data is available.

A catalog record for this book is available from the British Library.

ISBN 978-1-4214-5040-7 (hardcover)
ISBN 978-1-4214-5041-4 (ebook)

*Special discounts are available for bulk purchases of this book. For more information, please contact Special Sales at specialsales@jh.edu.*

We dedicate this book in memorial to Dr. Steve Wing (1952–2016), whose collaborative community-based research served as an informed voice for the vulnerable and marginalized who suffer the injustice of IFAP pollution. To ensure a continuing presence and focus on environmental injustice, former students, colleagues, and friends funded the annual Environmental Justice Lecture—Inspired by Steve Wing the People's Professor (his research community's academic title) at the UNC Gillings School of Global Public Health.

# CONTENTS

During the forty years I served as a representative and senator in the US Congress, I saw up close the transformation of livestock farming from traditional Iowa crop-livestock farms in the 1970–1980s to a livestock industry dominated by large corporate operations, most from out of state and some foreign owned. Over these years, I spoke with many independent farmers who found they could not compete with the integrators, could no longer raise livestock, and even lost their farms—especially during the farm crisis of the 1980s. As a member of the Senate Committee on Agriculture, Nutrition, and Forestry, I fought to provide support for the independent livestock farmer and preserve independent meat slaughter and processing plants. This proved to be, and continues to be, an uphill battle.

As the chair and longtime member of the Senate Committee on Health, Education, Labor, and Pensions and chair of the Senate Health, Education, Labor, and Pension Appropriations Subcommittee, I became heavily involved in promoting and funding health care and public health programs at the National Institutes of Health (NIH) and the Centers for Disease Control and Prevention (CDC). Because of the historic imbalance in funding between medical care and public health, I sought to promote and strengthen public health programs, especially those at the CDC. Agricultural health and safety was described to me by a CDC director as the "last frontier" in occupational health. To address this need, the National Agricultural Health and Safety Initiative was funded through the National Institute for Occupational Safety and Health supporting intramural research, research grants, and a nationwide network of Agricultural Health and Safety Centers. Other agricultural health and safety research was funded at the NIH and at the US Department of Agriculture. These multiple programs have contributed substantially to our understanding of agriculturally related health effects and injuries, as well as their prevention.

As I met with Iowa farmers over four decades, I saw and heard stories from Iowa farmers who lost fingers in corn pickers, limbs from power takeoffs, and more crippling injuries from tractor rollovers and other farm machinery. This experience helped inform me in authoring the Americans with Disabilities Act that has provided support and assistance to millions of Americans who live with disabilities but are now better able to contribute to society. I have heard of the hardships experienced by livestock farmers unable to compete with livestock corporations or even find an independent meat processing plant. More recently, I have heard from once independent livestock farmers forced to become corporate contract growers after remortgaging their farm to build the required facilities to raise thousands of chickens or pigs.

I have also heard numerous stories from farmers and their family members about living next to large livestock operations. These folks are used to living with farm odors, but the odor from living downwind from an animal feeding operation with thousands of pigs is something different. They describe how they have had to change how they live and how it has affected their health. Some have told me of children with hard to control asthma. Others have told me of bouts of bronchitis, wheezing, and shortness of breath when manure pits are pumped and manure is spread on nearby land. They complain about fish kills and contamination of their well water. Many livestock farmers have taken manufacturing jobs to make ends meet. And others have told me they have tried to sell their rural home but find its value has greatly decreased because of a large livestock operation that moved in next door.

The twelve chapters, written by national experts in each area, document the science that explains how the health of livestock workers, neighbors, and rural community residents has been impacted by industrial farm animal production. The book has been organized by faculty from two of the best schools of public health in the nation, the University of Iowa College of Public Health and the Johns Hopkins Bloomberg School of Public Health. The Johns Hopkins Press is the global leading publisher of public health journals and books. *Industrial Farm Animal Production, the Environment, and Public Health* will be of interest to many, including public and environmental health colleges, land grant universities, farm state agencies and legislators, livestock producers, defense and plaintiff attorneys, and concerned citizens.

Senator Tom Harkin

*Opposition is true friendship.*—WILLIAM BLAKE

The root of this book arose from our collaboration on the Pew Commission on Industrial Farm Animal Production that resulted in its 2008 report, *Putting Meat on the Table: Industrial Farm Animal Production in America*, and from recognition that a great deal of new research had been published since 2008. The report was the work of fifteen commissioners and a dedicated staff with expertise in animal agriculture, public health, animal health, medicine, rural sociology, and public policy who came together for eleven meetings; reviewed thousands of pages of submitted documents; were further informed by eight commissioned technical reports and site visits to cattle, broiler, hog, egg, and dairy industrial farm animal production (IFAP) operations; and benefited from two hearings with the general public. The peer-reviewed final report included chapters on public health, environmental risks, animal welfare, rural America, and the move toward sustainable animal agriculture, with 24 recommendations and 135 secondary recommendations. In the Preface to the report, Executive Director Robert P. Martin cited serious obstacles the Commission experienced in completing its work, stating that industrial agriculture greeted the report "with responses ranging from open hostility to wary cooperation. We found significant influence by the industry at every turn: in academic research, agricultural policy development, government regulation, and enforcement." Martin described an "agro-industrial complex—an alliance of agriculture commodity groups, scientists at academic institutions who are paid by the industry, and their friends on Capitol Hill."

James A. Merchant, MD, DrPH, then dean of the University of Iowa College of Public Health, represented public health on the Commission. He worked closely with an MD academic infectious disease specialist and a DVM academic veterinarian on the Commission's public health chapter and recommendations. He, and colleagues at the University of Iowa, submitted a technical report for the Commission: "Occupational and Community Impacts of Industrial Farm Animal Production." At the time of the Commission's first meeting and public hearing in Des Moines in June 2006, Merchant received a letter from representatives from the Iowa Farm Bureau and all Iowa agricultural commodity associations who purported to be the "Coalition to Support Iowa Farmers," complaining about a College of Public Health center's distribution of a summary publication of the 2002 Iowa State University and University of Iowa report, *Iowa Concentrated Animal Feeding Operation Air Quality Study*, about a faculty member who had been making presentations to community groups about the study, and in closing made a threat regarding the appropriation of the College of Public Health. While clearly intended as intimidation, a letter countering their assertions was sent to all, and Merchant continued his service for the Commission.

## Livestock Industry Pressure on Authors and Their Universities

Academic investigators working in the field of occupational and environmental health are all familiar with the necessity to gain access to workplaces, environmental habitats, and exposed populations. This requires a great deal of preparatory work with employers, often governmental agencies, and a wide variety of organizations and individuals to gain access, cooperation, and participation. While often challenging, independent investigators typically have considerable success in reaching their research goals, with the collection of reliable and valid data and the interpretation and publication of their findings. We, as well as several of the authors of the twelve chapters in this book, have encountered considerable interference with academic freedom as exerted directly by industrial agriculture or its pressure on academic administrators. Ensuring academic freedom, unbiased funding, and unbiased research is critical to a sustainable environment and to protect the public's health.

University of North Carolina (UNC) epidemiologist Steve Wing described pressure he, his university colleagues, and doctoral students (see chapter 7) faced in a 2002 *Environmental Health Perspectives* publication, "Social Responsibility and Research Ethics in Community-Driven Studies of Industrialized Hog Production." The pressure included industry harassment and intimidation of community residents, industry intrusion seeking to identify study subjects and research records, pressure applied to university administrators, and intimidation and litigation threats experienced by him as the principal investigator. Wing, with UNC support, was successful in protecting the identity of study subjects but was required to turn over all documents—including computerized files, statistical tabulations, and study-related correspondence and reports—to the North Carolina Pork Council attorney. Wing responded by documenting these several industry tactics and publishing their science-based results in peer-reviewed journals, concluding that "researchers may choose to walk away from pollution and conflict; community members who live with discrimination, pollution, and conflict have no choice but to accept or to fight injustice." Steve Wing, and his several doctoral students, did not walk away and chose to stand with community residents to fight injustice through science-based research and, ultimately, expert testimony during his terminal illness, in support of federal court litigation (see chapters 3, 4, 7, and 12).

Also in 2002, at the request of then Iowa governor Tom Vilsack, a group of twenty-five University of Iowa (UI) and Iowa State University (ISU) scientists produced a 220-page report, the *Iowa Concentrated Animal Feeding Operations Air Quality Study*. The report responded to five Vilsack administration questions in a consensus executive summary followed by ten chapters, each coauthored jointly by UI and ISU scientists (see chapters 3 and 4). While Governor Vilsack was pleased with the report that guided his administration's policy advocating for local control for siting concentrated animal feeding operations

(CAFOs), industry executives responded by threatening Iowa State administrators and scientists in a meeting to which they were summoned. When an ISU faculty member was later quoted in the *Des Moines Register* as expressing reservations about the report, the UI co-chair, Dean Merchant, called his ISU counterpart, asking, "Did your faculty not all sign off on the Executive Summary?" The ISU co-chair responded, "They did." But then added, "We were taken to the woodshed. It was terrible!" When Dean Merchant and an ISU representative were subsequently asked to testify before a joint General Assembly Agriculture Committee, Merchant defended the report's process and consensus findings and recommendations. Legislator responses were few but did include one distinct threat from a legislator, known to be a pork producer, regarding the appropriation for the UI College of Public Health. The ISU co-chair had been replaced by a then senior associate dean who testified, "Iowa State University has backed away from this report," thus betraying the academic freedom and consensus conclusions of the Iowa State faculty scientists. However, none of the faculty scientists withdrew from the report, which can still be cited (see chapter 3).

Iowa State University alumnus Senator Tom Harkin planned to donate his papers, from ten years in the US House of Representatives and thirty years in the US Senate, to ISU to benefit a new Harkin Institute of Public Policy. The formation of the Institute had been approved by the Iowa Board of Regents (BOR) in 2011. Two executives from the livestock industry served as members of the BOR. Email correspondence from these BOR leaders influenced an initial ISU memorandum of agreement that would have prevented the Harkin Institute from conducting agricultural research. After protest from the Institute's advisory board, ISU President Steven Leath substituted his own restrictions that would have required any Institute agricultural research to be vetted by the ISU Center for Agricultural and Rural Development. Leath was supported in this recommendation by then Iowa governor Terry Branstad. This continuing restriction of the academic freedom of the emerging Harkin Institute ultimately led its advisory board to recommend that the Institute and ISU part ways. In 2013, Harkin and the Institute's advisory board decided to transfer his congressional papers and the Harkin Institute to private Drake University, where it has thrived as The Harkin Institute—Connecting People and Policy.

The Keokuk County Rural Health Study (KCRHS), a $10 million (1990–2013) UI cooperative agreement with the National Institute for Occupational Safety and Health (NIOSH), was a prospective study of health and injury outcomes arising from rural and agricultural exposures experienced by one thousand families over three rounds of research. It resulted in dozens of scholarly publications, multiple spinoff grants with millions more in funding and published research, and many doctoral dissertations, master's theses, and postdoctoral and graduate student research papers. Among research publications arising from the KCRHS was a paper documenting the ease by which swine influenza was transmitted to livestock farmers, veterinarians, and meatpacking plant workers (see chapter 5). While swine flu in humans is usually mild, a novel swine influenza virus (H1N1) arising from a Mexican pork operation resulted in a 2009–2010 pandemic resulting in a World Health Organization estimate of 284,000 deaths. A second area of KCRHS research concerned childhood asthma arising from exposures to CAFO emissions. Two publications documented elevated rates of childhood asthma, especially among children living on farms with nearly all small deep-pit CAFOs but also dose-related asthma among children living within three miles of these CAFOs (see chapters 3 and 4). A third focus of KCRHS research was respiratory disease and impaired lung function associated with CAFO exposures, a focus that was continued through an institutional agreement between the UI and NIOSH that found increased respiratory disease among men who worked in swine and poultry CAFOs (see chapter 3).

During the years livestock industry executives served on the Iowa BOR, two new University of Iowa presidents were in office. Both Presidents Sally Mason and Bruce Harreld were nominated and promoted by industrial agriculture leaders. A new dean, Susan Curry, PhD, was selected to lead the UI College of Public Health when Dean Merchant elected to return to teaching and research after eleven years of service

(2008). UI Professor Kelly Donham had published the first paper (1977) documenting respiratory disease among veterinarians exposed to then small swine CAFOs (see chapter 3). In the 1980s and 1990s, Professor Donham and Dean Merchant collaborated on numerous research studies, publications, conferences, and policy reports concerning adverse health effects arising from CAFO exposures. In 2013, Dr. Donham planned to transition to an emeritus professorship but planned to continue help lead a five-year NIOSH agricultural health and safety training grant he had written and won. While clearly allowed by UI rules and routinely practiced across campus for grant-funded emeritus faculty, even in other departments of the College of Public Health, Donham was not allowed to do so as he lacked the required signoff of his department head and dean. In 2014, Dean Merchant planned to transition to emeritus status, and he too planned to continue his KCRHS research with support from extramural grant funds. His request to do so was also denied. Anticipating this might be the case, Merchant arranged for an extension of the existing KCRHS institutional agreement between the UI and NIOSH to cover all questionnaires, laboratory test results, and biological samples of frozen sera and DNA. In 2016, Merchant was contacted by the NIOSH division director who had expected to receive the biological samples. He included email correspondence, from the responsible UI administrator for all KCRHS data, informing him that several cited studies had already consumed nearly all of the biological samples. Two Freedom of Information Act requests to the office of the UI vice president for research, however, found no evidence of the cited studies and that nearly all (some had been consumed by known earlier studies) of the sera and DNA samples were in fact still in a UI biobank. NIOSH scientists were thereafter only able to publish from the original institutional agreement.

The Iowa Nutrient Research Center (INRC) at Iowa State University received $2 million in appropriation to build a one-of-a-kind water quality monitoring system and data platform that provided a real-time data from sixty stream locations throughout Iowa (see chapter 2). At least that much funding was devoted to human resources to operate and maintain the system and to generate research reports. Under an ISU contract with the University of Iowa, Chris Jones, PhD, a research engineer with the UI College of Engineering, directed the monitoring system, generated research reports, and also wrote a UI Water Quality Monitoring & Research blog. In his periodic blog postings, Jones translated research data into understandable evidence-based facts for the general public. His blog reports included "Iowa's Real Population," based on manure arising from the USDA Iowa farm animal census, to calculate Iowa's "fecal equivalent population (FEP)" of 134 million (3,193,000 citizens in 2021). In "50 Shades of Brown," Jones updated Iowa's real population to 168 million, in an Iowa map showing cities, states, and countries that produce as much waste as the FEP for that watershed. He and his colleagues also actively published peer-reviewed research showing that livestock manure was driving stream nitrate, thousands of private wells were contaminated with *Escherichia coli* and nitrate, 25% of Iowa's population required nitrate mitigation for their water supplies, and Iowa was the largest contributor to the Gulf of Mexico dead zone. The UI received complaints from industry, and Jones had to deal with censoring from the administration. Yet, with the support of his institute director, the blog continued until the 2023 session of the Iowa General Assembly, when an Iowa senator, whose son-in-law operated a controversial permitted 9,000 head cattle CAFO at the headwaters of Bloody Creek Run, sponsored legislation that was passed and signed into law. Despite being located in the fragile karst region of northeastern Iowa and numerous community protests, the proposed site had been approved by the Iowa Department of Natural Resources (IDNR). The legislation defunded the INRC by $500,000, the amount needed to maintain the water quality monitoring program. Jones had serially documented the degradation of Bloody Creek Run, one of only thirty-four outstanding Iowa waters that had supported this self-sustaining trout stream. Further, the sponsoring senator threatened to also defund the UI College of Engineering academic institute, where Jones was employed. So Jones, who was one year away from his intended retirement, retired in May 2023 while at the same time publishing a compellation of his blogs, with introductory and concluding chapters, in *Swine Republic* (Ice Cube Press, North Liberty, IA). This state-of-the-art water monitoring program thus joined an earlier CAFO air monitoring program, with a fleet of air monitoring trailers conducted by the UI Hygienic Laboratory, under contract with the IDNR, and the ISU Leopold Center for Sustainable Agriculture, both defunded by the state.

Academic freedom is increasingly imperiled, especially at public universities and state agencies in farm states. Industrial agriculture has enormous influence over state and federal funding, leading university administrators to be in conflict with the public interest, professional ethics, and academic responsibilities with which research universities were founded and still promote. It is an easy calculus for some university administrators to deny academic freedom and to rid their university of industry-offending independent scientists and academic units, the rationale being to protect state funding and tenure for the greater university. After being compromised by special interests, they are easy prey for subsequent requests and begin to censor the academic units for which they are responsible. It is in this perverse academic environment that several of the independent authors of the following twelve chapters published their peer-reviewed research.

There is a paradox within the agro-industrial complex. The multinational and large national corporations, through all stages of vertical integration, own the farm animals and their meat. But it is their grower contractors, who provide livestock facilities, service their mortgages, care for the animals, handle the manure, and deal with the air and water pollution affecting their neighbors, who have become "serfs," relatively powerless pawns, while the corporations reap billions (see chapters 1, 4, and 9). Nevertheless, it is the national and state-based grower member commodity associations, together with the state Farm Bureau federations, that serve corporate interests through their enormous influence over federal farm regulatory agencies and policy, farm state governors and legislators, state agencies, most county supervisors, and some university administrators and faculty members.

But the agro-industrial complex cannot control peer-reviewed science published by independent investigators or the contributions of journalists and engaged public citizens who illuminate the impact of this industry on the environment and the public's health. Nor can the industry suppress the deep and abiding values of community, home, and family that continue to serve as sources of resolve to seek justice and restitution when their family's most basic quality of life conditions and property are violated.

# ACKNOWLEDGMENTS

We acknowledge and thank the dozens of peer reviewers, two or three per chapter, who provided thoughtful comments and needed edits. Their essential contributions have made *Industrial Farm Animal Production, the Environment, and Public Health* a much better book.

We thank the Johns Hopkins Bloomberg School of Public Health's Center for a Livable Future for their steadfast support and commitment in cosponsoring this publication. We would also like to thank the Johns Hopkins University Press for their support and guidance in bringing this work to the public.

James A. Merchant, MD, DrPH
Founding Dean Emeritus, College of Public Health
Professor Emeritus, Colleges of Public Health and Medicine
University of Iowa

Robert P. Martin, Director Emeritus
Food System Policy
Center for a Livable Future
Bloomberg School of Public Health
Johns Hopkins University

# CONTRIBUTORS

VINEY P. ANEJA, PHD, is a professor in the Department of Marine, Earth and Atmospheric Sciences at North Carolina State University.

LOKA ASHWOOD, PHD, Community and Environmental Health, University of Wisconsin, and now professor of sociology at the University of Kentucky.

DEBBIE BERKOWITZ, BA (Oberlin College) is currently a Fellow at the Kalmanovitz Initiative for Labor and the Working Poor, Georgetown University. She previously served as worker safety and health program director for the National Employment Law Project and as the chief of staff and senior policy advisor for the director of OSHA.

GREGORY C. GRAY, MD (University of Alabama) and MPH (Johns Hopkins Bloomberg School of Public Health), is now the Robert E. Shope, MD, Professor of Infectious Disease Epidemiology, Department of Internal Medicine, the University of Texas Medical Branch, Galveston, Texas. Dr. Gray was the founding director of the Center for Emerging Infectious Diseases in the College of Public Health at the University of Iowa.

VIRGINIA T. GUIDRY, PHD (epidemiology), UNC Gillings School of Public Health, now leads the Occupational and Environmental Epidemiology Branch at the North Carolina Department of Health and Human Services.

TOM HARKIN, JD, Catholic University, author and politician who served as US senator from Iowa from 1985 to 2015. He was previously US representative for Iowa's fifth congressional district from 1975 to 1985. He served as a member and chair of the Senate Committee on Health, Education, Labor, and Pensions (HELP) and the HELP Appropriations Subcommittee. He is credited with sponsoring the Americans with Disabilities Act and Title IV: Prevention of Chronic Disease and Improving Public Health of the Affordable Care Act. In his capacity as long-time chair of and ranking member of the HELP Appropriations Subcommittee, he was widely recognized by the national biomedical research and public health communities for his stead-fast leadership in passage and funding health care research, promotion, and prevention programs at the National Institutes of Health and the Centers for Disease Control and Prevention. He served as the chair and ranking member of the Senate Agriculture Committee and led passage of two farm bills. He is credited with creation of the US Department of Agriculture federal fresh fruit and vegetable nutrition program for public primary schools and for legislation requiring menu labeling. He continues his long national service through the Harkin Institute for Public Policy and Citizen Engagement at Drake University.

SARAH HATCHER, PHD (environmental sciences and engineering), UNC Gillings School of Global Public Health, and now Climate and Health Program lead, Occupational and Environmental Epidemiology Branch, North Carolina Department of Health and Human Services.

CHRISTOPHER D. HEANEY, PHD (epidemiology, UNC Gillings School of Global Public Health), is associate professor in the Department of Environmental Health and Engineering and the Department of Epidemiology at the Johns Hopkins Bloomberg School of Public Health. He leads the Community Science for Environmental Justice Initiative at the Johns Hopkins Center for a Livable Future.

N. WILLIAM HINES, JD (University of Kansas) is now Joseph F. Rosenfield Professor and Dean Emeritus, and Director Emeritus of the Agricultural Law Clinic, College of Law, University of Iowa. Dean Hines tracked the livestock industry transition in the 1980s from hogs raised by individual farm families to that of the vertically integrated swine industry relying on large CAFOs.

JOHN E. IKERD, PHD (University of Missouri) is now a professor emeritus of agricultural economics at the University of Missouri. Ikerd had a thirty-year career at North Carolina State University, Oklahoma State University, and the University of Missouri before retiring in 2000. He is the author of six books, including *Sustainable Capitalism, Crisis and Opportunity, Sustainability in American Agriculture*, and *Small Farms and Real Farms*. He writes and speaks on issues related to agricultural and economic sustainability.

AIMEE IMLAY, PHD (sociology, University of Kentucky), is now assistant professor of sociology at Mississippi State University.

CHRISTOPHER JONES, PHD, is a research engineer and adjunct associate professor at the University of Iowa College of Engineering. Jones earned his

PhD in analytical chemistry at Montana State University and previously served as a laboratory supervisor for the Des Moines Water Works and as an environmental scientist with the Iowa Soybean Association. He has directed the Iowa statewide real-time continuous water monitoring network, published articles on the interface between agriculture and water quality, and is author of *The Swine Republic*.

JAMES A. MERCHANT, MD, University of Iowa, DrPH (epidemiology), UNC Gillings School of Global Public Health, Founding Dean and Professor Emeritus (Occupational and Environmental Health) in the College of Public Health, and Professor Emeritus (Pulmonary, Critical Care, and Occupational Medicine), College of Medicine, University of Iowa. He previously served as the head of the UI Department of Preventive Medicine and Environmental Health, director of the UI Institute of Rural and Environmental Health, and the director of the NIOSH Division of Respiratory Disease Studies.

BILL NIMAN was one of two livestock ranchers who served on the Pew Commission on Industrial Farm Animal Production. He was the cofounder of Niman Ranch and BN Ranch, two sustainable meat companies, and has advised Whole Foods and Chipotle restaurants on their purchasing criteria. He brought to the Pew Commission his humane and sustainable philosophy for raising high-quality livestock and recommended industry reforms that would, if implemented, lead to a more sustainable livestock production.

NICOLETTE HAHN NIMAN, JD (Michigan). Nicolette is an environmental advocate, writer, speaker, and now cattle rancher. She is the author of the *Righteous Porkchop—Finding a Life and Good beyond Factory Farms*, and *Defending Beef, the Ecological and Nutritional Case for Meat*.

DAVID OSTERBERG, MS, in Water Resource Management, MA in Economics, University of Wisconsin, is a clinical Professor Emeritus in the Department of Occupational and Environmental Health, College of Public Health, University of Iowa, and founder of the Iowa Policy Project.

TOM PHILPOTT is a senior research associate in the Department of Environmental Health and Engineering at the Johns Hopkins Bloomberg School of Public Health and Johns Hopkins Center for a Livable Future. For many years, Philpott was the food and agriculture correspondent for *Mother Jones Magazine*. He is the author of *Perilous Bounty: The Looming Collapse of American Farming and How We Can Prevent It*.

GUDIGOPURAM REDDY is a retired professor and former head of the Department of Natural Resources and Environmental Design at North Carolina Agricultural & Technical State University, Greensboro.

JESSICA RINSKY, PHD (epidemiology), UNC Gillings School of Global Public Health. She received an MPH from the University of Kentucky and is now writing independently.

WAYNE T. SANDERSON, PHD (epidemiology), UNC Gillings School of Global Public Health, CIH, is now professor of biosystems and agricultural engineering and professor of epidemiology at the University of Kentucky.

JERALD L. SCHNOOR, PHD, is professor, civil and environmental engineering, Allen S. Henry Chair in Engineering, and professor of occupational and environmental health.

TARA C. SMITH, PHD (University of Toledo) is now a professor of epidemiology at Kent State University College of Public Health. With Gregory C. Gray she continues their research on zoonotic diseases, actively publishing in peer-reviewed journals, providing public commentary on zoonotic diseases, and promoting One Health as an approach to control epizootics, epidemics, and pandemics arising from novel microbial agents.

ARIEL A. SZOGI is a senior scientist in the USDA Agricultural Research Service in Florence, South Carolina.

KENDALL M. THU, PHD in anthropology, University of Iowa, and Professor and Head Emeritus, Department of Anthropology, and Presidential Engagement Professor, Northern Illinois University.

MATIAS VANOTTI is a senior scientist in the USDA Agricultural Research Service in Florence, South Carolina.

D'ANN L. WILLIAMS, DRPH, is an assistant scientist in the Department of Environmental Health and Engineering at the Johns Hopkins Bloomberg School of Public Health and leads the Animal Agriculture and Public Health focus at the Johns Hopkins Center for a Livable Future.

# INDUSTRIAL FARM ANIMAL PRODUCTION, THE ENVIRONMENT, AND PUBLIC HEALTH

# CHAPTER 1

# Industry History, Structure, and Trends

Nicolette Hahn Niman and Bill Niman

America's meat industry is consolidated, standardized, and industrial-ized. Like other economic sectors over the past century, meat supply chains have become more mechanized and uniform, from farm to fork. Agricultural animal flocks and herds are now mostly raised by the thou-sands in crowded metal sheds resembling large warehouses, which are often lined up in rows like barracks. Large agribusiness corporations like Cargill, Tyson, and Smithfield own these animals. The companies have consolidated and concentrated in the name of progress, maxi-mized productivity, and food supply safety and predictability. They raise a handful of particular animal breeds, use certain feeds and sup-plements, and follow standardized animal husbandry methods. All of which is designed to generate animals and food products of uniform shapes, sizes, and quality and control costs of production. The meat in-dustry touts this system as the best way—the only way, even—to feed a swelling global population.

This approach to food production is now dominant in the industri-alized world but is actually quite recent. Not so long ago, America's farm animals were physically diverse and widely dispersed. Farming prized and encouraged creativity and experimentation in breeding. The

Boston Poultry Show of 1849, for instance, displayed more than a thousand bird varieties. Chickens came in a plethora of sizes and colors—from shiny greenish-black to fluffy red. Their eggs were speckled, brown, beige, white, and even pale blue.[1]

The late nineteenth to the early twentieth century was still an era of "farm chickens." Small, colorful flocks with a few score birds were everywhere. They nourished farm families and workers with eggs and meat while also providing "egg money" from the sale of surplus eggs, a valuable supplement to the family income.[2] In 1910, chicken flocks averaged eighty birds and were kept on 88% of US farms.[3] Feeding and raising chickens involved minimal capital investment: human skill and care were the keys.

Already, though, there were signs of an emerging transformation of attitudes and practices in animal farming. Large-scale mechanical incubation had been introduced in Petaluma, California, in the 1880s. A poultry history notes (approvingly) that these incubators set poultry farming "on an unerring industrial course."[4] Arguably, it was the widespread adoption of this invention that first drove not just chicken farming but all animal farming toward segmentation, specialization, and, ultimately, industrialization.

Before incubators, farms relied on the savviness and instincts of chickens themselves. Hens had long been famous for their attentive mothering. They laid their eggs, sat broodily on their nests, and then zealously trained and safeguarded their chicks from every danger. Greek philosopher Plutarch, who often wrote admiringly of poultry, observed that "there is no part of [hens'] bodies with which they do not wish to cherish their chicks if they can." Oppian, a poet of ancient Greece who lived just after Plutarch, also revered the hen's parental devotion:

> With how much love the playful hen nourishes her tender young ones! If
> she sees a hawk descending, cackling in a loud voice, her feathers raised
> high, her neck curved back, [she] spreads her swelling wings over the
> clucking chicks. Then the frightened chick chirps and bides himself under
> these high walls, and the fearful mother gathers the long line of young

chicks under her plumage; careful mother that she is, she attacks the bold attacker and frees her dear chicks from the mouth of the rapacious bird.[5]

Incubators disrupted this age-old natural system. Eggs would now be laid in one location and then removed to hatcheries, where they were incubated in machines resembling giant ovens. Thousands of eggs of distinct origins were mixed. Baby chicks were then boxed and shipped like biscuits, by the hundreds, to far-flung locations around the country. No chick would know its siblings or mother, let alone be taken care of by her. Chickens were rendered as fungible as widgets.

By the early twentieth century, some farmers were experimenting with dramatically increasing flock sizes. Disease outbreaks and other health problems (such as rickets, from sun deprivation) had long constrained the size of flocks and prevented their continual confinement. Early attempts at expanded flock sizes, in the 1920s, saw typical death losses quadrupled, jumping from 5% to 20%.[6]

Farmers and their family still carried out the daily care and feeding of poultry. But machines were entering the picture. Along with specialization and larger flocks, automation was yet another harbinger of the industrialization of animal farming. Typifying the trend were Big Dutchman feeders invented in the 1930s by the DeWitt brothers of Zeeland, Michigan.[7] Such automated feeders and waterers saved labor but also meant that individual animals received much less human care.

Meanwhile, to stem death losses in larger, confined flocks, managers began to routinely add pharmaceuticals to feed. And because being kept indoors limited movement and caused chickens to lose their appetites, arsenic, which triggers hunger, was often put into the mix.[8] Poultry pioneers like Joseph Salsbury wrote prolifically for farm journals and set up a popular "poultry course" that, by the mid-1950s, had been attended by more than ten thousand people in the business. In everything he did, Salsbury encouraged liberal use of medications. His arsenic-based feed additive Ren-O-Sal, said to both keep coccidiosis at bay and increase appetite, became the first drug widely added to chickens' daily feed.[9]

By the mid-twentieth century, the United States had truly entered a new farming era. It left behind *farm chickens* and moved into the era of *chicken farms*. Even before the country formally entered World War II, President Franklin Delano Roosevelt used his Fireside Chats to encourage American farmers and ranchers to contribute to the war effort by increasing the numbers and amounts of animals and crops. "Food will win the war and write the peace," became a US Department of Agriculture (USDA) slogan.[10] Concerted efforts were made to raise more animals in fewer locations. Feed and transport companies and hatcheries ran ads encouraging farmers to support American troops by growing "defense chicks."[11] During the war, it was characterized as patriotic to ramp-up output. And once the war ended, government subsidies incentivized raising grains to be shipped overseas to feed hungry people in war-torn areas. Public financing of row crops also brought down the cost of animal feeds.

By 1950, poultry feed was plentiful and cheap. Many farms added in manufactured vitamin D3 and antibiotics. These factors combined to make it physically possible and economically viable, for the first time, to successfully keep large, continuously confined indoor chicken flocks.

Chicken farming gradually split into two distinct sectors. One type of chickens (so-called broilers) was raised for meat, while another variety (so-called layers) was raised specifically for eggs.[12] Meat chickens were selected for traits like rapid growth and large breasts while egg-laying chickens were chosen for prolific egg generation. A single breed, then a single bloodline, became dominant for each chicken type. Most farmers of both types of chickens would soon commit to contracts with large agribusiness concerns.

Entrepreneurs like Georgia businessman Jesse Dixon Jewell fostered the shift to "contract growers," an idea he promoted to faltering cotton farmers. Jewell supplied farmers with the birds and feed; farmers provided the labor, land, and buildings. Farmers also kept the chicken manure, commonly called "litter." Once Jewell built his own hatchery and processing plant, in 1940, he gained control over every aspect of production—from baby chicks to processed meat. He even boosted his bottom line by recycling his slaughterhouse wastes as an ingredient in his chicken feed. Jewell was an early pioneer of fully vertically integrated meat production. Thus he, and others influenced by him, "laid the foundation for an agribusiness concept—the idea where a farmer-businessman team would produce food efficiently and effectively on an assembly line basis," wrote an industry insider.[13]

In this midcentury period, as chicken farming was being transformed, it became standard practice to keep egg-laying hens continually confined in small, wire cages. They were lined up and stacked upon each other in batteries and thus became known as "battery cages." A feed dealer from the era touted the benefits of this system by saying, "What they did was to organize the hens in a production line where you can use more machinery, cut way down on labor, and allow just a few people to take care of a tremendous number of birds."[14] Quality of life for hens, who had always had the run of the barnyard, plummeted.

Placing hens in cages affected more than animal welfare. Keeping the birds away from sunlight and foraging vegetation also changed the nutritional value and appearance of the eggs. Yolks lost their omega-3s and took on a dull, grayish look instead of the deep golden hue one expects from the "sun" in "sunny side up." The industry's marketers soon recognized that consumers would reject such drab-looking eggs. To address the aesthetic problem, egg producers began to add red dye to hen feed so the yolks would appear more yellowish. (This is still common practice today.) However, for most eggs, the nutritional shortcomings remain.[15]

Egg-laying facilities were comparatively modest in size when battery cages were first introduced. A Georgia outfit raised eyebrows in the 1950s when it announced plans to build an egg operation with 100,000 hens. Over the following decades, that size would become the norm. Today, operations with millions of hens are commonplace.[16]

These many husbandry changes were accompanied by a notable attitudinal shift. The 1867 *Practical Poultry Keeper* advised farmers, "Fowls should not be kept unless proper and regular attention can be given them; and we would strongly urge that this needful attention should be *personal*."[17] But as flocks expanded from dozens to hundreds, then to thousands and tens of thousands, the very idea of the individual chicken evaporated from poultry manuals and textbooks. It was replaced by two calculations: first, how many pounds of feed it takes to produce a pound of chicken flesh or dozen eggs and, second, how much total cost goes into raising the live animal. In modern farming, breeding of meat chickens targets rapid growth and high feed conversion rates; breeding of egg-laying hens focuses on getting more eggs using less feed.

Pig farming followed a strikingly similar trajectory. Until the mid-twentieth century, pigs of all sorts lived on farms throughout the country. Farmers selected pig breeds to match their local climate, soils, and available water. Culinary preferences, often tied to cultural heritage, also influenced breed choices. Farms cultivated crops as animal feeds. But much of the pig diet was various edible bits that would otherwise have become wastes. Pigs spent their days out-of-doors, lying in the sun, foraging, and rooting, their bodies naturally protected from heat and cold by their own thick layers of subcutaneous fat. Iowa, with soils and rain conducive to corn and soy cultivation, produced more pork than any other state. All parts of the pig were valued—providing everything from leaf lard to bacon to leather. Pork nourished farm families and supplied local restaurants and markets.

Pigs were also uniquely helpful in boosting farm ecology and economy. An early twentieth-century agriculture book extolled hogs' manifold virtues for efficiently transforming food scraps and excess farm products into delicious meat. "No other farm animal can convert, so economically and profitably, the wastes and by-products of the farm into finished products of high quality and constant value throughout the year."[18]

But industrialization in pig farming was further catalyzed in 1962 by Wendell Murphy, a North Carolina school teacher who raised hogs on the side. That year, Murphy constructed a feed mill on his parents' property in the small town of Rose Hill. Closely following the trail blazed by poultry pioneer Jesse Dixon Jewell, Murphy offered his neighbors a fee to raise animals for him. Murphy provided the pigs and the feed while farmers provided land, buildings, and labor. Like Jewell's contract grower model, farmers also kept the manure (and accompanying liability).[19] Murphy encouraged a swine housing model in which pigs were kept confined twenty-four hours a day. As in poultry farming, this was accompanied by a variety of pharmaceutical and other feed amendments to keep the pigs alive despite being deprived of sunshine, fresh air, and exercise.[20]

By the 1970s, Murphy's influence was felt beyond North Carolina, and hog farming throughout the United States was being transformed. Pig herds, which had typically had a few dozen animals and been allowed freedom to root and roam outdoors, were being replaced by concentrated swine-raising facilities with thousands of pigs.

Murphy's ambitions later grew to governance, and in 1983, he successfully ran for a seat in the state legislature. He rose to a position of influence in the assembly, eventually becoming vice chair of both the agriculture and appropriations committees. This enabled him to oversee the passage of various laws promoting and protecting the North Carolina concentrated hog industry. The statutes shielded industrial animal facilities from nuisance lawsuits and (purportedly) from the requirement to comply with environmental laws, like the federal Clean Water Act.[21]

Assisted by Wendell Murphy, pig production in North Carolina quadrupled from 2.5 million pigs in 1989 to 10 million in 2003. Notably, though, during the same time period, the number of farms with pigs shrank from 12,500 to 2,800.[22]

Keeping farm animals continually crowded indoors causes a host of problems for animal health and welfare. To enable survival in such conditions and to speed their growth, up to 97% of industrially raised hogs are given antibiotics in their daily feed during their final life stages.[23] It had long been common knowledge that for pigs (like children) to be healthy, they need plenty of time outdoors, fresh air, and exercise.

The highly regarded book *Swine Management* by Iowa State University professor Arthur Anderson (published in 1950) repeatedly emphasized the importance of outdoor exercise for the raising of healthy pigs. A typical passage states, "Encourage sufficient exercise. Exercise plays an important part in the development of strong bones, strong muscles, with resultant healthy pigs. Plenty of exercise, therefore, should be encouraged, preferably on pasture, or at any rate on a dirt run. Avoid confinement to concrete or other floors that keep pigs from the soil."[24] Animal confinement facilities offer no access to pasture and little opportunity for exercise, especially as the pigs grow larger and pens become more crowded. At the numerous facilities we have visited, pigs were listless, appeared depressed, and barely moved around. Total confinement is a recipe for creating unhealthy animals.

A robust body of scientific research also reveals its environmental harms. Dr. Joanne Burkholder, a North Carolina State University biology professor, documented a 500% increase in ammonia in North Carolina's Neuse River estuary in the decade of hog industry expansion.[25] Biologist Dr. Bill Showers conducted research tracing industrial animal pollution using a nitrogen isotope found only in animal waste. His work documented that nitrate levels from hog waste are as much as ten times higher downstream from hog operations than upstream. "To say that [industrialized hog operations] are not exporting nitrogen is hydrologically impossible," Showers has said.[26]

The work of biologist Dr. Mike Mallin, at the University of North Carolina's Center for Marine Science, reinforced the strong link between animal confinement facilities and water pollution. For a decade, Dr. Mallin regularly checked water quality at dozens of sampling stations on rivers in eastern North Carolina, many of which flow past hog operations but little else. During that time period, Mallin and his team found a 265% increase in ammonia in the Black River. In the nearby Northeast Cape Fear River, he documented an ammonia increase of 315%. Both river basins have millions of confined hogs.[27]

Beef and lamb production have also become industrialized. But the histories of those meats are quite distinct from chicken and pork. Chickens and pigs are omnivores; they benefit from grazing but must be provided some sort of feed, usually in confinement. Cattle and sheep, on the other hand, are grazing animals; their husbandry has always been closely tied to grass. Domesticated sheep and cattle first arrived in the Americas in 1492 and 1493, respectively, with Christopher Columbus's first and second voyages. In 1591, the original seed stock for Latin American cattle herds was brought by Spanish merchant Gregorio de Villalobos. In the early 1600s, European settlers were landing on North America's eastern shores with early British and Continental bovine breeds, primarily for labor and milk rather than beef.

As settlers pushed south and west, cattle were part of the migrations, proliferating particularly in areas with abundant grasslands. Many early livestock ranches were in the South, especially in Georgia and the Carolinas. "The long grazing season, mild winters, sparsely wooded uplands were especially favorable for beef production," notes a cattle history. "It was said a steer could be raised as cheaply as a hen."[28]

By the mid-1800s, plenty of ranches were being established in the grasslands of the Far West. But the bulk of the nation's cattle raising was in the heart of the country. "Prior to the Civil War, the Ohio and upper Mississippi Valley states constituted the center of the [US] beef cattle industry. On practically every farm of this area was a herd of beef [mother] cows."[29]

Meanwhile, poor crop farming practices were eroding America's rich topsoil at an alarming rate. Pioneer farmers first plowing up Midwestern prairies had been greeted by chest-high grasses and topsoil up to six feet deep. But by 1934, precipitated by years of serious drought and crop failure, a 100-million-acre dead zone on those lands caused epic dust storms as far away as New York City. The center of the country, once a vast, ecologically diverse prairie maintained by large grazing herbivores, became known as the Dust Bowl. In 1935, under President Franklin Delano Roosevelt's leadership, the US government created the Soil Conservation Service, hoping to reverse the perilous trend.

Thankfully, within its first decade, Soil Conservation research was revealing solutions to the problem of agriculture. It showed that regularly rotating croplands into pastures—especially diverse pastures with mixes of grasses and legumes like vetch and clover—can reverse much of the damage done by row crop cultivation. This research demonstrated that such meadows not only feed grazing animals but are also fundamental to creating a permanent farming system that can regenerate itself and produce nourishing food for generations to come. The precise science behind these findings is now better understood. Soil Conservation research at that time was effectively showing that by capturing carbon and assisting subterranean micro-organisms, mixes of grasses and legumes could restore soil fertility, organic matter, and tilth (soil's texture and capacity to hold water), along with controlling insect pests and weeds. Field trials found grass cover to be 200 to 2,000 times more effective than plowed row crops in protecting the earth from soil losses.[30]

Such research fostered optimism among agriculture experts of the day that US farming was on the dawn of a promising new era of ecological and economic sustainability. The USDA's official annual *Yearbook of Agriculture* for 1948, entitled simply *Grass*, hopefully described a newly emerging "grassland philosophy," touting the plant's forthcoming Golden Age. The volume's foreword, by then Secretary of Agriculture Clinton P. Anderson, calls grass "our alliance with nature" and the "foundation of security in agriculture." He notes that farming based on grass produces nourishing food that could improve national health.[31] Around the same time, the American Society of Agronomy's former president, H. G. Hughes, authored a hefty tome called *Forages*, in which he wrote, "That adapted grasses and legumes are the chief tools in soil building, improvement and conservation is now generally recognized."[32]

Regrettably, the optimistic belief that American food production and farming would advance closely tied to grass turned out to be incorrect. Historical events pushed agriculture in a very different direction. As World War II wound down, factories constructed to produce munitions were repurposed to manufacture agricultural chemicals. The use of human-made fertilizers soon doubled. As noted earlier, government policies of this time subsidized and encouraged maximum grain output. These pro-production policies simultaneously disincentivized grass.

Specifically, they pushed farmers away from ecologically beneficial practices such as keeping permanent pastures, rotating crop fields into grass, diversifying farming with animals, and using grass buffers.[33]

Agriculture continued its evolution toward more specialization and segmentation. Laboratory-produced vitamin D and antibiotics were making it easier to restrict animals indoors around the clock. Grass habitats for most farm animals were being abandoned in favor of crowded confinement systems. Fields were plowed fencerow to fencerow, and chemicals became the basis for fertility, pest control, and weed suppression.[34]

Dairy cows were arguably the most affected by this dramatic shift. In the first half of the twentieth century, most US milk was still coming from smaller-scale farms where cows roamed and grazed grassy meadows most of the year. This changed midcentury. Wisconsin, America's leading dairy state until 1994, lost more than three-quarters of its dairy farms between 1959 and 1997. At the same time, cow herds were expanded and put into continual confinement. In 1945, the average Wisconsin herd had just 15 cows. The average had risen to 34 by 1975, was 71 by 2002, and reached 212 by 2022. The averages do not tell the full story. They fail to illuminate the emergence of dairies with over 1,000 cows, which are now commonplace in Wisconsin, as well as California, New York, Idaho, Texas, and other dairy-producing states.[35] By 1994, when California became the nation's largest dairy producer, it had 1,800 dairies with more than 200 cows, and by 2006, California had more than 1,000 dairies with more than 500 cows. Few of these milking cows had any connection to grass.

Turning away from grass and toward industrial animal confinement systems has had sweeping effects. Most important, it doomed billions of pigs, turkeys, chickens, and dairy cows to miserable lives. The majority of beef cattle and sheep, while rarely kept totally confined, now spend the latter part of their lives in outdoor dirt pens known as feedlots. While feedlots are less objectionable than the concentrated animal feeding operations used to raise pigs, poultry, and dairy cows, they are not ideal for animal welfare or the environment.

Concentrating animals has, in fact, done widespread ecological damage. It stripped soils and waters of their stalwart guardian as millions of acres of grassland were plowed to raise feed crops, with grass buffers and grass crop rotations nearly abandoned. Over the past two centuries, replacement of grasslands with plowed cropland has caused the United States to lose 30% of its topsoil.[36] The nonprofit Environmental Working Group reports that soil erosion continues at an alarming rate today, "many times higher than official estimates." Agriculture is now the nation's leading source of water pollution as well as a significant air polluter and contributor to climate change.[37]

Perverse incentives continue to push farmers to plow up their lands. These include the abandonment of landmark soil conservation practices adopted in 1980s and energy policies that encourage corn ethanol. Researchers at South Dakota State University used government satellite imagery to calculate the amount of native grassland being lost annually. Their research, published in the *Proceedings of the National Academy of Sciences*, found that between 2006 and 2011, farmers in the Dakotas, Minnesota, Nebraska, and Iowa plowed up 1.3 million acres of native grasslands to plant corn and soybeans. The research team noted that the region's land-use changes parallel some of the worst deforestations in the world. The Nature Conservancy has called grasslands the world's most imperiled ecosystem, noting that (among other harms) their demise has negative consequences for climate change.[38]

The industrialization that crept first into chicken farming and then moved into pig farming now affects all types of animal agriculture. Over the past century, large agribusiness interests have gained control over each sector of the animal-derived foods industry. Today, about 86% of the beef industry, 64% of the pork industry, 56% of the meat chicken industry, and 51% of the turkey industry are controlled by the top four agribusiness companies of the respective sectors. Some 60% of eggs are produced by vertically integrated corporations while almost all of the rest are raised for the companies under contract. Iowa State University agricultural economist Dr. Neil Harl has said that the effect of such monopolies has been to turn family farmers into "serfs." "A producer without meaningful competitive options is a relatively powerless pawn in the production process," Harl has said.[39]

Iowa State University agricultural economist Dr. Mike Duffy has noted that, counter to popular belief, the shift to agriculture controlled by agribusiness is not driven by a quest for improved efficiency. "It's not about efficiency at all," says Duffy, "It's about power." In both marketplace and politics, agribusiness dominates family farms.[40] It has gained market advantages and lowered its costs by exerting political and economic clout.

Agribusiness also lowers its expenses by deftly avoiding paying the true costs of doing business. Many state regulators are hamstrung by inadequate budgets for environmental enforcement. A study by the nonprofit Izaak Walton League documented that environmental enforcement is seriously deficient not only in Iowa but across much of Midwest farm country. It concluded, "Every state program in the Upper Midwest is under-staffed and under-funded to provide the adequate oversight needed for livestock [operations]."[41]

In our decades of experience working in the livestock industry, we have never witnessed federal or state agencies fully and fairly enforcing environmental laws and regulations against industrial animal operations. The ability to evade environmental enforcement translates to lowered costs for industrial farming operations, giving them an unfair competitive advantage over smaller, family-run operations.

Additionally, agribusiness has long made use of its political power to obtain substantial public supports. Such subsidies are yet another way of foisting agribusiness's true costs onto the US taxpayers. From 1995 to 2021, US subsidies for agriculture totaled $487 million, according to the Environmental Working Group.[42] Politicians are fond of portraying the payouts as helping small family farms. But a study of subsidies from 2003 to 2005 revealed that 84% of federal farm subsidies were paid to the largest one-fifth of farms.[43]

All of these factors make it harder for true family farmers to fairly compete.

Industrial animal farming facilities also pose many different types of risks to human health. The overuse of antibiotics has been shown to contribute to the rise and spread of antibiotic-resistant infectious diseases.[44] Humans encounter such bacteria in waters and air near industrial animal facilities as well as in the foods produced by such operations. Scores of studies (many done in Europe, where research funding is less dependent on agribusiness) have linked the gases of industrial animal operations to various human ailments. These include lung diseases, nausea, nosebleeds, depression, and even brain damage.[45]

For decades, people have been led to believe that these sorts of harms are a necessary evil to producing sufficient food to feed the world. But we strenuously reject that idea. In our experience, truly regenerative food systems provide both people and animals better lives, foster healthy ecosystems, and produce nutrient-rich, delicious foods. They exist in every part of the world and, importantly, can be replicated. With the support of state and federal governments, along with consumers, a food system that is ecologically and morally robust can be built. Exactly what that looks like will vary from place to place depending on multiple factors like the climate, topography, and human resources available. But creating a regenerative food system is both possible and necessary. Let's all get to work.

**NOTES**

1. Nicolette Hahn Niman, *Righteous Porkchop, Finding a Life and Good Food Beyond Factory Farms* (New York: Harper Collins, 2009), 40.

2. Hahn Niman, *Righteous Porkchop*, 41.

3. Hahn Niman, *Righteous Porkchop*, 40.

4. G. Sawyer, *The Agribusiness Poultry Industry: A History of Its Development* (New York: Exposition Press, 1971), 27.

5. Plutarch and Oppian quoted in P. Smith and C. Daniel, *The Chicken Book* (Athens: University of Georgia Press, 2000), 159–160.

6. Hahn Niman, *Righteous Porkchop*, 46.

7. Hahn Niman, *Righteous Porkchop*, 41.

8. Hahn Niman, *Righteous Porkchop*, 47.

9. Hahn Niman, *Righteous Porkchop*, 46.

10. A. Matusow, *Farm Policies and Politics in the Truman Years* (Cambridge, MA: Harvard University Press, 1967), 3.

11. Sawyer, *The Agribusiness Poultry Industry*, 91.

12. It is important to note that with this specialization, males chicks of the egg-laying variety became a "by-product" and were thrown away en masse soon after hatching.

13. Sawyer, *The Agribusiness Poultry Industry*, 143.

14. Sawyer, *The Agribusiness Poultry Industry*, 216.

15. Some companies use feed additives designed to raise the omega-3 content of eggs, although it is unknown whether such supplements provide the same nutritional quality as the omega-3 that occurs naturally in eggs from foraging flocks. Hahn Niman, *Righteous Porkchop*, 53.

16. Hahn Niman, *Righteous Porkchop*, 54.

17. Emphasis in original. L. Wright, *The Practical Poultry Keeper* (New York: Orange Judd Company, 1867, 1).

18. H. C. Dawson, *The Hog Book* (Buford, GA: Sanders Publishing, 1911), 21.

19. Hahn Niman, *Righteous Porkchop*, 93–94.

20. Hahn Niman, *Righteous Porkchop*, 94.

21. Hahn Niman, *Righteous Porkchop*, 94.

22. Hahn Niman, *Righteous Porkchop*, 12.

23. Hahn Niman, *Righteous Porkchop*, 99.

24. A. L. Anderson, *Swine Management* (Chicago: J. B. Lippincott, 1950), 188.

25. Hahn Niman, *Righteous Porkchop*, 21.

26. Hahn Niman, *Righteous Porkchop*, 25.

27. Hahn Niman, *Righteous Porkchop*, 26.

28. Nicolette Hahn Niman, *Defending Beef: The Ecological and Nutritional Case for Meat* (White River Junction, VT: Chelsea Green, 2021), 62.

29. Hahn Niman, *Defending Beef*, 62.

30. Hahn Niman, *Defending Beef*, 63.

31. Hahn Niman, *Defending Beef*, 64.

32. Hahn Niman, *Defending Beef*, 64.

33. Hahn Niman, *Defending Beef*, 64.

34. Hahn Niman, *Defending Beef*, 65.

35. Hahn Niman, *Righteous Porkchop*, 179.

36. J. Rogers and P. G. Feiss, *People and the Earth: Basic Issues in Sustainability of Resources and Environment* (Cambridge: Cambridge University Press, 1998), 63.

37. Hahn Niman, *Defending Beef*, 65.

38. Hahn Niman, *Defending Beef*, 66.

39. Hahn Niman, *Righteous Porkchop*, 242.

40. Hahn Niman, *Righteous Porkchop*, 241.

41. Hahn Niman, *Righteous Porkchop*, 242.

42. EWG Farm Subsidy Database, EBSCO Information Service, https://www.ebsco.com.

43. EWG Farm Subsidy Database.

44. Hahn Niman, *Righteous Porkchop*, 248–249.

45. Hahn Niman, *Righteous Porkchop*, 16.

# CHAPTER 2

# Water Pollution—Regional, National, and Global Impacts

Christopher Jones

The increased commercial availability of macronutrients in the decades following World War II enabled farmers to decouple the production of commodity crops from livestock production. For example, use of nitrogen fertilizers derived from the Haber Bosch process of ammonia synthesis[1] increased 13-fold from 1945 to 1972.[2] As a result, farmers no longer needed to rely on nutrients supplied by animal manures or, in the case of nitrogen, biological fixation of atmospheric nitrogen by legumes in symbiosis with bacteria.[3]

As the demand for meat has continued to remain strong, especially in First World countries,[4,5] food animals have been concentrated onto fewer and fewer farms where efficiencies of production can be optimized. In the US state of Iowa, the number of farmers raising hogs decreased from 65,000 in 1980 to 10,000 in 2002 and to fewer than 5,000 at present.[6] However, the average number of hogs raised by an individual farmer has increased from 200 to 4,700 in that time span, while the total number of hogs in the state has grown from 13 million to 25 million.[6] Similar scenarios have played out with other farm animals. The number of egg-laying chickens in Iowa increased from 21.5 million in 1997 to 56.5 million in 2021, and an astonishing 19 of

20 Iowa chickens reside in operations that house 100,000 or more birds.[6] For beef cattle, the number of operations with greater than 500 head increased 82% between 1997 and 2017.[7] Clustering animals in this manner has occurred in other parts of the United States as well as the European Union, Eastern Europe, China, and many other countries.

Concentrating livestock animals in animal feeding operations (concentrated animal feeding operation [CAFO]) has meant more reliance on feedstuffs composed of corn (*Zea mays*) and soybeans (*Glycine max* [L.] Merr.) and less reliance on forage crops and small grains. Likewise, US Corn Belt farmers choosing not to raise livestock have been able to simplify their crop production systems to continuous corn, a two-year rotation of corn–soybean, or a two-year rotation of corn–soybean/ wheat double crop in the eastern portion of the region. The introduction of soybean, which displaced not corn but rather crops like oat, alfalfa, clovers, and sorghum, correlates strongly with the use of commercial fertilizer for corn (Fig. 2.1).

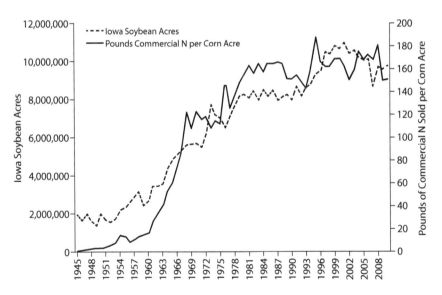

FIGURE 2.1. Area planted to soybeans in the US state of Iowa and the pounds of nitrogen fertilizer sold per planted acre of corn. *Data sources*: Census of Agriculture, National Agriculture Statistics Service.

Concentrating animals on fewer and fewer farms coupled with the displacement of diverse crop rotations by soybean meant a greater reliance on chemical fertilizers. At the same time, the total number of animals continued to increase, and thus manure nutrients have also been concentrated into smaller geographical areas. This has had consequences for the environment in places where livestock production is intense: Iowa (hogs and chickens), Wisconsin (dairy and beef cattle), and the western Lake Erie basin (hogs, cattle, poultry), to name three.

Managing manure from concentrated livestock operations can be a colossal challenge. For example, the manure waste generated by a hog contains about 3 times as much nitrogen and phosphorus as a human being (8), and thus an Iowa operation raising the average number of hogs (4,700) is managing the nutrient waste equivalent of a community with a population greater than 14,000 people. When the volume of hog waste is considered, the challenge appears even larger. The waste just from Iowa's hog population exceeds that excreted by the human population by 20–30 times.[8] This waste is stored in belowground pits or surface lagoons for 6–12 months before it is applied to crop fields.[8–10]

In Iowa, large livestock operations are required to create a manure storage and application plan as part of the permitting process for CAFO construction.[9] This Manure Management Plan maps the fields where waste will be applied, along with the timing and amount of application. The amounts are weakly restricted by the yield goal formula for nitrogen (N)[11] and the phosphorus (P) index for that nutrient, neither of which has been shown to be protective of water quality.[12] The credibility of the 50-year-old yield goal formula (multiply the expected corn yield potential in bushels per acre by 1.2 for pounds per acre N application) has been questioned, if not wholly discredited, as a sound approach for optimum environmental and agronomic outcomes.[13,14] All available forms and sources of nitrogen need to be considered for efficient management of that nutrient and optimization of environmental outcomes. These include mineralization of soil organic matter (mobilization) and biological fixation in addition to synthetic products and manure. Immobilization of nitrogen within the soil matter also occurs as inorganic forms are incorporated into biomass through biological processes. Monitoring and managing these pools of nitrogen in synchrony can help align inputs with crop nutrient demands. Farmers, however, can be highly motivated to overapply manure because of economic considerations related to transport of the material, which is much less nutrient dense than commercial formulations (Fig. 2.2).[10]

Dissolved and solid forms of nitrogen (ammonia, ammonium, nitrate, nitrite, organic forms) contained within manure wastes can off-gas to the atmosphere as ammonia ($NH_3$), nitrous oxide ($N_2O$), nitric oxide (NO), and nitrogen gas ($N_2$). Volatilization losses of N from both pit and lagoon storage are also difficult to control and minimize, and atmospheric deposition of N, usually ammonia ($NH_3$), ammonium ($NH_4^+$), and nitrate ($NO_3^-$), sourced to these facilities is a significant environmental consideration. There is evidence that much of the volatilized N is deposited within 1 km of the confinement operation,[15] and McGinn et al.[16] reported a 50% decline in deposition 200 m from a cattle confinement. In most circumstances, the farmer is not required to consider these inputs in their fertilization scheme, and Jackson et al.[9] concluded that in some scenarios, it makes clear economic sense for large livestock confinements to maximize N volatilization losses. Thus, in some circumstances, manure becomes a waste product and the practice of squandering manure nutrients is not necessarily economically wasteful.[17,18]

## Effect of Livestock Production on Water Resources

The post–World War II transition from diverse, multispecies farms to operations devoted to cash crops like corn and soybean, with a subset raising livestock at high densities, has produced both efficiencies and negative environmental consequences. It has long been known that

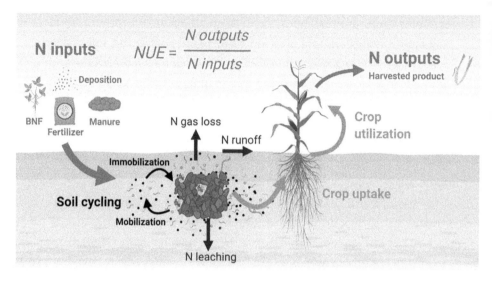

FIGURE 2.2. Conceptual model of nitrogen inputs and flow paths in a corn production system. BNF = biological N fixations; NUE = nitrogen use efficiency. *Source:* Udvardi, M., F. E. Below, M. J. Castellano, A. J. Eagle, K. E. Giller, J. K. Ladha, X. Liu, T. M. Maaz, B. Nova-Franco, N. Raghuram, and G. P. Robertson. (2021). A research road map for responsible use of agricultural nitrogen. *Frontiers in Sustainable Food Systems* 5:660155.

nitrogen fertilization correlates with stream nitrate pollution in the US Corn Belt[19] with impacts on municipal water supply[20] and Gulf of Mexico hypoxia.[20] Nitrate is a regulated pollutant in the United States under the federal Safe Drinking Water Act and an important driver of eutrophication in both freshwater and marine environments. Infants consuming high-nitrate water alone or with that mixed with baby formula are vulnerable to methemoglobinemia, which impairs red blood cells' ability to transport oxygen throughout the body.[21]

Because nitrogen inputs to crops cycle through plant biomass and into and out of soil organic matter, and because of the time lag of pollutant transport to streams via groundwater pathways,[22] it is nearly impossible to trace stream nitrate back to commercial fertilizer, animal manure, legumes, or soil organic matter. Hence, many have attempted to gain insights on nitrate sources and pathways using nitrogen budgeting.[23,24] Similar approaches have been used for the other major macronutrient driving eutrophication, phosphorus.[8,25] Much of this and other research has shown that nutrient and other types of water pollution tend to be particularly bad in watersheds with a high density of livestock.[10,26–28] A few of these are discussed below.

## Gulf of Mexico

Coastal Gulf of Mexico eutrophication driven by nutrient enrichment from livestock and crop production in the US Corn Belt draining to the Mississippi River basin has been observed and documented since at least 1974.[29] Waters off the coast of Louisiana become degraded as algae and phytoplankton exploit nutrient-rich water and bacterial consumption of their remains consumes dissolved oxygen (DO). Marine food webs are altered,[30] mobile species flee,[31,32] and immobile species perish[33] in areas where DO levels drop below 2 mg L$^{-1}$ (hypoxic/hypoxia areas). Economic consequences include decline of commercial fishing and shellfish catches and recruitment failure of valuable species.[34] In recent years, harmful algae blooms requiring closure of beaches on the Gulf Coast have been blamed on nutrient pollution in the Mississippi River.[35] Livestock animal waste is the third-leading contributor of both phosphorus and nitrogen to the Gulf of Mexico, while commercial fertilization of crops largely grown to feed these animals is the leading contributor of both (Fig. 2.3).[36,37]

A consortium of state agencies, tribal governments, and federal agencies was formed in 1997 to address the issues of Mississippi River basin nutrient pollution and Gulf of Mexico hypoxia, with an objective of reducing the areal extent of hypoxia to the 1980–1996 baseline average by 2015. Seeing this goal would go unmet, the task force pushed back the goal date to 2035 (Fig. 2.4).[38]

## Lake Erie

The shallowest of the five Great Lakes in North America, Lake Erie, has been plagued with algae blooms attributed to livestock, row crop

FIGURE 2.3. A plume (*left*) of freshwater enriched in nutrients and sediments enters the Gulf of Mexico from the Mississippi River. *Credit*: Nancy Rabalais, Louisiana Universities Marine Consortium.

production, and point sources in both the United States and Canada (Figs. 2.5 and 2.6). Point sources are pollutants sourced back to the end of a regulated pipe discharge; nonpoint sources are disperse and not easily traceable from the stream to the source(s). Although water quality in the lake improved in the 1980s and 1990s following the implementation of the US Clean Water Act, which regulated point source discharges, a "re-eutrophication" has occurred over the past 20 years linked to unregulated nonpoint sources of nutrients from agriculture.[39] Degrading amounts of N and P from productive agricultural land in Ohio, Indiana, Michigan, and Ontario drain to the western basin via rivers such as the Maumee, Raisin, and Thames, impairing the lake for recreation, aquatic life, and municipal drinking water.[40,41]

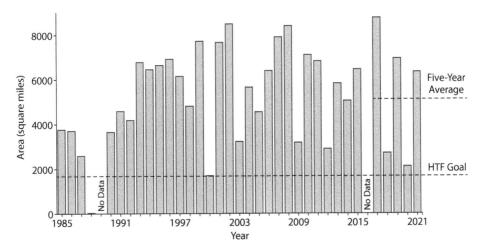

FIGURE 2.4. Gulf of Mexico hypoxia area. Also shown are the Environmental Protection Agency–led Hypoxia Task Force (HTF) improvement goal, along with the 5-year running annual average. *Data sources*: LUMCON/NOAA.

Unlike marine eutrophication in the Gulf of Mexico, where nitrogen is limiting,[42,43] anthropogenic sources of phosphorus are thought to be the main driver of eutrophication and degradation in Lake Erie.[39] The farmed landscape left level by glacial advance 2.5 million to 11,000 years ago requires constructed drainage in cropped fields to lower the water table, thereby drying out soggy soils and enhancing conditions for field work and increasing crop yields. This drainage consists primarily of networks of porous pipe (tile) installed to a depth of ~1 m that ultimately discharge to the stream network. Dissolved and particulate phosphorus, applied to or incorporated into the soil surface as manure or commercial fertilizer formulations, infiltrates to the tile via preferential pathways in the soil profile. Although commercial formulations have been found to contribute more than manure sources to the Maumee River, the proportion of applied manure phosphorus lost to Lake Erie is larger than the proportion of applied commercial P lost.[44] This is important since populations in the basin have increased since 2007, while the amount of commercial phosphorus application has likely declined since the 1970s.[45]

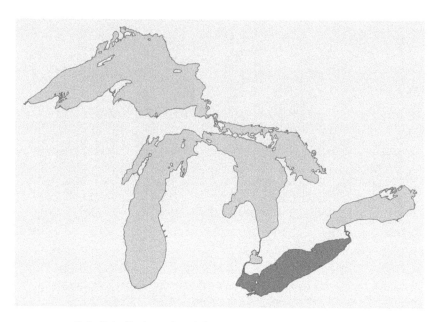

FIGURE 2.5. Lake Erie (dark gray) and the rest of the Great Lakes. *Source*: Wikimedia commons, CC BY-SA 3.0, https://commons.wikimedia.org/w/index.php?curid=26313431.

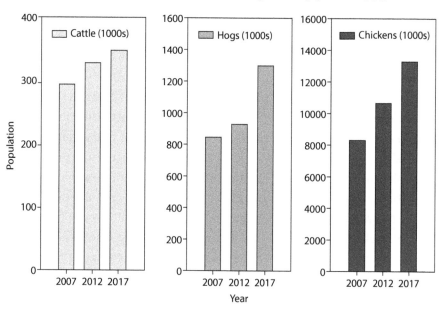

FIGURE 2.6. Livestock populations in the US portion of the Western Lake Erie basin. *Source*: USDA Quickstats (6).

## Chesapeake Bay

Land covering 64,000 square miles in six states drains to Chesapeake Bay, the largest estuary in the United States. Much of the land area in the Baltimore, Maryland, to Norfolk, Virginia, corridor is densely populated. The entire watershed is home to 17 million people, about 5% of the US population. By comparison, the area of the agricultural state of Iowa is only slightly less but is home to only 3 million people (Fig. 2.7).

Concern over degradation of water quality in Chesapeake Bay from nutrient and a myriad of other types of pollution was increasingly heightened during the 1960s and 1970s. The US Clean Water Act addressed many types of industrial and municipal discharges after its passage in 1972 but left nutrient pollution from nonpoint (disperse) sources mostly unregulated. Although only 22% of the land area is in agricultural production[46] (small compared to many areas of the US Corn Belt), these lands are disproportionately large contributors of both nitrogen (45%) and phosphorus (44%) to the Bay's feeder streams, which include the Potomac, Rappahannock, Susquehanna, and James rivers.[46]

Much of the Bay's nutrient pollution problems link to livestock production geographically decoupled from the production of the feed used to raise animals. As grain yields increased in the US Corn Belt and elsewhere with the widespread adoption of crop hybrids and chemical fertilizers following World War II, Chesapeake Bay livestock producers found it easier, more efficient, and economically prudent to feed their animals with grain formulations grown elsewhere. Import of animal feed also means import of nutrients (N and P) contained within the feed. Without adequate crop area to apply the excreted nutrients, nutrient imbalances result, and the excess enters the environment, which in this case means the Chesapeake Bay estuary. Areas draining to the Chesapeake Bay (Susquehanna, Rappahannock, Potomac, and James rivers, along with the Upper Chesapeake and Lower Chesapeake basins proper) are home to 1.2 million hogs, 2.4 million cattle, and 220 million chickens.[6] These animals excrete 158 million pounds of phosphorus and

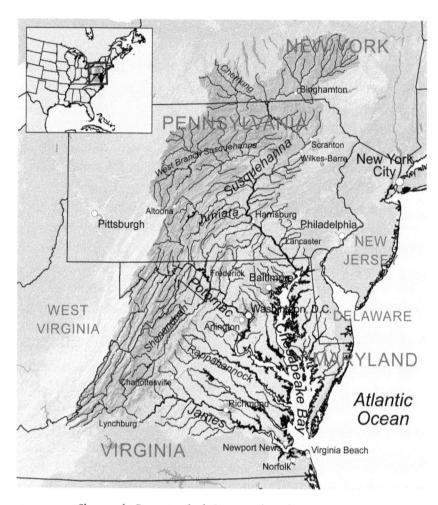

FIGURE 2.7. Chesapeake Bay watershed. *Source*: Wikimedia Commons, CC BY-SA 3.0, https://commons.wikimedia.org/w/index.php?curid=12520461.

560 million pounds of nitrogen in a year.[47] Our most nutrient-hungry crop, corn, needs about 25 pounds of phosphorus and 200 pounds of nitrogen per acre, meaning Chesapeake Bay animals excrete enough phosphorus and nitrogen to fertilize 5.5 million (P) and 2.8 million (N) acres of corn. Around 1.5 million acres of Chesapeake Bay land is committed to corn.[48] This illustrates the nutrient imbalances created by current configurations of livestock production in this region. These nu-

trient imbalances result in eutrophication of the estuary, reduced water clarity and biodiversity, and degraded recreational and aesthetic qualities of this major water resource, and once-thriving commercial fish and shellfish industries have been severely degraded.[46]

## Black Sea

The California-sized Black Sea is bordered by Russia, Ukraine, Bulgaria, Romania, Georgia, and Turkey. It receives freshwater from several major European rivers (especially the Danube), but Mediterranean Sea saltwater also intrudes through a hydrological connection known as the Bosphorus. Thus, Black Sea water is saltier than a lake but fresher than the ocean, producing a diverse ecosystem and productive fishery. Resorts along its shoreline have promoted Black Sea water as therapeutic for at least two centuries (Fig.2.8).

In the 1960s, USSR agricultural policy increased the use of chemical fertilizers. In addition, huge animal production systems were established in Soviet-bloc countries[49] (one Romanian CAFO had more than

FIGURE 2.8. Black Sea is shown in the middle of this map. *Source*: By Kamel 15-own work, CC BY-SA 3.0, https://commons.wikimedia.org/w/index.php?curid=5623/11.

a million hogs). By the 1970s, the Black Sea beaches of Ukraine and Romania were graveyards of fish, clams, and crabs doomed by a hypoxic dead zone in the Black Sea created by nitrogen and phosphorus pollution discharged by the Danube River. The excess of nutrients stimulated large blooms of phytoplankton, causing a collapse of the diverse brackish water ecosystem.

Following the collapse of the USSR in 1989, many of the huge CAFOs closed and use of chemical fertilizers declined. Only six years later in 1995, it was apparent that the Black Sea was recovering. By 2002, sensitive mussel beds were reestablished, and other ecological indicators were improving.

## Baltic Sea

Of the world's 400 or so known "dead zones" (i.e., low- or no-oxygen coastal areas degraded by excess nutrients), the Baltic Sea may host the largest and may in fact have seven distinct areas of reduced oxygen. Although nutrients from agriculture are also a main driver here, industrial and municipal discharge have contributed, along with the collapse of the cod fishery, which has caused ecosystem disruption favorable to harmful algae.

Large-scale hog production in Denmark, Poland, and other countries has been a strong contributor of nutrients to the Baltic Sea.[50] At any given time, Danish farmers are raising 13 million hogs[51] within the 16,600 mi$^2$ country, a density that exceeds even that of the largest hog-producing state in the United States, Iowa. And some individual Polish farms raise more than 60,000 hogs.[50] Management of manure nutrients from confined animal feeding operations is a difficult task on many farms.

The Baltic Sea is similar to the Black Sea in that they both are surrounded by land, are minimally connected to the larger ocean, and have salinity levels between that of the ocean and freshwater. The Baltic has also warmed substantially with climate change, a condition favorable for the algae that contribute to hypoxic zone formation. Water turnover rate is naturally slow (~30 years), and intrusion of salt water is restricted by shallow areas known as sills.[52] These natural conditions, coupled with anthropogenic inputs of nutrients, have expanded the Baltic Sea hypoxia zones 10-fold over the past century.[53]

## Iowa

The US Corn Belt state of Iowa has long been one of the country's leading producers of hogs, cattle, and poultry. Currently, Iowa exceeds all other states in egg and pork production and is fourth in production of feeder cattle.[6] Iowa has also been a leading producer of both corn and soybeans, frequently topping all other US states in harvested acres of these commodities.[6] To achieve this level of carbohydrate, protein, and vegetable oil production, nutrient inputs have been required that far exceed those present in the natural system that existed prior to European settlement. A consequence of this supercharged production system has been leakage of nutrients and other pollutants to the environment and especially the streams, lakes, and aquifers of the state (Fig 2.9).

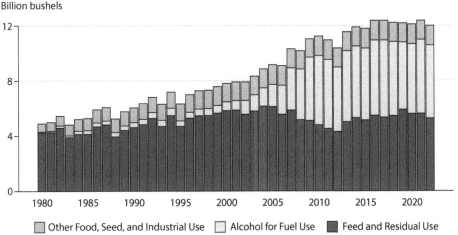

FIGURE 2.9. US domestic corn use. *Source*: US Department of Agriculture.

More than half of Iowa's corn is used to produce fuel ethanol, and most of the rest is used as livestock feed. Residuals from ethanol production—distillers dried grains (DDGs)—are also fed to livestock; in all, about half the calories contained within Iowa's corn crop end up in livestock feed. This is an enormous number of calories that nearly equals the caloric needs of the entire population of the United States. And an even greater percentage of the soybean crop is used in livestock feed.

While livestock production is geographically co-located with the growth of feed grain in a general way, most Iowa farms do not raise livestock; that is, most are committed solely to crop production. These crop farms do serve as end points for manure if a livestock producer has an inadequate crop area to dispose of the manure at rates that are allowed by Iowa rules. It has been found, however, that these rules do little to constrain farmers from applying manure and synthetic fertilizer nutrients far beyond recommended rates for crops.[9,10]

Livestock density strongly correlates with the nitrate concentration of adjacent streams in Iowa. Jones et al.[10] found that nitrate concentrations linked to total nitrogen inputs and generated manure but not with commercial nitrogen fertilizer amounts in nine Iowa watersheds. Manure nutrients applied to fields that were already fertilized with commercial nitrogen (implying a wastage of manure) created a surplus nitrogen condition that drives stream nitrate (Fig. 2.10).

Iowa has approximately 3,500 large concentrated animal feeding operations (CAFOs) as defined under the Clean Water Act[54] and several thousand smaller ones with even fewer regulations. CAFOs are operations that contain at least 700 dairy cows, 1,000 beef cows, 2,500 hogs, or 30,000 chickens. The state with the second-highest number of CAFOs, Minnesota, has only one-third as many (1,300). The neighboring states of Wisconsin and Illinois have fewer than 300. Livestock density in Iowa could explain why the state's stream phosphorus levels are two to three times higher than that of Illinois,

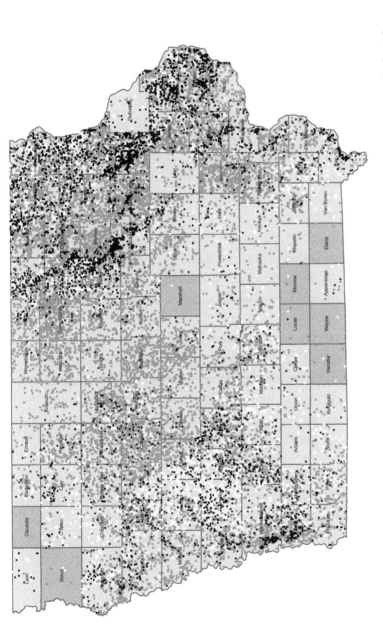

FIGURE 2.10. Correlations of 2017 watershed flow weighted average (FWA) NO3–N concentrations in nine Iowa watersheds with nitrogen (N) surplus (a); sum of commercial, manure, and fixation N (b); sum of commercial and manure nitrogen (c); commercial nitrogen (d); generated manure nitrogen (e); and area portion in corn and soybean (f). The dotted portion of the regression line in (a) is an extrapolation backward to a zero-surplus condition. FWA is defined as total NO3–N load divided by total discharge for 2017. Fixation is nitrogen sequestered into the soil in a microbe-mediated process with legumes, in this case, soybeans grown the previous year. *Source:* Anne Schechinger, Environmental Working Group.

even though Illinois has a large urban phosphorus contributor (Chicago metropolitan area) and about the same corn and soybean crop area as Iowa.[55]

Leakage of excess nutrients from Iowa's landscape has had dire environmental consequences that degrade recreational opportunities, reduce biodiversity, and increase the cost of drinking water for the state's residents. The largest city (Des Moines) and its surrounding area require nitrate removal at the municipal drinking water treatment plant, a process that creates a pollution stream of its own. Also, around 6,600 private wells (most in rural areas) in the state have tested above safe limits for nitrate since 2000, and many more have been contaminated with bacteria.[56]

Iowa streams drain to the Missouri and Mississippi rivers, and the nutrients contained within ultimately discharge to the Gulf of Mexico (Fig. 2.11). Iowa has been identified as a strong contributor of both nitrogen and phosphorus, the primary drivers of the Gulf's hypoxic (dead) zone.[55,56]

Iowa area comprises 3.3% of the Missouri River basin while contributing 12% of the water and 55% of the nitrate. Likewise, the state comprises 21% of the land area while contributing 21% of the water and 45% of the nitrate to the Upper Mississippi River basin. Finally, Iowa comprises 4.5% of the entire Mississippi basin area (including the Missouri River basin) while contributing 5.9% of the water and 29% of the nitrate,[57] as well as 15% of the phosphorus.[55]

Clearly, livestock populations and the crop production system that supports it are large drivers of degraded water quality in Iowa and in states downstream. Both Denmark and the Netherlands have livestock densities on the scale of Iowa. As a result, both countries have in the past suffered environmental consequences similar to Iowa's, but both countries' governments have intervened in more forceful ways than Iowa's leaders have. Going forward, desired environmental outcomes in this intense production system will need to be reconciled with economic and regulatory considerations important to the agricultural industry.

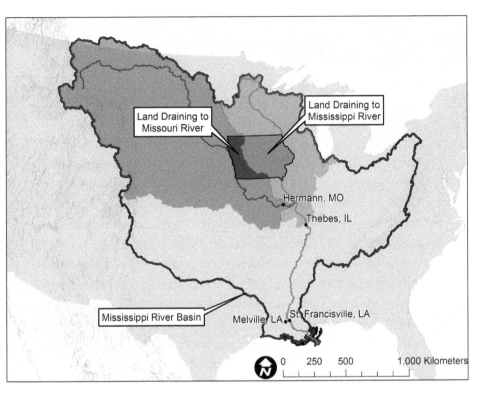

FIGURE 2.11. Areas of Iowa draining to the Missouri River and Mississippi River but not the Missouri River. *Source:* C. S. Jones, J. K. Nielsen, K. E. Schilling, and L. J. Weber. (2018). Iowa stream nitrate and the Gulf of Mexico. *PLOS ONE* 13(4): e0195930. https://doi.org/10.1371/journal.pone.0195930

## Potential Policies for Improved Environmental Outcomes

The existing livestock production schemes in the United States and other developed countries did not happen by accident—policy, or the absence thereof (such as weak regulatory frameworks), incentivizes the concentration of production in places like Iowa and the Western Lake Erie basin. Industrialized farm animal production (IFAP), which here could be defined as feeding animals cash crop grains in confined or restricted living conditions, links closely to other agricultural systems. For example, the US renewable fuel standard guarantees a market for corn. DDGs are a by-product of fuel ethanol production and can be fed to animals. Corn is a nutrient-hungry crop that can be fertilized with animal manure. Thus, ethanol production relates to mono-cropping corn (continuous corn versus corn–soybean rotation) and livestock production in indirect but important ways.

Efficiencies of production in concentrated animal schemes have influenced consumer prices. For example, the early stages of consolidation in the hog industry did reduce pork prices $29 per year for the average US customer.[58] These efficiencies can only be realized, however, when the costs of the externalities of water and air pollution and water resource depletion are distributed to the public at large and not to the farmers, packers, and retailers. This is where policy must intercede if improved environmental outcomes are to result.

What might these policies look like? Of course, this will depend on the type of production system. Incentivizing the return of cattle to pasture (from open feed lots and buildings) would be one first step. The renewable fuel standard catalyzed the conversion of pasture to corn crops and reduced available area for grazing.[59] Much of this converted land was marginally suitable for corn and thus more vulnerable to soil erosion and/or nutrient loss tied to corn production practices. Growing corn for ethanol also displaces forage crops like alfalfa, which could be grown without irrigation in much of the Corn Belt but require enormous amounts of irrigation water in the arid western United States (alfalfa/hay consumes the most irrigation water across all water sources).[60] This has had profound environmental and sociological consequences across the Colorado River basin and in fact most of the farmed western United States.[61] Likewise, corn grown for confinement cattle and fuel ethanol have helped to deplete the Ogallala aquifer in Kansas and other states to alarmingly low levels.[62] Around 6,000 years are required to recharge the aquifer naturally.[63]

Grazing cattle on pasture emulates the native grassland ecosystem that was grazed by bison and elk. Grazing would reduce the burden of manure management intrinsic to confined systems. Several existing policies help farmers construct water systems that enable them to restrict grazing animals from streams and eliminate or reduce stream degradation associated with animal wading. Programs of this sort, coupled with a retreat from the renewable fuel standard, could make meat production more sustainable.[64]

Recoupling livestock and crop production on individual farms could help farmers "close" nutrient cycling and avoid exporting grain to feed animals in distant areas that lack sufficient crop ground to utilize manure nutrients judiciously. Much of modern livestock production in the United States and elsewhere has been decoupled from crop production. Instead of grazing on forage crops, animals are fed with cash crop grains, mainly corn and soybeans, in a system designed for efficiency and rapid animal growth to market weights. This scheme requires large inputs of fossil fuel for nitrogen fertilizer, pesticides, grain drying, and equipment manufacturing, and other input costs, notably seeds modified with biotechnology, are also high. But because the renewable fuel standard guarantees a market for corn, these costs have become justified on lands that once were marginal for corn production but were productive pasture ground for grazing cattle. Thus, many Corn Belt farmers are indirectly incentivized to focus solely on crops, leaving a small minority to only raise livestock or link their own crop fertilization schemes to their animals' manure. The emergence of soybeans as a livestock feed helped that crop displace oats, alfalfa, and clovers, all crops with lower input costs and that degrade the environment far less than corn and soybean.[65] Return of Corn Belt land to alfalfa production could potentially reduce production of this crop in areas of the western United States where irrigation with dwindling water supplies is necessary. Feeding livestock with corn and soybean requires concentration of animals and subsequently has made manure management an enormous challenge, with consequences for both water and air.

A return of cattle to pasture would help diversify farms. Farmers are incentivized to crop marginally productive land when animals are confined and fed cash crop grains. These lands are often hilly and vulnerable to soil erosion, which increases losses of phosphorus to the stream network.[55] In the United States, federal cost share programs exist that help farmers set up fencing and watering systems that enable rotational grazing and restrict cattle from damaging stream banks and beds and defecating and urinating in streams. A return to these sorts of schemes very likely would reduce nutrient and other types of pollution. Likewise, a move away from the large hog confinement model and a return to hog production in pasture farrowing systems[66] would very likely increase the number of hog operations, bring diversity to farms, and make manure management less perilous to the environment. Animals can also be grazed in multispecies systems[67] that are more sustainable and humane environments for livestock.

Creative government policies favorable to these types of systems would produce positive environmental outcomes for the public. The transition away from these less intense production systems to the IFAP model was clearly made possible, at least in part, by the absence of regulations limiting CAFO pollution.

If animals are to remain in concentrated systems, laws that focus on and enforce measurable environmental outcomes could reduce the pollution inherent to these production systems. Such laws might include limiting the number of animals such that the watershed can meet water quality goals, government agency tracking of manure nutrients, aligning nutrient inputs to crops with their expected uptake, and prohibitions on manure application when the likelihood of loss from fields is high (i.e., winter, onto snow and frozen ground, just prior to expected storms, on steep slopes, near streambanks, etc.). Enforceable nutrient and pathogen standards for streams could force livestock facilities in those watersheds to suspend operation until they implement pollution-trapping or pollution-reducing methods. Stream nutrient standards have been used to help reduce phosphorus pollution of the Illinois River in Arkansas and Oklahoma.[68] The river and an impoundment on the river (Ten Killer Lake) are some of the most valuable and highly used water resources in Oklahoma. Poultry waste, primarily from concentrated broiler operations in Arkansas, is used to (over) fertilize pasture ground for cattle production, and its runoff seriously degrades the river and the lake.[69] Oklahoma sued Arkansas poultry producers in 2005 and ultimately won the case in 2023.[70] While the stream is improving, the limit of 0.037 mg/L phosphorus is still not being met at all times.[69] Similar regulatory frameworks that focus on air quality could also be developed in areas with high concentrations of livestock.

Many have considered anaerobic manure digesters as a means of making manure waste more manageable.[71] These also present the opportunity to reduce greenhouse gas emissions ($CO_2$ and methane-$CH_4$) from manure waste.[72] Methane has about 80 times the warming power of $CO_2$ and animal agriculture generates 32% of worldwide emissions.[73] Manure biogas systems (anaerobic digesters) potentially reduce emissions by capturing methane and then using it to displace the use of fossil fuels, namely, natural gas. This solution is intuitive, and in fact, the US federal government has tried to incentivize this strategy.[74] Digesters concentrate most of the manure nitrogen and phosphorus into a liquid that can then be used to fertilize crops. Solids are then usually applied as a soil amendment to farmed fields. This solution does have detractors, mainly because digesters do not reduce the overall volume of waste and fail to address the main driver of livestock-related water pollution: overpopulation of animals in polluted watersheds and consequently quantities of manure nutrients that exceed crop needs. Digesters are not mechanically foolproof and require skilled operators, and those that malfunction can seriously degrade nearby waterways.[75] There are also questions surrounding worker safety related to these systems.[76] Expense is also a concern for many operators.

Demand for meat products ultimately drives the level of production in many societies. Availability seldom limits consumption of meat in most Western countries where meat consumption is high. Globally, meat consumption increased 58% from 1998 to 2018, and only half of this was due to human population increase.[77] The United States leads the world in per capita meat consumption (except for Hong Kong) at 128 kg/year,[78] an amount that has increased 45% since 1961. Total meat consumed in the United States has increased fivefold since 1909.[79]

This demand for meat clearly links to the environmental consequences of livestock production. In Europe, total meat consumption, especially meat from ruminant animals, explains most of the country-to-country variation in the environmental footprint of food production.[80] In the modern era, the biomass contained within human bodies outweighs that of Earth's wild mammals 8:1, and when we add in our domesticated food animals, that ratio jumps to 23:1.[81] This last ratio must be enormous in places like Iowa and Denmark, where livestock production is intense, and where water quality and other environmental degradation is a serious concern.

Policymakers take great risks when they attempt to improve animal welfare and environmental outcomes by steering consumer choices toward alternatives. Attitudes about food and eating in general can be strongly held and are embedded within a myriad of religious, cultural, geographical, and economic factors. While meat rationing was common among countries during World War II, even then strong moral appeals were needed to convince people of the necessity of the policy.[82] It seems unlikely that this approach would be politically viable in the present day, especially in high-income countries. Certainly, some people are aware of the environmental consequences of meat consumption and feel those outcomes are unavoidable and a fair trade-off for the pleasure of consuming meat.

If farmers, food processors, and retailers were required through regulation to reduce the environmental pollution resulting from meat production, and those costs were passed on to the consumer, would meat consumption decline? The evidence is not clear. Modestly increasing the price of beef (£0.20 per meal) did not reduce consumption in the United Kingdom,[83] while another study in the same country showed consumption declining with price increases.[84] And it is a near certainty that many people would be unhappy with price increases linked to environmental objectives. These are difficult problems for countries to confront, but a reckoning will be imperative. Climate change, air and water pollution, increased wealth in developing countries, and continued population growth may force societies into more sustainable food production systems.

## REFERENCES

1. Mittasch, A., and W. Frankenburger. 1929. The historical development and theory of ammonia synthesis. *Journal of Chemical Education* 6 (12): 2097.
2. Commoner, B. 1977. Cost-risk-benefit analysis of nitrogen fertilization: A case history. *Ambio* 157–161.
3. Fujita, K., K. G. Ofosu-Budu, and S. Ogata. 1992. Biological nitrogen fixation in mixed legume-cereal cropping systems. *Plant and Soil* 141 (1): 155–175.
4. Yates-Doerr, E. 2012. Meeting the demand for meat? *Anthropology Today* 28 (1): 11–15.
5. Delgado, C., M. Rosegrant, H. Steinfeld, S, Ehui, and C. Courbois. 2001. Livestock to 2020: The next food revolution. *Outlook on Agriculture* 30 (1): 27–29.
6. USDA, National Agricultural Statistics Service (NASS). https://www.nass.usda.gov/
7. Legislative Services Agency, Iowa Legislature. 2019. Livestock inventory historical trends. https://www.legis.iowa.gov/docs/publications/IR/1048437.pdf
8. Libra, R. D., C. F. Wolter, and R. J. Langel. 2004. Nitrogen and phosphorus budgets for Iowa and Iowa watersheds. https://s-iihr34.iihr.uiowa.edu/publications/uploads/Tis-47.pdf
9. Jackson, L. L., D. R. Keeney, and E. M. Gilbert. 2000. Swine manure management plans in north-central Iowa: Nutrient loading and policy implications. *Journal of Soil and Water Conservation* 55 (2): 205–212.
10. Jones, C. S., C. W. Drake, C. E. Hruby, K. E. Schilling, and C. F. Wolter. 2019. Livestock manure driving stream nitrate. *Ambio* 48 (10): 1143–1153.
11. Stanford, G. 1966. Nitrogen requirements of crops for maximum yield. Agricultural anhydrous ammonia technology and use (agriculturalanh): 237–257.
12. Mallarino, A. P., B. M. Stewart, J. L. Baker, J. D. Downing, and J. E. Sawyer. 2002. Phosphorus indexing for cropland: Overview and basic concepts of the Iowa phosphorus index. *Journal of Soil and Water Conservation* 57 (6): 440–447.
13. Fox, R. H., and W. P. Piekielek. 1987. Yield response to N fertilizer and N fertilizer use efficiency in no-tillage and plow-tillage corn. *Communications in Soil Science and Plant Analysis* 18 (5): 495–513.
14. Camberato, J. 2012. A historical perspective on nitrogen fertilizer rate recommendations for corn in Indiana (1953–2011). Purdue Extension. https://extension.purdue.edu/extmedia/ay/ay-335-w.pdf
15. Loubet, B., W. A. Asman, M. R. Theobald, O. Hertel, Y. S. Tang, P. Robin, M. Hassouna, U. Dämmgen, S. Genermont, P. Cellier, and M. A. Sutton. 2009. Ammonia deposition near hot spots: processes, models and monitoring methods. In *Atmospheric Ammonia: Detecting Emission Changes and Environmental Impacts*, edited by Mark A. Sutton, Stefan Reis, and Samantha M. H. Baker, 205–267. Springer.

16. McGinn, S. M., H. H. Janzen, T. W. Coates, K. A. Beauchemin, and T. K. Flesch. 2016. Ammonia emission from a beef cattle feedlot and its local dry deposition and re-emission. *Journal of Environmental Quality* 45 (4): 1178–1185.

17. Fleming, R. A., B. Babcock, and E. Wang. 1998. Resource or waste? The economics of swine manure storage and management. *Applied Economic Perspectives and Policy* 20 (1): 96–113.

18. Sheriff, G. 2005. Efficient waste? Why farmers over-apply nutrients and the implications for policy design. *Applied Economic Perspectives and Policy* 27 (4): 542–557.

19. Klepper, R. 1974. Fertilizer application rates and nitrate concentrations in Illinois surface waters. National Agricultural Library. http://agris.fao.org/agris -search/search.do?recordID=US201300533223

20. Hatfield, J. L., L. D. McMullen, and C. S. Jones. 2009. Nitrate–nitrogen patterns in the raccoon river basin related to agricultural practices. *Journal of Soil and Water Conservation* 64:190–199.

21. Fan, A. M., and V. E. Steinberg. 1996. Health implications of nitrate and nitrite in drinking water: An update on methemoglobinemia occurrence and reproductive and developmental toxicity. *Regulatory Toxicology and Pharmacology* 23 (1): 35–43.

22. Van Meter, K. J., N. B. Basu, and P. Van Cappellen. 2017. Two centuries of nitrogen dynamics: Legacy sources and sinks in the Mississippi and Susquehanna river basins. *Global Biogeochemical Cycles* 31:2–23.

23. David, M. B., L. E. Gentry, D. A. Kovacic, and K. M. Smith. 1997. Nitrogen balance in and export from an agricultural watershed. *Journal of Environmental Quality* 26:1038–1048.

24. Jones, C. S., A. Seeman, P. M. Kyveryga, K. E. Schilling, A. Kiel, K.-S. Chan, and C. F. Wolter. 2016. Crop rotation and raccoon river nitrate. *Journal of Soil and Water Conservation* 71:206–219.

25. Alexander, R. B., R. A. Smith, G. E. Schwarz, E. W. Boyer, J. V. Nolan, and J. W. Brakebill. 2008. Differences in phosphorus and nitrogen delivery to the Gulf of Mexico from the Mississippi River basin. *Environmental science & technology*, 42 (3): 822–830.

26. Mee, L. 2006. Reviving dead zones. *Scientific American* 295:78–85.

27. Wang, J., Q. Liu, Y. Hou, W. Qin, J. P. Lesschen, F. Zhang, and O. Oenema. 2018. International trade of animal feed: Its relationships with livestock density and N and P balances at country level. *Nutrient Cycling in Agroecosystems* 110:197–211.

28. Oenema, O., D. Oudendag, and G. L. Velthof. 2007. Nutrient losses from manure management in the European Union. *Livestock Science* 112: 261–272.

29. Oetking, P., R. Back, R. Watson, and C. Merks. 1974.. *Hydrography on the nearshore continental shelf of south central Louisiana: Final Report of Offshore Ecology Investigation for Gulf Universities Research Consortium, Galveston, Texas.* Corpus Christi, TX: Southwest Research Institute. Project. (03±3720).

30. Justić, D., N. N. Rabalais, and R. E. Turner. 1995. Stoichiometric nutrient balance and origin of coastal eutrophication. *Marine Pollution Bulletin* 30 (1): 41–46.
31. Leming, T. D., and W. E. Stuntz. 1984. Zones of coastal hypoxia revealed by satellite scanning have implications for strategic fishing. *Nature* 310 (5973): 131–138.
32. Renaud, M. L. 1986. Hypoxia in Louisiana coastal waters during 1983: Implications for fisheries. *Fishery Bulletin* 84 (1): 19–26.
33. Ferber, D. 2001. Keeping the stygian waters at bay. *Science* 291:968–973.
34. Diaz, R. J., and A. Solow. 1999. Ecological and economic consequences of hypoxia. Topic 2 report for the integrated assessment on hypoxia in the Gulf of Mexico. https://repository.library.noaa.gov/view/noaa/21436
35. Tian, H., R. Xu, S. Pan, Y. Yao, Z. Bian, W. J. Cai, C. S. Hopkinson, D. Justic, S. Lohrenz, C. Lu, and W. Ren. 2020. Long-term trajectory of nitrogen loading and delivery from Mississippi River basin to the Gulf of Mexico. *Global Biogeochemical Cycles* 34 (5): e2019GB006475.
36. Greenhalgh, Suzie, and Paul Faeth. 2001. A potential integrated water quality strategy for the Mississippi River basin and the Gulf of Mexico. *The Scientific World Journal* 1:982595. https://doi.org/10.1100/tsw.2001.354
37. Armstrong, B. N., M. K. Cambazoglu, and J. D. Wiggert. 2021. Modeling the impact of the 2019 Bonnet Carré Spillway opening and local river flooding on the Mississippi Sound. In *OCEANS 2021: San Diego–Porto*, 1–7. IEEE.
38. Rabalais, N. N., and R. E. Turner. 2019. Gulf of Mexico hypoxia: Past, present, and future. *Limnology and Oceanography Bulletin* 28 (4): 117–124.
39. Kane, D. D., J. D. Conroy, R. P. Richards, D. B. Baker, and D. A. Culver. 2014. Re-eutrophication of Lake Erie: Correlations between tributary nutrient loads and phytoplankton biomass. *Journal of Great Lakes Research* 40: 496–501.
40. Ludsin, S. A., M. W. Kershner, K. A. Blocksom, R. L. Knight, and R. A. Stein. 2001. Life after death in Lake Erie: Nutrient controls drive fish species richness, rehabilitation. *Ecological Applications* 11 (3): 731–746.
41. Steffen, M. M., T. W. Davis, R.M.L. McKay, G. S. Bullerjahn, L. E. Krausfeldt, J. M. Stough, M. L. Neitzey, N. E. Gilbert, G. L. Boyer, T. H. Johengen, and D. C. Gossiaux. 2017. Ecophysiological examination of the Lake Erie Microcystis bloom in 2014: Linkages between biology and the water supply shutdown of Toledo, OH. *Environmental Science & Technology* 51 (12): 6745–6755.
42. Turner, R. E., N. N. Rabalais, and D. Justic. 2006. Predicting summer hypoxia in the northern Gulf of Mexico: Riverine N, P, and Si loading. *Marine Pollution Bulletin* 52 (2): 139–148. https://doi.org/10.1016/j.marpolbul.2005.08.012
43. Howarth, R. W., and R. Marino. 2006. Nitrogen as the limiting nutrient for eutrophication in coastal marine ecosystems: Evolving views over three decades. *Limnology and Oceanography* 51 (1, pt 2): 364–376.
44. Kast, J. B., A. M. Apostel, M. M. Kalcic, R. L. Muenich, A. Dagnew, C. M. Long, G. Evenson, and J. F. Martin. 2021. Source contribution to phosphorus loads from the Maumee River watershed to Lake Erie. *Journal of Environmental Management* 279:111803.

45. Han, H., J. D. Allan, and N. S. Bosch. 2012. Historical pattern of phosphorus loading to Lake Erie watersheds. *Journal of Great Lakes Research* 38 (2): 289–298.
46. Beegle, D. 2013. Nutrient management and the Chesapeake Bay. *Journal of Contemporary Water Research & Education* 151 (1): 3–8.
47. Libra, R. D., C. F. Wolter, and R. J. Langel. 2004. Nitrogen and phosphorus budgets for Iowa and Iowa watersheds. https://s-iihr34.iihr.uiowa.edu /publications/uploads/Tis-47.pdf
48. Baxter, R., A. Plakkat, G. Camargo, M. Dubin, C. A. Rotz, G. Roth, and T. L. Richard. 2009. Biofuels for the bay: Cellulosic double crops in the Chesapeake watershed. In ASABE - Bioenergy Engineering Conference 2009, 259–264. American Society of Agricultural and Biological Engineers.
49. Mee, L. 2006. Reviving dead zones. *Scientific American* 295 (5): 78–85.
50. Wetzels, H. 2020. Poland, drowning in algae: Dead zones in the Baltic Sea. Paper presented at the Agriculture and Rural Convention, November 18. https://www .arc2020.eu/poland-drowning-in-algae-dead-zones-in-the-baltic-sea/#:~:text =Marine%20life%20in%20the%20Baltic,largely%20unchecked%20by%20EU%20 regulations
51. Statista. Number of pigs on farms in Denmark from 2011 to 2021. https://www .statista.com/statistics/643196/number-of-pigs-on-farms-in-denmark/
52. Carstensen, J., and D. J. Conley. 2019. Baltic Sea hypoxia takes many shapes and sizes. *Limnology and Oceanography Bulletin* 28 (4): 125–129.
53. Carstensen, J., J. H. Andersen, B. G. Gustafsson, and D. J. Conley. 2014. Deoxygenation of the Baltic Sea during the last century. *Proceedings of the National Academy of Sciences* 111 (15): 5628–5633.
54. Rock, K. 2018. Growing number of concentrated animal feeding operations raises water quality concerns. Center for Rural Affairs, January 18. https://www .cfra.org/blog/growing-number-concentrated-animal-feeding-operations-raises -water-quality-concerns
55. Schilling, K. E., M. T. Streeter, A. Seeman, C. S. Jones, and C. F. Wolter. 2020. Total phosphorus export from Iowa agricultural watersheds: Quantifying the scope and scale of a regional condition. *Journal of Hydrology* 581:124397.
56. Environmental Working Group and Iowa Environmental Council. 2019. Iowa's private wells contaminated by nitrate and bacteria. https://www.ewg.org /interactive-maps/2019_iowa_wells/
57. Jones, C. S., J. K. Nielsen, K. E. Schilling, and L. J. Weber. 2018. Iowa stream nitrate and the Gulf of Mexico. *PLoS ONE* 13 (4): e0195930.
58. U.S. hog giant transforms Eastern Europe. 2009. *New York Times*, May 5. https://www.nytimes.com/2009/05/06/business/global/06smithfield.html
59. Lark, T. J., N. P. Hendricks, A. Smith, N. Pates, S. A. Spawn-Lee, M. Bougie, E. G. Booth, C. J. Kucharik, and H. K. Gibbs. 2022. Environmental outcomes of the US renewable fuel standard. *Proceedings of the National Academy of Sciences* 119 (9): e2101084119.

60. Ruess, P. J., M. Konar, N. Wanders, and M. Bierkens. 2023. Irrigation by crop in the Continental United States from 2008 to 2020. *Water Resources Research* 59 (2): e2022WR032804.

61. Wheeler, K. G., B. Udall, J. Wang, E. Kuhn, H. Salehabadi, and J. C. Schmidt. 2022. What will it take to stabilize the Colorado River? *Science* 377 (6604): 373–375.

62. Rhodes, E. C., H. L. Perotto-Baldivieso, E. P. Tanner, J. P. Angerer, and W. E. Fox. 2023. The declining Ogallala aquifer and the future role of rangeland science on the North American High Plains. *Rangeland Ecology & Management* 87: 83–96.

63. Little, J. B. 2009. The Ogallala aquifer: Saving a vital U.S. water source. *Scientific American*, March 1.

64. Jackson, R. D. 2022. Grazed perennial grasslands can match current beef production while contributing to climate mitigation and adaptation. *Agricultural & Environmental Letters* 7 (1): e20059.

65. Hatfield, J. L., L. D. McMullen, and C. S. Jones. 2009. Nitrate-nitrogen patterns in the Raccoon River basin related to agricultural practices. *Journal of Soil and Water Conservation* 64 (3): 190–199.

66. Reich, D., and J. B. Kliebenstein. 2006. Economics of breeding, gestating and farrowing hogs in "natural pork" production; financial comparison. *Iowa State University Animal Industry Report* 3 (1). https://porkgateway.org/wp-content/uploads/2015/07/economics-of-breeding-gestating-and-farrowing-hogs-in-natural-pork-production-financial-comparison1.pdf

67. Martin, G., K. Barth, M. Benoit, C. Brock, M. Destruel, B. Dumont, M. Grillot, S. Hübner, M. A. Magne, M. Moerman, and C. Mosnier. 2020. Potential of multi-species livestock farming to improve the sustainability of livestock farms: A review. *Agricultural Systems* 181:102821.

68. Oklahoma Water Resources Board. XXXX. Water quality standards. 2020–2021 Illinois River watershed total phosphorus criterion. https://www.owrb.ok.gov/rules/wqs/revisions/totalphosphorous.php

69. Crawford, G. 2023. Report: Phosphorus in river watershed still too high. *Tahlequah Daily Press*, February 23. https://www.tahlequahdailypress.com/news/report-phosphorus-in-river-watershed-still-too-high/article_fdb58ac6-c0e9-55fc-b22b-4254f863adc1.html

70. Thompson, D. 2023. Arkansas poultry companies pollute Illinois River, federal judge rules. *Arkansas Democrat Gazette*, January 20. https://www.arkansasonline.com/news/2023/jan/20/arkansas-poultry-companies-pollute-illinois-river/

71. Khanal, S. K. 2011. *Anaerobic biotechnology for bioenergy production: Principles and applications.* John Wiley & Sons.

72. Lazenby, R. 2022. Rethinking manure biogas. Policy considerations to promote equity and protect the climate and environment. Vermont Center for Agriculture and Food Systems. https://www.vermontlaw.edu/academics/centers-and-programs/center-for-agriculture-and-food-systems/reports/manure-biogas

73. Willett, W., J. Rockström, B. Loken, M. Springmann, T. Lang, S. Vermeulen, T. Garnett, D. Tilman, F. DeClerck, A. Wood, and M. Jonell. 2019. Food in the Anthropocene: The EAT–Lancet Commission on healthy diets from sustainable food systems. *The Lancet* 393 (10170): 447–492.

74. Schneider, K. 2023. 'A national scandal': How US climate funding could make water pollution worse. *The Guardian*, February 8. https://www.theguardian.com/environment/2023/feb/08/biden-climate-law-pollution-midwest

75. Strong, J. 2022. Company filled massive manure container despite signs of a leak, DNR says. *Iowa Capital Dispatch*, July 6.

76. Jordan, E. 2021. No OSHA probe of man who died in dive into farm digester. *Cedar Rapids Gazette*, June 17.

77. Whitnall, T., and N. Pitts. 2019. Global trends in meat consumption. *Agricultural Commodities* 9 (1): 96–99.

78. Ritchie, H., P. Rosado, and M. Roser. 2019. Meat and dairy production. Our World in Data. https://ourworldindata.org/meat-production

79. Barclay, E. 2012. A nation of meat eaters: See how it all adds up. National Public Radio, June 27. https://www.npr.org/sections/thesalt/2012/06/27/155527365/visualizing-a-nation-of-meat-eaters#:~:text=As%20Allison%20Aubrey%20and%20Dan,plants%20to%20raise%20and%20transport

80. Mertens, E., A. Kuijsten, H. H. van Zanten, G. Kaptijn, M. Dofková, L. Mistura, L. D'Addezio, A. Turrini, C. Dubuisson, S. Havard, and E. Trolle. 2019. Dietary choices and environmental impact in four European countries. *Journal of Cleaner Production* 237:117827.

81. Kolbert, E. 2019. Louisiana's disappearing coast. *The New Yorker*, April 1.

82. Carruth, A. 2009. War rations and the food politics of late modernism. *Modernism/Modernity* 16 (4): 767–795.

83. Garnett, E. E., A. Balmford, T. M. Marteau, M. A. Pilling, and C. Sandbrook. 2021. Price of change: Does a small alteration to the price of meat and vegetarian options affect their sales? *Journal of Environmental Psychology* 75:101589.

84. Charlebois, S., M. McCormick, and M. Juhasz. 2016. Meat consumption and higher prices: Discrete determinants affecting meat reduction or avoidance amidst retail price volatility. *British Food Journal* 118 (9): 2251–2270.

## Other Resources

Clark, M., J. Hill, and D. Tilman. 2018. The diet, health and environment trilemma. *Annual Review of Environment and Resources* 43:109–134. https://doi.org/10.1146/annurev-environ-102017-025957.

Iowa Corn Growers Association. https://www.iowacorn.org/corn-uses/ethanol#:~:text=57%25%20of%20Iowa's%20corn%20is,for%20you%20and%20your%20family!

Lemaire, G., A. Franzluebbers, P. César de Faccio Carvalho, B. Dedieu. 2014. Integrated crop–livestock systems: Strategies to achieve synergy between agricultural production and environmental quality. *Agriculture, Ecosystems and Environment.* http://dx.doi.org/10.1016/j.agee.2013.08.009.

Magdoff, F., L. Lanyon, and B. Liebhardt,1997. Nutrient cycling, transformations, and flows: Implications for a more sustainable agriculture. *Advanced Agronomy* 60:1–73. https://doi.org/10.1016/S0065-2113(08)60600-8.

Martin, M., M. Moraine, J. Ryschawy, M.A. Magne, M. Asai, J.-P. Sarthou, M. Duru, and O. Olivier. 2016. Crop–livestock integration beyond the farm level: A review. *Agronomy for Sustainable Development* 36:53.

Rabalais, N. N., R. E. Turner, and W. J. Wiseman Jr. 2002. Gulf of Mexico hypoxia, aka "the dead zone." *Annual Review of Ecology and Systematics* 33: 235–263.

Sulc, R. M., and B. Tracy. 2007. Integrated crop–livestock systems in the U.S. Corn Belt. *Agronomy Journal* 99:335–345.

# CHAPTER 3

# Air Pollution I

Occupational, Community, Regional, and Global Health Effects

James A. Merchant, Jerald L. Schnoor, Wayne T. Sanderson, D'Ann L. Williams, and David Osterberg

Air emissions arising from industrial farm animal production (IFAP) facility concentrated animal feeding operations, of all sizes (CAFOs), are public health hazards for workers, their neighbors, proximate rural communities, and regional community residents. In the 1970s, when small animal feeding operations were first found to cause respiratory symptoms among veterinarians and livestock farmers, these deep-pit facilities contained only a few hundred pigs. Nevertheless, respiratory symptoms were documented, as were numerous deaths among farmers and pigs from exposure to high concentrations of hydrogen sulfide when pits were agitated or pumped. At the same time, industrialization of poultry operations had growing quickly, with poultry CAFOs housing tens of thousands of birds. This was soon accompanied by rapid industrialization of swine operations and dairy and cattle feedlots that contained thousands to tens of thousands of animals producing air pollution and enormous amounts of manure, far greater than needed to fertilizer available crop land.

Particulate and gaseous emissions that arise from CAFOs, while varying in proportions, contain endotoxin-rich primary particles ($PM_{10}$, $PM_{2.5}$) and ammonia-rich secondary particles ($PM_{2.5}$), ammonia ($NH_3$)

and often hydrogen sulfide ($H_2S$) and other gases, hundreds of volatile organic compounds (VOCs), and other irritant and odorous chemicals—all of which expose CAFO workers, proximate rural neighbors, and rural community residents (Fig. 3.1). IFAP-dense regions receive wet and dry pollutant deposition to land and water bodies. Secondary particles arising from emitted ammonia play a dominant role in the production of ambient $PM_{2.5}$. IFAP facilities are also major sources of methane and oxides of nitrogen, both potent global warming gases.

## Occupational Exposures

CAFO workers breathe high concentrations of a complex mixture of dust particles, bioaerosols, gases, and vapors that are threats to their health. This is a self-selected workforce, as those with acute symptoms frequently leave IFAP employment. Neighbors and rural community residents, some of whom are more vulnerable children, the elderly, asthmatics, and those with allergies and chronic obstructive lung disease, cannot easily relocate and are exposed to lower, but still hazardous, levels of CAFO emissions.

Because of the large number of animals in confined spaces, workers are often exposed to high concentrations of airborne organic dust particles, bioaerosols, and gases.[1,2] Particulate exposures include dusts generated from feeds (hay and grains), bedding, feathers, animal dander (skin and hair cells), and manure.[3] Attached to these aerosolized organic particles, or suspended independently, are a vast array of bioaerosols—bacteria, fungi, and viruses and their constituent compounds: endotoxins and glucans.[4] Endotoxins are a toxic heat-stable lipopolysaccharide substance present in the outer membrane of most Gram-negative bacteria that are released when the bacteria lyse. (1→3)-β-D-glucans are a group of glucose poylsaccharides in the cell walls of cereals, bacteria, and fungi.[5] Industrial farming operations also provide an environment for the spread of zoonotic pathogens such as *Salmonella*, *Leptospira*, and *Escherichia coli*.[6] Workers are at risk of infection through direct contact with animals or animal wastes.

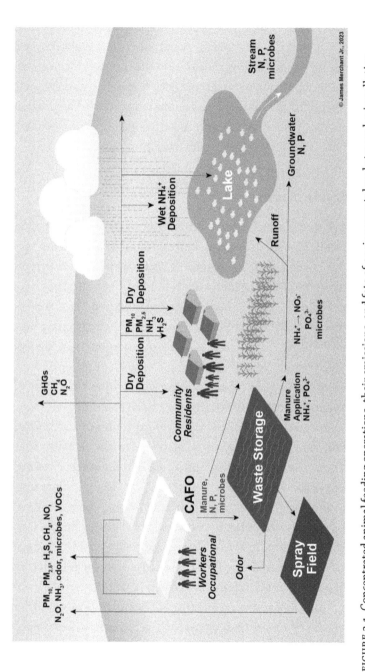

FIGURE 3.1. Concentrated animal feeding operations, their emissions, and fate of environmental and atmospheric pollution.

Pesticides are often used in CAFOs to control insect pests and diseases. Workers may be exposed through direct application, drift, or residues on surfaces.[7,8] The health effects from pesticide exposure range from skin irritation to respiratory and neurological effects. Several types of antibiotics are often added to animal feeds to prevent infections and increase growth. These antibiotics become airborne and inhaled by workers, causing allergic reactions and antibiotic resistance to bacterial infections.[9]

Toxic gas exposures include ammonia, hydrogen sulfide, methane, and carbon monoxide.[10] Ammonia forms from the biological and chemical breakdown of manure proteins, uric acid, and urea during storage and decomposition. Ammonia concentrations in industrial animal operations can reach levels that are highly irritating to the eyes and respiratory system. Hydrogen sulfide, produced by the decomposition of organic matter, can cause headaches, nausea, and, with high concentrations from agitation of manure, respiratory distress and death.[11,12] Methane is produced by the fermentation of animal waste and carbon dioxide when expired by animals. In high concentrations, these gases can displace oxygen and cause disorientation, suffocation, and death.

Industrial farming operations rarely monitor the levels of the particulates, bioaerosols, and gases. Federal and professional agencies have established criteria for safe levels of ammonia, carbon monoxide, and hydrogen sulfide in industrial work environments. However, there are currently no established criteria for safe levels of the organic particulates, bioaerosols, or endotoxin in CAFOs. Yet, workers are exposed to these multiple agents and often at concentrations greater than those encountered by most other occupations.

Fresh air ventilation can be provided through natural air currents or mechanical ventilation to reduce worker exposures to dusts and gases. However, this is often not done during cold weather due to heating costs. Implementing proper personal protective equipment and education for work in industrial farming operations, especially during high dust and gas concentrations, are essential components of worker health and safety programs. Regular monitoring of gas levels and referencing established occupational exposure limits, to ensure that workers are not overexposed to toxic gases, is another essential program component. Industrial hygiene measures coupled with a medical surveillance program to document respiratory symptoms and lung function, hearing protection, biomonitoring for novel pathogens and infections, and vaccination for endemic influenza and coronaviruses are all parts of a comprehensive CAFO health and safety program.

## Neighbor and Rural Community Exposures

IFAP facilities create air pollution that adversely affects neighbors and nearby communities but also regional populations and the environment. Primary particles ($PM_{10}$ and $PM_{2.5}$), animal dander, and endotoxin-laden dusts are emitted from industrial animal production facilities.[13] The Environmental Protection (EPA) has primary and secondary standards for $PM_{2.5}$ (average standards with levels of 12.0 μg/m$^3$ and 15.0 μg/m$^3$, respectively), as well as 24-hour standards with 98th percentile levels of 35 μg/m$^3$ and $PM_{10}$ 24-hour standards with one-expected exceedance and levels of 150 μg/m$^3$. Currently, the EPA proposes to retain primary 24-hour $PM_{2.5}$ standards and lower only the primary annual $PM_{2.5}$ standard from 12 μg/m$^3$ to 9–10 μg. EPA air quality monitoring, the primary source of available air emission data, is collected in municipalities with high populations, while air emissions monitoring in rural areas is limited, creating gaps in our understanding of rural air quality.

Some polluting gases are precursors in the formation of secondary fine particles ($PM_{2.5}$) such as ammonium nitrate ($NH_4NO_3$) and ammonium sulfate (($NH_4)_2SO_4$) aerosols, which, at a regional scale, contribute large proportions of anthropogenic $PM_{10}$ and even higher proportions of $PM_{2.5}$ in livestock dense regions.[14] Primary ($PM_{10}$) particles often contain endotoxin, and secondary organic dust particles often contain adsorbed $NH_3$. Other particles can be very small in diameter ($PM_{2.5}$) and penetrate deep into the lungs of exposed individuals.[14,15] In addition, toxic gases such $H_2S$ and $NH_3$, VOCs, and nitric oxide (NO) are emitted to the atmosphere with potential neighbor and rural community health effects.

Many states have regulated $H_2S$, $NH_3$, and odor concentrations at the property boundary of livestock operations. For example, Minnesota Rule 7009.0080 sets forth its $H_2S$ standard as follows: $H_2S$ exceeding 30 ppb (30-minute average) is not to be exceeded more than twice in a 5-day period and 50 ppb (30-minute average) more than twice in one year. However, producers are afforded an enforcement exemption during manure storage agitation and land application for a period of 21 days every year.[16,17] A second method states use to limit CAFO exposures is through required setback distances from CAFO structures to residences, businesses, churches, schools, and public use area. Iowa requires a setback distance of 1,875 feet for any type of manure storage lagoon associated with a confinement building containing up to 500 animal units (AU).[18] The distance increases to 1,259 ft. for CAFOs 501 to <1,000 AU, to 1,875 ft. for 1,000 to <3,000 AU, and to 2,375 ft. for CAFOs containing 3,000 or more AU. CAFOs with anaerobic lagoons and >3,000 AU have a setback distance of 3,000 ft. Animal feeding operations with 500 or fewer AU and covered manure storage structures require no setback distance. The Iowa Department of Natural Resources (DNR) allows groupings of 500 AU or less CAFOs owned by different family members that avoid any setback distance. This has contributed to an explosion of CAFOs in Iowa, having quadrupled to over 10,000 since documented by the Iowa Air Quality Study in 2002.[16,19] The total number and location of all small Iowa CAFOs is unknown. It is clear that a few thousand more than 10,000 exist based on an aerial survey of CAFOs, in a section of northwestern Iowa, that identified hundreds of additional small feeding operations. The Iowa DNR also manages a lax "Master Matrix" scoring method that allows 97% of CAFO applications to be approved.[19]

Odors from animal operations also cause workers, neighbors, and nearby residents to become symptomatic, impairing their quality of life (see chapter 4). Of the hundreds of documented VOCs and fixed gases in emissions detected from North Carolina swine facilities, most of these compounds were found individually to be at concentrations below published odor and irritation thresholds. Yet, human assessments of odor and irritant sensation remained strong, even at 1,000 meters, and have been detected miles from these facilities.[20,21]

While the concentration of primary particles rapidly declines once emitted from CAFOs, they are still measurable at least up to 1.5 miles from swine CAFOs, as endotoxin and as a specific DNA markers of pig protein, Pig-2-Bac.[12,22,23] A study of the spatial and temporal variation of endotoxin and $PM_{10}$ in a dense livestock farming region of the Netherlands provided estimates for 1,875- and 3,000-ft. buffer zones.[24] Temporal measurements were found to be more strongly related to $PM_{10}$ concentrations, while spatial livestock-related factors were more strongly related to endotoxin concentrations. The observed variability in these measurements led investigators to conclude that exposure estimates should be based on a broader set of sampling locations.

To more accurately estimate distant exposures from CAFO gases, O'Shaughnessy and Altmaier used the plume dispersion model, AERMOD, to determine the spatial distribution of hydrogen sulfide in the vicinity of 10 large Iowa swine CAFOs.[25] Their model utilized flux rates based on CAFO floor area, wind speed and direction, and rural dispersion coefficients to calculate an emission factor that closely modeled actual $H_2S$ measurements. The model revealed that the highest $H_2S$ concentrations could exceed 30 ppb for large CAFOs for distances within 0.5 km but that there was a long decay in $H_2S$ concentration to 2 ppb at 6 km (Fig. 3.2). Pavalonis et al., who studied mainly small swine animal feeding operations in Keokuk County, Iowa, also used AFO area ($m^2$), distance between the AFO and the residence (m), and a function of low wind speed and direction to calculate a resident's relative AFO exposure ($E_{relative}$).[26]

It is difficult to accurately characterize exposures from CAFO emissions of particles, bioaerosols, irritant gases, and odiferous compounds because of the constantly changing dynamics of plume dispersion and varying locations of nearby residents. Various methods employing stationary sampling devices are limited in their ability to collect adequate

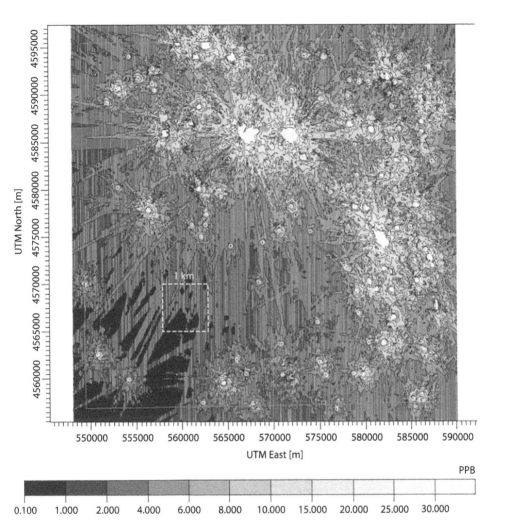

FIGURE 3.2. AERMOD-based model, Keokuk County, Iowa, H2S dispersion.
*Source*: O'Shaughnessey P, Altmaier R. (2011). Use of AERMOD to determine a hydrogen sulfide emission factor for seine operations by inverse modeling. Atmos Environ 45(27):4617–4625.

measurements to prevent exposure misclassification. Therefore, the primary method by which neighbors and rural resident health indices have been associated with CAFO pollution has been via the use of environmental proxies, distance from CAFOs, or use of numbers of CAFOs in buffer zones. This strategy has been successful in documenting higher prevalence rates of adverse health effects closer to, or with more dense clusters of, livestock operations.[21,26-33] Several studies have incorporated area sampling of specific air pollutants, as proxies, of CAFO pollution: Schinasi.[34] ($PM_{10}$, $PM_{2.5}$, endotoxin, $H_2S$, subjective odor by panel members), Guidry et al.[35] ($H_2S$), Smit et al.[33] ($PM_{10}$, endotoxin), Schulze et al.[32] ($NH_3$), Blanes-Vidal et al.[36] ($NH_3$), and Williams et al.[37] ($NH_3$, $PM_{10}$, cow allergen).

## Regional and Global Exposures

Regional and global effects arise from potent greenhouse gases (GHGs), methane ($CH_4$) and nitrous oxide ($N_2O$), which are emitted from IFAP facilities and operations. Methane causes 27.9 times the greenhouse radiative effect of carbon dioxide ($CO_2$), and nitrous oxide contributes 273 times greater effect than $CO_2$ measured as Global Warming Potential (GWP) over a 100-year period.[38] Even though concentrations of pollutants are diluted by a greater mixing volume of air as they are transported away from the facilities by wind velocity and turbulence, their GHG potential is unaffected.[12,17] Nevertheless, hydrogen sulfide concentrations emanating from hog confinement operations can reach concentrations at least as high as 671 ppm in the vicinity of animal operations, where they are as deadly as acute occupational exposures.[17,39] Concentrations are highest during agitation and mixing of manure to transport for manure application, to lagoons, or for waste treatment operations.

The largest class of industrial emissions of ammonia in the United States is from agricultural operations, as has been well documented in the highly concentrated swine and poultry production regions of North Carolina and in the Netherlands.[40,41] Concentrations downwind from animal feeding operations in northeastern Colorado were found to be approximately 200 ppb for $NH_3$ and 2,600 ppb for $CH_4$ at a distance of 120 m.[42] Total emissions for three counties in northeastern Colorado were substantial at $1.9 \times 10^9$ g month$^{-1}$ for $NH_3$ and $10.6 \times 10^9$ g month$^{-1}$ for $CH_4$. $PM_{2.5}$ and gases are transported through atmospheric circulation and dispersed from facilities to distant receptors. Their fate and transport are influenced by weather conditions, atmospheric turbulence and mixing, humidity, temperature, vegetative surfaces, and precipitation. Toxic gases, $H_2S$ and $NH_3$, as well as $PM_{2.5}$, can expose community residents located within several thousand feet of the animal production operations.[43] Dry deposition in nearby fields results when $PM_{2.5}$ particles and gases are deposited on vegetation and other surfaces in the absence of precipitation.

Wet deposition occurs when the airborne pollutants fall to the ground or water surfaces by rainfall, snowfall, or hail/sleet. Contamination of water bodies can occur when manure is applied to the land as fertilizer with subsequent runoff. Ammonium, phosphate, and nitrate ($NH_4^+$, $PO_4^{3-}$, $NO_3^-$) are of particular concern in this regard.[40] Wet deposition is directly proportional to the concentration of pollutants intercepted by the rain, snow, or ice phase. Hydroxyl radicals in the atmosphere are responsible for oxidizing $H_2S$ and VOCs to more innocuous products. When ammonia mixes with sulfur oxides and nitrogen oxides in the atmosphere, secondary aerosol particles ($PM_{2.5}$) are formed and can be transported over large distances and last for days to weeks.[40,41]

Potent greenhouse gases, $CH_4$ and $N_2O$, disperse from the boundary layer near the earth to the troposphere and upper atmosphere, where they exert their warming potential on planet Earth. Globally, livestock-related nitrous oxide emissions are estimated to total between 1 and 2 million metric tons of nitrous oxide–N each year.[43] Animal production facilities are considered one of the main sources of $CH_4$ and $N_2O$ to the atmosphere from humans. Of total anthropogenic emissions, ~37% of $CH_4$ and 65% of $N_2O$ emanate from animal production.[44]

## Occupational Health Effects

Workers in CAFOs are exposed daily to a wide variety of gases, vapors, bioaerosols, dusts, and other chemicals that cause respiratory symptoms, lung function impairment, and pulmonary diseases. The first description of health hazards among animal confinement facility workers was documentation of respiratory symptoms among veterinarians by Donham and colleagues.[45] This study was followed by documentation of deaths from pulmonary edema, later recognized as acute respiratory distress syndrome (ARDS), from high exposures (>500 ppm to hydrogen sulfide during agitating, emptying, and sometimes entering manure pits.[46,47] These events were often accompanied by the deaths of an entire population of pigs in a confined facility.

A number of other respiratory manifestations, including sinusitis, asthma, bronchitis, airway obstruction, and organic toxic dust syndrome (ODTS), have been documented among CAFO workers. The most common health effects are bronchitis, asthma, and an asthma-like condition accompanied chest tightness, wheezing, and acute and chronic airway obstruction.[47,48] High-concentration enclosed space exposures to these organic dust mixtures can cause ODTS.[49] This flu-like illness is characterized by headache, joint and muscle pain, fever, weakness, cough, shortness of breath, and fatigue, often lasting a few days.

Non-allergic asthma, sometimes referred to as an asthma-like condition and accompanied by cross-shift declines in expiratory flow rates of 5% to 10%, were first documented in Iowa swine farmers, often accompanied by fixed airway obstruction that was greater in winter, among smokers and those with longer durations of exposure.[50,51] Importantly, cross-shift declines in expiratory flow rates have been associated with increased dust and endotoxin concentrations, as well as by loss of lung function over time.[51,52] The use of disinfectants in livestock facilities has been found to increase atopic sensitization and asthma among Dutch livestock workers.[53] Multiple later studies of respiratory disease among swine, poultry, dairy, and cattle CAFO workers in the United States, Canada, and Europe have replicated and confirmed these early studies.[54–58]

## Neighbor and Community Health Effects

For many reasons, the Agency for Toxic Substances and Disease Registry (ATSDR) health-based guidelines, the EPA standards, and state-based community health regulations must be stricter than for those exposed occupationally.[16] Such protection is necessary because CAFO neighbors and nearby communities include susceptible subgroups, including children, the elderly, and vulnerable populations with preexisting conditions, including asthma, chronic obstructive lung disease, and those with allergies and compromised immunity. Workers, who are exposed to higher concentrations a few hours a day, have a choice as to where they work. But, CAFO neighbors and nearby rural community residents have little to no choice where they live and are exposed 24 hours a day for many days of the year. Therefore, community exposures arising from CAFOs, including $PM_{10}$, $PM_{2.5}$, hydrogen sulfide, ammonia, VOCs, allergens, and endotoxin-laden bioaerosols, are all expected to have adverse health effects at lower concentrations, especially among those most susceptible. IFAP facility neighbors and nearby rural community residents must therefore have greater margins of safety to provide necessary protection from these airborne hazards.

## Increased Childhood Asthma

Children are particularly vulnerable to environmental exposures given their growing lungs and increased respiration. Differing global rates of childhood asthma are thought to be largely attributable to variations in environmental exposures.[59] International Study of Asthma and Allergies in Childhood questionnaire surveys were carried out in two intensive farming Iowa counties among children ages 6–9 and 10–14 years.[60] Wheezing in the past year was reported by 19.1% and doctor-diagnosed asthma by 13.4%, both similar to urban prevalence rates, suggesting no asthma-protective effect from intensive livestock farming exposures.

Research from the Keokuk County Rural Health Study (KCRHS), a three-round prospective study of 1,000 families, provided a rich data set from which to study childhood asthma.[61,62] Nearly all CAFOs, predominantly swine feeding operations, contained fewer than 500 animals and were deep-pit facilities. Four "asthma outcomes" (doctor-diagnosed asthma, doctor diagnosed asthma/medication for wheeze, current wheeze, and cough with exercise) were documented. Round 1 prevalence of doctor-diagnosed asthma, known to be underdiagnosed, was 12%, while a more accurate estimate of asthma prevalence, doctor-diagnosed asthma/medication for wheeze, was 16.7%. The prevalence of any asthma outcome among children living on a farm raising swine was 42.9%, compared to 26.6% among non–swine farm children, and was 55.8% among children living on swine farms that added antibiotics to feed. Children born on a farm reported fewer allergies than children not born on a farm. Spirometry and methacholine challenge outcomes did not differ between children living on a farm and those not living on a farm. Multivariate models, accounting for multiple asthma risk factors, found three of the four asthma outcomes (doctor-diagnosed asthma/medication for wheeze, current wheeze, and cough with exercise) were significantly increased for farms raising swine and adding antibiotics to feed. The high prevalence of asthma and asthma symptoms among this cohort of children was striking but, as stated by the authors, was likely to be in part attributable to occupational levels of exposure among some of these children who did chores in the animal facilities.

Sigurdson and Kline studied two rural Iowa elementary schools, one school within a half a mile of a large CAFO housing 3,800 hogs, while the control school was located more than 10 miles from any CAFO.[30] Prevalence of doctor-diagnosed asthma was 19.7% among children in the CAFO-proximate school, while the control school prevalence was a significantly lower 7.3%. The adjusted odds ratio for doctor-diagnosed asthma was a highly significant 5.71. Possible confounding factors were considered but not found to be significant in multivariate models.

In 2006, Mirabelli and colleagues published two papers on childhood asthma among North Carolina schoolchildren.[21,63] Based on a sample of public schools, they estimated potential exposure using both record-based and survey-based exposure indices. Of the sample of 226 schools, the nearest swine CAFO ranged from 0.2 to 42 miles. Sixty-six schools were located within 3 miles of any CAFO. Livestock odor was reported in 21% of the surveyed schools, while in 8%, the odor was noticeable indoors, including in classrooms and hallways. In schools reporting livestock odor, the ratings of the strength of the odor decreased with increasing distance to the nearest swine CAFO. An accompanying paper assessed exposure to airborne CAFO odor and asthma symptoms among adolescents, ages 12–14 years.[63] During the 1999–2000 school year, 58,169 adolescents answered questions about their respiratory symptoms, allergies, medications, socioeconomic status, and household environments. Estimates of school-based exposures were calculated from 265 schools and 2,343 swine operations. The prevalence of wheezing, adjusting for confounders, was slightly higher at schools exposed to odor from CAFOs. Among students who had reported allergies, the prevalence of wheezing was significantly increased by 5% among children living within 3 miles of a CAFO and was 24% higher at schools in which livestock odor was noticeable twice per month, as compared to those in schools with no reported odor. Students with allergies, who lived within 3 miles of a CAFO, also reported higher rates of doctor-diagnosed asthma, doctor/emergency room visits, asthma medication, activity limitation, and days of missed school.

Data from round 2 of the KCRHS allowed analysis of the prevalence of childhood asthma among children living in proximity (within 3 miles) of a Keokuk County feeding operation.[26] The prevalence of doctor-diagnosed asthma did not differ significantly from that of round 1, but doctor-diagnosed asthma/medication for wheeze was increased to 22.7%. Relative exposure to CAFO emissions ($E_{relative}$), based on feeding operation footprint, distance to feeding operations, and low wind speed and direction, was developed to assess relative environmental exposure to CAFO emissions among children living apart from a livestock farm. Children with higher $E_{relative}$ measures had significantly increased odds for both asthma outcomes, while those with doctor-diagnosed asthma/medication for wheeze were found to have dose-related increases in asthma with an increasing $E_{relative}$. This study is important as it documented, even for small CAFOs for which no required siting or setback limits are required in Iowa, that a dose-related increase in childhood asthma existed among neighboring children.

A prospective panel study was carried out among 58 school-age children who received asthma health care from the Yakima Valley Farm Worker Health Clinics, a network of federally qualified clinics serving farmworker families in a high-intensity large fruit orchard and dairy operation region of eastern Washington.[64] Asthma symptoms and quick-relief medication use were assessed weekly via phone-administered surveys ($n = 2,013$), and peak flow meters were used daily to measure forced expiratory volume in 1 second ($FEV_1$). Regional $PM_{2.5}$ was measured at a single centrally located monitoring station. Exposure to ammonia was associated with decreases in $FEV_1$. An interquartile range (IQR) increase in weekly $PM_{2.5}$ of 6.7 $\mu/m^3$ was associated with an increase in reported asthma symptoms, including wheezing, limitation of activities, and nighttime waking. $FEV_1$, as a percentage of predicted, decreased by 0.9% for each IQR increase in $PM_{2.5}$ and by 1.4% when restricted to children with atopic asthma.

Kiss et al. documented the association of residential proximity to mixed livestock farms and modeled $PM_{10}$ concentrations in association with lung function in adolescents as part of the Dutch prospective PIAMA study.[65] Spirometry ($FEV_1$ and forced vital capacity or FVC) was measured among nonfarm youth at age 16 living within a 3-km (1.86 miles) buffer from a livestock farm. Higher exposures to farming were consistently associated, for all types of livestock, with a lower $FEV_1$ (−1.4%) but not FVC. Youth living close to a larger number of farms within 3 km, as well as youth experiencing higher concentrations of $PM_{10}$ from livestock farming, were associated with 1.8% and 0.9% lower $FEV_1$ levels, respectively.

While there is evidence that children living on smaller rural farms early in life garner protection from atopic sensitization, asthma, and wheezing due to early livestock exposures that expose them to endotoxin and other microbial toxins,[66-69] higher exposures to endotoxin among school-age children, even when exposed early in life, have been found to result in increased risk.[70] This finding is consistent with studies of school-age children, especially among those with atopy who live

J. A. MERCHANT, J. L. SCHNOOR, W. T. SANDERSON, D. WILLIAMS, AND D. OSTERBERG

close to industrial farm animal facilities, all of which have found higher prevalence rates of asthma and/or asthma-related symptoms.

## Increased Airway Disease among Rural Adults

A primary objective of the KCRHS was to evaluate and compare respiratory symptoms and lung function among farm family, rural nonfarm family, and town family members.[61] The assessment of the effect of farming was confounded because over two-thirds of adult males had grown up on a farm, were engaged in mixed livestock and crop farming, or had farmed in the past. The prevalence of current smokers among farmers was significantly lower that among nonfarm and town adult men. Unexpected and strikingly, low odds ratios (ORs) for attacks of wheezing/shortness of breath, ever having asthma, and asthma confirmed by a doctor (ORs = 0.50–0.52) were found among adult men. Migration out of Keokuk County was not considered likely enough to explain these findings. Consistent with this unexpected observation was a follow-up study of all three rounds of the KCRHS, which found no evidence that occupational exposures among nonsmokers posed a risk to airway obstruction.[71] However, airflow obstruction, with or without chronic bronchitis, in this three-round cohort was significantly associated with ever working in a hog or chicken CAFO.[72]

Well-controlled epidemiological studies of neighbors and rural community residents include a large community-based study of adults ($n = 6,917$) living in four rural German towns proximate to high-density swine CAFOs who were surveyed by questionnaire.[32] Exposure was measured by collecting data on a 4-point scale of odor annoyance together with data on the number of CAFOs within 500 m (1,641 ft.) from homes. Analyses were restricted to those not working in farming. The prevalence of wheezing without a cold, doctor-diagnosed asthma, and allergic rhinitis were all significantly increased with higher levels of odor annoyance (none, somewhat, moderately, strongly). Increased CAFO density, as measured by the number of animal houses within

500 m, was associated with significant increases in wheezing without a cold (27.1% with 12 CAFOs) and doctor-diagnosed asthma (10.4% with 12 houses). Importantly, subjects living within 500 m of 12 CAFOs had significantly lower levels of $FEV_1$ (−7.4%), as compared with age- and height-adjusted predicted levels. The authors concluded these findings were likely due to an "asthma-like syndrome" arising from exposure to CAFO emissions.

Wing and colleagues studied 101 nonsmoking volunteers living within 1.5 miles of swine CAFOs in 16 rural neighborhoods in eastern North Carolina.[73] Based on twice-daily odor diaries over a 2-week period, subjective measures of odor were compared to objective measures of components of swine odor—hydrogen sulfide, particulate ($PM_{10}$, $PM_{2.5}$), and endotoxin. Swine odor was reported in more than half of the 1,655 episode reports. Self-reported CAFO odor measures were found to increase in a dose-related pattern with objective measures of $H_2S$, $PM_{10}$, temperature, and wind speed. Further analyses of this study population found these repeated measures (hundreds) were related to acute eye irritation (odor, $H_2S$, and $PM_{10}$).[34] Respiratory symptoms in the previous 12 hours were associated with unit-dose increases in odor and $H_2S$, and difficulty breathing was increased with unit-dose increases of odor. An increase in wheezing and a decrease in $FEV_1$ were associated with an increased concentration of $PM_{2.5}$. Increased sore throat, chest tightness, and nausea were dose related to increases in the level of endotoxin. The authors concluded, and an independent commentary concurred, that measured emissions within 1.5 miles of swine CAFOs were related to acute physical symptoms and changes in lung function and that these findings were protected from unmeasured confounding by an innovative study design.[74]

A Dutch electronic record study included 92,548 patients in 27 general medicine practices in a high-density livestock region.[75] Distance between livestock farms and home address, presence of livestock within 500 m, and $PM_{10}$ from farms within 500 m were modeled as proxies for farm exposure. A current diagnosis of asthma, allergic rhinitis, and chronic obstructive pulmonary disease (COPD) was found to be inversely associated with $PM_{10}$, as did the presence of swine, goat, and sheep farms, whereas mink farms were positively associated with increased $PM_{10}$ concentrations. Adjustment for potential confounding in an embedded case-control study did not change these results, and endotoxin levels in neighboring homes were not associated with proximate farm exposures. However, exacerbations of airway infections, cough, and dyspnea occurred more frequently among patients with asthma and COPD living close to livestock farms. The authors cited literature finding a protective effect for respiratory allergies among children with early life farm exposures and concluded such protection may continue and occur in adulthood.[75–77]

A further study by these investigators studied 14,875 Dutch adults for the prevalence of COPD and asthma using a respiratory questionnaire evaluating respiratory health, smoking, and personal characteristics.[78] The prevalence of COPD and asthma was both lower among residents living within 100 m of a livestock farm. But exposure to more than 11 farms within 1,000 m, as compared with fewer than 4 farms within 1,000 m, was associated with increased wheezing among COPD patients. This study suggested a protective effect of livestock farm emissions on the respiratory health of neighboring residents, but COPD patients were found to be at higher risk to exacerbations. Spirometry, a respiratory questionnaire, and measurement of $PM_{10}$ and $NH_3$ were further studied in a sample of 2,308 of these subjects.[79] Spatial exposures were evaluated by the number of farms within 500 m and 1,000 m of a livestock farm and modeled $PM_{10}$ concentrations within the two buffer zones. Temporal exposure was evaluated as week-average $PM_{10}$ and $NH_3$ concentrations. A spatial association was found between the number of livestock farms within 1,000 m and decreased maximal mid-expiratory flow (MMEF), and a temporal association was found between decreased $FEV_1$, $FEV_1/FVC$, and MMEF and week-average $NH_3$. Dutch investigators also conducted an 82-patient COPD panel study of twice-daily spirometry over a 3-month period, daily diary entries of respiratory symptoms and odor annoyance, and daily $PM_{10}$ and $NH_3$ concentrations from regional air monitoring stations.[80] Decrements in morning $FEV_1 > 20\%$

were found to be associated with increased $NH_3$, demonstrating acute effects of livestock-related air pollution among COPD patients.

A representative and population-based cohort study of Wisconsin adults ($n = 5,338$), based on the 2008–2016 Survey of Health of Wisconsin (SHOW), documented self-reported doctor-diagnosed allergies, asthma, episodes of asthma, asthma medication use in the past 12 months, and spirometry, in relation to distance (1.5 miles and 5 miles) from a CAFO (dairy cow, hog, chicken, or turkey).[81] Living within 1.5 miles, compared to living more than 5 miles away from a CAFO, was associated with significantly increased odds of self-reported allergies, lung allergies, asthma, asthma medication, and uncontrolled asthma in the past 12 months.

Proximity to IFAP and asthma exacerbations were evaluated using electronic medical records of 35,269 asthma patients at the Pennsylvania Geisinger Clinic. A lower than predicted $FEV_1$ (−7.72%) was found among residents living within 1.5 miles of a swine or veal CAFO when compared with those living more than 3 miles from a CAFO.[82] Hospitalizations, emergency encounters, and new oral corticosteroid (OCS) orders were also evaluated among asthmatics living in proximity (within 3 miles) of a CAFO when compared to asthmatics living more than 3 miles from a CAFO. In adjusted models, proximity to CAFOs was positively associated with OCS orders and hospitalizations, but not emergency encounters.

**Increased Risk of Pneumonia**

Also using Geisinger Clinic electronic medical records was a nested case-control study of pneumonia and chest imaging that identified 11,910 child and adult cases of community-acquired pneumonia (CAP) that were analyzed using an estimated poultry operation exposure metric that incorporated animal number, facility size, and location.[83] A comparison of patients living in the highest versus the lowest quartile of the poultry operation metric found a 66% increased odds of a CAP diagnosis.

These findings are consistent with a series of Dutch studies that found significantly increased medical record–based rates of pneumonia associated with proximity to goat and poultry farms,[84–86] as well as mixed (pig, cattle, poultry, and goat) intensive livestock farming.[87] A 2022 Dutch study calculated odds for individuals with a laboratory-confirmed severe acute respiratory virus coronavirus 2 (SARS-CoV-2) test living in proximity to livestock farms (cattle, goat, sheep, pig, poultry, horse, rabbit, and mink).[88] Significantly increased odds ratios were found among SARS-CoV-2 patients living within all four zones less than 1,000 m of a livestock farm when compared to patients living more than 1,000 m from a livestock farm.

## Increased Mortality from Living Close to a CAFO

A national census-based cohort of all inhabitants from rural and semi-urban areas of the Netherlands was used to evaluated respiratory mortality (respiratory system diseases, chronic lower respiratory diseases, pneumonia) from 2005–2012 among resident living within four zones within 2,000 m of a livestock farm (cattle, pigs, chickens, mink).[89] Living within 2,000 m was found to be associated with increased mortality from chronic lower respiratory disease. Living within 1,000 m of farms with low numbers of pigs found a Cox hazard ratio (HR) of 1.06 (1.02, 1.10), while living within 1,000 m of farms with high numbers of pigs had an HR of 1.18 (1.13, 1.24).

A similar mortality study was carried out examining risk of cause-specific mortality associated with CAFOs in North Carolina for 2000–2017.[90] Estimates of exposure, presence or absence of a CAFO within a 15-mile buffer, and four levels of exposure (no, low, medium, and high) were based on the number of CAFOs within the 15-mile buffer. Individual (sex, race/ethnicity, age, education) and community-level factors (median household income, urbanicity, and region) were considered. All people living within the 15-mile buffer were found to have significantly higher cardiovascular mortality. For those living near CAFOs, compared to the no CAFO exposure group, increased odds ratios for cardiovascular mortality were 1.01 (95% confidence interval, 1.00–1.03), 1.04 (1.03–1.06), and 1.06 (1.05–1.07) for low, medium, and high CAFO exposure, respectively, indicating an increased cardiovascular mortality trend of higher risk with higher CAFO exposures.

Over the last 50 years numerous mortality studies have documented a consistent decrease in lung cancer mortality among cotton textile workers (25 studies) and farmers (39 studies), both among men and women.[91] While most of these studies attribute lower lung cancer incidence and mortality to lower rates of smoking, alcohol consumption, physical activity, and other lifestyle factors, a systematic review and meta-analysis based on high-quality studies supports the hypothesis that occupational exposure to endotoxin is protective against lung cancer.[91]

## Regional Air Pollution Health Effects

Agriculture is well recognized to be a major contributor to $PM_{2.5}$ air pollution.[92–94] Food production negatively impacts human health from primary $PM_{2.5}$ and secondary $PM_{2.5}$ arising from $NH_3$, $NO_x$, $SO_2$, and VOCs.[92,93] There is now convincing evidence that air pollution, specifically $PM_{2.5}$, contributes to increased cardiopulmonary mortality.[93,95–97,98] Large U.S. and European cohort studies estimated mortality per 10 $\mu g/m^3$ of long-term exposure to $PM_{2.5}$ and found significantly elevated hazard ratios for mortality for all causes; cardiopulmonary, cardiovascular, cerebrovascular diseases, respiratory diseases, and lung cancer.[95,97] Both comprehensive European and US low-exposure studies ($PM_{2.5}$) found significantly elevated natural cause morality below $PM_{2.5}$ of 10 $\mu g/m^3$.[97,98] For 2011, $PM_{2.5}$ pollution in the United States was estimated to result in 107,000 premature deaths at a societal cost of $886 billion.[92] Of these deaths, 15% were estimated to be caused by agricultural activities. Of ground-level emissions, the largest single contribution to total anthropogenic economic damage was ground-level release of $NH_3$ from agriculture (i.e., application of manure and fertilizers) that contributed 12% of total impacts.[92]

Based on an analysis of 95 attributable agricultural commodities and 67 final food products that encompass more than 99% of agricultural production in the United States, agriculture-related $PM_{2.5}$ pollution has been estimated to result in a total of 17,900 annual air quality deaths, of which 12,700 were estimated to be attributed to animal-based food production.[94] It was further estimated that on-farm interventions could reduce $PM_{2.5}$-related mortality by 50%. These interventions included primarily improved animal waste management practices but also improved control of fertilizer application and tillage practices, field burning, and farm machinery emissions. It was also estimated that a shift toward more plant-based foods that maintain protein and other dietary needs could reduce agricultural air quality–related mortality by 68% to 83%.[94] For the European Union, a theoretical estimated health and economic benefit from a complete phase-out of air pollution from agriculture could lead to an estimated reduction in $PM_{2.5}$-related mortality by greater than 50%, a reduction of 140,000 deaths, and an associated economic benefit of $407 billion.[99]

A final pressing public health issue is the impact of industrial farm animal production emissions on climate change from greenhouse gases. As previously discussed, of total anthropogenic GHG emissions, about 37% of methane and 65% of nitrous oxide arise from animal production.[43,44] Transitioning to sustainable animal production practices would reduce these GHG emissions. A second agricultural contribution to GHG arises from dietary choices. Systematic reviews of the contributions of GHG emissions from food consumption have found the greatest positive impacts would come from changes in human diets—eating less meat and dairy from ruminant animals and eating more plant-based foods.[100–102] Such diets are also well known to enhance health and decrease mortality.[103]

## Conclusion

The industrialization of farm animal production over the past 60 years has resulted in well-documented air pollution exposures to farmers and farm workers, IFAP facility neighbors, proximate rural communities, and residents living in livestock-dense regions. Occupational health effects include chronic bronchitis, asthma, acute and chronic impairment of lung function, ARDS and death from high exposures to hydrogen sulfide gas. Those living in proximity to CAFOs, especially children, those with preexisting conditions, and those living close to and in areas with higher numbers of CAFOs, have been found to suffer from increased exposure-related asthma, acute and chronic airway obstruction, increased exacerbations of COPD, increased rates of pneumonia, and exposure-related increased mortality from chronic respiratory and cardiovascular diseases. Primary and secondary particles ($PM_{2.5}$), primarily from ammonia, arise from IFAP facilities and are important contributors to regional air pollution associated with increased mortality from cardiovascular, cerebrovascular, pulmonary diseases, and lung cancer. IFAP facilities are also a primary source of greenhouse gases and are responsible for a substantial proportion of anthropogenic emissions of methane and oxides of nitrogen.

These multiple IFAP air pollution–related public health impacts, now well documented and understood, make a compelling case for policy interventions. As clearly articulated by the Pew Commission on Industrial Farm Animal Production, current industrialized farm animal production agriculture is not sustainable and is known to adversely affect the public's health.[104] The need for policies to redirect farm animal production to a sustainable model has never been more urgent.

## Recommended Policy

Numerous policy changes are needed nationally, for livestock-producing states, and at the local level for the rural communities most impacted by IFAP air pollution. The goal should be to not only limit and control IFAP-related exposures for workers, rural neighbors and communities, and residents of livestock-dense regions but also promote policies, programs, and practices that will allow a transition to sustainable farm animal production. The following are recommendations for policy changes at the federal, state, and community levels that, if implemented, would greatly benefit rural, national, and global communities.

**Federal**

- Based on convincing European and US evidence of excess mortality from $PM_{2.5}$ at 10 µg/m$^3$, regulate $PM_{2.5}$ at 8–9 µg/m$^3$ and continue environmental sustainability efforts to reach the World Health Organization recommended limit of 5 µg/m$^3$.[105]
- Redefine and strengthen EPA regulations for swine, poultry, dairy, and cattle CAFOs as source categories under 111 of the Clean Air Act.
- Promulgate a comprehensive Occupational Safety and Health Administration standard to protect the health and safety of workers in large-scale (1,000 AU) farm animal production facilities.
- Revise and authorize the Fair Labor Standards Act to bring regulations for IFAP and other industrial farm child labor in line with that of child labor in other regulated workplaces.
- Support farm system reform legislation that places an immediate moratorium on new large-scale CAFOs and halts expansion of unregistered CAFOs.
- Support legislation that funds a 10-year voluntary buy-out program to encourage large CAFO owners to exit animal production or change industrial farm animal production to proven sustainable livestock production practices.
- Fund proven USDA manure handling and processing technologies that substantially reduce CAFO toxic emissions and global warming gases while preserving nutrients for agricultural and nonagricultural use.

**State**

- Enforce existing environmental regulations of industrial farm animal production requiring CAFOs to abide by environmental laws applicable to other comparable industries while eliminating existing regulatory exemptions for CAFOs.

- Replace outmoded and ineffective CAFO siting schemes to require setback requirements for animal feeding operations for all-sized facilities.
- Implement ammonia and hydrogen sulfide environmental exposure limits at the property lines of IFAP facilities.
- Develop and incorporate statewide spatial plans that include approval of CAFO siting at the county level for siting new and replacement CAFOs.
- Challenge state laws that seek to prevent lawsuits brought because of medical or nuisance harm arising from CAFO emissions.
- Challenge state ag-gag laws and right-to-farm laws that seek to hide industrial farm animal production practices from the public and take away the rights of residents and local communities to protect their property through nuisance suits.
- Give local, county, and state boards of health the authority to regulate and/or address CAFO public health impacts.
- Promote and support civic organizations that seek to protect the public's health and the environment through engagement of policymakers in meetings/hearings through civic action.

**County and Community**
- Organize to influence county supervisors and local health departments to enact ordinances, or seek authority to pass ordinances, that allow local control of siting or expansion of existing CAFOs.
- Promote and engage in community-based education, organization, and promotion of programs that inform citizens of the public health and environmental impacts of IFAP.
- Ensure enforcement of state and local environmental programs through inquiry and participation in meetings/hearings and citizen science.
- Provide citizen suit provisions similar to those afforded to people under the Clean Water Act and Clean Air Act, so people

have the ability to ensure enforcement when regulatory agencies fail to act.

## Acknowledgment

The authors thank James A. Merchant Jr. for creating the Figure 3.1 graphic based on an original sketch by Jerald Schnoor and with revisions made by Wayne Sanderson, Christopher Heaney, Christopher Jones, and James Merchant.

**REFERENCES**

1. Schenker M, Christiani D, Cormier Y, Dimich-Ward, Doekes G, Dosman J, Dowes J, Dowling K, Enarson D, Green F (1998). Respiratory health hazards in agriculture. Am J Resp Crit Care Med 158(5):S1–S76.
2. O'Shaughnessy P, Donham K, Peters L, Taylor C, Altmaier R, Kelly K (2010). A task-specific assessment of swine worker exposure to airborne dust. J Occup Environ Hyg 7:7–13.
3. Basinas I, Sigsgaard T, Kromhout H, Heederik D, Wouters I, Schlunssen V (2015). A comprehensive review of levels and determinants of personal exposure to dust and endotoxin in livestock farming. J Expo Sci Environ Epidemiol 25:123–137.
4. Douglas P, Roberson S, Gay R, Hansell A, Gant T (2018). A systematic review of the public health risks of bioaersols from intensive farming. Int J Hyg Environ Health 221:134–173.
5. Cyprowski M, Buczynska A, Kozjda A, Sowiak M, Brodka K, Szdkowska-Stanczyk I (2012). Exposure to (1–3)-beta-D-glucans in swine farms. Aerobiologia 28:161–169.
6. Neyra R, Vogesen L, Davis M, Price L, Silbergeld E (2012). Antimicrobial-resistant bacteria: an unrecognized work-related risk in food animal production. Safe Health Work 3:85–91.
7. Fenske R (2005). State-of-the-art measurement of agricultural pesticide exposures. Scand J Work Environ Health 31(Suppl. 1):67–73.
8. Calvert G, Karnik J, Mehler L, Beckman B, Morrissey B, Sievert B, Barrett R (2005). Acute pesticide poisonings among agricultural workers in the United States, 1998–2005. Am J Ind Med 51(12):883–898.
9. Murphy M, Sanderson W, Vargo J (2007). Airborne antibiotic concentrations in a swine feeding operation. J Agr Safety Health 13(4):357–366.
10. Heederik D, Sigsgaard T, Thorne P, et al. (2007). Health effects of airborne exposures from concentrated animal feeding. Environ Health Perspectives 115(2):298–302.
11. Donham K, Knapp, Monson R, Gustafson K (1982). Acute toxic exposure to gases from liquid manure. J Occup Med 24:142–145.

12. Thorne P, Ansley A, Perry S (2009). Concentrations of bioaerosols, odors, and hydrogen sulfide inside and downwind from two types of swine livestock operations. J Occup Environ Hyg 6:211–220.

13. Pavilonis B, Anthony T, O'Shaughnessy P, Humann M, Merchant J, Moore G, Thorne P, Weisel C, Sanderson W (2013). Indoor and outdoor particulate matter and endotoxin concentrations in an intensely agricultural county. J Expo Sci Environ Epidemiology 23(3):299–305.

14. Wyer K, Kelleghan D, Blanes-Vidal V, Shauberger G, Curran T (2022). Ammonia emissions from agriculture and their contribution to fine particulate matter: a review of implications for human health. J Environ Manage 323:116285.

15. Cambra-Lopez M, Aarnink A, Zhao Y, Calvet S, Torres A (2010). Airborne particulate matter from livestock production systems: a review of an air pollution problem. Environ Pollut 158(1):1–17.

16. Merchant J, Kline J, Donham K, Bundy D, Hodne C; ISU-UI Study Group (2002). Human health effects. In: *Iowa Concentrated Animal Feeding Operations Air Quality Study*. Iowa City: University of Iowa, College of Public Health. http:// www.ehsrc.uiowa.edu/cafo air quality study.html

17. Tengman C, Goodwin R, Biucudo J (2006). Hydrogen sulfide concentrations around swine farms. Pork Information Gateway. https://porkgateway.org /resource/hydrogen-sulfide-concentrations-around-swine-farms/

18. Iowa Department of Natural Resources (2021). DNR Form 542–1420. Minimum separation distances for construction or expansion of confinement feeding operation structures. https://www.iowadnr.gov.

19. Merchant J, Osterberg D (2018). The explosion of CAFOs in Iowa and its impact on water quality and public health. https://www.iowapolicyproject.org/2018docs /180125-CCAFO.pdf

20. Shiffman S, Bennett J, Raymer J (2001). Quantification of odors and odorants from swine operations in North Carolina. Agr Forest Meteorol 108:213–240.

21. Mirabelli M, Wing S, Marshall S, Wilcosky T (2006). Race, poverty, and potential exposure of middle-school students to air emissions from confined swine feeding operations. Environ Health Perspect 114(4):591–595.

22. Schultz A, van Strien R, Ehrenstein V, Schierl R, Kuchenhoff H, Radon K (2006). Ambient endotoxin level in an area with intensive livestock production. Ann Agr Environ Med 13(1):87–91.

23. Heaney C, Myers K, Wing A, Hall D, Baron, D, Stewart J (2015). Source tracking swine fecal waste in surface water proximal to swine concentrated animal feeding operations. Sci Total Environ 211:676–683.

24. de Rooij M, Heederik D, van Nunen J, van Schothorst J, Maassen C, Hoek G, Wouters I (2018). Spatial variation of endotoxin concentrations measured in ambient $PM_{10}$ in a livestock-dense area: implementation of a land-use regression approach. Environ Health Perspect 126(1):017003.

25. O'Shaughnessey P, Altmaier R (2011). Use of AERMOD to determine a hydrogen sulfide emission factor for seine operations by inverse modeling. Atmos Environ 45(27):4617–4625.

26. Pavalonis B, Sanderson W, Merchant J (2011). Relative exposure to swine animal feeding operations and childhood asthma prevalence in an agricultural cohort. Environ Res 122:74–80.
27. Wing S, Wolf S (2000). Intensive livestock operations, health, and quality of life among eastern North Carolina residents. Environ Health Perspect 108(3):233–238.
28. Elliott L, Yeatts K, Loomis D (2004). Ecological associations between asthma prevalence and potential exposure to farming. Eur Respir J 24(6):938–941.
29. Avery R, Wing S, Marshall S, Schiffman S (2004). Odor from industrial hog farming operations and mucosal immune function in neighbors. Arch Environ Health 59:101–108.
30. Sigurdson S, Kline J (2006). School proximity to concentrated animal feeding operations and prevalence of asthma in students. Chest 129:1486–1491.
31. Radon K, Schulze A, Ehrenstein V, van Strien R, Praml G, Nowak D (2007). Environmental exposure to confined animal feeding operations and respiratory health of neighboring residents. Epidemiology 18:300–308.
32. Schultze A, Rommelt H, Ehrenstein V, vanStrien R, Praml G, Kuchenhoff H, Nowak D, Radon K (2011). Effects on pulmonary health of neighboring residents of concentrated animal feeding operations: exposure assessed using optimized estimation technique. Arch Environ Occup Health 66(3):146–154.
33. Smit L, Hooivelf M, van der Sman-de F, et al. (2014). Air pollution from livestock farms and asthma, allergic rhinitis and COPD among neighbouring residents. Occup Environ Med 71(2):134–140.
34. Schinasi L, Horton R, Guidry V, Wing S, Marshall S, Morland K (2011). Air pollution, lung function, and physical symptoms in communities near concentrated swine feeding operations. Epidemiology 22(2):208–215.
35. Guidry V, Kinlaw A, Johnston J, Hall D, Wing S (2016). Hydrogen sulfide concentrations at three middle schools near industrial livestock facilities. J Exposure Sci Environ Epidemiol 27:1–8.
36. Blanes-Vidal V, Baelujm J, Nadimi E, Lofstrom P, Christensen L (2014). Chronic exposure to odorous chemicals in residential areas and effects on human psychosocial health: Dose-response relationships. Sci Total Environ 490:545–554.
37. Williams D, Breysse P, McCormack M, Diette G, McKenzie S, Geyh A (2011). Airborne cow allergen, ammonia and particulate matter at homes vary with distance to industrial scale dairy operations: an exposure assessment. Environ Health 10(1):1–9.
38. Intergovernmental Panel on Climate Change (2021). The physical science basis of climate change, table of greenhouse gas lifetimes, radiative efficiencies and metrics. 7SM-24. https://www.ipcc.ch
39. Abt Associates (2000). Air quality impacts of livestock waste. https://management consulted.com
40. Aneja V, Roelle P, Murray G, Southerland J, Erisman J, Fowler D, Asman W, Patni N (2001) Atmospheric nitrogen compounds II: emissions, transport, transformation, deposition and assessment, Atmos Environ 35(11)1903 1911.

41. Hendriks C, Kranenburg R, Kuenen J, van Gijlswijk R, Kruit R, Segers A, van der Gon H, Schaap M (2013). The origin of ambient particulate matter concentrations in the Netherlands. Atmos Environ 69:289–303.

42. Golston LM, Pan D, Sun K, Tao L, Zondlo MA, Eilerman SJ, Peischl J, Neuman JA, Floerchinger C (2020). Variability of ammonia and methane emissions from animal feeding operations in northeastern Colorado. Environ Sci Technol 54(18):11015–11024.

43. Baak BH, Todd RW, Cole NA, Koziel JA (2005). Ammonia and hydrogen sulfide flux and dry deposition velocity estimates using vertical gradient method at a commercial beef cattle feedlot. In: *State of the Science Animal Manure and Waste Management*, January 4–7, 2005, San Antonio, Texas. 2005 CDROM. https://www.ars.usda.gov/research/publications/publication/?seqNo115=175192

44. Rivera JE, Chará J (2021). CH4 and N2O emissions from cattle excreta: a review of main drivers and mitigation strategies in grazing systems. Front Sustain Food Syst 5:657936.

45. Donham K, Rubino M, Thedell T, Kammermeyer J (1977). Potential health hazards to agricultural workers in swine confinement buildings. J Occup Med 19:383–287.

46. Osbern L, Crapo J (1981). Dung lung: a report of toxic exposure to liquid manure. Ann Intern Med 95:312–314.

47. Donham K, Zavala D, Merchant J (1984). Acute effects of the work environment on pulmonary function of swine confinement workers. Am J Ind Med 5:367–376.

48. Donham K, Zavala D, Merchant J (1984). Respiratory symptoms and lung function among workers in swine confinement buildings: a cross-sectional epidemiological study. Arch Environ Health 39(2):96–101.

49. Donham K, Haglind P, Peterson Y, Rylander R (1986). Environmental and health studies in swine confinement buildings. Am J Ind Med 10:289–293.

50. Schwartz D, Landas S, Lassise D, Burmeister L, Hunninghake G, Merchant J (1992). Airway injury in swine confinement workers. Ann Intern Med 116(8):630–635.

51. Schwartz D, Donham K, Olenchock S, Popendorf W, Van Fossen D, Burmeister L, Merchant J (1995). Determinants of longitudinal changes in spirometric function among swine confinement operators and farmers. Am J Respir Crit Care Med 151(1):47–53.

52. Reynolds S, Donham K, Whitten P, Merchant J, Burmeister L, Popendorf W (1996). Longitudinal evaluation of dose-response relationships for environmental exposures and pulmonary function in swine production workers. Am J Ind Med 29(1):33–40.

53. Preller L, Doekes G, Heederik D, Vermeuler R, Vogelzang P, Boleij J (1996). Disinfectant use as a risk factor for atopic sensitization and symptoms consistent with asthma: an epidemiological study. Eur Respir J 9(7):1407–1413.

54. Zejda J, Hurst T, Rhodes C, Barber E, McDuffie H, Dosman J (1993). Respiratory health of swine producers: focus on young workers. Chest 103(3):702–709.

55. Kirychuk S, Senthilselvan A, Dosman J, et al. (2003). Respiratory symptoms and lung function in poultry confinement workers in Western Canada. Can Respir J 10:375–380.

56. Dalphine J-C, Dubiez A, Monnet E, Gora D, Westeel V, Pernet D, Polio JC, Gibey R, LaPlante J-J, Depierre A (1998). Prevalence of asthma and respiratory symptoms in dairy farmers in the French province of Doubs. Am J Respir Crit Care Med 158:1493–1498.

57. Guilliem A, Soumagne R, Dalphin J-C, Degano B (2019). COPD, airflow limitation and chronic bronchitis in farmers: a systematic review and meta-analysis. Occup Environ Med 76(1):58–68

58. Plembon S, Henneberger P, Humann M, Liang X, Doney B, Kelly K, Cox-Ganser J (2022). The association of chronic bronchitis and airflow obstruction with lifetime and current farm activities in a sample of rural adults in Iowa. Int Arch Occup Environ Health 95:1741–1754.

59. Lai C, Beasley R, Crane J, Foliaki S, Shah J, Weiland S; the ISAAC Phase Three Study Group (2009). Global variation in the prevalence and severity of asthma symptoms: phase three of the International Study of Asthma and Allergies in Childhood (ISAAC). Thorax 64:476–483.

60. Chrischilles E, Ahrens R, Kuehl A, Kelly K, Thorne P, Burmeiseter L, Merchant J (2004). Asthma prevalence and morbidity among rural Iowa school children. J Allergy Clin Immunol 113(1):66–71.

61. Merchant J, Stromquist A, Kelly K, Zwerling C, Reynolds S, Burmeister L (2002). The epidemiology of chronic disease and injury in an agricultural county: the Keokuk County Rural Health Study. J Rural Health 18(4):521–535.

62. Merchant J, Naleway A, Swendsen E, et al. (2005). Asthma and farm exposures in a cohort of rural Iowa children. Environ Health Perspect 113:350–356.

63. Mirabelli M, Wing S, Marshall W, Wilcosky T (2006). Asthma symptoms among adolescents who attend public schools that are located near confined swine feeding operations. Pediatrics 111:e66–e75.

64. Loftus C, Yost M, Sampson P, Arias G, Torres E, Vasquez V, Bhatti P, Karr C (2015). Regional $PM_{2.5}$ and asthma morbidity in an agricultural community: a panel study. Environ Res 136:505–512.

65. Kiss P, de Rooij M, Koppelman G, et al. (2022). Residential exposure to livestock farms and lung function in adolescence—the PIAMA birth cohort study. Environ Research 219:115134.

66. Braun-Fahrlander C, Gassner M, Grize L; SCARPOL team (1999). Prevalence of hay fever and allergic sensitization in farmer's children and their peers living in the same rural community. Swiss study on childhood allergy and respiratory symptoms with respect to air pollution. Clin Exp Allergy 29:28–34.

67. Reidler J, Braun-Fahrlander C, Eder W, et al. (2001). Exposure to farming in early life and development of asthma and allergy: a cross-sectional survey. Lancet 358:1129–1133.

68. Alfven T, Braun-Fahrlander C, Brunekreef B, et al. (2006). Allergic diseases and atopic sensitization in children related to farming and anthroposophic lifestyle—the PARSIFAL study. Allergy 61:414-21.

69. von Ehrenstein O, Von Mutius E, Illi S, et al. (2000). Reduced risk of hay fever and asthma among children of farmers. Clin Exp Allergy 30:187–193.

70. Braun-Farhlander C, Riedler J, Herz U, et al. (2002). Environmental exposure to endotoxin and its relation to asthma in school-age children. N Engl J Med 347(12):869–877.

71. Henneberger P, Humann M, Liang X, Doney B, Kelly K, Cox-Ganser (2020). The association of airflow obstruction with occupational exposures in a sample of rural adults in Iowa. J Chron Obstruct Pulmon Dis 17(4):401–409.

72. Plombon S, Henneberger P, Humann M, Liang X, Doney B, Kelly K, Cox-Ganser J (2022). The association of chronic bronchitis and airflow obstruction with lifetime and current farm activities in a sample of rural adults. Int Arch Occ Environ Hlth 95:1741–1754.

73. Wing S, Horton R, Marshall S, Thu K, Tajik M, Schinasi L, Shiffman S (2008). Air pollution and odor in communities near industrial swine operations. Environ Health Perspect 116(10):1362–1368.

74. Merchant J (2011). Advancing industrial livestock production: health effects research and sustainability. Epidemiology 22(2):216–218.

75. Leynaert B, Neukirch C, Jarvis D, et al (2001). Does living on a farm during childhood protect against asthma, allergic rhinitis, and atopy in adulthood? Am J Respir Crit Care Med 164:1829–1834.

76. Portegnen L, Sigsgaard T, Omland O, et al (2002). Low prevalence of atopy in young Danish farmers and farming students born and raised on a farm. Clin Esp Allergy 32:247–353.

77. Pecchlivanis S, von Mutius E (2020). Effect of Farming on Asthma. Narrative Review Acta Medica Academica 49(2):144–155.

78. Borlee F, Yzermans C, van Dijk C, Heederik D, Smit L (2015). Increased respiratory symptoms in COPD patients living in the vicinity of livestock farms. Eur Respir J 46:1605–1614.

79. Borlee F, Yzermans J, Aalders B, Rooijackers J, Krop E, Maassen C, Schellevis F, Brunekreef B, Heederik D, Smit L (2017). Air pollution from livestock farms is associated with airway obstruction in neighboring residents. Am J Respir Crit Care Med 196(9):1152–1161.

80. van Kersen W, Oldenwening M, Aalders B, Gloemsma L, Borlee F, Heederik D, Smit L (2020). Acute respiratory effects of livestock-related air pollution in a panel of COPD patients. Environ Int 136:105426.

81. Schultz A, Peppard P, Gangnon R, McMalecki K (2019). Residential proximity to concentrated animal feeding operations and allergic and respiratory disease. Environ Int 130:104911.

82. Rasmussen S, Casey J, Bandeen-Roche K, Schwartz B (2017). Proximity to industrial food animal production and asthma exacerbations in Pennsylvania. Int J Environ Res Public Health 14(4):362.

83. Poulsen M, Pollak J, Sills D, Casey J, Nachman K, Cosgrove S, Steward D Schwartz B (2018). High density poultry operations and community-acquired pneumonia in Pennsylvania. Environ Epidemiol 2:e013.

84. Freidl G, Spruijt I, Borlee F, Smit L, van Gageldonk-Lafeber A, Heederk D, Yzermans J, van Dijk C, Maassen C, Van der Hoek W (2017). Livestock associated

risk factors for pneumonia in an area of intensive animal farming in the Netherlands. PLoS One 12:e0174796.

85. Klous G, Smit L, Freidl G, Borlee F, van der Hoek W, Yzermans C, Kretzchmar M, Heederik D, Coutinho R, Huss A (2018). Pneumonia risk of people living close to goat and poultry farms—taking GPS derived mobility patterns into account. Environ Int 115:150160.

86. Post P, Hogerwerf L, Huss A, et al. (2019). Risk of pneumonia among residents living near goat and poultry farms during 2014–2016. PLoS One 14:e02236601.

87. Baliatsas C, Duckers M, Smit L, Heederik D, Yzermans J (2020). Morbidity rates in an area with high livestock density: a registry-based study including different groups of patients with respiratory health problems. Int J Environ Res Public Health 17(5):1591.

88. Hogerwerf L, Post P, Bom B, van der Hoek W, van de Kasssteele J, Stemerding A, de Vries W, Houthuijs D (2022). Proximity to livestock farms and COVID-19 in the Netherlands, 2020–2021. Int J Hyg Environ Health 245:114022.

89. Simoes M, Janssen N, Heederik D, Smit L, Vermeulen R, Huss A (2022). Residential proximity to livestock animal and mortality from respiratory diseases in The Netherlands: a prospective census-based cohort study. Environ Int 161:107140.

90. Son J-Y, Miranda M, Bell M (2021). Exposure to concentrated animal feeding operations (CAFOs) and risk of mortality in North Carolina, USA. Sci Total Environ 799:149407.

91. Lenters V, Basinas I, Bean-Freeman L, Boffetta P, Checkoway H, Coggon D, Poetengen L, Sim M, Wouters I, Heedrik D, Vermeulen R (2010). Endotoxin exposure and lung cancer risk: a systematic review and meta-analysis of the published literature on agriculture and cotton textile workers. Cancer Causes and Control 21:523-555.

92. Goodkind A, Tessum C, Coggins J, Hill J, Marshall J (2019). Fine-scale damage estimates of particulate matter air pollution reveal opportunities for location-specific mitigation of emissions. PNAS 116(18):8775–8780.

93. Pond Z, Hernandez C, Adams P, et al. (2021). Cardiopulmonary mortality and fine particulate air pollution by species and source in a national U.S. Cohort. Environ Sci Technol 56:7212–7223.

94. Domingo N, Balasubramanian S, Thakrar S, et al. (2021). Air quality-related health damages from food. PNAS 118(20):e2013637118.

95. Pope C, Lefler J, Ezzati M, et al. (2019). Mortality risk and fine particulate air pollution in a large, representative cohort of U.S. adults. Environ Health Perspect 127:99002.

96. Kioumourtzoglou M-A, Schwartz J, James P, Dominici F, Zanobetti A (2016). $PM_{2.5}$ and mortality in 207 U.S. cities: modification by temperature and city characteristics. Epidemiology 26(2):221–227.

97. Brunekreef B, Strak M, Chen J, Andersen Z, Atkinson R, Bauwelinck M, et al. (2021). Mortality and morbidity effects of long-term exposure to low-level $PM_{2.5}$, BC, $NO_2$, and $O_3$: an analysis of European cohorts in the ELAPSE Project. Research Report 208. Boston, MA: Health Effects Institute.

98. Dominici F, Zanobetti A, Schwartz J, Braun D, Sabath B, Xiao W (2022). Assessing adverse health effects of long-term exposure to low levels of ambient air pollution: implementation of causal inference methods. Research Report 211. Boston, MA: Health Effects Institute.

99. Giannadaki D, Giannaki E, Pozzeer A, Lelievelf J (2018). Estimating health and economic benefits of reductions in air pollution from agriculture. Sci Total Environ 622–623:1304–1316.

100. Reay D (2006). Green House Gas Online.org.http://www.ghgonline.org/nitrous /livestock.htm. Westhoek H, Lesschen J, Rood T, Wagner S, DeMarco A, Murphy-Bokern D, Leip A, van Grinsven H, Sutton M, Oenema O (2014). Food choices, health and environment: effects of cutting Europe's meat and dairy intake. Global Environ Change 26:196–205.

101. Kim B, Santo R, Scatterday A, et al. (2020). Country-specific dietary shifts to mitigate climate and water crises. Global Environ Change 62:101926.

102. Ivanovich C, Sun T, Gordon D, Ocko I (2023). Future warming from global food consumption. Nat Climate Change 13:297–302.

103. Willet W, Skerrett P (2002). *Eat, Drink and Be Healthy: The Harvard Medical School Guide to Healthy Eating.* New York, NY: Simon and Schuster.

104. The Pew Commission on Industrial Farm Animal Production (2008). *Putting Meat on the Table: Industrial Farm Animal Production in America.* www.pewtrusts .org.5106

105. World Health Organization. Air quality guidelines. http://c40knowledgehub .org/s/article/WHO-Air-Quality-Guidelines?language=eng

# CHAPTER 4

# Air Pollution II

Nuisance, Quality of Life, and Behavioral Health Impacts

James A. Merchant, Kendall M. Thu, Christopher D. Heaney, and David Osterberg

Health, as defined by the World Health Organization, is "a state of complete physical, mental and social wellbeing."[1] This broad definition of health is widely recognized and is increasingly being adopted by employers as they seek to enhance the health, productivity, and well-being of their employees, as well as by communities as they seek to make decisions about industrial and agricultural development. It is an appropriate definition to apply when considering industrial farm animal production (IFAP) concentrated animal feeding operation (CAFO) emissions as they adversely affect the health and well-being of neighbors and nearby communities. Health should be defined broadly because the nature of harm involves the nature of home. Residents associate their family and home life as the center of their well-being and are entitled to have a sense of health and security. A nuisance arises from an impairment of the use and enjoyment of homestead, and it takes into account the fact that a homeowner and family members have a right to the use, enjoyment, and comfort of their home. This impairment includes the conduct and effects that cause material physical discomfort, irritation, significant annoyance, and quality of life deterioration.

Nuisances arise most commonly from CAFO odor, but also from water contamination, flies, buzzards, noise, dust, and devaluation of property. Common complaints involve annoyance, an array of behavioral and physiological mediated symptoms, and interference with use and value of property. These experiences have been found to be common among those exposed to all types of CAFOs. The same patterns of conditions, symptoms, and limitations in daily life have been documented and affirmed in numerous studies associated with quantifiable, qualitative, reliable, and valid behavioral and physiological measures.

While the source of an annoying CAFO odor is usually obvious, the contributions to CAFO odor may come from other industrial or livestock facilities, especially with low wind speeds. Documentation of the CAFO as the source of the air or water pollutant emission is clearly important in making a complaint. It is equally important to identify the owner of the pollution. Corporate livestock companies are often called "integrators" as they control all stages of animal production from the birth of the animal to its slaughter, packaging, and distribution. Integrator contracts typically seek to make the grower responsible for the waste from the animals owned by the integrator. A recent legal decision made clear that the ownership of the animal and its waste cannot be separated—the ownership of the animal determines the responsible party.[2] This determination is underscored by nuisance law: "One who employs an independent contractor to do work which the employer knows to be likely to involve a trespass upon the land of another or the creation of a public or a private nuisance, is subject to liability for harm resulting to others from such trespass or nuisance."[3] The grower, who raises the animals to the specification of the integrator, nevertheless, has to contend with the complaints—and often ire—of neighbors and nearby community residents.

## Odor Exposures

Emissions from CAFOs, of all sizes, are a complex mixture of particles composed of feed, animal dander, bioaerosols, microbes, antibiotics, and a vast array of chemicals, including numerous irritants, neurotoxins, and volatile organic compounds (VOCs). Important emissions are ammonia ($NH_3$), hydrogen sulfide ($H_2S$), $PM_{10}$ and fine $PM_{2.5}$ particles, and hundreds of VOCs containing chemical irritants, odorants, and neurotoxins. Odor arising from manure from all types of IFAP facilities—confinement buildings, waste storage sites, and biogas facilities—is the particular problem. Of all of the gases, vapors, particles, and aerosols arising from swine CAFOs, over 24 odorous chemicals, often referred to as odorants, have been identified.[4] Volatile acids, mercaptans, and amines are odorous even in miniscule concentrations. Ammonia and hydrogen sulfide are pungently aromatic irritants. Schiffman and colleagues quantified odors and odorants from swine facilities in North Carolina.[5] A total of 331 different volatile organic compounds and fixed gases were identified by gas chromatography and mass spectrometry. The compounds "were diverse and included many acids, alcohols, aldehydes, amides, amines, aromatics, esters, eithers, fixed gases, halogenated hydrocarbons, hydrocarbons, ketones, nitriles, other nitrogen-containing compounds, phenols, sulfur-containing compounds, steroids, and other compounds." Most of these compounds were found to be individually at concentrations below published odor and irritation thresholds. However, in combination and when adsorbed onto particles, they become potent sources of odor and irritation. Depending on weather conditions, odorous gases may travel several miles.[6,7]

Complaints arising from IFAP facility neighbors and proximal communities are almost always about odor. A 2021 global, systematic review and meta-analysis of industrial odor and human health that included health symptoms (wheezing, cough, headache, nausea and vomiting), stress-related symptoms, and altered mood states found that animal feeding operations and their waste were the most common industrial source.[8] An earlier review of emissions and community exposures to CAFOs, including $NH_3$, $H_2S$, methane, VOCs, and endotoxin, also discussed dispersion models to predict downwind concentrations of pollutants released from CAFOs.[9] A 2020 review of measurement techniques and models to assess odor annoyance describes dynamic olfactometry, standardized field inspections, recordings by residents, and their respective advantages and disadvantages.[10] Also included in this review are the advantages and disadvantages of using gas chromatography, measurement of a tracer gas proxies, and the use of an electronic nose. Several air dispersion models were evaluated and stated to be especially useful as they provide simulation of spatial and temporal variations in odor concentrations, for both current and future emission scenarios, to determine setback distances. Evaluation of the Dutch long-term frequency distribution model (LTFD) found a strong relation between modeled odor exposure and odor annoyance.[11] Evaluation of the Austrian odor dispersion model (AODM) and comparisons with some other countries (Germany, Switzerland, The Netherlands, and the United States) for agricultural odors found that guideline separation distances were less than their model calculations.[12]

While measurements of air emissions from CAFOs in the community setting (see chapter 3) have focused on particulate matter (PM, $PM_{10}$, and $PM_{2.5}$), semi-volatile PM, endotoxin, VOCs, methane, oxides of nitrogen, and livestock allergens, more recently, fecal microbial source tracking (MST) has been introduced. MST marker technology involves the detection and quantification of the DNA of microbes that are sensitive and specific to the presence of fecal material from particular livestock species. Pig-2-bac is a highly sensitive and specific MST marker of swine-specific fecal material.[13,14] Detection of pig-2-bac DNA has been reported in surface waters proximal to swine CAFO lagoons and spray field systems,[13,14] the anterior nares of industrial hog operation workers,[15] and air and surface settled dust samples,[16] demonstrating the utility of MST technology to trace the source and route of pollution from IFAP facilities. A full complement of observational and analytical methods was used to assess exposures to neighbors from several Smithfield swine CAFOs and their spray fields, including the use of MST technology to measure pig-2-bac at neighbors' homes.[16] Fourteen of 17 homes within 0.47 miles of a CAFO tested positive for settled fecal dust (pig-2-bac), and all six yard dust samples using air filtration devices also tested positive for pig-2-bac. Several candidate MST markers of poultry-specific fecal contamination exist, although their sensitivity and specificity are not as high as for pig-2-bac. This technology continues to be developed, optimized, and further validated. It possesses great utility in the documentation of the fate, transport, and impact of IFAP pollution.

## Behavioral and Physiological Health Effects Arising from Odor

Exposure to environmental odor, arising from VOCs that contain both odorants and irritants in varying combinations, has been linked to worry, annoyance, and physical symptoms.[17-23] A Duke University workshop summarized health effects arising from livestock operations[20] and described health symptoms that have been reported with increasing frequency arising from manure and biosolids: "most frequently reported health effects include eye, nose and throat irritation, headache, nausea, diarrhea, hoarseness, sore throat, cough, chest tightness, nasal congestion, palpitations, shortness of breath stress, drowsiness, and alteration in mood." The workshop further observed that these symptoms usually occur shortly following exposure but that hypersensitive individuals, like asthmatics and those with chronic obstructive lung disease, may have their condition exacerbated with persisting symptoms. This Duke report described three pathways, or paradigms, by which environmental odor may cause health effects: (1) Symptoms occurring at odor concentrations below that expected from irritants when CAFO odors are perceived as unpleasant can impair mood. Both the perceived odor and cognitive expectations about a chemical can affect individual response. It was also recognized that individuals working in odorous environments may adapt to odor with longer-term exposures. (2) Symptoms may occur from combinations of irritants that may be additive or synergistic in their effect and typically occur at odor concentrations below that when odor is first detected. (3) Odorants may contribute to symptoms and changes in lung function as a part of a mixture that contains bioactive pollutants, such as organic dusts, endotoxin, glucano, allergens, microorganisms, and other toxins.[5,22] All of these pathways may be involved at the same time or in sequence depending on the timing, chemical makeup, and concentration of the exposure. For the majority of chemicals, olfactory stimulation precedes sensory irritation, and for many irritant chemicals, like ammonia, mucous membrane irritation occurs at levels two to five times that first elicited by olfaction, while for nonreactive VOCs, olfactory and irritant thresholds are separated by a variable factor of 10–500.[18] Schusterman described an adapted odor impact model for hydrogen sulfide where odor detection begins at 1 ppm, odor recognition begins at 2 ppm, annoyance begins at 10 ppm, but irritancy does not begin until 1,000 ppm.[18]

## Behavioral Health Effects Arising from Odor

An important early behavioral health study of swine odor was that of Schiffman and colleagues.[19] Twenty-two North Carolina neighbors living close to swine operations were compared to a control group of 22 control participants with no livestock operation exposure who were matched on gender, race, age, and years of education. The sources of swine CAFO odor were from ventilation air exhaust, waste handling systems, lagoons, and land application of manure. All subjects completed a Profile of Mood States (POMS) questionnaire, which is sensitive to transient mood shifts. The 65 questions on the POMS allow assessment of six domains: tension/anxiety, depression/dejection, anger/hostility, vigor/activity, fatigue/inertia, and confusion/bewilderment on a scale of 0 (not at all) to 4 (extremely). Results found that subjects living near swine operations, and who experienced odor, reported more tension, more depression, more anger, less vigor, more fatigue, and more confusion than did control subjects. Those exposed to swine odor, based on total POMS scores, also had more total mood disturbance than control subjects.

Bullers evaluated the effect of environmental stressors and perceived loss of control among 48 residents living close to North Carolina industrial hog facilities and a control group of 34 residents with no exposure to hog facilities.[24] Perceived lack of control over odor, the intermittent nature of odor, the lack of control over one's own property's degradation, loss of property value, and loss of enjoyment were all cited as contributors to psychological distress. Living near an industrial hog facility was found to be associated with decreased perception of control and increases in 12 of the 22 surveyed physical symptoms. Both perceived control and psychological distress measures were significantly increased among residents living close to an industrial hog facility as compared with unexposed control residents.

Malodor as a trigger of stress and negative mood was the subject of another eastern North Carolina study of 101 nonsmoking adults living in 16 low-income neighborhoods located within 1.5 miles of at least one industrial hog facility.[25] Based on twice-daily diary entrees, malodor was found to be associated with stress and four mood states. Significantly increased odds ratios were found for a one-unit change on a 0–8 odor scale for feeling nervous or anxious for a 1-ppb change in hydrogen sulfide concentration and for a 1-$\mu$g/m$^3$ change in semi-volatile particulate matter ($PM_{10}$). In the same study population, increases in both diastolic and systolic blood pressure were found to be associated with $PM_{10}$ and $H_2S$.[26] Also, subjects kept diaries on whether they were asleep or awake each hour for 2 weeks. Among study subjects, nightly (across a 12-hour period) swine odor was associated with lower sleep duration (mean duration −14.3 minutes) as compared to odor-free nights.[27] Increased awakening was found to be associated with measurement of hydrogen sulfide at a central location in each community, when compared to nights when no hydrogen sulfide was detected.

In collaboration with a local community organization concerned with CAFO odor, 15 nonsmoking residents from five neighborhood clusters of eastern North Carolina residents living within 1.5 miles of an industrial hog operation were asked to provide saliva samples twice a day and to rate odor on a 0–8 scale for 2 weeks in order to evaluate psycho-physiologically mediated immunosuppressive effect on secretory immunoglobulin A.[28] A decrease in secretory rate with increased hog odor was observed in this small study. The authors suggested this

finding was likely an immunosuppressive effect of malodor on mucosal immunity.

Measures of annoyance, behavioral interference, and health risk perception were related to measures of exposure to animal waste/farm-
ing odors in six randomly selected nonurban Danish regions.[29] A total
of 1,120 households were randomly selected and mailed a questionnaire
on indoor climate and timed to coincide with the period when animal
waste was most often applied. A 5-point odor annoyance scale was related to measures of $NH_3$ as a proxy of airborne exposures of livestock
odor. An estimated prevalence of odor annoyance (18% annoyed 10%
of the time) exceeded the cited World Health Organization (WHO)
threshold level (5% annoyed 2% of the time). Forty-five percent of the
respondents reported increases in annoyance, health risk perception,
and behavioral interference with unit increases in $NH_3$ exposure.
Annoyance was found to be a strong mediator of exposure-related behavioral interference (altering plans to avoid exposure) and exposure-
related health risk perception.

## Physiological Health Effects Arising from Odor

Early studies of physical symptoms triggered by odor include that of
Thu and colleagues, who studied 18 residents living within 2 miles of a
4,000 sow-swine CAFO with six hog sheds and a two-stage lagoon, as
well as a comparable group of residents with minimal exposure to
livestock operations.[30] Those living close to the CAFO experienced
symptoms similar to those experienced by CAFO workers: burning
eyes, runny nose, plugged ears, increased cough and phlegm, shortness of breath, wheezing, and chest tightness. Questions designed to
indicate depression and anxiety revealed no differences between the
two groups. Wing and Wolf studied nonfarming residents, including
23 living within 2 miles of a 6,000-head swine CAFO, 13 living within
2 miles of an intensive cattle operation, and 19 living in a rural area
without any livestock operation.[21] Residents in the vicinity of the hog
CAFO reported increased rates of headache, runny nose, sore throat,

excess coughing, diarrhea, and burning of the eyes when compared with unexposed control community residents.

Mirabelli and colleagues surveyed 58,169 North Carolina schoolchildren regarding prevalence of respiratory symptoms and allergies associated with livestock odor detected in 21% of 265 schools within 0.2 to 42 miles from 2,343 swine operations.[6,31] The prevalence of wheezing was found to be slightly higher in schools where livestock odor was reported but was significantly increased by 5% among students living within 3 miles of a CAFO and was 24% higher in schools in which livestock odor was noticeable at least twice per month, as compared to schools that reported no livestock odor. Students with allergies and who lived within 3 miles of a CAFO reported higher rates of doctor-diagnosed asthma, doctor and/or emergency room visits, asthma medication, activity limitation, and days of missed school.

A large epidemiological study of nonfarm community residents ($n = 6,917$) living in four rural German towns, close to high-density swine CAFOs, were surveyed by questionnaire.[33] Exposure was measured using a 4-point scale of odor annoyance together with geocoded data regarding the number of CAFOs within 500 m (1,641 ft.). Increased CAFO density, as measured by the number of CAFOs within 500 m, was found to be associated with increased prevalence of wheezing without a cold, increased prevalence of doctor-diagnosed asthma, and significantly lower levels of forced expiratory volume in 1 second ($FEV_1$ −7.4%) as compared with age- and height-adjusted predicted levels.

Wing and colleagues studied 101 nonsmoking volunteers living within 1.5 miles of swine CAFOs in 16 rural neighborhoods in eastern North Carolina.[32] Based on twice-daily odor diaries over a 2-week period, objective measures of swine odor were made at subject homes— hydrogen sulfide, particulate ($PM_{10}$, $PM_{2.5}$), and endotoxin. Swine odor was reported in more than half of the 1,655 episode reports. Detection of odor was correlated to $H_2S$, $PM_{10}$, temperature, and wind speed. The study demonstrated that repeated self-reported measures of odor were related to objective measures of well-recognized CAFO pollutants, thereby validating residents' subjective reports of odor episodes.

Further analyses of this study population found these repeated measures (odor, $H_2S$, and $PM_{10}$) were related to acute eye irritation.[34] Also, an increase in wheezing and decreases in $FEV_1$ were found to be associated with increased concentrations of $PM_{2.5}$. Increased sore throat, chest tightness, and nausea were found to be positively correlated to increases in endotoxin concentration. The study concluded that objective measures of CAFO exposures were significantly related to physical symptoms and changes in lung function. An independent review concurred and commented that these findings were protected from unmeasured confounding by an innovative study design.[35]

Schulze and colleagues studied 457 nonfarm residents in the German Lower Saxony Lung Study.[36] Annual ammonia emissions were optimized using cluster analysis. Residents exposed to higher levels of ammonia were found to be more likely to be sensitized to common allergens than lower-exposed residents and had significantly lower $FEV_1$ levels. Loftus and colleagues conducted a longitudinal panel study of 58 asthmatic children exposed to ammonia odor from industrial dairy farms in an agricultural region of Washington State.[37] Ammonia was sampled in 18 representative sites allowing calculation of daily plume exposures. Significant decrements in $FEV_1$ were observed one day following elevated livestock plume exposures. The 2023 Dutch Prevention and Incidence of Asthma and Mite Allergy (PIAMA) cohort study assessed associations between residential exposure to mixed livestock plumes ($PM_{10}$ exposure as the proxy pollutant) and changes in spirometry among 16-year-old youth.[38] The operational priority substances (OPS) dispersion model was used to model mixed livestock plumes. Lower levels of $FEV_1$ were found to be consistently associated with increased $PM_{10}$ exposure concentrations.

## Quality of Life and Well-Being

With the rapid increase in industrial livestock production in Iowa in the 1990s, Iowa Farm and Rural Life Polls reported substantial concern among CAFO neighbors.[39,40] Three-fourths of farmers surveyed lived within three-quarters of a mile of a CAFO neighbor. In the 1998 poll, 14% were unwilling to tolerate odor from a neighbor's livestock operation more than 2 days a year, 34% were willing to tolerate only a week or less, and 50% viewed odor a "major nuisance" if it affected them as many as 10 times a year. Respondents agreed with the following statement: "Increasingly, manure management is a major issue in the livestock industry" 61% of the time in 1992 and 85% in 1998.

The 1999 Wing and Wolf study also evaluated quality of life (QoL), as indicated by the number of times residents could not open their windows or go outside even in nice weather.[21] QoL was similar between residents living near an intensive cattle operation and rural control residents not living near livestock operations but was greatly reduced among residents living within 2 miles of a swine CAFO. Problems cited by swine CAFO neighbors included limited child and adult recreation, unable to open windows, contaminated wells, and decreased property values. In a subsequent eastern North Carolina study, Tajik and colleagues conducted detailed interviews, using both open-ended and semi-structured questionnaires designed to assess the impact of CAFO exposure on neighbors' QoL.[41] All 49 participants were adult nonsmokers, nearly 90% were Black, and all lived within 1.5 miles of a swine CAFO. The authors cited recurring themes related to beneficial use of property in almost all interviews: cannot sit outside, have guests over, have cookouts, or have family reunions; cannot play, garden, or work outside; cannot use well water or need to buy bottle water; had to buy air conditioner/dryer; and had a hard time sleeping at night.

A study of four Lower Saxony, Germany, towns located close to high-density swine CAFOs surveyed 3,112 nonfarm residents by questionnaire.[42] Exposure was evaluated using a 4-point scale of odor annoyance, together with geocoded data on the number of CAFOs within 500 m (1,641 ft.) from homes. Sixty-one percent of respondents complained about odor. Over 90% of respondents attributed the source of odor they experienced at home to nearby livestock facilities. Analyses found that self-assessed level of odor was a strong negative predictor of QoL, as assessed by the Short Form 12 Health Survey (SF-12).

## National Meeting, Commission, Governmental, and Legal Proceeding Reports

In 1998, the North Carolina Health Director Dennis McBride issued a report, "The Association of Health Effects with Exposure to Odors from Hog Farm Operations," based on results from five focus groups.[43] The primary complaint of participants was annoyance from odor and concerns about health risk arising from odor exposure. Another complaint was that they had very little control over their living environment and that they had received very little communication from hog facility owners or from state government agencies. Based on these findings and a review of available literature, McBride concluded that hog farm odor was a public health risk and that facility owners, operators, and regulators should take action to minimize odor and other emissions in order to protect hog facility workers and neighbors.

In 2001, the Minnesota Environmental Quality Board published a Generic Environmental Impact Statement on Animal Agriculture.[44] The "Technical Working Paper of Social and Community Impacts" found that neighbors of both poultry and swine CAFOs had "the greatest quality of life concerns." Concerns centered on reduced value of property and included not being able to enjoy a walk or exercise, garden, barbeque on the deck, or have company over for fear of embarrassment. The same year, the Natural Resources Defense Council issued a report, concluding, "Studies consistently show that lagoons emit toxic airborne chemicals that can result in human health problems through inflammatory, immunologic, irritant, neurochemical, and psychophysiological mechanisms."[45]

In 2001, then Iowa governor Tom Vilsack, in response to numerous odor complaints to the Iowa Department of Natural Resources (DNR), requested that Iowa State University and the University of Iowa address five questions regarding health effects, exposures, and remediation strategies regarding air emissions arising from CAFOs.[46] Twenty-seven scientists from both universities issued a consensus executive summary and individually authored 10 chapters in a 220-page report that concluded that CAFO emissions "may constitute a public health hazard" and that precautions should be taken to minimize exposures to hydrogen sulfide, ammonia, and odor. In chapter 7 of that report, Flora and colleagues reviewed available literature on social and community impacts and commented that "an important aspect of community quality of life is social capital, which includes mutual trust, reciprocity, and shared norms and identity. In general, communities with greater social capital provide greater quality of life."[47]

The study group recommended that a new statewide spatial siting plan should be developed, that local siting guidelines should be implemented, and that available odor and gas reduction technologies should be undertaken to benefit both the producer and community residents.[46] The Iowa legislature rejected the Vilsack administration recommendation for local CAFO siting but did increase setback distances for large CAFOs. The DNR then implemented a CAFO siting "Master Matrix," purportedly to account for environmental issues, annoyance, and health concerns of neighbors and nearby community residents. In 20 years of operation, The Matrix has proven to do none of the above. Rather, it has been manipulated to approve combinations of small animal confinement facilities to avoid rules concerning setback distance, resulting in approval of 97% of applications.[48]

A committee of the National Research Council of the National Academy of Sciences, supported by the US Environmental Protection Agency and the US Department of Agriculture, published "Air Emissions from Animal Feeding Operations: Current Knowledge, Future Needs."[49] The committee assessed the potential importance of CAFO emissions and found that hydrogen sulfide and particulates were "significant" on the local scale and that odor was of "major" importance. The primary adverse effect of concern arising from VOCs, $H_2S$, and odor was on quality of life. Also in 2003, the Canadian government sponsored a systematic literature review, entitled "Hog Farms and Their Impact on Quality of Life of Rural Populations."[50] The study group concluded, "Impacts on overall quality of life also appear to be clear: livestock production farms, including hog farms, can have a negative impact on the quality of life perceived by the surrounding population. Odours are the exposure source most frequently cited in connection with this impact, but they are not the only one. The impact is also influenced by proximity and age."

In 2008, the Pew Commission on Industrial Farm Animal Production published "Putting Meat on the Table: Industrial Farm Animal Production in America."[51] The report was based on the review of thousands of publications, regional testimonies from stakeholders, and several commissioner nationwide site visits to industrial livestock facilities. The report section on "Industrial Agriculture and Quality-of-Life" concluded that odors from industrial animal production "can have dramatic consequences for surrounding communities."[51] Pew also published a technical report on the "Occupational and Community Impacts of Industrial Farm Animal Production."[52] The report concluded that "recurrent strong odors, the degradation of water bodies, and increases in populations of flies are among the problems caused by CAFOs that make it intolerable for neighbors and their guests to participate in normal outdoor recreational activities in and around their homes."

In 2010, the National Association of Local Boards of Health, supported by the Centers for Disease Control and Prevention, published "Understanding Concentrated Animal Feeding Operations and Their Impact on Communities."[53] The purpose of the report was to inform local board of health members regarding issues related to animal feeding operations so that they could "mitigate potential problems associated with CAFOs." The report section on neighbors' lifestyles concluded, "CAFO odors can cause severe lifestyle changes for individuals in the surrounding communities and can alter many daily activities. When odors are severe, people may choose to keep their windows closed, even in high temperatures when there is no air conditioning. People also may choose to not let their children play outside and may even keep them home from school."

In 2017, the EPA director of external civil rights compliance wrote a letter in response to a civil rights complaint alleging that minority neighbors of CAFOs in North Carolina bear a disproportional burden regarding quality of life impacts and health symptoms.[54] Based on its interviews of rural residents living close to CAFOs and site visits to observe these CAFOs, the investigation found that those living near facilities operating under a 2005 General Permit suffered from "nausea and headaches; odors that prevented them from enjoying their yards and outdoors; concerns about impacts to groundwater and surface water; and increase flies and other pests." The 2005 EPA General Permit had previously recognized that industrial hog operations had a negative impact on nearby residents, particularly with respect to objectionable odors and other nuisance problems that can affect their quality of life.[55]

In 2019, the American Public Health Association adopted its second IFAP public health policy statement,[56] a "Moratorium on Concentrated Animal Feeding Operations." This statement notes that large amounts of manure and other untreated waste created by concentrated animal feeding operations pose threats to air quality, drinking water, and human health, and it urges the federal government to remove such operations from reporting exemptions related to environmental emissions. It calls on policymakers to enforce the Clean Water Act as it relates to such operations, as well as strengthen regulations on the monitoring of air emissions.

## Legal Proceeding Investigations

It is unusual for a lawsuit to challenge the largest livestock producer in the world. But, as recounted in *Wastelands, the True Story of Farm Country on Trial* by Corban Addison, a multiyear science-based nuisance lawsuit was brought against Smithfield Farms, owned by the Chinese WH Group, on behalf of over 500 poor, nearly all Black plaintiffs.[2,57] The subsidiary of Smithfield that owned the thousands of hogs in the several CAFOs located within a mile and one-half, and in some cases less than 1,000 feet, of plaintiff homes, was Murphy-Brown. Wendell Murphy was an early integrator who designed and implemented grower agreements that sought to profit the integrator while shielding it from complaints and liability arising from hog waste. This contract, with variations, is the model throughout the swine and poultry industry and is described well in Wastelands:[57]

> Murphy-Brown owns the hogs. It sets the schedule for the delivery trucks, feed trucks and dead trucks. It establishes the procedures that the growers have to abide by if they wish to keep pigs in their barns. The grower, by contrast, holds all of the risk. He pays the operating costs of the farm. He employs the workers and maintains the facilities and equipment. He keeps the property insured. When a hog dies in his care, he takes the loss. The grower, moreover, is required to dispose of the hog waste in accordance with state and federal law. When it rains, he cleans up after the floods and spills. He services the hundreds of thousands of dollars of debt that he took on to build the place, and any other debt that he has incurred to improve it.
>
> If Murphy-Brown isn't satisfied with the grower's yield—the number of suckling pigs born per sow, for instance, or the death rate of finished hogs—the company can demand that the grower upgrade his facilities, install new technology, or hire new employees, all at the grower's expense. If the grower fails to make these improvements—or can't afford them—the company can terminate the contract and depopulate the farm. The relationship is purely provisional. The grower must live with the constant risk of total loss, all to earn a subsistence income of a few dollars per marketable hog. Murphy-Brown, meanwhile, collects the fully grown hogs from its farms, slaughters them at its slaughterhouses, packages the meat for sale—or exports it to China or elsewhere overseas—and rakes in around a billion dollars a year in profits.
>
> The growers, in effect, are modern-day sharecroppers.

Social scientists and public health practitioners use oral history as a way to understand cultural norms and how individuals think of themselves in relation to the rest of the world. Through oral histories, individual, familial, and communal experiences can be captured and assessed.[58] Within this methodological framework, qualitative interviews with 102 individuals from 16 neighborhoods containing CAFO plaintiffs in eastern North Carolina were conducted to provide detailed background information for the Smithfield case. Interviews were conducted to ascertain patterns of quality of life disruption among plaintiffs, the nature of those patterns, and cultural norms for living in the rural environment for these communities.[59] these data provide an understanding of cultural norms concerning quality of life and how hog CAFO exposures interfere with normative expectations of quality of life.

There are several key findings from these interviews.[59] Central to these individuals' quality of life expectations were cultural values of outdoor experiences enculturated in their childhood upbringing. The interview information reflected a clear normative pattern of working and playing in the outdoors that characterized plaintiffs' childhoods that shaped central cultural principles and expectations for what constitutes quality of life. A central cultural tenet of their quality of life is the ability to enjoy the outdoors and use their home in a way that connects with the outdoors. All plaintiffs reported that they lived at their properties prior to the arrival of the hog CAFOs or are in families with ties and claims to the land predating the CAFOs.

Plaintiffs reported quality of life problems from odors, flies, truck traffic, and buzzards linked with hog CAFOs[59] Plaintiffs described that these problems did not exist prior to the advent of the CAFOs. Their homes and properties are central for their quality of life, which revolves around core cultural principles of family, faith, friends, and health. The odor, flies, trucks, and buzzards not only interfere with individual events isolated to particular time and days but also envelop and significantly undermine entire lifestyles and cultural norms that are the basis of plaintiffs' quality of life. Their homes have been turned into barriers against offensive odors rather than a complement to outdoor life. While odor is episodic, it cannot be predicted, and even in the absence of an odor event, neighbors expressed anxiety and apprehension over the potential for it to arrive at any time. This erratic frequency of the odor resulted in many plaintiffs describing keeping their windows and doors generally closed, as they could not time exactly when a given odor episode may occur. Some plaintiffs experienced living with and raising livestock, including hogs, while growing up. None could remember their outdoor experiences and quality of life being disrupted because the number of livestock was limited and the animals lived outside. By contrast, the odor from nearby hogs after the CAFOs arrived differed significantly in that it was much more intense and life-altering than their experiences with livestock growing up. The plaintiffs expressed experience with and drew contrasts between the modest size and volume of livestock rearing for home use that many of them experienced or participated in historically and the industrial-scale volume of hog production associated with CAFOs in their neighborhoods today.

Smithfield, after having lost all five trials of plaintiff classes in the US District Court in Raleigh, and with judgments in favor of the plaintiffs totaling over $500 million, then appealed to the Fourth Circuit Court of Appeals in Richmond, Virginia.[57] Despite what was generally agreed to be a conservative three-judge panel, it became clear to Smithfield that it was likely it would lose again and in doing so set a precedent that they, and the rest of the livestock industry, would have to live with well into the future. So, Smithfield settled with the provision that the terms of the settlement would be sealed. Elderly and conservative, circuit judge Harvey Wilkinson commented.[57]

> It is well-established—almost to the point of judicial notice—that environmental harms are visited disproportionately upon the dispossessed—here on minority populations and poor communities. But whether a home borders a golf course or a dirt road, it is a castle for those who reside in it. It is where children play and grow, friends sit and visit, and a life is built. Many plaintiffs in this suit have tended their hearths for generations—one family for almost 100 years. They are exactly whom the venerable tort of nuisance ought to protect.

## Property Values

Homes around CAFOs are less pleasant places. Evidence that the arrival of an animal feeding operation will decrease a neighbor's home value is often reported by community activists. A recent publication *The Effect of CAFOs on Neighboring House and Land Values* by Midwest Environmental Advocates in Madison, Wisconsin, relies on an often-cited survey publication.[60] That article by John A. Kilpatrick, in the *Appraisal Journal*, documents the extensive devaluation in property caused by proximity to a neighboring CAFO.[61]

Distance from the source and being downwind from a livestock facility appear to have the biggest effects on decreases in property value. That distance matters, and that the decrease in value is significant, is made clear by the following quote in the Kilpatrick article. He refers to CAFOs as animal operations (AOs):

> Overall, the empirical evidence indicates that residences near AOs are significantly affected, and the data seems to suggest a valuation impact of up to 26 percent for nearby properties, depending on distance, wind direction, and other factors. Further, there has been some suggestion that properties immediately abutting an AO can be diminished as much as 88 percent. One study estimates the total negative impact to property values in the United States at $26 billion. Mitigation makes a marginal impact. Not only are residences affected, but nearby small farms can be impacted by such factors as water degradation and insects.[63]

The Kilpatrick publication was often used by CAFO opponents after its publication. However, recently there has been an exchange of letters to the editor of the *Appraisal Journal* between Kilpatrick and fellow University of Missouri professor Ray Massey. Professor Massey evaluated seven of the peer-reviewed economic studies cited by Kilpatrick and claimed errors by the author.[62] This journal also printed responses from Professor Kilpatrick, who took issue with many of Massey's conclusions. While one might conclude that Massey disagreed with the overall conclusion of the negative effect of AOs on home values demonstrated by Kilpatrick, that would be incorrect. A publication by Massey and Horner produced a table reporting the results of 12 home value studies.[63] One paper they cite is from Minnesota, which found that housing values actually increased near animal feeding operations. The authors pointed out that the homes where this occurred were low-value structures, which influenced the result. Massey and Horner also observed that distance, a downwind location, and house value and semi-rural versus a rural location all play a part in what happens to the value of homes near animal facilities. Of the other 11 examples in their table, the nearest CAFO to the property had the following effect: 1 study reported a decrease beyond 3 miles that was "not significant by itself"; the other 10 found housing prices decreased, but with qualifications. One study found only houses downwind saw a decrease; in another, there was a decrease in value only in town and within 0.5 miles; and in the third, the effect was "none to negative," depending on the value of the house. The other seven studies all found a decrease in house values, and there were no stated qualifications in the table.

Kilpatrick's original article contains information, apart from economic papers, that shed light on home value decrease. Reports by county tax assessors find that reductions in the assessed value for houses near livestock facilities range from 20% to 40% of value in counties in farm states, including Colorado, Missouri, Michigan, Illinois, and Iowa.[61]

Residents of rural farmland or small rural towns have reason to fear that their home of moderate to high value will lose value if an animal facility moves in nearby. There are many reasons such facilities are not good neighbors. Home value loss in a major one.

## Conclusions

Over 30 years of public health research, including anthropological, epidemiological, psychological, economic, and biochemical studies, have consistently and overwhelmingly demonstrated that CAFOs create nuisance conditions for neighboring residents. The WHO definition of health as "a state of complete physical, mental and social wellbeing" is particularly fitting in understanding the confluence of social, physical, and mental factors that contribute to the deterioration of quality of life for CAFO neighbors.

Rural residents view their homes as a space and place where they raise and enjoy their family. It is a sacrosanct space central to their quality of life that includes connecting with the outdoors. When that space is encroached by emissions from nearby CAFOs, families experience a violation that fundamentally undermines their ability to enjoy their homes, surrounding yards and gardens, and socializing with friends and family. The physical properties of emissions from CAFOs create a constellation of health symptoms similar to well-documented symptoms among workers inside CAFOs. Research has demonstrated that complaints of CAFO odor from neighbors are accurate and not frivolous. In addition, declining property values that result from the building of CAFOs proximal to rural residents creates hardship and an economic loss. Who would be willing to buy a home near a CAFO? All of these problems are exacerbated with the construction of CAFOs in communities of color that often have fewer resources and connections to political power. The arrival of CAFOs is viewed as another chapter of ongoing injustice.

Court cases, such as the federal trials against Smithfield in North Carolina, demonstrate that the ability to rectify nuisance conditions created by CAFOs is extremely difficult. The amount of money and power to influence policymakers at the local, state, and federal levels creates a feeling of despair among CAFO neighbors that there is nothing they can do. In the wake of the Smithfield litigation, North Carolina modified its right to farm law to further take away people's rights, a pattern now seen across the nation. However, the deep and abiding values of community, home, and family will continue to serve as sources of unrelenting resolve to seek justice and restitution, particularly when the most basic quality of life conditions are violated.

**Recommended Policy**

See chapter 3.

## REFERENCES

1. World Health Organization (WHO) (1992). *Basic Documents*. 39th ed. Geneva, Switzerland: WHO.
2. Addison, Corban (2022). *Wastelands, the True Story of Farm Country on Trial*. New York, NY: Alfred A. Knopf.
3. Restatement (Second) of Torts; at Section 427B (1979). Am.L. Inst.
4. Cole D, Todd L, Wing S (2000). Concentrated swine feeding operations and public health: a review of occupational and community health effects. Environ Health Perspect 10 8:685–699.
5. Schiffman SS, Bennett JL, Raymer JH (2001). Quantification of odors and odorants from swine operations in North Carolina. Agr Forest Meteorol 108(3):213–240.
6. Mirabelli M, Wing S, Marshall S, Wilcosky T (2006). Race, poverty, and potential exposure of middle-school students to air emissions from confined swine feeding operations. Environ Health Perspect 114(4):591–595.
7. North Carolina Cooperative Extension, North Carolina State University. Understanding livestock odors. https://www.bae.ncsu.edu/extension/est-publications/air_quality/ag589-livestock-odors.pfg
8. Gudadalupe-Fernandez V, DeSario M, Vecchi S, Bauleo L, Michelozzi P, Davoli M, Ancona C (2021). Industrial odour pollution and human health: a systematic review and meta-analysis. Environmental Health 20:108.
9. Hoff S, Hornbuckle K, Thorne P, Bundy D, O'Shaughnessy P (2002). Emissions and community exposures from CAFOs. In: *Iowa Concentrated Animal Feeding Operations Air Quality Study: Final Report*. Iowa City: Environmental Health Sciences Research Center, University of Iowa. https://www.public-health.uiowa.edu/ehsrc/CAFOstudy.htm
10. Conti C, Guarino M, Bacenetti J (2020). Measurement techniques and models to assess odor annoyance: a review. Environ Int 134:105261.
11. Boers D, Geelen, Erbrink H, Smit L, Heederik D, Hooiveld M, Yzermans C, Huijbregts M, Wouters I (2016). The relation between modeled odor exposure from livestock farming and odor annoyance among neighboring residents. Int Arch Occup Environ Health 89:521–530.
12. Schauberger G, Piringer M, Petz E (2001). Separation distance to avoid odour nuisance due to livestock calculated by the Austrian odour dispersion model (AOEM). Agr Ecosyst Environ 87:13–28.
13. Heaney C, Myers K, Wing S, Hall D, Baron D, Stewart J (2015). Source tracking swine fecal waste in surface water proximal to swine concentrated animal feeding operations. Sci Total Environ 2015; 511:676–683. https://www.ncbi.nlm.nih.gov/pmc/articles/PMC4514616/
14. Mieszkin S, Furet J-P, Corthier G, Gourmelon M (2009). Estimation of pig fecal contamination in a river catchment by real-time PCR using two pig-specific *Bacteriodales* 16S rRNA genetic markers. Appl Environ Microbiol 75(10): 3045–3054.

15. Pisanic N, Nadimpalli M, Rinsky J, Stewart J, Wing S, Love D, Hall D, Heaney C (2016). Pig-2-Bac as a biomarker of occupational exposure to pigs and livestock-associated *Staphylococcus aureus* among industrial hog operation workers. Environ Res 143:93–97.

16. Rogers S (2018). Expert report in the United States District Court for the Eastern District of North Carolina Western Division. Master Case No. 5:15-CV-00013-BR. Case 7:14-cv-00180-BR. Document 328-15.S rRNA.

17. Shusterman D (1992). Critical review: the health significance of environmental odor pollution. Arch Environ Health 47:76–87.

18. Shusterman D (1999). The health significance of environmental odour pollution: revisited. J Environ Med 1:249–258.

19. Schiffman S, Miller E, Suggs M, Graham B (1995). The effect of environmental odors emanating from commercial swine operations on the mood of nearby residents. Brain Res Bull 37:369–375.

20. Schiffman S, Walker J, Dalton P, Lorig T, Raymer J, Shusterman D, Williams M (2000). Potential health effects of odor from animal operations, wastewater treatment, and recycling of byproducts. J Agromed 1:7–50.

21. Wing S, Wolf S (2000). Intensive livestock operations, health and quality of life among eastern North Carolina residents. Environ Health Perspect 108:233–238.

22. Schiffman S, Studwell C, Landerman L, Berman K, Sundy J (2005). Symptomatic effects of exposure to diluted air sampled from a swine confinement atmosphere on healthy human subjects. Environ Health Perspect 113(5):567–576.

23. Merchant J, Kline J, Donham K, Bundy D, Hodne C; ISU-UI Study Group. (2002). Human health effect. In: *Iowa Concentrated Animal Feeding Operations Air Quality Study*. Iowa City: University of Iowa, College of Public Health. http://www.ehsrc .uiowa,edu/ehsrc.CAFOstudy

24. Bullers S (2005). Environmental stressors, perceived control, and health: The case of residents near large-scale hog farms in eastern North Carolina. Hum Ecol 33(1):1–16.

25. Horton R, Wing S, Marshal S, Brownley K (2009). Malodor as a trigger of stress and negative mood in neighbors of industrial hog operations. Am J Public Health 99(Suppl. 3):S610–S615.

26. Wing S, Avery-Horton R, Rose K (2013). Air pollution from industrial swine operations and blood pressure of neighboring residents. Environ Health Perspect 121(1):92–96.

27. MacNeil N, Jackson C, Heaney C (2021). Relation of repeated exposures to air emissions from swine industrial operations to sleep duration and awakenings in nearby residential communities. Sleep Health 7:528–534.

28. Avery R, Wing S, Marshall S (2004). Odor from industrial hog farming operations and mucosal immune function in neighbors. Arch Environ Health 59(2):1001–1108.

29. Blanes-Vidal V, Baelum J, Nadimi E, Lofstrom P, Christensen L (2014). Chronic exposure to odorous chemicals in residential areas and effects on human psychosocial health: dose-response relationships. Sci Total Environ 490:545–554.

30. Thu K, Donham K, Ziegenhorn R, Reynolds S, Thorne P, Subramanian P, Whitten P, Stooksesberry J (1997). A control study of the physical and mental health of residents living near a large-scale swine operation. J Agr Saf Health 3(1):13–26.

31. Mirabelli M, Wing S, Marshall S, Wilcosky T (2006). Asthma symptoms among adolescents who attend public schools that are located near confined wine feeding operations. Pediatrics 118:e66–e75.

32. Wing S, Horton R, Marshall S, Thu K, Tajik M, Schinasi L, Schiffman S (2008). Air pollution and odor in communities near industrial swine operations. Environ Health Perspect 116(10):1362–1368.

33. Radon K, Schulze A, Ehrenstein V, van Strien R, Praml G, Nowak D (2007). Environmental exposure to confined animal feeding operations and respiratory health of neighboring residents. Epidemiology 18(3):300–308.

34. Schinasi L, Horton R, Guidry V, Wing S, Marshall S, Morland K (2011). Air pollution, lung function, and physical symptoms in communities near concentrated swine feeding operations. Epidemiology 22(2):208–215.

35. Merchant J (2011). Commentary: advancing industrial livestock production health effect research and sustainability. Epidemiology 22:2.

36. Schulze A, Rommelt H, Ehrenstein V, van Strien R, Prami G, Kuchenhoff H, Nowak D, Aradon K (2011). Effects on pulmonary health of neighboring residents of concentrated animal feeding operations: exposure assessed using optimized estimation technique. Arch Environ Occup Health 66(3):146–154.

37. Loftus C, Afsharinejad Z, Sampson P, Vedal S, Torres E, Arias G, Tchong-French M, Karr C (2020). Estimated time-varying exposures to air emissions from animal feeding operations and childhood asthma. Intern J Hyg Environ Health 223:187–198.

38. Kiss P, de Rooij M, Koppelman G, et al. (2023). Residential exposure to livestock farms and lung function in adolescence—the PIAMA birth cohort study. Environ Res 219:115–134.

39. Lasley P (1995). Iowa farm and rural life poll: 1995 summary report. Ames: Iowa State University Extension 1–16. PM 1628.

40. Lasley P (1998). Iowa farm and rural life poll: 1998 summary report. Ames: Iowa State University Extension 1–16.

41. Tajik M, Muhammad N, Lowman A, Thu K, Wing S, Grant G (2008). Impact of odor from industrial hog operations on daily living activities. New Solutions 18(2):193–198.

42. Radon K, Peters A, Praml G, Ehrenstein V, Schulze A, Hehl O, Nowak D (2004). Livestock odours and quality of life of neighbouring residents. Ann Agric Environ Med 11(1):59–62.

43. McBride A (1998). The association of health effects with exposure to odors from hog farm operations. http://infohouse.p2ricorg.ref.32.31217.htm

44. Wright W, Flora C, Kremer K, et al. (2001). Technical work paper on social and community impacts. Prepared for the Generic Environmental Impact Statement on Animal Agriculture and the Minnesota Environmental Quality Board.

45. Marks R (2001). Cesspools of shame: how factory farm lagoons and sprayfields threaten environmental and public health. Washington, D.C.: Natural Resources Defense Council and the Clean Water Network.
46. Iowa State University and University of Iowa Study Group (2002). Executive summary. In: *Iowa Concentrated Animal Feeding Operations Air Quality Study: Final Report.* Iowa City: Environmental Health Sciences Research Center, University of Iowa. https://www.public- health.uiowa.edu/ehsrc.CAFOstudy .htm
47. Flora J, Hodne C, Goudy W, Osterberg D, Kliebenstein J, Thu K, Marquez S (2002). Social and community impacts. In: *Iowa Concentrated Animal Feeding Operations Air Quality Study: Final Report.* Iowa City: Environmental Health Sciences Research Center, University of Iowa. https://www.public-health.uiowa .edu/ehsrc.CAFOstudy.htm
48. Merchant J, Osterberg D (2018). The explosion of CAFOs in Iowa and the impact on water quality and public health. Iowa Policy Project. January 25. https://www .commongoodiowa.org/media/documents/180125CAFO1_05C66C7611CC1.pdf
49. National Research Council, Ad Hoc Committee on Air Emissions from Animal Feeding Operations (2003). *Air Emissions from Animal Feeding Operations: Current Knowledge, Future Needs.* National Academies Press: Washington, D.C.
50. Brission G, Godbout S, Lemay S, Mercier G (2009). Hog farms and their impact on the quality of life of rural populations: a systematic review of the literature, Canada. National Collaborating Centre for Environmental Health. https://ncceh.ca
51. Pew Commission (2008). Putting meat on the table: industrial farm animal production in America. Report of the Commission on Industrial Farm Animal Production. http://pewtrusts.org/en/research-and-analysis/reports/2008/04/29 /putting-meat-on-the-table-industrial-farm-animal-production-in-america
52. Merchant J, Gray G, Hornbuckle K, Osterberg D, Thorne P (2008). Occupational and community impacts of industrial farm animal production. Report to the Pew Commission on Industrial Farm Animal Production. Washington, D.C. hsttp://pewtrusts.org/en/research-and-analysis/reports/2008/04/29 /occupational-and-community-impacts-of-industrial-farm-animal-production
53. Hribar C (2010). Understanding concentrated animal feeding operations and their impacts on communities. M. Schultz, Bowling Green, Ohio, National Association of Local Boards of Health. https://www.cdc.gov
54. US EPA (2017). External Civil Right Compliance Office, Office of General Counsel. Letter of Concern to William G. Ross, Jr., Acting Secretary, North Carolina Department of Environmental Quality. EPA File No. 11R-14-R4.
55. US EPA (2005). Animal feeding operations consent agreement and final order, 70FR 4957, 4957.
56. American Public Health Association (2003). Policy Statement No. 20037, 18 November 2003, precautionary moratorium on new concentrated animal feeding operations. https://www.apha.org/policies-and-advocacy/public-health-policy -statements/policy- database/2014/07/24/11/17/precautionary-moratorium-on -new-concentrated-animal-feeding-operations

57. Addison C (2022). *Wastelands—The True Story of Farm Country on Trial*. New York, NY: Alfred A. Knopf.
58. Lambert H, McKevitt C (2002). Anthropology in health research: from qualitative methods to multidisciplinary. BMJ 5:210–213.
59. Thu K (2018). Expert report in the United States District Court for the Eastern District of North Carolina Western Division. Master Case No. 5:15-CV-00013-BR (This document relates to all cases).
60. Midwest Environmental Advocates (2020). The effect of CAFOs on neighboring house and land values. http://midwesteadvocates.org/the-effect-of-cafos-on -neighboring-house-and-land-values
61. Kilpatrick J (2015). Animal operations and residential property values. Appraisal J 83:1. ABIINFORM Global.
62. Massey R (2019). Comment on animal operations and residential values by John A. Kilpatrick. Appraisal J. The Appraisal Institute, Chicago
63. Massey R, Horner J (2021). Animal feeding operations and housing values: summary of literature. http://extension.missouri.edu/media/wysiwyg /Extensiondata/Pub/pdf/mispubs.mpo748.

# CHAPTER 5

# Infectious Disease Health Effects

Tara C. Smith and Gregory C. Gray

In this chapter, we will review the impact modern livestock farming has had upon human infectious diseases. It seems appropriate to note that while there are multiple theories about how humans acquired pathogens from domestic animals, the number of these zoonotic sharings, as Morand et al. states,[1] "appears to be strongly related to the time since animal domestication." Johnson et al.[2] further found that the richness of zoonotic viruses correlated with the global abundance of domestic animal species, specifically farm animals. Recent reviews of influenza A virus prevalence in pigs supports this observation as farms with the highest prevalence of virus are those with the largest and most crowded animal populations.[3,4]

Humans could always acquire infections from direct contact with food animals and products from them (e.g., meat, milk, cheese, eggs). What is different today is the scale of the operations, the size and density of domestic animal population, and the rapid global distribution of food products. Pathways for the spread of microbes (and antibiotic residues and resistance genes) can be directly from live animals and their immediate environment to people but also include spread from waste that contaminates the environment and water that may be used for recreation or irrigating food crops. Food (animal products and produce and other items contaminated by them) is an important route of spread. Transmission can occur during transport, slaughter, and processing, and products may be mixed on an industrial scale, packaged, and dispersed around the globe.[5]

Modern livestock farming has globally adopted large, dense populations of domestic livestock in their production systems, and these large farms are increasing the number of human viral threats. For example, as swine farms have increased in size in many countries, the number of novel swine virus types has also increased.[6,7] This makes sense in that a specific viral strain never ceases to find susceptible animals to infect as these large farms have frequent introductions of immunologically naive juvenile animals. Hence, prolonged and intense human occupational exposure to domestic animals with numerous unique microbes provides the conditions necessary for an animal microbe to navigate the numerous barriers to spillover[8] and to infect the new human host. Hence, modern livestock farms that have large dynamic populations of animals harboring a large assortment of diverse zoonotic pathogens have a marked risk of accelerating zoonotic virus spillover events to humans.

For the purposes of this work, we will focus on animals raised in the United States for food production—namely, chickens, pigs, cattle, and sheep (arranged in descending order of US annual pounds of meat production). Certainly, other nations produce large quantities of meat from other species for human consumption, including goats, camels, horses, deer, rabbits, and dogs, but their infectious disease prevalence and production data are not thought to be as robust or available as for the leading US livestock species.

As described in previous sections of this book, while there have been some production losses due to the COVID-19 pandemic,[9] in general, in the United States as well as in many parts of the world, meat production has increased during the past 50 years with farms, especially pig farms,[10] growing larger and their number growing fewer. This is thought

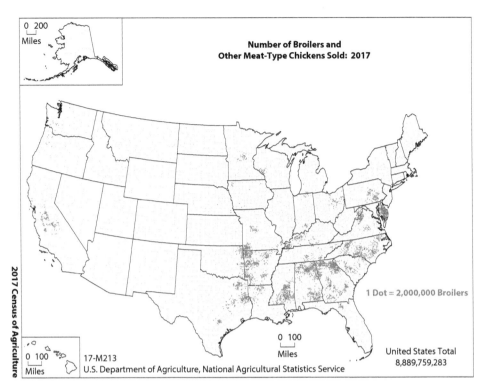

**Number of Broilers and Other Meat-Type Chickens Sold: 2017**

1 Dot = 2,000,000 Broilers

0 100 Miles

17-M213
U.S. Department of Agriculture, National Agricultural Statistics Service

United States Total
8,889,759,283

FIGURE 5.1. Geographical locations of farms (1 dot = 2,000,000 broilers) from which chickens and other meat-type chickens were sold in 2017. *Source*: US Department of Agriculture, Graphic 17-M213.

to reflect economies of scale, with larger farms being able to produce more meat at lower costs, supplanting smaller farms.

It is also important to note that the geographical distribution of livestock farms is not homogeneous. This is well demonstrated in the United States, where broiler (meat) chickens are largely concentrated in the southeastern United States (Fig. 5.1); pigs are chiefly farmed in the Midwest and North Carolina (Fig. 5.2); beef cattle farms are most prevalent in the Midwest (Fig. 5.3); milk cow farms are often located in relatively colder climates, including the Northeast (Fig. 5.4); and sheep are raised more commonly on farms in the West (Fig. 5.5).

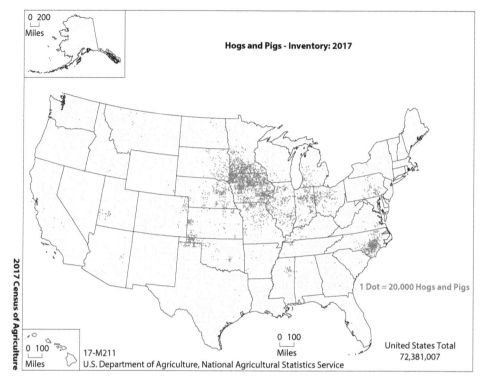

FIGURE 5.2. Geographical locations of farms (1 dot = 20,000 hogs and pigs) with pig holdings 2017. *Source*: US Department of Agriculture, Graphic 17-M211.

Hence, when one considers the impact livestock farms have had on human infectious diseases, it is important to consider animal densities, as well as temporal and geographical risk factors for livestock-driven zoonotic disease manifestations.

## Bacterial Exposures and Health Effects of Industrialized Farming

Livestock husbandry introduces health risks via microbial exposure in a number of ways. There can be direct transmission of pathogens originating in animals that can sicken humans. This may be on-farm, from animals to farmers or other animal caretakers; via contaminated food

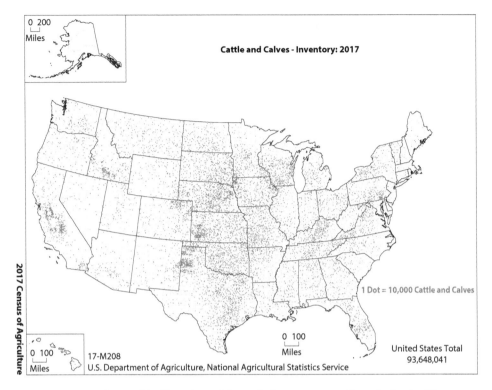

FIGURE 5.3. Geographical locations of farms (1 dot = 10,000 cattle and calves) with cattle and calves holdings in 2017. *Source:* US Department of Agriculture, Graphic 17-M208.

products that are distributed within the community; or via exposure to animal waste products due to application of manure in the environment. Some of these infections acquired from agriculture may lead to continued chains of human-to-human transmission (such as *Escherichia coli, Salmonella, Staphylococcus aureus,* and more), while some may infect an individual with no further downward spread (such as *Brucella*). Indeed, the most common route of transfer of most agricultural-associated pathogens to human is likely foodborne. A global population is reached by animal protein and fruits or vegetables that may be contaminated by livestock animal waste; a relatively small population, by contrast, has direct contact with food animals or their tissue via slaughter and processing plants, but these exposures are of a much

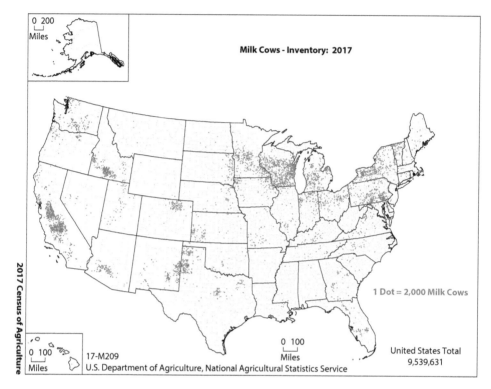

FIGURE 5.4. Geographical locations of farms (1 dot = 2,000 milk cow) from which milk cows were sold in 2017. *Source*: US Department of Agriculture, Graphic 17-M213.

greater intensity and, as such, are more likely to result in infection. Bacteria generated on farms may also be more likely to be resistant to antibiotics due to the use of antibiotics on farms for disease prophylaxis and treatment, which will be discussed in the next section.

## Escherichia coli

*Escherichia coli* is a highly diverse Gram-negative bacterial commensal that colonizes a variety of animal species, including humans. Although most *E. coli* strains are nonpathogenic, human pathogens can cause gastrointestinal or extraintestinal infections. Extraintestinal infections (caused by extraintestinal pathogenic *E. coli*, or ExPEC) include

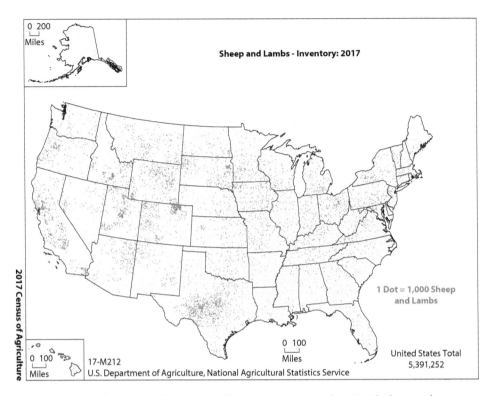

FIGURE 5.5. Geographical locations of farms (1 dot = 1,000 sheep) with sheep and lamb holdings in 2017. *Source*: US Department of Agriculture, Graphic 17-M212.

presentations such as urinary tract infections (UTIs), septicemia, and meningitis. Intestinal pathologies include severe diarrhea, sometimes with complications, by *E. coli* that can be categorized as enterotoxigenic, enteropathogenic, or enterohemorrhagic *E. coli* (ETEC, EPEC, or EHEC). EHEC infections can lead to hemolytic uremic syndrome (HUS), caused by a bacterial toxin that can lead to serious kidney damage and death.[11]

The most common strain of HUS-causing EHEC is serotype O157:H7, with livestock—particularly cattle—serving as a reservoir for zoonotic transmission.[12] O157:H7 has been considered an adulterant (a deleterious substance that may render it injurious to health) by the Food Safety and Inspection Service (FSIS) on meat products since 1994, following a large outbreak that killed 4 children and infected 732 people across four states. In 2012, six other non-O157 EHEC strains were also designated for surveillance.[13] Collectively, non-O157 serotypes likely produce more disease than O157.[14] Together, Shiga toxin–producing *E. coli* (STEC) infections are estimated to cause more than 265,000 illnesses, 3,600 hospitalizations, and 30 deaths each year.[15] An unknown additional number of individuals may require long-term dialysis or transplants due to kidney damage. Cattle are the primary source of EHEC infections in humans, either directly via contaminated meat[16] or indirectly due to fecal contamination of fruits or vegetables.[17,18] Other species can be colonized with EHEC as well, including sheep,[19] pigs,[20] and goats,[20] as well as wild animals including deer,[21] but are not thought to be as important regarding human infections as cattle.

ExPEC strains cause millions of infections every year in the United States,[22] including UTIs. Although many may perceive UTIs as minor infections, invasive UTIs may be deadly.[23] Recent studies examining strains of *E. coli* isolated from meat products and human clinical infection isolates have shown that many human UTIs are likely caused by common poultry strains, suggesting transmission from poultry to humans via contaminated meat products.[24–26]

Yersiniosis

*Yersinia* is part of the Enterobacteriaceae family. Of 18 species within, 3 are zoonotic and pathogenic for humans: *Y. pestis* (bubonic plague), *Y. enterocolitica* (yersiniosis), and *Y. pseudotuberculosis* (rodentiosis). As *Y. pestis* is not livestock associated and *Y. pseudotuberculosis* is more rare, causing self-limiting gastroenteritis and a condition called Far East scarlet-like fever (FESLF),[27] the focus here will be on *Y. enterocolitica* and yersiniosis.

*Y. enterocolitica* are Gram-negative, generally rod-shaped bacteria. They can be motile at temperatures below human body temperature. Human infection generally presents as diarrhea (sometimes bloody) with fever and abdominal pain but can cause sepsis in rare cases. Nonspecific symptoms may also be present, leading to misdiagnosis.[28]

Symptoms may persist for 1–2 weeks in adults or up to 4 weeks in children following a typical incubation period of 3–7 days.[29] *Y. enterocolitica* can also grow at refrigerator temperatures,[29] complicating control measures. In 2015, yersiniosis was the third most commonly reported zoonosis in the European Union, with 7,202 confirmed cases;[30] the Centers for Disease Control and Prevention (CDC) reports over 117,000 illnesses and 35 deaths yearly in the United States.[31]

Yersiniosis is typically foodborne. The organisms are present in the environment and have been isolated from raw milk, water contaminated with sewage, and a number of animal species, including pigs, poultry, cattle, sheep, and goats, as well as wild animals,[32] although pigs do not show any symptoms of infection and are generally thought to be most important in human disease transmission via contaminated meat products.

### Salmonella

*Salmonella* and *E. coli* are both members of the Enterobacteriaceae group. Collectively, they are one of the most common global causes of food poisoning. *Salmonella* species are estimated to account for up to 1 billion cases per year globally.[33,34] Named for researcher Daniel Salmon, the Gram-negative rods were first isolated during an examination of cholera in pigs. Collectively, *Salmonella* have a wide range of growth, which complicates control, with some growing at 54°C and others as low as 2°C.[35] The case fatality rate is low, but with such large numbers of infections, the total deaths are estimated yearly at 150,000, often in children under the age of 4.[36] Most infections are due to food-borne transmission, but *Salmonella typhi* is transmitted between humans and via contaminated water and will not be further discussed here. In the United States, an estimated 1 million *Salmonella* cases per year occur, with 26,000 hospitalizations and 420 deaths.[37]

*Salmonella* nomenclature is complicated and often changing. Currently, the genus is divided into two species, *S. enterica* and *S. bongori*; seven subspecies designated by number/letters (I, II, IIIa, IIIb, IV, V, and

VI); and over 2,500 serotypes.[38,39] *S. typhimurium*, *S. enteritidis*, *S. newport*, and *S. heidelberg* are most often responsible for food poisoning and are typically ingested via contaminated food products or water.[28] Bacteria may remain in the intestines for up to a month for adults, 7 weeks for children, and up to 1 year for a small percentage of individuals following resolution of symptoms.[40] Treatment for serious cases is generally fluid therapy, unless bacteremia is present, for which antibiotics are provided.[28]

Animals, their products, and their environments are the source of most nontyphoid *Salmonella* infections. Eggs and egg products are a key source of infection,[41] followed by pigs/pork products and cattle and dairy.[42-47] When contaminated, meat products typically acquire *Salmonella* during production via intestinal material from infected animals.

Campylobacteriosis

*Campylobacter* species are small, spirally curved, Gram-negative rods that move in a corkscrew path. In the United States, *Campylobacter* species are one of the most common causes of diarrheal illness, with *C. jejuni* responsible for approximately 850,000 illnesses and 76 deaths in the country each year,[48] with similar numbers in the European Union, causing approximately 229,000 cases of illness each year[49] and 500 million globally.[50]

The incubation period is generally 1–7 days, depending on the initial dose of exposure. Symptoms include diarrhea that may be watery to bloody, fever, abdominal pain, and vomiting, lasting 5–7 days.[51] As many as 1% of cases may be associated with complications, including Guillain-Barré syndrome, a neurological condition that follows various infections and can lead to paralysis, which may be permanent or temporary.[52] Reactive arthritis[53] and intestinal disorders, including irritable bowel syndrome (IBS),[54] may also result.

*Campylobacter* is found in the intestinal flora of a wide variety of animals, including cattle, sheep, goats, pigs, and poultry, as well as wild animals and pets.[29] Environmental sources such as groundwater can also be contaminated.[55] Cattle in particular seem to be susceptible to infection; when the bacteria enter a farm, up to 80% of animals may be infected,[28] whereas it is closer to 20% in sheep.[56] Pigs may be infected but are more likely to harbor *Campylobacter coli* than *jejuni*;[57] human infections from contaminated pork are rare. Poultry are much more likely to be infected and spread the bacterium rapidly through the facility.[58] In the United States, the most recent National Antimicrobial Resistance Monitoring System (NARMS) data suggest that *Campylobacter* contamination is decreasing, with approximately 4% of chicken breasts positive.[59]

## Brucella

Brucellosis is most commonly caused in humans by *Brucella abortus* but may be caused by related species *Brucella melitensis* and *Brucella suis*. Also referred to as undulant fever, Malta/Maltese fever, undulant fever, and more, it is caused by Gram-negative coccobacilli that affect multiple species of animals.[60] Transmission is generally due to consumption of contaminated foods and dairy products, occupational contact, or inhalation of infected aerosols (bacteria that are dispersed via the air).[61] While brucellosis was first recognized by David Bruce in 1887,[62] it was not until a 1918 publication by microbiologist Alice C. Evans that the organisms causing brucellosis in animals and Malta fever in humans were determined to be the same.[63]

A variety of species can harbor *Brucella* organisms. *B. abortus* typically infects cattle, but *B. suis* and *B. melitensis* may also be isolated from cattle.[64] Pigs, goats, yak, and camels may also harbor the organisms. Transmission between animals can occur due to environmental contamination and vertically via pregnant animals to the fetus, which generally suffer abortion.[64] In humans, farmers and others who work directly with animals may be directly exposed to *Brucella* via animal secretions or aerosolized organisms. The public has historically been exposed via unpasteurized milk or milk products,[65,66] including cheese. Exposure has also been reduced from historic levels due to farm-level interventions, including yearly testing of dairy herds in the United States and vaccination of cattle.[67]

*Brucella* infections have declined over the decades as pasteurization of milk has become common but still causes more than 500,000 infections globally each year.[60] It is relatively rare in the United States, with 115 cases reported to the CDC in 2010, generally due to occupational exposure to animals.[60] Clinical disease presents initially similar to influenza, with headache, fever, myalgia, fatigue, and sometimes vomiting, diarrhea, and abdominal pain. Miscarriage is common in pregnant individuals. One percent to 2% of cases are fatal. Treatment with combination antibiotics is recommended. Long-term complications resulting in chronic brucellosis may occur, leading to potentially extended disability.[68]

### *Staphylococcus aureus*

*Staphylococcus aureus* is a key cause of foodborne disease, responsible for an estimated 241,000 illnesses each year in the United States.[48] The Gram-positive bacterium is considered a commensal, which can result in a wide variety of infections, from toxin-mediated gastrointestinal upset and mild skin infections to life-threatening septicemia.[69] A wide variety of animals, including livestock, pets, wildlife, and humans, can carry the organism on the skin and mucous membranes, including the nares, throat, and intestine.[70] Foodborne contamination can result from adulteration during processing from animal sources or later contamination during handling by humans, resulting in a mixture of animal- and human-derived strains on and in food products,[71] complicating studies of origin.

*S. aureus* has long been an issue for dairy cattle, where the bacterium has been a leading cause of bovine mastitis.[72] This mastitis resulted in contaminated milk and other dairy products prior to routine use of pasteurization and today can led to economic losses and the need for antibiotic treatment of affected cattle, contributing to antibiotic resistance. In other livestock and poultry species such as pigs and chickens, *S. aureus* was occasionally identified as a cause of exudative epidermitis ("greasy pig disease")[73] or bumblefoot[74] in poultry but not considered a key pathogen in those animals. More recently, colonizing *S. aureus* (including methicillin-resistant *S. aureus*, MRSA) has been identified in farmers globally, originating due to exposure to livestock and poultry. These have been collectively termed "livestock-associated" or LA-MRSA.[75] Although these strains rarely cause clinical infections in colonized animals, they can be a public health issue as a cause of infection or death in exposed humans.[76]

*Listeria monocytogenes*

*Listeria* species are Gram-positive rods. Of 17 species of the organism, only *Listeria monocytogenes* is pathogenic for humans, and it can be found in a wide variety of environments including water, soil, and animal intestinal tracts.[77] Most cases of *L. monocytogenes* in humans are thought to be due to foodborne contamination, assisted by the ability of the organism to grow at low temperatures and thus multiply even during refrigeration. Listeriosis is most serious in the immunocompromised (including the elderly) and in pregnant women, in whom it can harm the individual and lead to spontaneous abortion. Although the incubation period is typically around 8 days, it can be lengthy—up to 70 days.[28] The mortality rate is on the higher side of foodborne pathogens, typically 20–30%[78] and potentially greater in the highest-risk groups.[79] Incidence, however, is low, with an estimated 1,600 cases yearly in the United States and 260 deaths.[80]

   *L. monocytogenes* can infect a number of domestic and wild animals, including cattle, sheep, goats, pigs, horses, and poultry, as well as fish and shellfish.[81] With this wide range of animal hosts, it is not surprising that contaminated food products are also varied, including meat and dairy products, fish, seafood, and even vegetables and fruits.[28]

## Antimicrobial Resistance

In addition to symptomatic infection or long-term carriage of bacterial pathogens following exposure via livestock or poultry or their products, industrial farm production can lead to the spread of antibiotic-resistant organisms or resistance genes.

Antibiotics have been used in livestock for over 70 years for treatment, metaphylaxis (treatment of a group of animals for disease prevention), and growth promotion.[82] The latter has fallen out of favor in the European Union; it was banned in 2006[83] and ended in the United States in 2017 for drugs that are considered medically important to humans. Still, livestock-use antibiotics, including those important for human medical purposes, are still a large fraction of global antibiotic use,[84] and 26% of 190 countries reporting on antibiotic use in animals still used antibiotics for growth promotion in 2019.[85] Human-use classes of antibiotics, including sulfonamides, fluoroquinolones, macrolides, and lincosamides, among others, have been detected in agricultural ecosystems.[86] Consumption for livestock use is expected to rise globally over the next decade, as demands for meat protein increase and additional countries shift to models of large-scale industrial agriculture where antibiotics are a necessary part of animal husbandry.[84] Antibiotic use in animals and human medical use together have led the World Health Organization to declare antibiotic resistance a threat,[87] and in 2019, antimicrobial resistance was estimated to lead to more global fatalities than HIV/AIDS or malaria.[88]

While human use of antibiotics plays a key role in this resistance, antibiotic use anywhere and for any purpose has the potential to lead to antibiotic resistance. With livestock antibiotic use, susceptible organisms are killed and resistant strains remain, spreading among animals, as well as between animals and people on farms; externally via processing or food products; or moving into the environment in manure or air. "Naked" antibiotic resistance genes, present on plasmids, transposons, or chromosomal DNA, can also move into the environment and be taken up by antibiotic-sensitive strains, providing them with drug resistance mechanisms that can cross genus or species barriers.[89] The use of antimicrobial metals, such as zinc and cadmium in livestock feed, can also co-select for antibiotic resistance genes, leading to resistance to antibiotics that may not even be used in livestock husbandry, including methicillin.[90] The industrial farm provides a setting where genetically similar animals live in close proximity and may share microbes and resistance genes. Their waste and microbes reach the environment, often with little or no treatment, and may flow into local streams and surface waters. Migratory birds or other wildlife may be part of an informal network that will carry agriculture microbes (or their resistance genes) to new geographic areas.

It has been well established that livestock and animal products can spread these resistant organisms and resistance genes to humans,[91-95] but it has been a long-term challenge to definitively link antibiotic resistance generated via livestock husbandry to human infections. Many bacterial species can be long-term colonizers, living for weeks to years on the mucus membranes, on the skin, or in the intestines. As such, tracing the origin of colonization can be difficult. Genomic sequencing has allowed close genetic matches to be determined between animal-origin strains and human colonization samples or infections.[24,96-99] An additional challenge is that access to live animals on the farms has become increasingly difficult in the United States.[10,100] There is concern that research findings may cause economic damage to farmers if pathogens are identified[100] and that finding pathogens of concern may keep animals from market.[10] Much information regarding animal strains has been ascertained by sampling food products, but bacteria isolated from retail meats and produce may reflect a mix of animal and human strains originating from farms and contamination during processing.

Resistance occurs in all of the bacterial species mentioned in the prior section. We will focus on a few well-studied examples below.

## Methicillin-Resistant *Staphylococcus aureus* (MRSA)

Livestock-associated methicillin-resistant *Staphylococcus aureus* (LA-MRSA) was first recognized in pig farmers in France and the

Netherlands.[101,102] Since this time, strains have been detected in a variety of livestock (including cattle, pigs, and poultry) and their handlers[103–106] as well as in wildlife.[107,108]

LA-MRSA has also spread beyond the livestock workers in whom they were initially recognized. Recent studies have demonstrated the feasibility of foodborne transmission into the community,[109] although this mechanism appears to be uncommon. LA-MRSA strain CC398 (the most common LA-MRSA type) does appear to be entering the community in some manner. Of 151 MRSA CC398 infections identified in Denmark from 1999 to 2011, 54 (36%) were in individuals with no livestock exposure.[110]

While initial studies of LA-MRSA focused primarily on colonization, several papers have demonstrated that these strains are capable of causing infections typical of other *S. aureus* strains, including skin and soft tissue infections (SSTIs), but also serious infections, including bloodstream infections (BSIs).[76] A recent paper found that LA-MRSA CC398 accounted for 17 cases of BSIs, 700 cases of SSTIs, and 76 cases of other infections in Denmark from 2010 to 2015. In the peak year of 2014, LA-MRSA CC398 accounted for 16% of all MRSA BSIs and 21% of all MRSA STTI in the country. As with the prior study examining CC398 infections, these data likewise showed that, although infected individuals lacking livestock contact tended to live in rural areas, 59% of those with MRSA CC398 BSIs lacked livestock contact, as did 32% of those with SSTIs.[97]

### E. coli

An emerging concern in *E. coli* and other species is colistin resistance, mediated by *mcr* (mobile colistin resistance) genes, 10 of which have been identified to date (*mcr-1* through *mcr-10*). This is a transposable genetic element that can rather easily be horizontally transferred between bacteria, spreading resistance to the antibiotic colistin. Colistin is an antibiotic generally used as a treatment of last resort for Gram-negative infections. Although it was first identified more than 60 years ago, its use has been limited due to concerns about nephrotoxicity and neurotoxicity.[111] With increasing resistance to alternatives such as aminoglycosides, colistin use has been revisited, but rising resistance puts its use as a top shelf/last resort antimicrobial into jeopardy.

Pigs and chickens are the primary animal species (besides humans) in which *mcr* genes have been identified (reviewed in Bastidas-Caldes et al.[112]), although *mcr*-containing strains have also been isolated from cattle in Europe.[113] The genes seem to be most common to date in Africa and Asia, followed by the Americas and Europe. In the United States, only *mcr*-1 and *mcr*-3 have been identified.[112,114,115] *mcr*-1 was first reported in China and remains high there, where colistin is widely used in agriculture, suggesting selection had driven an increase in the gene in populations of Enterobacteriaceae. Coresistance to other agents via resistance genes residing on the same plasmids may also facilitate selection via exposure to other antibiotics.[116] Transmission to humans occurred likely via direct contact with animals and food-borne exposures.[117,118]

## Human Viral Infections Associated with Industrialized Farming

### Background

Livestock farming has frequently been associated with viral infections in humans. Below we briefly summarize domestic animal viral zoonoses for the most prevalent livestock species in the United States. It is important to recognize that many specific human spillover events represent direct animal-to-human transmission such as among animal workers. In addition to suffering such infections, animal workers may also serve as a bridging population in transferring zoonotic viruses to their local communities. This was made clear through observations for the 2009 H1N1 pandemic. For instance, in our 2016 report,[119] we found evidence that swine feeding operations in North Carolina amplified H1N1 influenza A virus in humans in that human infection counts peaked earlier for counties with a high prevalence of swine farms.

Similarly, Quist et al.[120] found that people living near US swine farms were at increased risk of gastrointestinal diseases. More recently, Hogerwerf et al.[121] observed that people living in close proximity to livestock farms in The Netherlands were found to be at higher risk or severe acute respiratory syndrome coronavirus 2 (SARS-CoV-2) infection. Below we review primary zoonotic pathogen threats associated with the most abundant US livestock types. We suggest that as the world increasingly embraces industrialized farming, the transmission risk for these zoonotic viruses to cause human morbidity is likely to increase.

## Poultry

While chicken layers vastly outnumber poultry meat types, we also include turkeys, ducks, and quail in this category.

*Influenza A virus*—Avian influenza A viruses are among the most important zoonotic virus threats to humans. They are prevalent worldwide and in numerous hemagglutinin and neuraminidase subtypes. Human infections are generally rare and most common for H5N1, H7N9, and H9N2 strains, often occurring in association with poultry epizootics. China has largely controlled human H5 and H7 infections through bivalent H5/H7 vaccinations of poultry.[122] Human avian influenza morbidity is often subclinical or mild, but occasionally, it can be severe, leading to respiratory failure and death.

In developing countries, low-pathogenic avian influenza strains are often tolerated in poultry flocks and thought to subsequently contribute to novel emergent influenza strains, which may threaten humans.[123] In recent years, multiple other such novel influenza A types have occasionally infected humans.[123] While the influenza A viruses are not highly enzootic among US poultry, migrating birds often cause incursions to US domestic flocks. Currently, the United States is engaged in a widespread wild bird–led epizootic of avian H5 influenza A virus strains. Fortunately, despite thousands of documented cases of avian influenza virus infections in humans, the species barrier between poultry and humans is relatively high compared with similar species barriers between pigs and humans.[124]

While other poultry viruses such as Newcastle disease virus[125] and avian pneumovirus[126] have evidence for infecting humans and perhaps occasionally cause mild disease, no other poultry viruses rival avian influenza A virus' threat to humans.

## Cattle

Here we include both beef cattle and dairy cattle in this category. Compared to other common US livestock species, cattle infrequently have been found to transmit zoonotic viruses to humans.[127] The most prevalent threats are vector borne and located in specific geographical areas.

*Rift Valley fever virus*—This virus causes seasonal sporadic epidemics in ruminants in sub-Saharan Africa. Human infections with the virus are generally mild and influenza-like. Occasionally, humans manifest more severe disease involving inflammation of the eyes, the brain, and other organs.

*Crimean–Congo hemorrhagic fever virus*—This tick-borne disease has a geographical range that includes much of Africa, eastern Europe, and western Asia. Livestock workers are commonly infected. Human disease is manifest by influenza-like illness followed by petechial skill rash, jaundice, skin bruising, and nosebleeds.

*Tick-borne encephalitis virus*—Multiple tick species are competent vectors to carry this virus to humans. The virus in endemic in multiple areas in Europe and Asia. Thousands of human cases are reported each year. Approximately two-thirds of humans infected with the virus are without symptoms. Clinical human infections involve headache, muscle aches, and fatigue. Occasionally, severe disease occurs with brain or other neurologic system involvement.

*Influenza D virus*—This is newly recognized virus is thought to be highly enzootic in both beef and dairy cattle.[128–130] It is recognized as an important cause of bovine respiratory disease complex, one of the most prevalent causes of morbidity in modern cattle farming. The virus is thought to have a worldwide distribution. Early reports suggest the virus also infects humans,[131] although such infections are not well characterized.

*Rabies*—While cattle rabies reports are markedly less prevalent than carnivore-associated rabies infection in most parts of the world, cattle-associated rabies infections occasionally occur worldwide and result in human infections.

*SARS-CoV-2*—A number of experimental studies[132,133] have shown that a proportion of cattle challenged intranasally with SARS-CoV-2 have developed subclinical evidence of infection. However, at least for SARS-CoV-2 strains studied to date, cattle have not been shown to be efficient transmitters of the virus.

Two other less common, cattle-associated viruses have been shown to have potential to cause infections with mild or no symptoms in humans. These viruses include bovine papular stomatitis virus[134] and bovine enterovirus.[135] However, their risk of causing clinical human disease is low compared to the aforementioned viruses.

## Pigs

In many parts of the world, pigs are a leading source of protein. Compared to other common livestock, pigs pose a high number of zoonoses threats to humans.[136] Such zoonotic threats are significant because worldwide, pig husbandry is rapidly embracing industrialized farming methods, with pig farms growing larger and often harboring a greater number of unique zoonotic virus strains. In China, some hog farms are being built to house 84,000 sows at one time (four times the size of the largest swine farms elsewhere).[137] The potential for novel virus generation in these large confinement facilities is tremendous.[138]

*Influenza A virus*—In China,[139-141] Romania,[142] South Africa,[143] Malaysia,[144] and the United States,[145-147] we have conducted multiple One Health studies of influenza A on swine farms. Influenza A viruses are often highly enzootic in the pigs. The risk for swine workers to be infected with a emergent swine influenza virus is often quite high,[139,140,147] often making it very improbable that an immunologically naive swine worker would be spared from infection with a novel, emergent swine influenza A virus prevalent among farm pigs.

*Influenza B, C, and D virus*—Pigs are recognized to be competent reservoirs for each of these influenza virus types[148,149] and thought to have potential to transmit these viruses to humans. However, relatively few studies have been conducted to understand the risk or epidemiology of pig-to-human infection.

*Nipah virus*—Pigs are clearly recognized as amplifying reservoirs for Nipah virus and a bridging species between the bat (natural reservoir) and humans. As Nipah virus is enzootic in bats in multiple geographical areas, and human-to-human transmission has been documented, some believe pigs have potential to play roles in large-scale human Nipah virus epidemics.[150]

*Hendra virus*—While most Hendra virus detections in domestic animals have occurred in horses, experimental studies[151] have documented the potential for pigs to amplify the virus.

*Ebola viruses*—Pigs have been shown to be susceptible to both Ebola-Zaire[152] and Ebola-Reston viruses.[153] Pigs in the Philippines have harbored Ebola-Reston virus but are thought to be of only moderate risk of transmitting the disease to humans.[152]

*Japanese encephalitis virus*—Pigs are thought to be natural reservoirs for this virus and a reason the virus is endemic in much of Asia.[154] There is some evidence that the virus can be shed from pig to pig without the aid of its mosquito vectors.[155]

*Hepatitis E virus*—Hepatitis E has a worldwide distribution. Among the seven recognized genotypes, genotypes 3 and 4 often originate with pigs. The viruses can be transmitted to humans via poor hygiene, water contamination, and ingesting contaminated pork products.

*Menangle virus*—This virus is often the cause of losses in pig production and may occasionally spill over to cause serious illness among humans.[156,157]

*Vesicular stomatitis virus*—With a near-worldwide geographical distribution, this virus often causes illness in pigs and sometimes mild influenza-like illness in humans.

*Rotavirus*—Multiple strains of rotavirus have been found in pigs. Swine rotavirus strains have been associated with enteric disease in humans.[158]

*Pseudorabies virus*—Often detected in pigs, pseudorabies viruses have been implicated to rarely cause acute respiratory infections and encephalitis in humans.[159]

*Foot and mouth disease virus*—Recognized as a severe disease in pigs, foot and mouth disease viruses have occasionally caused cutaneous or mucosal signs in humans.[160]

## Sheep

*Rabies*—Sheep are sometimes infected with rabies virus, and rarely do these infections lead to herd epizootics.[161] Infected sheep manifest aggressiveness and other neurological signs. Occasionally, sheep rabies virus may spill over to infect humans.

*Crimean-Congo hemorrhagic fever virus (CCHFV)*—Sheep commonly have serological evidence of Crimean-Congo hemorrhagic fever virus infection in many geographical areas where the virus is endemic. In fact, CCHFV seroprevalence in sheep and goats is thought to be a good indicator that the virus is prevalent in area ticks.[162] Sheep are thought to be an important reservoir for CCHFV, and their infection may increase the risk of CCHFV infection in humans.

*Getah virus*—While more commonly detected in other domestic animals like pigs and cattle, sheep are occasionally infected with this arbovirus. Occasionally, high seroprevalences of Getah viruses have found in sheep such as that recently reported in northwest China.[163] As the virus may infect human cell lines and has been implicated as causing fever in humans, there is theoretically concern that the expanding geographical range of virus could in the future threaten human health.

*Hepatitis E virus*—Although more commonly recognized as enzootic in pigs, evidence for hepatitis E virus infection in sheep is recognized with a relatively high seroprevalence found in some geographical regions.[164]

*Cache Valley virus*—This mosquito-borne zoonotic virus has a wide geographic distribution in the Americas and has been found, serologically, to infect in small ruminants like sheep. In sheep, the virus can cause birth defects. Rarely has this virus been found to infect humans.[165]

*Middle East respiratory syndrome coronavirus (MERS-CoV)*—While not thought to be the primary reservoir, there is some serological evidence that MERS-CoV has spilled over to infect sheep.[166]

*Orf virus*—This virus causes pustular lesions in humans, often on the hands, and is thought to chiefly have been zoonotically acquired by exposure to sheep and goats.[167] The virus is thought to have a near-worldwide distribution.

*Rift Valley fever virus (RVFV)*—Sheep are thought to serve as a reservoir for this mosquito-borne zoonosis that is enzootic in large areas of sub-Saharan Africa.[168] Humans may be infected with RVFV through contact with infected animal tissues or mosquito bites. Most often, RVFV infection in humans is mild and flu-like. Occasionally, infected humans develop meningitis-like signs and symptoms.

*Borna disease virus*—This neurotropic virus is enzootic in horses, sheep, and other domestic animals. Occasionally, it infects humans and has been associated with a wide range of central nervous system signs and symptoms.[169] The ecology of this virus is a matter of investigation, as well as its associated psychiatric morbidity in humans.

*Alkhurma hemorrhagic fever virus*—This zoonotic virus has been implicated as a cause of human hemorrhagic fever in Saudi Arabia. Seroepidemiologic investigation has implicated contact with domestic animals like sheep and handling their raw meat products.[170]

*Tick-borne encephalitis virus*—This tick-transmitted virus causes severe encephalitis and has a high mortality in humans. It may also be transmitted to humans through human ingestion of raw sheep, goat, or cow milk. Epidemiologic studies of sheep milk may serve as an important indicator for the geographical endemicity of the virus.[171]

## Policy Implications

The industrial farm provides a unique setting where genetically similar animals live in close proximity and may share microbes with resistance genes. Animal waste and microbes reach the environment, often with little or no treatment, and may flow into local streams and surface waters. Migratory birds may be part of an informal network that will carry microbes, including viruses like avian influenza viruses, to new geographic areas. Modern animal husbandry practices, which exercise strong biosecurity and good animal housing, can reduce some of the emerging pathogen risk. However, there is an increasing need to conduct better surveillance for novel pathogens in the industrial farm environment, and this is often not being addressed.

Given the diverse set of pathogens that originate from livestock and cause health issues in humans, the policy recommendations to deal with their emergence are also varied. What unites all organisms described is the need for a One Health approach to investigation and control, as well as continued removal of "silos" of study that separate those studying primarily human, animal, or environmental health. Foodborne infections already cause an estimated 48 million illnesses and 3,000 deaths collectively each year in the United States, primarily due to contamination of products by animal-origin bacteria and viruses, and their severity is only rising as antibiotic resistance increases and bacterial cases become more difficult to treat. It has been suggested that antimicrobial-resistant infections caused more fatalities in 2019 than HIV/AIDS or malaria,[88] and recent work has predicted up to 10 million fatalities yearly by 2050.[172] While human medical policies also contribute to the issue of antibiotic resistance, a minority of the population spends time hospitalized each year. Everyone needs to eat, and while meat products were the primary vehicle for the spread of animal-origin pathogens from farm to table in this chapter, fruits and vegetables can also be contaminated due to contaminated manure used as crop fertilizer.[173] As such, it is difficult to impossible to avoid exposure to resistant organisms or resistance genes.

Many countries, including the United States, have instituted policies to reduce the use of antibiotics in agriculture. The effectiveness of such policies has been difficult to ascertain. In the United States, no use of antibiotics is tracked, making it difficult to ascertain the actual amount of product given to animals.[174] Sales have decreased since their historic high in 2015, have been relatively flat since 2017, and are once again increasing. However, these declines have been led primarily by drops of use in chickens, while sales of medically important antibiotics in cattle, swine, and turkey have increased since 2017.[174] The United States lacks additional tracking systems present in European Union states, which include the tracking of on-farm antimicrobial use.

The industrialization of farming in general has exacerbated many current infectious disease issues. The industrial model, moving from the stereotypical "little red barn" farm of the past to today's large-scale confined animal feeding operations, necessitates antibiotic use in order to stave off illness caused by production practices, including a high density of animals and shorter time between birth and weaning of animals. This high density and the homogenization of animal genetics also puts animals at higher risk of infectious disease spread within facilities. While strong biosecurity procedures on farms reduce the risk of entry of new pathogens, it does not eliminate it, as recently seen with H1N1 influenza in 2009[175] and African swine fever in China since 2018.[176]

## Conclusions

It is clear that modern agriculture, while more productive and cost-efficient, remains a frequent source of pathogens that are causing human illnesses. As government oversight has not been well received by the food industries, the best way forward seems for teams of food industry and human health professionals to partner together in finding ways to improve food safety and food security as the scale of industrialized farming continues to grow worldwide.

## REFERENCES

1. Morand S, McIntyre KM, Baylis M. Domesticated animals and human infectious diseases of zoonotic origins: domestication time matters. *Infect Genet Evol* 2014; **24**: 76–81.
2. Johnson CK, Hitchens PL, Pandit PS, et al. Global shifts in mammalian population trends reveal key predictors of virus spillover risk. *Proc Biol Sci* 2020; **287**(1924): 20192736.
3. Van Reeth K, Brown IH, Durrwald R, et al. Seroprevalence of H1N1, H3N2 and H1N2 influenza viruses in pigs in seven European countries in 2002–2003. *Influenza Other Respir Viruses* 2008; **2**(3): 99–105.
4. Baudon E, Peyre M, Peiris M, Cowling BJ. Epidemiological features of influenza circulation in swine populations: a systematic review and meta-analysis. *PLoS One* 2017; **12**(6): e0179044.
5. Choffnes ER, Institute of Medicine. Forum on microbial threats. Improving food safety through a One Health approach: workshop summary. Washington, D.C.: National Academies Press; 2012.
6. Watson SJ, Langat P, Reid SM, et al. Molecular epidemiology and evolution of influenza viruses circulating within European swine between 2009 and 2013. *J Virol* 2015; **89**(19): 9920–9931.
7. Vincent AL, Ma W, Lager KM, Janke BH, Richt JA. Swine influenza viruses: a North American perspective. *Adv Virus Res* 2008; **72**: 127–154.
8. Plowright RK, Parrish CR, McCallum H, et al. Pathways to zoonotic spillover. *Nat Rev Microbiol* 2017; **15**(8): 502–510.
9. Rahimi P, Islam MS, Duarte PM, et al. Impact of the COVID-19 pandemic on food production and animal health. *Trends Food Sci Technol* 2022; **121**: 105–113.
10. Gray GC, Baker WS. Editorial commentary: the problem with pigs: it's not about bacon. *Clin Infect Dis* 2011; **52**(1): 19–22.
11. Gould LH, Demma L, Jones TF, et al. Hemolytic uremic syndrome and death in persons with *Escherichia coli* O157:H7 infection, foodborne diseases active surveillance network sites, 2000–2006. *Clin Infect Dis* 2009; **49**(10): 1480–1485.
12. Manning SD, Motiwala AS, Springman AC, et al. Variation in virulence among clades of *Escherichia coli* O157:H7 associated with disease outbreaks. *Proc Natl Acad Sci U S A* 2008; **105**(12): 4868–4873.
13. USDA. USDA targeting six additional strains of E.coli in raw beef trim starting Monday. 2012. https://www.usda.gov/media/press-releases/2012/05/31/usda-targeting-six-additional-strains-ecoli-raw-beef-trim-starting
14. Hadler JL, Clogher P, Hurd S, et al. Ten-year trends and risk factors for non-O157 Shiga toxin-producing *Escherichia coli* found through Shiga toxin testing, Connecticut, 2000–2009. *Clin Infect Dis* 2011; **53**(3): 269–276.

15. Scallan E, Hoekstra RM, Angulo FJ, et al. Foodborne illness acquired in the United States—major pathogens. *Emerg Infect Dis* 2011; **17**(1): 7–15.
16. Tuttle J, Gomez T, Doyle MP, et al. Lessons from a large outbreak of *Escherichia coli* O157:H7 infections: insights into the infectious dose and method of widespread contamination of hamburger patties. *Epidemiol Infect* 1999; **122**(2): 185–192.
17. McCarthy M. *E coli* O157:H7 outbreak in USA traced to apple juice. *Lancet* 1996; **348**(9037): 1299.
18. Charatan F. FDA warns US consumers not to eat spinach after *E coli* outbreak. *BMJ* 2006; **333**(7570): 673.
19. Gencay YE. Sheep as an important source of *E. coli* O157/O157:H7 in Turkey. *Vet Microbiol* 2014; **172**(3–4): 590–595.
20. Keen JE, Wittum TE, Dunn JR, Bono JL, Durso LM. Shiga-toxigenic *Escherichia coli* O157 in agricultural fair livestock, United States. *Emerg Infect Dis* 2006; **12**(5): 780–786.
21. Dunn JR, Keen JE, Moreland D, Alex T. Prevalence of *Escherichia coli* O157:H7 in white-tailed deer from Louisiana. *J Wildl Dis* 2004; **40**(2): 361–365.
22. Foxman B. The epidemiology of urinary tract infection. *Nat Rev Urol* 2010; **7**(12): 653–660.
23. Flores-Mireles AL, Walker JN, Caparon M, Hultgren SJ. Urinary tract infections: epidemiology, mechanisms of infection and treatment options. *Nat Rev Microbiol* 2015; **13**(5): 269–284.
24. Liu CM, Stegger M, Aziz M, et al. *Escherichia coli* ST131-H22 as a foodborne uropathogen. *MBio* 2018; **9**(4): e00470-18.
25. Nordstrom L, Liu CM, Price LB. Foodborne urinary tract infections: a new paradigm for antimicrobial-resistant foodborne illness. *Front Microbiol* 2013; **4**: 29.
26. Liu C, Aziz M, Park DE, et al. Using source-associated mobile genetic elements to identify zoonotic extraintestinal *E. coli* infections. *One Health* 2023; **28**(16): 100518.
27. Amphlett A. Far East scarlet-like fever: a review of the epidemiology, symptomatology, and role of superantigenic toxin: *Yersinia pseudotuberculosis*-derived mitogen A. *Open Forum Infect Dis* 2016; **3**(1): ofv202.
28. Chlebicz A, Slizewska K. Campylobacteriosis, salmonellosis, yersiniosis, and listeriosis as zoonotic foodborne diseases: a review. *Int J Environ Res Public Health* 2018; **15**(5): 863.
29. Bintsis T. Foodborne pathogens. *AIMS Microbiol* 2017; **3**(3): 529–563.
30. Eurosurveillance Editorial Team. The European Union summary report on trends and sources of zoonoses, zoonotic agents and food-borne outbreaks in 2010. *Euro Surveill* 2012; **17**(10): 20113.
31. CDC. Yersinia enterocolitica (Yersiniosis). October 24, 2016. https://www.cdc.gov/yersinia/index.html
32. Rakin A, Garzetti D, Bouabe H, Sprague LD. *Yersinia enterocolotica*. In: Tang Y-W, Sussman M, Liu D, Poxton I, Schwartzman J, eds. *Molecular Medical Microbiology*. 2nd ed. San Diego, CA: Academic Press; 2015: 1319–1344.

33. Whiley H, Ross K. *Salmonella* and eggs: from production to plate. *Int J Environ Res Public Health* 2015; **12**(3): 2543–2556.
34. Coburn B, Grassl GA, Finlay BB. *Salmonella*, the host and disease: a brief review. *Immunol Cell Biol* 2007; **85**(2): 112–118.
35. Doyle MP, Diez-Gonzalez F, Hill C; Ohio Library and Information Network. *Food Microbiology: Fundamentals and Frontiers.* 5th ed. Washington, D.C.: ASM Press; 2019.
36. Evangelopoulou G, Kritas S, Christodoulopoulos G, Burriel AR. The commercial impact of pig *Salmonella* spp. infections in border-free markets during an economic recession. *Vet World* 2015; **8**(3): 257–272.
37. CDC. *Salmonella*. March 23, 2023. https://www.cdc.gov/salmonella/index.html
38. Brenner FW, Villar RG, Angulo FJ, Tauxe R, Swaminathan B. *Salmonella* nomenclature. *J Clin Microbiol* 2000; **38**(7): 2465–2467.
39. Chen HM, Wang Y, Su LH, Chiu CH. Nontyphoid *salmonella* infection: microbiology, clinical features, and antimicrobial therapy. *Pediatr Neonatol* 2013; **54**(3): 147–152.
40. Buchwald DS, Blaser MJ. A review of human salmonellosis: II. Duration of excretion following infection with nontyphi *Salmonella*. *Rev Infect Dis* 1984; **6**(3): 345–356.
41. Gast RK, Dittoe DK, Ricke SC. *Salmonella* in eggs and egg-laying chickens: pathways to effective control. *Crit Rev Microbiol* 2022; **50**(1): 39–63.
42. Hurtado A, Ocejo M, Oporto B. *Salmonella* spp. and *Listeria monocytogenes* shedding in domestic ruminants and characterization of potentially pathogenic strains. *Vet Microbiol* 2017; **210**: 71–76.
43. Bonardi S. *Salmonella* in the pork production chain and its impact on human health in the European Union. *Epidemiol Infect* 2017; **145**(8): 1513–1526.
44. Arguello H, Alvarez-Ordonez A, Carvajal A, Rubio P, Prieto M. Role of slaughtering in *Salmonella* spreading and control in pork production. *J Food Prot* 2013; **76**(5): 899–911.
45. Zeng H, De Reu K, Gabriel S, Mattheus W, De Zutter L, Rasschaert G. *Salmonella* prevalence and persistence in industrialized poultry slaughterhouses. *Poult Sci* 2021; **100**(4): 100991.
46. Antunes P, Mourao J, Campos J, Peixe L. Salmonellosis: the role of poultry meat. *Clin Microbiol Infect* 2016; **22**(2): 110–121.
47. Beach JC, Murano EA, Acuff GR. Prevalence of *Salmonella* and *Campylobacter* in beef cattle from transport to slaughter. *J Food Prot* 2002; **65**(11): 1687–1693.
48. Scallan E, Hoekstra RM, Angulo FJ, et al. Foodborne illness acquired in the United States—major pathogens. *Emerg Infect Dis* 2011; **17**(1): 7–15.
49. Eurosurveillance Editorial Team. The 2013 joint ECDC/EFSA report on trends and sources of zoonoses, zoonotic agents and food-borne outbreaks published. *Euro Surveill* 2015; **20**(4): 21021.
50. Kashoma IP, Kassem II, Kumar A, et al. Antimicrobial resistance and genotypic diversity of *Campylobacter* isolated from pigs, dairy, and beef cattle in Tanzania. *Front Microbiol* 2015; **6**: 1240.

51. Kaakoush NO, Castano-Rodriguez N, Mitchell HM, Man SM. Global epidemiology of *Campylobacter* infection. *Clin Microbiol Rev* 2015; **28**(3): 687–720.
52. Nyati KK, Nyati R. Role of *Campylobacter jejuni* infection in the pathogenesis of Guillain-Barre syndrome: an update. *BioMed Res Int* 2013; **2013**: 852195.
53. Pope JE, Krizova A, Garg AX, Thiessen-Philbrook H, Ouimet JM. Campylobacter reactive arthritis: a systematic review. *Semin Arthritis Rheum* 2007; **37**(1): 48–55.
54. Scallan Walter EJ, Crim SM, Bruce BB, Griffin PM. Postinfectious irritable bowel syndrome after Campylobacter infection. *Am J Gastroenterol* 2019; **114**(10): 1649–1656.
55. Stanley K, Cunningham R, Jones K. Isolation of *Campylobacter jejuni* from groundwater. *J Appl Microbiol* 1998; **85**(1): 187–191.
56. Epps SV, Harvey RB, Hume ME, Phillips TD, Anderson RC, Nisbet DJ. Foodborne *Campylobacter*: infections, metabolism, pathogenesis and reservoirs. *Int J Environ Res Public Health* 2013; **10**(12): 6292–6304.
57. Qin SS, Wu CM, Wang Y, et al. Antimicrobial resistance in *Campylobacter coli* isolated from pigs in two provinces of China. *Int J Food Microbiol* 2011; **146**(1): 94–98.
58. Whiley H, van den Akker B, Giglio S, Bentham R. The role of environmental reservoirs in human campylobacteriosis. *Int J Environ Res Public Health* 2013; **10**(11): 5886–5907.
59. Mujahid S, Hansen M, Miranda R, Newsom-Stewart K, Rogers JE. Prevalence and antibiotic resistance of *Salmonella* and *Campylobacter* isolates from raw chicken breasts in retail markets in the United States and comparison to data from the plant level. *Life (Basel)* 2023; **13**(3) 642.
60. Hayoun MA, Muco E, Shorman M. *Brucellosis*. Treasure Island, FL: StatPearls; 2023.
61. Amjadi O, Rafiei A, Mardani M, Zafari P, Zarifian A. A review of the immunopathogenesis of brucellosis. *Infect Dis (Lond)* 2019; **51**(5): 321–333.
62. Bruce D. Note on the discovery of a micro-organism in Malta fever. *Practitioner* 1887; **39**: 161–170.
63. Evans AC. Further studies on *Bacterium abortus* and related bacteria II. A comparison of *Bacterium abortus* with *Bacterium bronchisepticus* and with the organism which causes Malta fever. *J Infect Dis* 1918; **22**(6): 580–593.
64. Khurana SK, Sehrawat A, Tiwari R, et al. Bovine brucellosis—a comprehensive review. *Vet Q* 2021; **41**(1): 61–88.
65. Dadar M, Fakhri Y, Shahali Y, Mousavi Khaneghah A. Contamination of milk and dairy products by *Brucella* species: a global systematic review and meta-analysis. *Food Res Int* 2020; **128**: 108775.
66. CDC. CDC Food Safety Alert: *Brucellosis* exposures from raw milk. 2019. https://www.cdc.gov/media/releases/2019/s0211-brucellosis-raw-milk.html
67. Pinn-Woodcock T, Frye E, Guarino C, et al. A one-health review on brucellosis in the United States. *J Am Vet Med Assoc* 2023; **261**(4): 451–462.
68. Shakir R. Brucellosis. *J Neurol Sci* 2021; **420**: 117280.
69. Lowy FD. *Staphylococcus aureus* infections. *N Engl J Med* 1998; **339**(8): 520–532.

70. Butaye P, Argudin MA, Smith TC. Livestock-associated MRSA and its current evolution. *Curr Clin Microbiol Rep* 2016; **3**(1): 19–31.
71. Kadariya J, Smith TC, Thapaliya D. *Staphylococcus aureus* and staphylococcal food-borne disease: an ongoing challenge in public health. *BioMed Res Int* 2014; **2014**: 827965.
72. Campos B, Pickering AC, Rocha LS, et al. Diversity and pathogenesis of *Staphylococcus aureus* from bovine mastitis: current understanding and future perspectives. *BMC Vet Res* 2022; **18**(1): 115.
73. Foster AP. Staphylococcal skin disease in livestock. *Vet Dermatol* 2012; **23**(4): 342–351, e63.
74. Szafraniec GM, Szeleszczuk P, Dolka B. Review on skeletal disorders caused by *Staphylococcus* spp. in poultry. *Vet Q* 2022; **42**(1): 21–40.
75. Smith TC, Pearson N. The emergence of *Staphylococcus aureus* ST398. *Vector Borne Zoonotic Dis* 2011; **11**(4) 327–339.
76. Smith TC, Wardyn SE. Human infections with *Staphylococcus aureus* CC398. *Curr Environ Health Reports* 2015; **2**(3): 41–51.
77. Gahan CG, Hill C. *Listeria monocytogenes*: survival and adaptation in the gastrointestinal tract. *Front Cell Infect Microbiol* 2014; **4**: 9.
78. Madjunkov M, Chaudhry S, Ito S. Listeriosis during pregnancy. *Arch Gynecol Obstet* 2017; **296**(2): 143–152.
79. Choi MH, Park YJ, Kim M, et al. Increasing incidence of listeriosis and infection-associated clinical outcomes. *Ann Lab Med* 2018; **38**(2): 102–109.
80. CDC. Listeria. April 7, 2023. https://www.cdc.gov/listeria/index.html
81. McIntyre L, Wilcott L, Naus M. Listeriosis outbreaks in British Columbia, Canada, caused by soft ripened cheese contaminated from environmental sources. *BioMed Res Int* 2015; **2015**: 131623.
82. Landers TF, Cohen B, Wittum TE, Larson EL. A review of antibiotic use in food animals: perspective, policy, and potential. *Public Health Rep* 2012; **127**(1): 4–22.
83. European Commission. Ban on antibiotics as growth promoters in animal feed enters into effect. 2005. https://ec.europa.eu/commission/presscorner/detail/en/IP_05_1687
84. Van Boeckel TP, Brower C, Gilbert M, et al. Global trends in antimicrobial use in food animals. *Proc Natl Acad Sci U S A* 2015; **112**(18): 5649–5654.
85. World Organisation for Animal Health. *OIE Annual Report on Antimicrobial Agents Intended for Use in Animals, Fifth Report*. Paris: World Organisation for Animal Health; 2020.
86. Williams-Nguyen J, Sallach JB, Bartelt-Hunt S, et al. Antibiotics and antibiotic resistance in agroecosystems: state of the science. *J Environ Qual* 2016; **45**(2): 394–406.
87. Larkin H. Increasing antimicrobial resistance poses global threat, WHO says. *JAMA* 2023; **329**(3): 200.
88. Antimicrobial Resistance Collaborators. Global burden of bacterial antimicrobial resistance in 2019: a systematic analysis. *Lancet* 2022; **399**(10325): 629–655.

89. Silbergeld EK, Graham J, Price LB. Industrial food animal production, antimicrobial resistance, and human health. *Annu Rev Public Health* 2008; **29**: 151–169.

90. Nair R, Thapaliya D, Su Y, Smith TC. Resistance to zinc and cadmium in *Staphylococcus aureus* of human and animal origin. *Infect Control Hosp Epidemiol* 2014; **35(Suppl 3)**: S32–S39.

91. Johnson JR, Kuskowski MA, Smith K, O'Bryan TT, Tatini S. Antimicrobial-resistant and extraintestinal pathogenic *Escherichia coli* in retail foods. *J Infect Dis* 2005; **191**(7): 1040–1049.

92. Ferber D. Antibiotic resistance. Superbugs on the hoof? *Science* 2000; **288**(5467): 792–794.

93. Levy SB, FitzGerald GB, Macone AB. Spread of antibiotic-resistant plasmids from chicken to chicken and from chicken to man. *Nature* 1976; **260**(5546): 40–42.

94. Smith TC. Livestock-associated *Staphylococcus aureus*: the United States experience. *PLoS Pathog* 2015; **11**(2): e1004564.

95. Smith TC, Male MJ, Harper AL, et al. Methicillin-resistant *Staphylococcus aureus* (MRSA) strain ST398 is present in midwestern U.S. swine and swine workers. *PLoS ONE* 2009; **4**(1): e4258.

96. Johnson TJ, Aziz M, Liu CM, et al. Complete genome sequence of a CTX-M-15-producing Escherichia coli strain from the H30Rx subclone of sequence type 131 from a patient with recurrent urinary tract infections, closely related to a lethal urosepsis isolate from the patient's sister. *Genome Announcements* 2016; **4**(3) e00334-16.

97. Larsen J, Petersen A, Larsen AR, et al. Emergence of livestock-associated methicillin-resistant *Staphylococcus aureus* bloodstream infections in Denmark. *Clin Infect Dis* 2017; **65**(7): 1072–1076.

98. Price LB, Stegger M, Hasman H, et al. *Staphylococcus aureus* CC398: host adaptation and emergence of methicillin resistance in livestock. *MBio* 2012; **3**(1): e00305-11.

99. Wardyn SE, Stegger M, Price LB, Smith TC. Whole-genome analysis of recurrent *Staphylococcus aureus* t571/ST398 infection in farmer, Iowa, USA. *Emerg Infect Dis* 2018; **24**(1): 153–154.

100. Gray GC, Cao WC. Editorial commentary: variant influenza A(H3N2) virus: looking through a glass, darkly. *Clin Infect Dis* 2013; **57**(12): 1713–1714.

101. Voss A, Loeffen F, Bakker J, Klaassen C, Wulf M. Methicillin-resistant *Staphylococcus aureus* in pig farming. *Emerg Infect Dis* 2005; **11**(12): 1965–1966.

102. Armand-Lefevre L, Ruimy R, Andremont A. Clonal comparison of *Staphylococcus aureus* isolates from healthy pig farmers, human controls, and pigs. *Emerg Infect Dis* 2005; **11**(5): 711–714.

103. Nemati M, Hermans K, Lipinska U, et al. Antimicrobial resistance of old and recent *Staphylococcus aureus* isolates from poultry: first detection of livestock-associated methicillin-resistant strain ST398. *Antimicrob Agents Chemother* 2008; **52**(10): 3817–3819.

104. Silva NC, Guimaraes FF, Manzi MP, et al. Methicillin-resistant *Staphylococcus aureus* of lineage ST398 as cause of mastitis in cows. *Lett Appl Microbiol* 2014; **59**(6): 665–669.

105. Tavakol M, Riekerink RG, Sampimon OC, van Wamel WJ, van Belkum A, Lam TJ. Bovine-associated MRSA ST398 in the Netherlands. *Acta Vet Scand* 2012; **54**(1): 28.

106. Nemeghaire S, Roelandt S, Argudin MA, Haesebrouck F, Butaye P. Characterization of methicillin-resistant *Staphylococcus aureus* from healthy carrier chickens. *Avian Pathol* 2013; **42**(4): 342–346.

107. Gomez P, Gonzalez-Barrio D, Benito D, et al. Detection of methicillin-resistant *Staphylococcus aureus* (MRSA) carrying the *mecC* gene in wild small mammals in Spain. *J Antimicrob Chemother* 2014; **69**(8): 2061–2064.

108. Gomez P, Lozano C, Camacho MC, et al. Detection of MRSA ST3061-t843-*mecC* and ST398-t011-*mecA* in white stork nestlings exposed to human residues. *J Antimicrob Chemother* 2016; **71**(1): 53–57.

109. Larsen J, Stegger M, Andersen PS, et al. Evidence for human adaptation and foodborne transmission of livestock-associated methicillin-resistant *Staphylococcus aureus*. *Clin Infect Dis* 2016; **63**(10): 1349–1352.

110. Larsen J, Petersen A, Sorum M, et al. Methicillin-resistant *Staphylococcus aureus* CC398 is an increasing cause of disease in people with no livestock contact in Denmark, 1999 to 2011. *Euro Surveill* 2015; **20**(37): 30021.

111. Li J, Nation RL, Turnidge JD, et al. Colistin: the re-emerging antibiotic for multidrug-resistant Gram-negative bacterial infections. *Lancet Infect Dis* 2006; **6**(9): 589–601.

112. Bastidas-Caldes C, de Waard JH, Salgado MS, et al. Worldwide prevalence of *mcr*-mediated colistin-resistance *Escherichia coli* in isolates of clinical samples, healthy humans, and livestock: a systematic review and meta-analysis. *Pathogens* 2022; **11**(6): 659.

113. Hernandez M, Iglesias MR, Rodriguez-Lazaro D, et al. Co-occurrence of colistin-resistance genes *mcr*-1 and *mcr*-3 among multidrug-resistant *Escherichia coli* isolated from cattle, Spain, September 2015. *Euro Surveill* 2017; **22**(31): 30586.

114. Meinersmann RJ, Ladely SR, Plumblee JR, et al. Colistin resistance *mcr*-1-gene-bearing *Escherichia coli* strain from the United States. *Genome Announcements* 2016; **4**(5): e00898-16.

115. Meinersmann RJ, Ladely SR, Plumblee JR, Cook KL, Thacker E. Prevalence of *mcr*-1 in the cecal contents of food animals in the United States. *Antimicrob Agents Chemother* 2017; **61**(2): e02244-16.

116. Sun J, Yang RS, Zhang Q, et al. Co-transfer of *bla*(NDM-5) and *mcr*-1 by an IncX3-X4 hybrid plasmid in *Escherichia coli*. *Nat Microbiol* 2016; **1**: 16176.

117. Alba P, Leekitcharoenphon P, Franco A, et al. Molecular epidemiology of *mcr*-encoded colistin resistance in *Enterobacteriaceae* from food-producing animals in Italy revealed through the EU harmonized antimicrobial resistance monitoring. *Front Microbiol* 2018; **9**: 1217.

118. Zajac M, Sztromwasser P, Bortolaia V, et al. Occurrence and characterization of *mcr-1*-positive *Escherichia coli* isolated from food-producing animals in Poland, 2011–2016. *Front Microbiol* 2019; **10**: 1753.

119. Lantos PM, Hoffman K, Hohle M, Anderson B, Gray GC. Are people living near modern swine production facilities at increased risk of influenza virus infection? *Clin Infect Dis* 2016; **63**(12): 1558–1563.

120. Quist AJL, Holcomb DA, Fliss MD, Delamater PL, Richardson DB, Engel LS. Exposure to industrial hog operations and gastrointestinal illness in North Carolina, USA. *Sci Total Environ* 2022; **830**: 154823.

121. Hogerwerf L, Post PM, Bom B, et al. Proximity to livestock farms and COVID-19 in the Netherlands, 2020–2021. *Int J Hyg Environ Health* 2022; **245**: 114022.

122. Wu J, Ke C, Lau EHY, et al. Influenza H5/H7 virus vaccination in poultry and reduction of zoonotic infections, Guangdong Province, China, 2017-18. *Emerg Infect Dis* 2019; **25**(1): 116–118.

123. Mostafa A, Abdelwhab EM, Mettenleiter TC, Pleschka S. Zoonotic potential of influenza A viruses: a comprehensive overview. *Viruses* 2018; **10**(9): 497.

124. Borkenhagen LK, Salman MD, Ma MJ, Gray GC. Animal influenza virus infections in humans: a commentary. *Int J Infect Dis* 2019; **88**: 113–9.

125. Ul-Rahman A, Ishaq HM, Raza MA, Shabbir MZ. Zoonotic potential of Newcastle disease virus: old and novel perspectives related to public health. *Rev Med Virol* 2022; **32**(1): e2246.

126. Kayali G, Ortiz EJ, Chorazy ML, et al. Serologic evidence of avian metapneumovirus infection among adults occupationally exposed to Turkeys. *Vector Borne Zoonotic Dis* 2011; **11**(11): 1453–1458.

127. McDaniel CJ, Cardwell DM, Moeller RB, Jr., Gray GC. Humans and cattle: a review of bovine zoonoses. *Vector Borne Zoonotic Dis* 2014; **14**(1): 1–19.

128. Liu R, Sheng Z, Huang C, Wang D, Li F. Influenza D virus. *Curr Opin Virol* 2020; **44**: 154–161.

129. Sreenivasan CC, Sheng Z, Wang D, Li F. Host range, biology, and species specificity of seven-segmented influenza viruses: a comparative review on influenza C and D. *Pathogens* 2021; **10**(12): 1583.

130. Nissly RH, Zaman N, Ibrahim PAS, et al. Influenza C and D viral load in cattle correlates with bovine respiratory disease (BRD): emerging role of orthomyxo-viruses in the pathogenesis of BRD. *Virology* 2020; **551**: 10–15.

131. White SK, Ma W, McDaniel CJ, Gray GC, Lednicky JA. Serologic evidence of exposure to influenza D virus among persons with occupational contact with cattle. *J Clin Virol* 2016; **81**: 31–33.

132. Frazzini S, Amadori M, Turin L, Riva F. SARS CoV-2 infections in animals, two years into the pandemic. *Arch Virol* 2022; **167**(12): 2503–2517.

133. Fiorito F, Iovane V, Pagnini U, et al. First description of serological evidence for SARS-CoV-2 in lactating cows. *Animals (Basel)* 2022; **12**(11): 1459.

134. de Sant'Ana FJ, Rabelo RE, Vulcani VA, Cargnelutti JF, Flores EF. Bovine papular stomatitis affecting dairy cows and milkers in midwestern Brazil. *J Vet Diagn Invest* 2012; **24**(2): 442–445.

135. Gur S, Gurcay M, Seyrek A. A study regarding bovine enterovirus type 1 infection in domestic animals and humans: an evaluation from the zoonotic aspect. *J Vet Med Sci* 2019; **81**(12): 1824–1828.

136. Uddin Khan S, Atanasova KR, Krueger WS, Ramirez A, Gray GC. Epidemiology, geographical distribution, and economic consequences of swine zoonoses: a narrative review. *Emerg Microbes Infect* 2013; **2**(12): e92.

137. Patton D. Flush with cash, Chinese hog producer builds world's largest pig farm. 2020. https://www.reuters.com/article/us-china-swinefever -muyuanfoods-change-s/flush-with-cash-chinese-hog-producer-builds-worlds -largest-pig-farm-idUSKBN28H0MU

138. Saenz RA, Hethcote HW, Gray GC. Confined animal feeding operations as amplifiers of influenza. *Vector Borne Zoonotic Dis* 2006; **6**(4): 338–346.

139. Ma MJ, Wang GL, Anderson BD, et al. Evidence for cross-species influenza A virus transmission within swine farms, China: a One Health, prospective cohort study. *Clin Infect Dis* 2018; **66**(4): 533–540.

140. Anderson BD, Ma MJ, Wang GL, et al. Prospective surveillance for influenza. virus in Chinese swine farms. *Emerg Microbes Infect* 2018; **7**(1): 87.

141. Borkenhagen LK, Wang GL, Simmons RA, et al. High risk of influenza virus infection among swine workers: examining a dynamic cohort in China. *Clin Infect Dis* 2020; **71**(3): 622–629.

142. Coman A, Maftei DN, Krueger WS, et al. A prospective study of Romanian agriculture workers for zoonotic influenza infections. *PLoS One* 2014; **9**(5): e98248.

143. El Zowalaty ME, Abdelgadir A, Borkenhagen LK, Ducatez MF, Bailey ES, Gray GC. Influenza A viruses are likely highly prevalent in South African swine farms. *Transbound Emerg Dis* 2022; **69**(4): 2373–2383.

144. Borkenhagen LK, Mallinson KA, Tsao RW, et al. Surveillance for respiratory and diarrheal pathogens at the human-pig interface in Sarawak, Malaysia. *PLoS One* 2018; **13**(7): e0201295.

145. Gray GC, McCarthy T, Capuano AW, et al. Swine workers and swine influenza virus infections. *Emerg Infect Dis* 2007; **13**(12): 1871–1878.

146. Ramirez A, Capuano AW, Wellman DA, Lesher KA, Setterquist SF, Gray GC. Preventing zoonotic influenza virus infection. *Emerg Infect Dis* 2006; **12**(6): 996–1000.

147. Myers KP, Olsen CW, Setterquist SF, et al. Are swine workers in the United States at increased risk of infection with zoonotic influenza virus? *Clin Infect Dis* 2006; **42**(1): 14–20.

148. Bailey ES, Choi JY, Fieldhouse JK, et al. The continual threat of influenza virus infections at the human-animal interface: what is new from a one health perspective? *Evol Med Public Health* 2018; **2018**(1): 192–198.

149. Lee J, Wang L, Palinski R, et al. Comparison of pathogenicity and transmissibility of influenza B and D viruses in pigs. *Viruses* 2019; **11**(10): 905.

150. Luby SP. The pandemic potential of Nipah virus. *Antiviral Res* 2013; **100**(1): 38–43.

151. Li M, Embury-Hyatt C, Weingartl HM. Experimental inoculation study indicates swine as a potential host for Hendra virus. *Vet Res* 2010; **41**(3): 33.
152. Penas JA, Miranda ME, de Los Reyes VC, Sucaldito MNL, Magpantay RL. Risk assessment of Ebola Reston virus in humans in the Philippines. *Western Pac Surveill Response J* 2019; **10**(3): 1–8.
153. Barrette RW, Metwally SA, Rowland JM, et al. Discovery of swine as a host for the Reston ebolavirus. *Science* 2009; **325**(5937): 204–206.
154. Mulvey P, Duong V, Boyer S, et al. The ecology and evolution of Japanese encephalitis virus. *Pathogens* 2021; **10**(12): 1534.
155. Ricklin ME, Garcia-Nicolas O, Brechbuhl D, et al. Vector-free transmission and persistence of Japanese encephalitis virus in pigs. *Nat Commun* 2016; **7**: 10832.
156. Chant K, Chan R, Smith M, Dwyer DE, Kirkland P. Probable human infection with a newly described virus in the family Paramyxoviridae. The NSW Expert Group. *Emerg Infect Dis* 1998; **4**(2): 273–275.
157. Barr JA, Smith C, Marsh GA, Field H, Wang LF. Evidence of bat origin for Menangle virus, a zoonotic paramyxovirus first isolated from diseased pigs. *J Gen Virol* 2012; **93**(Pt 12): 2590–2594.
158. Wu FT, Liu LT, Jiang B, Kuo TY, Wu CY, Liao MH. Prevalence and diversity of rotavirus A in pigs: evidence for a possible reservoir in human infection. *Infect Genet Evol* 2022; **98**: 105198.
159. Liu Q, Wang X, Xie C, et al. A novel human acute encephalitis caused by pseudorabies virus variant strain. *Clin Infect Dis* 2021; **73**(11): e3690–e3700.
160. Bauer K. Foot- and-mouth disease as zoonosis. *Arch Virol Suppl* 1997; **13**: 95–97.
161. Zhu Y, Zhang G, Shao M, Lei Y, Jiang Y, Tu C. An outbreak of sheep rabies in Shanxi province, China. *Epidemiol Infect* 2011; **139**(10): 1453–1456.
162. Schuster I, Mertens M, Mrenoshki S, et al. Sheep and goats as indicator animals for the circulation of CCHFV in the environment. *Exp Appl Acarol* 2016; **68**(3): 337–346.
163. Shi N, Qiu X, Cao X, et al. Molecular and serological surveillance of Getah virus in the Xinjiang Uygur Autonomous Region, China, 2017–2020. *Virol Sin* 2022; **37**(2): 229–237.
164. Caballero-Gomez J, Garcia-Bocanegra I, Jimenez-Martin D, et al. Epidemiological survey and risk factors associated with hepatitis E virus in small ruminants in southern Spain. *Zoonoses Public Health* 2022; **69**(4): 387–393.
165. Waddell L, Pachal N, Mascarenhas M, et al. Cache Valley virus: a scoping review of the global evidence. *Zoonoses Public Health* 2019; **66**(7): 739–758.
166. Weidinger P, Kolodziejek J, Camp JV, et al. MERS-CoV in sheep, goats, and cattle, United Arab Emirates, 2019: virological and serological investigations reveal an accidental spillover from dromedaries. *Transbound Emerg Dis* 2022; **69**(5): 3066–3072.
167. Thompson HJ, Harview CL, Swick B, Powers JG. Orf virus in humans: case series and clinical review. *Cutis* 2022; **110**(1): 48–52.
168. Adamu AM, Enem SI, Ngbede EO, et al. Serosurvey on sheep unravel circulation of Rift Valley fever virus in Nigeria Ecohealth 2020; 1/(3): 393–397.

169. Niller HH, Angstwurm K, Rubbenstroth D, et al. Zoonotic spillover infections with Borna disease virus 1 leading to fatal human encephalitis, 1999–2019: an epidemiological investigation. *Lancet Infect Dis* 2020; **20**(4): 467–477.
170. Alzahrani AG, Al Shaiban HM, Al Mazroa MA, et al. Alkhurma hemorrhagic fever in humans, Najran, Saudi Arabia. *Emerg Infect Dis* 2010; **16**(12): 1882–1888.
171. Wallenhammar A, Lindqvist R, Asghar N, et al. Revealing new tick-borne encephalitis virus foci by screening antibodies in sheep milk. *Parasit Vectors* 2020; **13**(1): 185.
172. O'Neill J. Tackling drug-resistant infections globally: final report and recommendations. 2016. https://apo.org.au/node/63983
173. Zalewska M, Blazejewska A, Czapko A, Popowska M. Antibiotics and antibiotic resistance genes in animal manure—consequences of its application in agriculture. *Front Microbiol* 2021; **12**: 610656.
174. Wallinga D, Smit LAM, Davis MF, Casey JA, Nachman KE. A review of the effectiveness of current US policies on antimicrobial use in meat and poultry production. *Curr Environ Health Rep* 2022; **9**(2): 339–354.
175. Anderson TK, Chang J, Arendsee ZW, et al. Swine influenza A viruses and the tangled relationship with humans. *Cold Spring Harb Perspect Med* 2021; **11**(3): a038737.
176. Ata EB, Li ZJ, Shi CW, Yang GL, Yang WT, Wang CF. African swine fever virus: a raised global upsurge and a continuous threaten to pig husbandry. *Microb Pathog* 2022; **167**: 105561.

# CHAPTER 6

# Social and Community Impacts

Aimee Imlay and Loka Ashwood

Rural agricultural communities in the United States continue to experience substantial shifts in the agricultural political economy driven by
farm consolidation and the emergence of industrial food animal production (IFAP). Until the near end of the twentieth century, most farm
animals were raised on diversified farms with a variety of crops and
animals. Farm communities contained an abundance of small- and
mid-sized producers that facilitated vibrant rural economies and close
community relations. Between 1850 and 1920, the number of US farms
rapidly increased to more than six million farms, yet since the peak in
1935, the number of farms declined substantially, and overall farm size
continued to increase (Brown and Schafft 2019). During 2021, there
were just over two million farms in the United States (United States
Department of Agriculture [USDA] 2022), and during 2020, about 89%
of all farms were classified as small family farms (Whitt, Todd, and
Keller 2021). Large and very large industrial farms comprise only about
4% of all farms, yet account for more than 40% of production and sales,
indicating a significant shift in agricultural concentration (Brown and
Schafft 2019). In terms of industrial animal production, roughly 99%
of all animals raised for food are raised in industrial facilities, including

concentrated animal feeding operations (CAFOs) and animal feeding operations (AFOs) (Humane Society of the United States 2012). CAFOs and their parallel, AFOs, are different ways of talking about IFAP. IFAP is a system of production that confines animals for feeding, separates the production of feed and livestock, involves large and specialized farms, and requires vertical linkages with buyers (MacDonald 2018), resulting in serious consequences for rural places globally.

Industrial agriculture involves large-scale, intensive production of both crops and animals and is driven by mechanization and technological developments (e.g., chemical inputs), resulting in widespread farm consolidation and fewer actors in global agrifood production. While the US poultry industry was the first animal sector to utilize industrial farming (Constance 2002), this intensive model of production has since spread across domestic and global animal sectors. The most powerful companies at the helm of industrial agriculture transcend nation-state. For example, the largely Brazilian-owned and financed conglomerate JBS dominates ownership and production in cattle, poultry, hogs, and turkey in the United States and across the globe.

Today, some rural communities in the United States face a unique set of socioeconomic challenges, including population loss, less diversified labor markets, high rates of unemployment, lower investment in human capital due to diminished local revenue flow, and less access to quality health care (Berry 2014; Ulrich-Schad and Duncan 2018). Rates of both rural poverty and reliance on nutritional programs (i.e., Supplemental Nutrition Assistance Program) are higher than national averages (DeWitt et al. 2020; Farrigan 2022). Additionally, poverty is more persistent in rural areas, and rural America contains the only extreme poverty counties in the nation (Farrigan 2020).[1] Still, rural communities are not a monolith, and there is substantial variation between rural areas in terms of community well-being. Yet on the aggregate, rural communities continue to experience difficulties with adequate service provision and economic development. Industrial animal agriculture is touted to stimulate economic growth and development in communities with stalled economic growth and/or high rates of poverty while initially lowering on-the-shelf food prices for consumers. Through government subsidies, agribusinesses now enjoy such oligopoly and monopoly power that they coordinate to raise prices on the shelf and lower them for farmers, largely with impunity (Moss and Taylor 2014). Meanwhile, the social and community costs are profound and borne by vulnerable populations and animals.

This chapter highlights how industrial farm animal production has gained such prominence and continues to have devastating impacts on rural communities in the United States. In doing so, we detail how corporate subsidization and market power in the agricultural sector consolidated farms and paved the way for the proliferation of IFAP. We then discuss the impact of industrial animal production in rural communities by discussing the changes to quality of life and community ties, impacts on property rights and values, changes in civic participation, and shifts in animal husbandry and animal welfare. We close with policy recommendations and pathways for future research that encourage structural transformation of industrial animal agriculture and foster vibrant and healthy rural communities.

## Corporate Subsidization and Market Power in Agriculture

CAFOs are a product of government subsidization, concentration of ownership, and exclusive markets for the most powerful. Access to credit has played a central role in farm consolidation and the rise of industrial feeding operations. The government-sponsored enterprise Farm Credit System (FCS) was first established in 1916 through the Federal Farm Loan Act. FCS encouraged farmers to adopt more intensive technologies by taking on debt, making them acutely vulnerable during the Great Depression (Larzelere and Law 1943). More recently, FCS encouraged farmers to build confinements. After the 1998 hog market crash, where prices hit their lowest level since 1964, the FCS approached farmers to gauge their interest in putting up more intensive operations (Ashwood et al. 2022b). Today, FCS holds nearly as much US farm debt as private lenders (Monke 2018). As a result of FCS's decisions to fund the largest of operations, it now is the major financial firm upholding the largest pork powerhouses in the United States. It plays a key role in the financial network enabling Smithfield Foods and JBS, whose holdings and operating decisions largely trace back to ultimate beneficiaries in China and Brazil, respectively (Ashwood et al. 2022b).

CAFOs could not ensure a steady revenue for investors or financial solvency to banking entities providing loans without subsidization from the US government. Subsidies in the United States continue to follow US Secretary of Agriculture Earl Butz's mantra: "Get big or get out." As recently as 2019, then US Secretary of Agriculture Sony Perdue told Wisconsin dairy farmers, some of whom at the time were taking their lives in despair, that "in America, the big get bigger and the small go out" (Bell et al. 2021). Policies enforce this view, regardless of protest by farmers and communities who bear the most acute cost, as intensive qualitative case studies have demonstrated (De Lind 1995; Dudley 2000; Ashwood 2021). For example, the USDA's 2022 Spot Market Hog Pandemic program provided a payment of fifty-four dollars per head for up to ten thousand hogs. "Legal entities" could apply for the funds separately, meaning that many subsidiaries held underneath one conglomerate, like Smithfield Foods, could each receive such support (USDA n.d.). The USDA has long emphasized top-heavy subsidy payments that benefited the largest producers at the expense of smaller producers (President's National Advisory Commission on Rural Poverty 1967). Early on, these top-heavy payments put smaller producers out of business as they were unable to afford their farms, which contributed to less robust local economies as farms shuttered in rural communities. Today, this trend continues, as farm subsidy schemes benefit the largest producers with household incomes well above the average farm household income (White and Hoppe 2012; Hoppe, Banker, and MacDonald 2005). Farm subsidies such as crop insurance and commodity payments are calculated in terms of acreage; therefore, often the largest operations receive the largest payments. As a result, livestock feed is heavily subsidized by crop insurance and commodity program payments awarded to wheat, corn, and soy producers

(Howard 2019). Direct subsidization of animals per head and indirect subsidization via feed costs all displace integrated farms operating on a per-unit and more self-contained, community-embedded form.

The willing indifference to the ultimate beneficiaries receiving public subsidies in animal production has put the public purse behind foreign ownership of US agriculture. A Government Accountability Office (GAO) review of the 2020 Coronavirus Food Assistant Program put livestock producer payments at $9.8 billion. In a subset of these applications, the office found that over half of the applications were potentially improper and referred them to the Office of Inspector General. Another 10% of the applicants did not even establish clear ownership of the commodities they claimed payment for (GAO 2022). To date, anticorporate farming laws regularly make exceptions for animal operations (Ashwood et al. 2023). Attempts to track foreign national corporate ownership typically rest with the Farm Service Agency and the inadequately maintained Agricultural Foreign Investment Disclosure Act of 1978 (AFIDA), which focuses on land. The ultimate beneficiaries of these entities are not publicly known, as even a company that exists in a particular nation may have investors ultimately benefiting in different locations (Ashwood et al. 2022a).

The use of the corporate form, either within private or public organizational structures, is the lynchpin of concentration in market power and likewise obfuscation to avoid antitrust culpability in animal production (Ashwood, Diamond, and Thu 2014; Ashwood, Pilny, et al. 2022). Across sectors—poultry, turkey, grains, seeds, chemicals, cattle, tractors and equipment, fertilizer, and hogs—a web of relations connects firms across what are sometimes mistaken as distinct farm markets (James, Hendrickson, and Howard 2012). Interwoven financial ties between companies—subsidiary, shareholder, debtor–creditor, members of the board, officers, legal successors, partners—make companies dependent upon one another while also practicing power across sectors (Howard 2021). For example, JBS, Cargill Inc., National Beef Packing Co, and Tyson Inc. have been accused of fixing prices across beef, pork, and poultry sectors, resulting in millions of dollars in settlement litigation based on an antitrust framework (Stempel 2022). Traditionally, measurements of oligopoly and monopoly power centered on one specific farm market, like beef, but the intersectoral power and financial interdependency of firms calls for more network-focused analysis of just how consolidated industrial production is (Ashwood et al. 2022b).

## Farm Consolidation Impact on Rural Communities

Taken together, top-heavy corporate subsidization squeezes out small and midsized producers, while sharply increasing large-scale production (Roberts and Key 2008; Bruckner 2016). In conjunction with the decline of farm operations, the average farm size increased from an average of 145 acres between 1880 and 1935 (Park and Deller 2021) to an average of 445 acres per farm during 2021 (USDA 2022). This consolidation is most pronounced among animal producers, particularly hog and dairy producers. Between 1978 and 2017, the number of hog operations declined by more than 87% and the number of dairy producers declined by more than 81% (Ashwood et al. 2023), as displayed in Table 6.1. Meanwhile, the total inventory of hogs and dairy cattle increased from more than 58 million hogs during 1978 to more than 72 million hogs during 2017 (see Table 6.2). For dairy, the inventory has slightly decreased from more than 10 million dairy cows during 1978 to roughly 9.5 million during 2017 (United States Bureau of the

Table 6.1  Change in Number of Farm Operations by Sector: 1978–2017

| | Number of Operations | | |
|---|---|---|---|
| | 1978 | 2017 | Percent Change |
| Dairy | 512,292 | 66,439 | −87.03 |
| Hogs | 221,007 | 40,336 | −81.75 |
| Poultry | 368,181 | 267,294 | −27.40 |
| Turkeys | 26,638 | 23,173 | −13.00 |
| Cattle (beef) | 1,032,952 | 729,046 | −29.42 |

*Source*: Data compiled from 1978 Census of Agriculture and 2017 Census of Agriculture.

Table 6.2  Change in Inventory by Commodity: 1978–2017

| | Inventory | | |
| | 1978 | 2017 | Percent Change |
| --- | --- | --- | --- |
| Dairy cows | 10,354,979 | 9,539,631 | –7.87 |
| Hogs | 58,809,991 | 72,381,007 | 23.08 |
| Poultry (broilers) | 645,989,949 | 1,621,400,316 | 150.99 |
| Turkeys | 36,066,309 | 104,322,709 | 189.25 |
| Cattle (beef) | 35,186,693 | 31,722,039 | –9.85 |

*Source*: Data compiled from 1978 Census of Agriculture and 2017 Census of Agriculture.

Census 1981; USDA 2019). The significant increase in hog inventory and relatively stable inventory of dairy cows, coupled with the sharp decline in total number of operations, demonstrates extreme consolidation of the industries.[2] Much of this rise in total inventory of hogs is not for domestic use but rather foreign exports that profit multinational corporations (Winders and Ransom 2019; Ashwood et al. 2022b).

While most farms in the United States are classified as small family farms, the loss of midsized producers has a significant impact on rural communities. The decline of the middle bifurcates the structure of agriculture, where smaller producers often lack political and social capital and market power in comparison to large producers (Guptil and Welsh 2014). Midsized farms are important for retaining the vibrancy of rural farming economies, as midsized operations are linked to greater levels of nonfarm economic output (Henry et al. 1987) and overall greater community well-being (Lobao, Hooks, and Tickamyer 2007). Perhaps the earliest study of the social and community impacts of the rise of large-scale farming was conducted by Walter Goldschmidt in 1944 when he investigated the impact of large-scale agricultural production in three California communities. His germinal findings unleashed a following of still ongoing research that documents the relationship between large-scale agricultural operations and adverse economic conditions, such as a diminished middle class, increased rates of hired farm labor, lower household incomes, and higher rates of poverty as compared to farming communities where small farms were numerous

(Goldschmidt 1947). In his study, Goldschmidt (1947) found that the effects of large-scale agriculture were not limited to economic conditions. These communities also had poorer-quality schools, reduced local service provision, and diminished civic engagement. The consolidation of agriculture gives rise to exploitative industrial labor relations (Thu 2009). While this work was initially controversial, Goldschmidt's findings have influenced decades of additional research and policy approaches.[3] He specifically called for more qualitative work to document the devastation wrought on rural communities by industrial agriculture.

Follow-up studies, including a later study by Goldschmidt, have connected changes in class structures to the concentration of industrial operations in communities. Goldschmidt (1978) argued that continued expansion of industrial agriculture in rural America would transform these communities into a two-class system of owners and workers. Harris and Gilbert (1982) found that large-scale farming was related to a decline in rural income, but when considering the possible effect of local class structure (i.e., the number of lower-class farm workers) on rural income, they found that large-scale farming is related to an increase in rural income overall as large-scale farming is also related to an increase in low-wage farmworkers in this study. Gilles and Dalecki (1988) found that more hired laborers was related to a decline in socioeconomic well-being. When considering the impact of farm scale, larger operations were related to better overall economic conditions (Gilles and Dalecki 1988), indicating that in this study, the dependency on farmworkers, representing a shift in the class structure, had a greater negative effect on community socioeconomic conditions than the size of the agricultural operations. For example, Latino farmworkers at CAFOs in Missouri labor in dangerous conditions, with little of the protective equipment they need (Ramos, Fuentes, and Trinidad 2016). Industrial processing plants regionally proximate to CAFOs are notoriously dangerous and oppressive for workers, often operated by vulnerable immigrants and sometimes even by children, like those doing the dangerous and hazardous night cleaning at JBS USA plants (Genoways 2014; United States Department of Labor 2022).

Other studies have considered the relationship between industrial farming and income inequality in rural communities. Heady and Sonka (1974) found that while large-scale production decreases food costs, it lowers community income. Greater small-scale production, they concluded, leads to greater rural community income. Other work found that industrialized farming is related to an increase in higher-income inequality and increased poverty over time (Lobao 1990). A study on hog farming communities in Iowa found a relationship between large-scale hog farming and a decline in small- and midsized producers, as well as a general decline in economic well-being (Durrenberger and Thu 1996). In communities where large-scale and industrial hog farming dominated, reliance on food stamps is higher than in communities where small- and midsized hog production is prominent (Durrenberger and Thu 1996). Low growth in per capita income is connected to the growth of large-scale farms, as demonstrated by an examination of farming communities between 1990 and 1995 (Deller, Gould, and Jones 2003).

The relationship between community well-being, rural poverty, industrial animal agriculture, and poverty is important, yet underexplored. Many studies have indicated that CAFOs are in communities that have high rates of poverty and are disproportionately nonwhite (Wing and Wolf 2000; Wilson et al. 2002; Mirabelli et al. 2006; Donham et al. 2007; Khanjar et al. 2022). In some states, like Mississippi and North Carolina, these facilities locate in communities experiencing persistent poverty. As Kelly-Reif and Wing (2016) write, "The intersection of rurality with race and class exacerbates environmental injustices, causing synergistic impacts larger than the sum of each type of injustice" (351). Rural poverty scholars highlight the importance of community well-being and robust economies as a predictor of deep and persistent poverty. Persistent poverty in rural communities is linked to a variety of community markers or outcomes, including bifurcated class structures (Duncan 1996, 2014), poor local social provision (Ulrich-Schad and

Duncan 2018), poor access to health care (Berry 2014), reduced levels of and investment in human capital (Tickamyer 2006), high rates of unemployment (Weber and Miller 2017), and diminished social capital (Duncan 1996, 2014). CAFOs diminish these markers of community well-being. Rural communities often struggle to provide services like adequate health care, education, and human capital investment. Escaping poverty thus remains difficult. Adjacent CAFOs, with their devastating community effects, exacerbate the struggle. Vibrant communities create opportunities that shield their residents from persistent rural poverty and for communities adjacent to CAFOs, the very industry touted to revitalize these vulnerable communities rather diminishes them. In essence, given the substantial adverse impacts of industrial animal agriculture, CAFOs create, or at the very least worsen, poverty traps.

## Quality of Life and Community Ties

Industrial animal production is related to a decline in quality of life and changes to community ties for adjacent residents. Odor, noise, and increased traffic result from IFAP, significantly impacting the neighbors' quality of life by interfering with the routine activities of daily living. Odor and flies from CAFOs may result from waste lagoons, dead farm animals, or the trucks that remove the dead animals (McMillan and Schulman 2003). Odor from these facilities is often so strong that it impacts the recreation and leisure activities of residents living nearby, including the frequency at which residents open their windows (Wing and Wolf 2000), their ability to enjoy outdoor recreation without exposure to strong odors (Thu and Durrenberger 1994; Wing and Wolf 2000; McMillan and Schulman 2003; Constance and Tunistra 2005), and children's ability to enjoy picnics and outdoor recreation (Wing and Wolf 2000; McMillan and Schulman 2003), and in some cases, relatives have stopped visiting their family members who reside nearby these facilities (Thu and Durrenberger 1994). In North Carolina, interview participants report trying not to breathe to avoid the strong odor from nearby swine CAFOs (Wing and Wolf 2000). During certain times of the day, the noise interferes with routine activities and their desire to go outdoors (Wright et al. 2001).

Neighbors' exposure to noise and odor frays social relations with the operators of IFAP facilities. Rifts form between producers and nonproducers or small- and medium-sized farmers versus large ones (De Lind 1998; McMillan and Schulman 2003; Constance and Tunistra 2005; Jackson-Smith and Gillespie 2005; Ashwood 2021). Jackson-Smith and Gillespie (2005) found that in dairy-producing communities, operators with large herds were less likely to know their neighbors and more likely to have dealt with complaints. They found herd size was a greater predictor of neighbor complaints than generational ownership of the farm, presence of children, and operator age (Jackson-Smith and Gillespie 2005). In East Texas, industrial poultry production increased resentment between producers and nonproducers, where the latter reported feeling as if the producers summarily disregard the impact the odor (Constance and Tunistra 2005). De Lind (1998) highlights the community toll industrialized animal production can have on a community in addition to the environmental and public health consequences of industrial animal production. In Parma, Michigan, during the 1980s, community members organized against an expansion of swine CAFOs, but the conflict resulted in harassment and intimidation of residents, property destruction, threats of violence, damage to marriages and longstanding friendships, and the tragic early death of an activist due to stress from the community conflict (De Lind 1998). In Illinois, farmers who broke away from the Farm Bureau, a powerful agribusiness group, to fight large-scale hog confinements faced ridicule from some industry representatives but were then embraced by their communities more generally (Ashwood 2021). At the core, CAFOs significantly strain or break the ties that bind communities together, including reciprocity, mutual trust, shared norms, and the sense of a shared identity. When community members are divided based on their position to industrial animal agriculture (i.e., producers and nonproducers), the social fabric of communities frays and the case studies described here are illustrative of these shifts.

## Property Rights and Values

Another substantial community consequence of IFAP involves a decline in the value of property proximate to industrial facilities. Several studies have documented a decline in property values and/or a growing concern among residents regarding the value of their property (Thu and Durrenberger 1994; Palmquist et al. 1997; Constance and Tunistra 2005; Kuethe and Keeney 2012). In North Carolina, a study investigating the impact of industrial hog operations on adjacent property values found that the greatest decline occurs when a home is located within a half-mile of a manure lagoon (Palmquist et al. 1997). In Minnesota, a study highlighted that feedlots are related to a decline in home values, and the impact grows the closer the home is to the operation (Taff, Tiffany, and Weisberg 1996). Other work has indicated that CAFOs located within 3 miles of a home decrease home value by 6.6% and homes within a tenth-mile of a CAFO undergo an 88% drop (Hamed, Johnson, and Miller 1999; Kilpatrick 2001). Other work has demonstrated that the impact on property value varies based on distance to the facility and the preexisting value of the home. Kuethe and Keeney (2012) found that in Indiana, the effects of animal feeding operations on property values vary across the distribution of home prices. Here, they found that the effects on home values are greatest for homes with above-median sales prices. The loss in property value related to adjacent facilities is the result of stigma and environmental contamination resulting from proximity to AFOs and CAFOs (Kilpatrick 2001).

These significant decreases in monetary value have not gone uncontested. In some cases, those living proximate to CAFOs have sued for nuisances, when pollution impacts their ability to enjoy their home; negligence, in which the operators of such facilities know how to farm less harmfully but do not; and trespass, when pollution from one property improperly comes onto another. These bundles of rights traditionally are attached to property and codified in common-law jurisprudence as well as state and federal constitutions (Ashwood, Diamond, and Walker 2019). However, right-to-farm (RTF) laws increasingly stripped these protections away from residents living adjacent to CAFOs.

RTF laws, first introduced during the late 1970s, were advocated by legislators as a crucial tool to protect farmland and family farms from suburban sprawl. However, the impact on rural communities is much more insidious. Today, such laws exist in all fifty states and offer a suite of protections to agricultural operations, most notably, protection from nuisance suits (Ashwood et al. 2023). Provisions within RTF statutes often disincentivize neighbors and community members from bringing a nuisance suit. For example, some states require plaintiffs (typically a landowner or resident) to pay attorney costs and fees if they lose, but not the defendant (often a business firm or CAFO). Statutes often provide immunity if the operation is up and running for more than a year, regardless of whether a long-standing farm was there prior. Further, operations receive protection from suits if they adhere to "generally accepted agricultural" or "best management" practices, the meaning of which is murky and typically plays out in court to the benefit of the largest of operators (Ashwood et al. 2023). Among all party types, when CAFOs go to court, they are most likely to win. The party type least likely to win in court utilizing RTF laws are sole-proprietor farmers, the ideal type used to justify the passage of such laws in the first place (Ashwood et al. 2023). Taken together, such laws demonstrate a stark disparity between who is protected by RTF laws and the rhetoric claiming to protect the family farm (Ashwood et al. 2023). Given that RTF statutes offer CAFOs a host of protections, including protections from noise and odor stemming from the operations, the laws act as both a deterrent and a block to local residents seeking to defend their property rights. The inability to defend their land has serious consequences for rural communities and the environment, as the property rights most conducive to safeguard home, air, and water are stripped away (Diamond et al. 2022).

## Civic Participation

Industrial farm animal production in rural communities has altered how rural residents view the state and interact with local government. De Lind's (1998) work in Parma, Michigan, demonstrates that CAFOs have the capacity to shift residents' understanding of the role of the state in relation to protecting residents' interests. The residents of Parma, prior to the hog CAFO siting, largely felt that the local government would protect their interests. After the CAFO was sited, their perceptions shifted to understanding the state as selling out local interests in the name of profit. McMillan and Schulman (2003) document similar trends in their work in North Carolina. Here, citizens expressed discontent due to perceived lack of governmental oversight over the facilities and the hog industry more generally. Citizens felt as if the quality of local governance had declined due to perception of corruption between local regulators and farmers, and thus their concerns about odor, noise, and pollution remained largely unaddressed by local government officials, resulting in resentment and anger toward local government (McMillan and Schulman 2003). In communities with CAFOs, local control of politics diminishes as industrial operators circumvent democratic governance (McMillan and Schulman 2003). In addition to shifting perceptions of local government, civic participation within such communities changes. Lyson and Welsh (2001) found that absentee-owned large-scale farms are negatively associated with a civically engaged middle class. A robust middle class is linked to a variety of community well-being markers, including lower rates of violent crime, lower rates of teen pregnancy, lower rates of poverty, and lower rates of unemployment. This suggests that the presence of large-scale operations diminishes the middle class, with broad implications for political engagement and local decision-making.

While distrust in the state has long been linked to rural political sentiment, some communities have abandoned traditional party politics and traditional forms of civic participation to address immediate concerns in their communities, including protesting proposed CAFO through direct action that transcends traditional political boundaries (Ashwood 2021). Additionally, this study of two rural community organizations that successfully fought CAFO placements, Rural Residents for Responsible Agriculture (RRRA) and Neighbors Opposing a Polluted Environment (NOPE), details how rural emancipation can sidestep the state and allow rural communities to seek solutions to immediate problems while retaining their community self-determination (Ashwood 2021).

## Animal Husbandry and Animal Welfare

IFAP represents a profound shift in animal husbandry where farm animals raised in CAFOs are relegated to unsanitary and inhumane conditions. Animals raised in CAFOs experience stress and boredom due to the overcrowding and inability to engage in their natural behaviors (Humane Society of the United States 2012). These animals often undergo painful procedures (e.g., chicken debeaking) to prevent loss of profit and are subject to conditions that restrict movement to keep their meat tender, as in the case of veal cattle (Human Society of the United States 2012).

Traditional animal husbandry is vastly different from "best management" and "accepted" practices used in IFAP. For most of history, animals raised for food were given room to roam, had access to fresh air, and, in the case of dairy cows and egg-laying hens, produced milk and eggs in accordance with their cycles. Intensive animal production involves confining animals indoor, restricting movement, artificial insemination, and feed different from traditional and diversified diets of farm animals. The shift toward an industrial model of animal agriculture reduces the life longevity for animals, denigrates the relationship between animals and humans, and reinforces a worldview of domination and exploitation. Furthermore, CAFOs centralize risk for the animal and the worker, making both vulnerable to zoonotic disease transmission and contraction. Similar to how IFAP alienates farmers from production and their labor, IFAP alienates animals from their species.

There are a host of laws that protect industrial animal practices. Farm animals are often exempt from state anticruelty statutes, although recent legislation and ballot initiatives address the treatment of these animals (e.g., California's Proposition 12 passed during 2018). Most states protect best management practices for the industry, which exempts farm animals from state anticruelty statutes (Walton and Jaiven 2020). Federally, the Animal Welfare Act (AWA) protects companion animals, animals used for exhibition purposes (i.e., circus animals), and animals used for vivisection, yet farm animals have no such rights (Walton and Jaiven 2020; Prisco 2022). The other federal law, the Human Methods of Slaughter Act (HMSA), seeks to ensure that farm animals are treated in accordance with the law, yet a number of exemptions result in little to no enforcement of the act (Walton and Jaiven 2020). Importantly, poultry is exempt from any protections under the HMSA (Walton and Jaiven 2020; Prisco 2022).

At the state level, "ag-gag" laws criminalize a variety of activities meant to expose the treatment of farm animals, including videorecording, observation of farm activities, and use of drones to record activity at CAFOs (ASPCA 2022). As of 2022, five states have ag-gag laws on the books, and these states are Alabama, Arkansas, Missouri, North Dakota, and Wyoming (ASPCA 2022). Iowa's ag-gag law was deemed unconstitutional during 2022, and legislation is still pending. Idaho, Kansas, Montana, North Carolina, and Utah have determined that such laws are unconstitutional (ASPCA 2022). Eighteen other states have introduced ag-gag legislation, but these bills have failed either through ballot initiatives or stalling in legislative session (ASPCA 2022). A recent study demonstrates that when consumers were provided information on industrial animal production practices, they were increasingly opposed to current animal farming practices (Harris, Ladak, and Mathur 2022). Simply put, IFAP relies on animal mistreatment and exploitation as the industrial model requires confinement and overcrowding to maximize both production and profit. Animal welfare related laws are part and parcel of the social ecology broken by the industrial system of animal production.

## Conclusion and Recommendations

Rural communities are situated at the intersection of the agricultural political economy and decades of socioeconomic change precipitated by the industrialization of agriculture. CAFOs are an acute environmental justice issue, impacting people most according to their rurality, their race, and their poverty. The consequences for the animals within them, the water flowing beside them, and the air flowing through them are also acute. CAFOs worsen the socioeconomic conditions in which they arise, including a shift in the class structures, which has led to an increase in income inequality in some places, a general decline in the quality of life of residents, a tension in community ties, a decline in property values and a loss of property rights, and shifts in the nature of civic participation.

We recommend a multipronged approach to transforming the impacts of CAFOs. We have highlighted the role of the state in engendering IFAP through top-heavy subsidization of corporate agriculture, the role of RTF laws in protecting CAFOs at the expense of rural residents, and the failure of state and federal laws to protect farm animals. The largest multinational companies compile wealth and, following a power-law distribution, position themselves to get richer by dispossessing rural smallholders (Ashwood et al. 2022b). Redistributing economic power democratically calls for public disclosure of the ultimate beneficiaries of subsidies provided by the USDA and likewise those holders behind corporate farmland purchases. Transparency can help farm subsidies become more redistributive. Small- and midsized producers are linked to healthy and vibrant rural communities (Guptil and Welsh 2014), yet current US farm policy rewards the largest producers and often excludes smaller producers from receipt of program payments (Hoppe, Banker, and MacDonald 2005). Commodity subsidies are linked to an increase in poverty in rural Midwestern counties with a high concentration of large farms, and the billions of dollars awarded in the form of commodity subsidies have little to no poverty-mitigating effect in other Midwestern counties, particularly following the most recent changes to commodity programs implemented during 2014 (Imlay 2023). Possible pathways for a more equitable farm policy subsidy design involve an introduction of a redistributive payment, similar to the payment awarded to small producers in the European Union (EU) that explicitly seeks to protect farming as a viable livelihood strategy and the well-being of rural communities within its policy design. The introduction of a similar policy in the United States could reinvigorate rural farming economies experiencing stalled economic growth and a decline in general community well-being.

We recommend substantial reform of RTF laws to instead promote agriculture as a viable livelihood strategy while simultaneously protecting the well-being of rural communities (Ashwood et al. 2023). One option is the overall repeal of RTF laws, as on the aggregate, they provide the most protection to business firms and CAFOs, regardless of whether they are owned domestically. However, targeted steps in changing statutory language also can help. Returning to local governments their power to control land-use decisions is a democratic step forward, and likewise giving communities the provision to determine acceptable agricultural practices (Ashwood et al. 2023). Additionally, the "there first" and "one year up and running" protections afforded to agricultural operations in RTF laws ought to be reconsidered by state legislatures. These provisions distort traditional common-law nuisance law by disallowing residents to defend their property based on who utilized the land first, and repealing these provisions returns nuisance law to its common-law origins (Diamond et al. 2022).

Reform of federal and state anticruelty laws offers a salient pathway to disassembling the industrial model of animal production. The public is increasingly sympathetic to the plight of farm animals, as recently evidenced by California's Proposition 12, passed during 2018, which requires veal calves, breeding pigs, and egg-laying hens to be raised in accordance with stands for freedom of movement, cage-free designs, and a specified minimum floor space. Additionally, the law explicitly states that farmers are prohibited from knowingly confining these animals in a "cruel manner" and bans the sale of products in the state that are produced in a noncomplying manner. The National Pork Producers Council (NPPC) and the American Farm Bureau Federation (AFBF) asked the Supreme Court to overturn the legislation citing violations of the interstate commerce clause, but the Court allowed California's law to stand.[4] We anticipate that California's law will initiate some industry reform, paving the way to make some of the cruelest confinement practices, like farrowing and gestation sites in facilities housing thousands of hogs, obsolete (Ashwood, Diamond, and Thu 2014).

In short, CAFOs are the result of corporate subsidization and farm consolidation, and they operate, in part, due to exemptions within anticruelty laws that fail to protect farm animals. Our approach to transforming industrial animal agriculture involves substantial reform of each of the legal and regulatory frameworks that perpetuate this model of production. We maintain that a joint approach to reforming the laws and policies that bolster industrial animal agriculture has the potential to revitalize rural communities, elevate the distributive orientation of property centered around enjoyment and home, protect farm animals, and re-democratize agriculture to create bright futures for rural communities.

## NOTES

1. A persistent poverty county is a county that has a poverty rate great than 20% for three consecutive decennial census years. An extreme poverty county is a county that has poverty rates greater than 40%.

2. These are point-in-time inventory numbers; they do not reflect the number of hogs and/or dairy cows sold or slaughtered each year.

3. Scholars interested in the relationship between industrial farming and rural community well-being have employed measures of either farm scale or farm structure. Farm scale is captured by considering the size of farms, which may involve acreage, income, and/or sales, whereas farm structure involves examination of ownership, including corporate ownership, contract production, and/or amount of hired labor (Lobao and Stofferahn 2008). While each approach has a set of methodological and theoretical advantages and disadvantages, a full discussion of these approaches is beyond the scope of this chapter. We utilize the term "industrial farming" here to capture changes in both structure and scale.

4. National Pork Producers Council et al. v. Ross, Secretary of the California Department of Food and Agriculture et al., 598 U.S. 2 (2023).

## REFERENCES

Ashwood, Loka. "'No Matter If You're a Democrat or a Republican or Neither':
Pragmatic Politics in Opposition to Industrial Animal Production." *Journal of
Rural Studies* 82 (2021): 586–94.

Ashwood, Loka, John Canfield, Madeleine Fairbairn, and Kathy Master. "What Owns
the Land: The Corporate Organization of Farmland Investment." *Journal of
Peasant Studies* 49, no. 2 (2022a): 233–62.

Ashwood, Loka, Danielle Diamond, and Kendall Thu. "Where's the Farmer? Limiting
Liability in Midwestern Industrial Hog Production." *Rural Sociology* 79, no. 1
(2014): 2–27.

Ashwood, Loka, Danielle Diamond, and Fiona Walker. "Property Rights and Rural
Justice: A Study of US Right-to-Farm Laws." *Journal of Rural Studies* 67 (2019):
120–29.

Ashwood, Loka, Aimee Imlay, Lindsay Kuehn, Allen Franco, and Danielle Diamond.
*Empty Fields, Empty Promises: A State-by-State Guide to Understanding and
Transforming the Right to Farm.* Chapel Hill: University of North Carolina Press,
2023.

Ashwood, Loka, Andy Pilny, John Canfield, Mariyam Jamila, and Ryan Thomson.
"From Big Ag to Big Finance: A Market Network Approach to Power in Agriculture." *Agriculture and Human Values* 39, no. 4 (2022b): 1421–34.

ASPCA. "What Is Ag-Gag Legislation?" 2022. https://www.aspca.org/improving-laws
-animals/public-policy/what-ag-gag-legislation

Bell, Michael, Loka Ashwood, Isaac Leslie, and Laura Schlachter. *An Invitation to
Environmental Sociology.* 6th ed. Thousand Oaks, CA: Sage, 2021.

Berry, E. Helen. "Thinking about Rural Health." In *Rural America in a Globalizing
World: Problems and Prospects for the 2010s*, edited by Conner Bailey, Leif Jensen,
and Elizabeth Ransom. Morgantown: West Virginia University Press, 2014.

Brown, David L., and Kai A. Schafft. *Rural People and Communities in the 21st Century:
Resilience and Transformation.* 2nd ed. Medford, MA: Polity Press, 2019.

Bruckner, Traci. "Agricultural Subsidies and Farm Consolidation." *American Journal
of Economics and Sociology* 75, no. 3 (2016): 623–48.

Constance, Douglas H. "Globalization, Broiler Production, and Community Contro-
versy in East Texas." *Southern Rural Sociology* 18, no. 2 (2002): 31–55.

Constance, Douglas H., and Reny Tunistra. "Corporate Chickens and Community
Conflict in East Texas: Growers' and Neighbors' Views on the Impacts of the
Industrial Broiler Production." *Culture & Agriculture* 27, no. 1 (2005): 45–60.

De Lind, Laura. "The State, Hog Hotels, and the 'Right to Farm': A Curious Relationship." *Agriculture and Human Values* 12, no. 3 (1995): 34–44.

De Lind, Laura. "Parma: A Story of Hog Hotels and Local Resistance." In *Pigs, Profits,
and Rural Communities*, edited by Kendall M. Thu and E. Paul Durrenberger.
Albany: State University of New York Press, 1998.

Deller, Steven C., Brian W. Gould, and Bruce Jones. "Agriculture and Rural Economic
Growth." *Journal of Agricultural and Applied Economics* 35, no. 3 (2003): 517.

DeWitt, Emily, Rachel Gillespie, Heather Norman-Burgdolf, Kathryn M. Cardarelli, Stacey Stone, and Alison Gustafson. "Rural SNAP Participants and Food Insecurity: How Can Communities Leverage Resources to Meet the Growing Food Insecurity Status of Rural and Low-Income Residents?" *International Journal of Environmental Research and Public Health* 17, no. 17 (2020): 6037.

Diamond, Danielle, Loka Ashwood, Allen Franco, Lindsay Keuhn, Aimee Imlay, and Crystal Boutwell. "Agricultural Exceptionalism, Environmental Injustice, and U.S." *Right-to-Farm Laws, Environmental Law Reporter* 52, no. 9 (2022): 10727–48.

Donham, Kelley J., Steven Wing, David Osterberg, Jan L. Flora, Carol Hodne, Kendall M. Thu, and Peter S. Thorne. "Community Health and Socioeconomic Issues Surrounding Concentrated Animal Feeding Operations." *Environmental Health Perspectives* 115, no. 2 (2007): 317–20.

Dudley, Kathryn Marie. *Debt and Dispossession: Farm Loss in America's Heartland.* Chicago: University of Chicago Press, 2000.

Duncan, Cynthia. "Understanding Persistent Poverty: Social Class Context in Rural Communities." *Rural Sociology* 61, no. 1 (1996): 103–24.

Duncan, Cynthia M. *Worlds Apart: Poverty and Politics in Rural America.* 2nd ed. New Haven, CT: Yale University Press, 2014.

Durrenberger, E. Paul, and Kendall M. Thu. "The Expansion of Large Scale Hog Farming in Iowa: The Applicability of Goldschmidt's Findings Fifty Years Later." *Human Organization* 55, no. 4 (1996): 409–15.

Farrigan, Tracey. "Extreme Poverty Counties Found Solely in Rural Areas in 2018." *Amber Waves.* United States Department of Agriculture Economic Research Service, 2020. https://www.ers.usda.gov/amber-waves/2020/may/extreme-poverty-counties-found-solely-in-rural-areas-in-2018/

Farrigan, Tracey. "Rural Poverty and Well-Being." United States Department of Agriculture Economic Research Service, 2022. https://www.ers.usda.gov/topics/rural-economy-population/rural-poverty-well-being/

Genoways, Ted. 2014. *The Chain: Farm, Factory, and the Fate of Our Food.* New York: HarperCollins.

Gilles, Jere Lee, and Michael Dalecki. "Rural Well-being and Agricultural Change in Two Farming Regions." *Rural Sociology* 53, no. 1 (1988): 40–55.

Goldschmidt, Walter. "Large-Scale Farming and the Rural Social Structure." *Rural Sociology* 43, no. 3 (1978): 362–66.

Goldschmidt, Walter. *As You Sow: Three Studies in the Social Consequences of Agribusiness.* Montclair, NJ: Allanheld, Osmun, 1947.

Government Accountability Office (GAO). "Coronavirus Food Assistance Program: USDA Should Conduct More Rigorous Reviews of Payments to Producers," September 8, 2022. https://www.gao.gov/products/gao-22-104397

Guptil, Amy, and Rick Welsh. "The Declining Middle of American Agriculture: A Spatial Phenomenon." In *Rural America in a Globalizing World: Problems and Prospects for the 2010s,* edited by Conner Bailey, Leif Jensen, and Elizabeth Ransom. Morgantown: West Virginia University Press, 2014.

Hamed, Mubarek, Thomas Johnson, and Kathleen Miller. "The Impacts of Animal Feeding Operations in Rural Land Values." Report R-99-02, University of Missouri Columbia Community Policy Analysis Center, 1999.

Harris, Craig K., and Jess Gilbert. "Large-Scale Farming, Rural Income, and Goldschmidt's Agrarian Thesis." *Rural Sociology* 47, no. 3 (1982): 449–58.

Harris, Jamie, Ali Ladak, and Maya B. Mathur. "The Effects of Exposure to Information about Animal Welfare Reforms on Animal Farming Opposition: A Randomized Experiment." *Anthrozoos* 35, no. 6 (2022): 773–88.

Heady, Earl O., and Steven T. Sonka. "Farm Size, Rural Community Income, and Consumer Welfare." *American Journal of Agricultural Economics* 56, no. 3 (1974): 534–42.

Henry, Mark S., Agapi Somwaru, Gerald Schluter, and William Edmonson. "Some Effects of Farm Size on the Nonfarm Economy." *North Central Journal of Agricultural Economics* 9, no. 1 (1987): 1–11.

Hoppe, Robert A., David E. Banker, and James M. MacDonald. "Growing Farm Size and the Distribution of Commodity Program Payments." *Amber Waves* 3, no. 1 (2005): 10–11.

Howard, Philip H. *Concentration and Power in the Food System: Who Controls What We Eat?* London: Bloomsbury Academic, 2021.

Howard, Philip. "Corporate Concentration in Global Meat Processing: The Role of Feed and Finance Subsidies." In *Global Meat: Social and Environmental Consequences of the Expanding Meat Industry*, edited by Bill Winders and Elizabeth Ransom, 31–54. Cambridge, MA: MIT Press, 2019.

Humane Society of the United States. *An HSUS Report: The Welfare of Intensively Confined Animals in Battery Cages, Gestation Crates, and Veal Crates*, July 2012. https://www.humanesociety.org/sites/default/files/docs/hsus-report-animal-welfare-of-intensively-confined-animals.pdf

Imlay, Aimee. "Placing Rural Poverty in the Political Economy: Farm Policy in the American Midwest." PhD diss., University of Kentucky, 2023.

Jackson-Smith, Douglas, and Gilbert W. Gillespie. "Impacts of Farm Structural Change on Farmers' Social Ties." *Society and Natural Resources* 18 (2005): 215–40.

James, H. S., M. K. Hendrickson, and P. H. Howard. "Networks, Power and Dependency in the Agrifood Industry." In *The Ethics and Economics of Agrifood Competition*, 99–126. Dordrecht: Springer, 2012.

Kelly-Reif, Kaitlin, and Steve Wing. "Urban-Rural Exploitation: An Underappreciated Dimension of Environmental Injustice." *Journal of Rural Studies* 47 (2016): 350–58.

Khanjar, Niya, Jonathan Hall, Joseph Galarraga, Isabelle Berman, Camryn Edwards, Daniel Polsky, Rianna Murray, Lucy Kavi, Julie Thompson, and Sacoby Wilson. "Environmental Justice and the Mississippi Farming Industry." *Environmental Justice* 15, no. 4 (2022): 235–45.

Kilpatrick, John A. "Concentrated Animal Feeding Operations and Proximate Property Values." *The Appraisal Journal* (2001): 301–6.

Kuethe, Todd H., and Roman Keeney. "Environmental Externalities and Residential Property Values: Externalized Costs along the House Price Distribution." *Land Economics* 88, no. 2 (2012): 241–50.

Larzelere, H. E., and D. K. Law. "Farm Debt Adjustment in Michigan through the St. Paul Federal Land Bank, 1933–1940." *Special Bulletin* 326 (1943).

Lobao, Linda. *Locality and Inequality: Farm and Industry Structure and Socioeconomic Conditions.* Albany: State University of New York Press, 1990.

Lobao, Linda, and Curtis Stofferahn. "The Community Effects of Industrialized Farming: Social Science Research and Challenges to Corporate Farming Laws." *Agriculture and Human Values* 25 (2008): 219–40.

Lobao, Linda M., Gregory Hooks, and Ann R. Tickamyer. *The Sociology of Spatial Inequality.* Albany: State University of New York Press, 2007.

Lyson, Thomas A., and Rick Welsh. "Scale of Agricultural Production, Civic Engagement, and Community Welfare." *Social Forces* 80, no. 1 (2001): 311–27.

MacDonald, James M. "CAFOs: Farm Animals and Industrialized Livestock Production." In *Oxford Research Encyclopedia of Environmental Science*, edited by H. H. Shugart. Oxford: Oxford University Press, 2018.

McMillan, MaryBe, and Michael D. Schulman. "Hogs and Citizens: A Report from the North Carolina Front." In *Communities of Work: Rural Restructuring in Local and Global Contexts*, edited by William W. Falk, Michael D. Schulman, and Ann R. Tickamyer. Athens: Ohio University Press, 2003.

Mirabelli, Maria C., Steve Wing, Stephen W. Marshall, and Timothy C. Wilcosky. "Race, Poverty, and Potential Exposure of Middle-School Students to Air Emissions from Confined Swine Feeding Operations." *Environmental Health Perspectives* 114, no. 4 (2006): 591–96.

Monke, Jim. "Agricultural Credit: Institutions and Issues." CRS Report No. RS21988 Version 38. Washington, DC: Congressional Research Service, 2018.

Moss, Diana L., and C. Robert Taylor. "Short Ends of the Stick: The Plight of Growers and Consumers in Concentrated Agricultural Supply Chains." *Wisconsin Law Review* 2 (2014): 338–68.

Palmquist, Raymond B., Fritz M. Roka, and Tomislaw Vukina. "Hog Operations, Environmental Effects, and Residential Property Values." *Land Economics* 73, no. 1 (1997): 114–24.

Park, SooJin, and Steven Deller. "Effect of Farm Structure on Rural Community Well-Being." *Journal of Rural Studies* 87 (2021): 300–13.

President's National Advisory Commission on Rural Poverty. *The People Left Behind.* Washington, D.C.: US Government Printing Office, 1967.

Prisco, Andrea. "The Rise of Concentrated Animal Feeding Operations, Their Effects, and How We Can Stop Their Growth." *Dickinson Law Review* 126, no. 3 (2022): 883–906.

Ramos, Athena K., Axel Fuentes, and Natalia Trinidad. "Perception of Job-Related Risk, Training, and Use of Personal Protective Equipment (PPE) among Latino Immigrant Hog CAFO Workers in Missouri: A Pilot Study" *Safety* 2, no. 4 (2016): 25. https://doi.org/10.3390/safety2040025

Roberts, Michael J., and Nigel Key. "Agricultural Payments and Land Concentration: A Semiparametric Spatial Regression Analysis." *American Journal of Agricultural Economics* 90, no. 3 (2008): 627–43.

Stempel, Jonathan. "JBS Reaches 'Icebreaker' Settlement of Beef Price-Fixing Claims." *Reuters*, February 2, 2022.

Taff, Steven J., Douglass Tiffany, and Sanford Weisberg. *Measured Effects of Feedlots on Residential Property Values in Minnesota: A Report to the Legislature.* Staff Paper Series. Minneapolis: University of Minnesota, 1996.

Thu, Kendall. "The Centralization of Food Systems and Political Power." *Culture & Agriculture* 31, no. 1 (2009): 13–18.

Thu, Kendall, and E. Paul Durrenberger. "North Carolina's Hog Industry: The Rest of the Story." *Culture & Agriculture* 14, no. 49 (1994): 20–23.

Tickamyer, Ann R. "Rural Poverty." In *Handbook of Rural Studies*, edited by P. J. Cloke, T. Marsden, and P. Mooney. Thousand Oaks, CA: Sage, 2006.

Ulrich-Schad, Jessica, and Cynthia M. Duncan. "People and Places Left Behind: Work, Culture and Politics in the Rural United States." *The Journal of Peasant Studies* 45, no. 1 (2018): 59–79.

United States Bureau of the Census. "Table 18. Livestock and Poultry—Inventory and Sales: 1978, 1974, and 1969." In *1978 Census of Agriculture, Volume 1: Geographic Area Series, Part 51: United States, Chapter 1: State Data.* Washington, D.C.: United States Department of Commerce, 1981.

United States Department of Agriculture (USDA). *Farms and Land in Farms: 2021 Summary.* Washington, D.C.: USDA National Agricultural Statistics Service, 2022.

United States Department of Agriculture (USDA). "Table 17. Milk Cow Herd Size by Inventory and Sales: 2017." In *2017 Census of Agriculture*, Vol. 1. Geographic Areas Series, Part 51: United States Summary and State Data. Washington, D.C.: United States Department of Agriculture, 2019.

United States Department of Agriculture (USDA). "Table 19. Hogs and Pigs— Inventory: 2017 and 2012." In *2017 Census of Agriculture*, Vol. 1. Geographic Areas Series, Part 51: United States Summary and State Data. Washington, D.C.: United States Department of Agriculture, 2019.

United States Department of Agriculture (USDA). "Spot Market Hog Pandemic Program," Farm Service Agency, n.d. https://www.farmers.gov/archived/smhpp?utm_medium=email&utm_source=govdelivery

United States Department of Labor. "Court Enters Permanent Injunction against Food Sanitation Contractor to End Oppressive Child Labor Practices; Requires Hiring Outside Compliance Specialist." Wage and Hour Division. Case: 40220cv093246. December 6, 2022. https://www.dol.gov/newsroom/releases/whd/whd20221206-3

Walton, Lindsay, and Kristen King Jaiven. "Regulating CAFOs for the Well-Being of Farm Animals, Consumers, and the Environment." *Environmental Law Reporter* 50, no. 6 (2020): 10485–97.

Weber, Bruce, and Kathleen Miller. "Poverty in Rural America Then and Now." In *Rural Poverty in the United States*, edited by Ann R. Tickamyer, Jennifer Sherman, and Jennifer Warlick. New York, NY: Columbia University Press, 2017.

White, T. Kirk, and Robert A. Hoppe. "Changing Farm Structure and the Distribution of Farm Payments and Federal Crop Insurance, EIB-91." Washington, D.C.: U.S. Department of Agriculture, Economic Research Service, 2012.

Whitt, Christine, Jessica E. Todd, and Andrew Keller. "America's Diverse Family Farms: 2021 Edition." Washington, D.C: Economic Research Service, Economic Information Bulletin Number 231, 2021.

Wilson, Sacoby M., Frank Howell, Steve Wing, and Mark Sobsey. "Environmental Injustice and the Mississippi Hog Industry." *Environmental Health Perspectives* 110, no. 2 (2002): 195–201.

Winders, Bill, and Elizabeth Ransom. "Expanding Production, Consumption, and Trade." In *Global Meat: Social and Environmental Consequences of the Expanding Meat Industry*, edited by Bill Winders and Elizabeth Ransom, 1–24. Cambridge, MA: MIT Press, 2019.

Wing, Steve, and Susanne Wolf. "Intensive Livestock Operations, Health, and Quality of Life Among Eastern North Carolina Residents." *Environmental Health Perspectives* 108, no. 3 (2000): 233–38.

Wright, Wynne, Cornelia Butler Flora, Kathy S. Kramer, Willis Goudy, Clare Hinrichs, Paul Lasley, Ardith Maney, et al. "Technical Work Paper on Social and Community Impacts" Prepared for the Generic Environmental Impact Statement on Animal Agriculture and the Minnesota Environmental Quality Board, 2001. https://www.lrl.mn.gov/docs/pre2003/mandated/010457.pdf

# CHAPTER 7

# Environmental Justice

Virginia T. Guidry, Jessica Rinsky, and Sarah Hatcher

*America is segregated and so is pollution.* —DR. ROBERT BULLARD

## Background

Like other polluting industries, industrial food animal production (IFAP) facilities are more likely to be located in communities with less power to resist them. Concentration of the IFAP industry and its disproportionate impacts were first documented in communities of color and low-income communities,[1] but any community that lacks the necessary political and economic power to make decisions is vulnerable to the resulting pollution.[2]

> The hog industry in eastern North Carolina began in the early 80s, then the next thing we know it's 10 million of these animals in North Carolina. With the majority of them being in predominantly African American, Native American, and Latino communities, we feel like that was no mistake, we call those the avenues of least resistance. (Naeema Muhammad, community organizer)[3]

The concentration of polluting industries and resulting environmental inequity contributes to racial and economic disparities in health and quality of life. The recognition of these inequities and their widespread impacts sparked the environmental justice movement, which seeks equal access to a healthful environment for all, regardless of race, ethnicity, or income.

## History of the Environmental Justice Movement

The environmental justice movement began in 1982, when North Carolina sited a landfill for soil contaminated with polychlorinated biphenyls (PCBs) in the rural, majority Black community of Warren County. This community had no role in generating the PCB-contaminated soil, and the landfill siting prompted months of protests by local residents and other supporters, including arrests for civil disobedience. When jailed in Warren County during the protests, Reverend Ben Chavis famously said, "This is racism. This is environmental racism."[4] Ultimately, the landfill was installed, along with a promise from then governor Jim Hunt to clean up the landfill if the technology ever became available. That promise was fulfilled and the landfill was decontaminated in 2002.[5] However, some residents feel that the community suffered long-term economic and possibly health damage due to the landfill, with insufficient steps taken to rectify the harm.

In response to the Warren County events and subsequent investigations into the siting of toxic waste facilities and other polluting industries,[6] multiple organizations have developed definitions of environmental justice (Table 7.1). These definitions typically include a recognition of disproportionate effects and the importance of meaningful involvement of affected communities in decision-making toward solutions.

These definitions of environmental justice focus on an ideal to which we should strive. However, the current situation is one of injustice, with a range of contributing social, historical, political, and economic processes that result in demographic differences between communities that are and are not experiencing environmental injustice.[7] Consequently, we define environmental injustice not as an attribute of the

## Table 7.1 Selected Definitions of Environmental Justice

| Author/Organization | Definition |
| --- | --- |
| North Carolina Environmental Justice Network[a] | The right to a safe, healthy, productive, and sustainable environment for all, where "environment" is considered in its totality to include the ecological (biological), physical (natural and built), social, political, aesthetic, and economic environments . . . the conditions in which such a right can be freely exercised, whereby individual and group identities, needs, and dignities are preserved, fulfilled, and respected in a way that provides for self-actualization and personal and community empowerment. |
| Dr. Bunyan Bryant[b] | Those cultural norms and values, rules, regulations, behaviors, policies, and decisions [that] support sustainable communities where people can interact with confidence that the environment is safe, nurturing, and productive. This goal is served when people can realize their highest potential . . . where both cultural and biological diversity are respected and highly revered and where distributive justice prevails. |
| US Environmental Protection Agency (EPA)[c] and Centers for Disease Control and Prevention (CDC)[d] | The fair treatment and meaningful involvement of all people regardless of race, color, national origin, or income, with respect to the development, implementation, and enforcement of environmental laws, regulations, and policies. . . . This goal will be achieved when everyone enjoys: the same degree of protection from environmental and health hazards, and equal access to the decision-making process to have a healthy environment in which to live, learn, and work. |
| US Institute of Medicine[e] | A concept that addresses in a cross-cutting and integrative manner the physical and social health issues related to the distribution of environmental benefits and burdens among populations, particularly in degraded and hazardous physical environments occupied by minority or disadvantaged populations. |

[a] North Carolina Environmental Justice Network, "Defining Environmental Justice."
[b] Environmental Transformation Movement of Flint, "What Are Environmental Justice & Restorative Practices?"
[c] US EPA, "Learn about Environmental Justice."
[d] Centers for Disease Control and Prevention, "Environmental Justice Index (EJI) Fact Sheet."
[e] Institute of Medicine, Committee on Environmental Justice, "1, Introduction and Executive Summary."

negatively impacted community but as a characteristic of the relation-ships between communities.[8] Here, we will further explore the patterns of environmental injustice associated with IFAP.

## IFAP as an Environmental Injustice

Pollution resulting from IFAP represents an important environmental injustice in the United States. IFAP facilities are concentrated in rural communities[9] across the country,[10] often where populations historically have not had equal say in decision-making around the location, opera-tion, or regulation of facilities. This structure stems "from differentials in economic, social, and political power that lead to disproportionate hazard exposure."[11]

Although attempts have been made to evaluate the environmental injustice of IFAP nationally,[12] understanding environmental injustice related to IFAP must be contextualized locally and with an understand-ing of the history of systemic and institutionalized racism in the United States.[13] Many impacted rural communities are in the south-ern United States, where the legacy of slavery is the strongest. In the mid-Atlantic, Northeast, and Midwest, however, communities of color are more commonly clustered in urban areas. The most well-studied examples of the environmental injustice of IFAP in the United States that illustrate these concepts are the cases of North Carolina and Iowa, two of the biggest hog-producing states in the country.[14]

## North Carolina

In North Carolina, the landscape of industrial hog—and, later, poultry—production transformed from approximately 11,000 small-scale, pasture-raised animal farms producing approximately 3 million hogs per year in the 1980s to approximately 2,500 facilities producing more than 8 million hogs per year today.[15] As part of this shift, many small-scale farmers who could no longer compete with the economies of scale created by IFAP lost their livelihood, including substantial loss of land for Black farmers.[16]

In the 1990s, community members began to notice that primarily African American, poor, and aging communities were being targeted for the location of industrial hog facilities.[17] Research confirmed that industrial hog facilities were disproportionately located near Black, indigenous, and Hispanic communities, and communities with low socioeconomic status in the Coastal Plain region,[18] as shown in Figure 7.1. Specifically, Wing and Johnston showed that census blocks with the highest poverty levels had approximately seven times the number of industrial hog facilities than census blocks with the lowest poverty levels. Similarly, they found that census blocks with the highest nonwhite population had approximately five times the number of industrial hog facilities than those with the lowest. Information about the communities affected by other types of IFAP in North Carolina, specifically poultry facilities, is more limited because data about the location and characteristics of these facilities are not always publicly available (Box 7.1).

## Iowa

Iowa is the largest producer of swine in the United States.[19] The state has large amounts of farmland suitable for the types of manure disposal systems required of IFAP facilities, a favorable legal climate for the IFAP industry (e.g., minimal regulation and lack of local power to limit the location of industrial facilities), and proximity to the corn and soy crops used to feed industrially produced hogs.[20] All counties in Iowa have at least one industrial hog facility, but these facilities are concentrated in northwest, central, and southeastern Iowa. Manure spills from these facilities, a reportable event in the state, were similarly clustered in northwest and north-central Iowa. Although in Iowa, the areas with higher IFAP concentrations have lower percentages of people living in poverty or nonwhite populations than areas with lower IFAP concentrations, Carrel et al. (2016) suggest that a more nuanced consideration of environmental injustice is necessary. Impacted areas are home to

A.

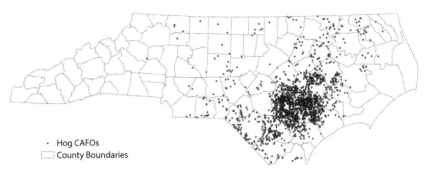

- Hog CAFOs
☐ County Boundaries

B.

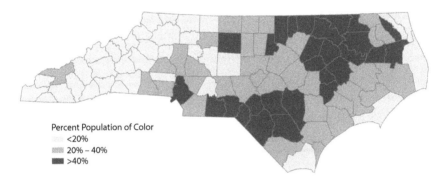

Percent Population of Color
  <20%
  20% – 40%
  >40%

C.

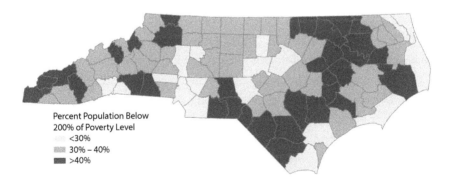

Percent Population Below
200% of Poverty Level
  <30%
  30% – 40%
  >40%

FIGURE 7.1. Distribution of (a) hog industrial food animal production (IFAP) facilities, (b) the percentage of the population of color, and (c) the percentage of the population below 200% of the federal poverty level by county—North Carolina, 2022. *Source*: Johns Hopkins Center for a Livable Future.

populations with larger proportions of people having less than a college education compared with other areas, which may be an indication of a power differential compared to more educated communities. In addition, there may be downstream negative effects of swine production, manure spills, and antibiotics from swine production that are more difficult to measure.[21]

## Other States

Community groups and research studies have called attention to similar patterns in other states, although information is more limited. In Mississippi, as in North Carolina, researchers found that industrial hog facilities were inequitably located in both African American communities and communities living in poverty.[22] Similarly, industrial poultry facilities were located primarily in low-income communities in Mississippi, but their location was not associated with the location of communities of color.[23]

Research focused on northern states shows patterns more similar to Iowa. In Ohio, researchers found swine, dairy, and poultry IFAP facilities meeting the definition of a concentrated animal feeding operation (CAFO) are generally clustered in the western part of the state and not associated with the percentage of Black and low-income

populations. Rather, dairy and swine CAFOs in Ohio were disproportionately located near Hispanic communities and in communities with
higher proportions of children less than 15 years of age.[24] In Delaware,
poultry IFAP facilities were concentrated in rural areas and were found
to disproportionately affect Hispanic populations and populations living below the poverty line; the number of poultry IFAP facilities was
also associated with the percentage of the population with less than
a high school education.[25] The location of poultry IFAP facilities in
Maryland follows a similar pattern, where facilities are clustered in the
Eastern Shore in rural areas and areas with some of the lowest median
household incomes in the state, but not communities of color.[26]

In areas across the United States where IFAP research has not yet
been conducted, community groups, documentaries, and media coverage have helped to document the experiences of other communities
impacted by IFAP.[27] In addition, although we focus on the environmental justice issues associated with living near IFAP facilities, persons
who work in animal production, slaughter, and processing facilities also
face injustices. The livestock industry employs a large proportion of
persons of color and those who are foreign born.[28] A substantial proportion of workers have a primary language other than English, are un-
documented, and live below the poverty line. These vulnerabilities
may keep them working in jobs shown to experience high rates of work-
related injuries and illnesses.[29] See chapter 9 for a detailed discussion
of slaughter and processing plant workers.

## Disproportionate Effects of IFAP

*"We've taken the right to farm to the point where it can easily be called the
right to harm. The right to take away other people's rights."*—John Ikerd,
Professor Emeritus of Agricultural Economics at the University of
Missouri[30]

The clustering of IFAP facilities results in a disproportionate distribution of the negative effects of IFAP on the rural communities described above. Communities near IFAP facilities experience water and

air pollution, and they are affected by odors emanating from these facilities and their waste management activities.[31] Research has demonstrated that proximity to IFAP facilities is associated with negative health and quality of life effects among neighbors such as increased blood pressure, stress, and anxiety levels; irritation of the eyes, nose, and throat; respiratory symptoms; and negative effects on mood.[32] The specific pollutants and related negative impacts on health are discussed in more detail in chapters 2 and 3.

Impacts on quality of life have also been documented. IFAP facility neighbors in North Carolina described an inability to enjoy beneficial use of their property such as sitting, playing, or working outside; entertaining guests; planting a garden; or visiting with neighbors because of the unpredictability of odor from these operations.[33] The same study reported that residents also needed to make costly changes to their lifestyle because of odors, such as purchasing air conditioners to avoid leaving windows open or purchasing a dryer because they can no longer dry their clothes outside.

Proximity to IFAP facilities is also associated with a reduction in property values.[34] A study in Iowa found that homes located within 1.5 miles of an IFAP facility could have up to a 26% reduction in property value depending on proximity to and whether the home is upwind or downwind of the IFAP facility.[35] Studies in Missouri found that within 3 miles of a CAFO, average loss of residential land value ranged between $58 and $112 per acre.[36] Reduced land use and property values experienced by communities in proximity to an IFAP facility are a threat to rural life and the community and may limit an individual's ability to leave if desired.

The adverse effects of IFAP facilities are often compounded because of the history of institutional discrimination in the United States. The same communities may also deal with proximity to other polluting industries, poor housing, limited resources, poor underlying health status, and lack of access to services and medical care.[37] Increasing severity of weather events such as hurricanes, floods, and droughts has also further exacerbated environmental conditions affecting many of these communities.[38] The health of rural communities and impacts of IFAP is discussed in more depth in chapter 6.

## Underlying Structures Supporting the Environmental Injustice of IFAP

*"We just keep trying to bring it to the attention of those people who are in these positions that are supposed to make decisions, waiting for them to do the right thing. We've been shut out . . . we've just been shut out."*—Elsie Herring, rural resident of North Carolina (*Right to Harm*, n.d.)

The IFAP industry has historically influenced agricultural policy, regulation, and enforcement, which has resulted in the prioritization of industry interests over community interests.[39] Some have referred to this pattern as the "agro-industrial complex: an alliance of agriculture commodity groups, scientists at academic institutions who are paid by the industry, and their friends on Capitol Hill."[40] Without political power, significant resources, or options for legal action, it is difficult for rural communities, communities of color, and low-income communities to represent their interests to government officials and the IFAP industry. The following are examples of some structural barriers to achieving environmental justice with respect to IFAP.

## Legislation

All 50 states have some form of right-to-farm legislation that protects the ability of the agricultural industry to do business, and some states go as far as prohibiting local actions that could limit what businesses are allowed to do, even to protect the environment or public health.[41] During the past few years, multiple state legislatures have amended these laws to further protect IFAP industry interests, for example, by limiting damages that could be awarded in agriculture-related nuisance claims after several such claims were found in favor of the community plaintiffs.

As of 2019, 10 states have enacted "ag-gag" laws, which criminalize or provide civil penalties or damages for misrepresenting oneself with motives to commit an unauthorized act, or recording or photographing an agricultural facility without permission.[42] These laws often also prevent community members, reporters, researchers, and others from documenting concerns about agricultural facilities.

## Regulation and Enforcement

The United States relies on a fragmented and incomplete system of laws and enforcement to regulate IFAP, which is not focused on protecting community health and varies by state, animal type, size, waste system, and other characteristics.[43] At the federal level, the US Environmental Protection Agency (EPA) has limited regulations applicable to IFAP facilities meeting the definition of a CAFO, mainly focused on the ability to discharge into US waterways.[44] However, the EPA also offers an exemption to permitting requirements for agricultural stormwater related to "normal" farming activities.[45] Authority for CAFO designation, monitoring, and response to violations has been granted to state agencies on behalf of the EPA.[46] Most states have enacted laws that require manure management plans for facilities that meet the definition of a CAFO.[47] However, because of the agricultural stormwater exemption, most states permit CAFOs as nondischarge facilities despite research demonstrating that these facilities discharge pollutants into US waterways through various routes, including stormwater runoff.[48] In addition, facilities that do not meet the definition of a CAFO are not subject to the same set of regulations yet may result in similar exposures and community effects. Further, despite US livestock production emitting a range of air pollutants, challenges in quantifying emissions from IFAP facilities and industry opposition to regulation have resulted in air pollutants from IFAP facilities remaining essentially unregulated.[49]

Regulation of IFAP facilities is further complicated because in most states, no single agency has ownership of monitoring, regulation, and response to IFAP facility emissions.[50] Often, environmental or agriculture agencies with authority to regulate IFAP lack public health juris-diction, resources (e.g., funding and staff), and health expertise to monitor the IFAP industry effectively.[51] These barriers may result in limited inspection of facilities or enforcement of existing regulations.[52] Further, in some states, legal and legislative actions have reduced the ability of local governments to regulate or limit IFAP.[53] The lack of reg-ulation limits the ability for communities to report problems or for governmental agencies to take action.[54]

The current regulatory situation prompted the American Public Health Association (APHA) to issue a policy statement calling for leg-islators to consider a moratorium on the establishment of new and ex-pansion of existing IFAP facilities until policies protecting the public's health are in place.[55]

### Monitoring Health Impacts

State and local health departments may be aware of the environmen-tal justice and health concerns related to IFAP facilities in their juris-diction but often lack the ability to act because they are not formally part of the regulatory, enforcement, or monitoring structure and lack resources. Further, some public health authorities, along with regula-tory agency employees, have encountered barriers from state gov-ernments that believe the financial incentive of the IFAP industry outweighs the health and environmental concerns.[56] Without clear authorities, health departments encounter challenges in obtaining data to monitor and evaluate environmental justice and health impacts re-lated to IFAP to inform policy and action.

### Political Influence

The structural inadequacies described above are supported by political influence of the IFAP industry. For example, Wendell Murphy, owner of Murphy Farms, served as a North Carolina state representative and senator. In 1991, during his time in the North Carolina legislature,

Murphy cosponsored a law known as "Murphy's Law," which "shields large-scale animal farms from local zoning regulations."[57] Many other state legislators in North Carolina have been personally involved in IFAP, and the majority receive political donations from the industry.[58]

The IFAP industry has used this influence to attempt to interfere with research documenting environmental injustices related to IFAP facilities. In a 2002 commentary, Dr. Steve Wing detailed the actions taken by the pork industry in North Carolina to intimidate him, his research team, and community members who participated in research studies.[59] These actions were possible because of the political influence the industry had in the state, including within the legislature and the University of North Carolina Board of Governors.

## Limited Options for Legal Recourse

Community options for legal recourse in the context of environmental justice are limited and highly burdensome. Current environmental laws fail to offer sufficient protection from environmental hazards and do not account for disparate racial/ethnic impact of such hazards.[60] Title VI of the Civil Rights Act of 1964 prohibits discrimination on the basis of race and ethnicity by recipients of federal funds and has been a common path of recourse for environmental justice complainants.[61] However, in 2001, the Supreme Court issued a ruling that requires civil environmental justice cases to provide evidence of intentional discrimination.[62] The EPA also has a poor track record of enforcing Title VI,[63] and multiple investigations have called for an overhaul in the EPA's enforcement of Title VI, including the US Commission on Civil Rights.[64]

## Addressing the Environmental Injustice of IFAP

Many efforts have been directed at recognizing the environmental injustice of IFAP. Unfairly, the burden of proof of environmental injustice and adverse effects from IFAP is placed on affected communities. Communities have organized to share their stories and bring attention to the issue; engage with researchers, journalists, lawyers, and policymakers to publicly identify and recognize the problem; and take action to address the injustice.[65]

## Community Action

In the late 1990s in Halifax County, North Carolina, local citizens formed the Concerned Citizens of Tillery and Halifax Environmental Loss Prevention when they learned that hundreds of new IFAP facilities were planned for their county. The county passed a livestock ordinance that prevented the siting of many facilities. These efforts and plans to locate an industrial hog facility near a wealthy community prompted a state law that placed a moratorium on the construction of new hog facilities.[66] Later, concerned citizens of Chatham County, North Carolina, which neighbors the nearby University of North Carolina and the growing Research Triangle Park, successfully lobbied their local health department and county commissioners to develop and enforce local regulation regarding IFAP facilities.[67] Similarly, citizens of Bayfield, Wisconsin, prevented the siting of an industrial hog facility in their community.[68] However, many other communities have struggled to garner such local support, often due to the personal and financial ties of local government officials to the IFAP industry.[69] Further, several state legislatures, such as North Carolina, have pre-empted municipal efforts to control siting decisions for IFAP facilities.[70] These examples demonstrate how communities with more real or perceived economic, social, or political power often have more success in preventing concentration of IFAP facilities in their communities, compared to communities with less power.

## Media Coverage

Impacted communities and their collaborators have worked extensively to describe the environmental injustice of IFAP through interviews, presentations, and documentaries. The written, audio, and visual documentation of the lived experiences of community members provides powerful evidence of the community impacts of IFAP that have increased public awareness and kept the topic in the public eye.[71]

## Community-Driven Research

Community-driven research has also been an important tool in building the scientific evidence base that pollution related to IFAP is measurable and causes or contributes to adverse health effects in nearby communities.[72] Community-driven research approaches, including community-based participatory research (CBPR), can also improve research validity. For example, by involving communities affected by industrial hog operations, Wing et al. demonstrated that community participation improved the relevance of their hypotheses, validity, and interpretation of their results, with almost no attrition of participants despite a detailed study protocol. When community-driven approaches are implemented effectively, they can also promote social change through community education and action.[73]

## Legal Action

Community-driven action, media coverage, and research have developed enough evidence to support legal actions to address current IFAP-related injustices. For example, in North Carolina, community groups aided by environmental lawyers filed a Title VI complaint against the North Carolina Department of Environment and Natural Resources (NC DENR) "for issuing a general permit that allows industrial swine facilities in North Carolina to operate with grossly inadequate and outdated systems of controlling animal waste and little provision for government oversight, which has an unjustified disproportionate impact on the basis of race and national origin against African Americans, Latinos and Native Americans in violation of Title VI of the Civil Rights Act of 1964."[74] This complaint resulted in changes to the department's permit and work related to environmental injustice in the state. The

Southern Environmental Law Center filed another Title VI complaint on behalf of community members in 2021 (with a supplement in 2022), indicating that NC DENR, now named the North Carolina Department of Environmental Quality (NC DEQ), continues to authorize "swine waste management systems that lack necessary protections against air and water pollution."[75] Community members have also filed nuisance lawsuits in multiple states to draw public attention to the damage to communities surrounding IFAP; multiple suits have now been decided in favor of community plaintiffs with large damages awarded.[76]

## Limited Industry Solutions

Despite some successes for communities affected by IFAP and the identification of technological solutions by researchers, the solutions deemed acceptable by the IFAP industry are often narrow in focus, addressing isolated impacts of IFAP without addressing the larger environmental issues and injustices. For example, biogas production, or the use of methane produced during anaerobic digestion of manure as a source of energy, has been proposed to reduce methane emissions from IFAP facilities. This may help farmers reduce fuel costs on a smaller scale, but scaling this approach requires significant investment in infrastructure for transporting methane gas and does not sufficiently reduce the volume of manure that must be stored or used.[77] Further, the hog industry may use the production of biogas as a motivation to maintain the lagoon and spray field system instead of investing in better solutions, potentially resulting in continued or worsening pollution.

## Conclusions

IFAP represents an environmental injustice in which communities near IFAP facilities absorb the externalized health and environmental costs of the production system while the IFAP industry maintains its profits and the general population receives access to artificially inexpensive meat. IFAP in the United States is concentrated in rural communities and often in low-income, underserved communities or communities of color. Many affected communities have fought to protect their environment, health, and quality of life. However, the injustice of the current IFAP system is a systemic problem that requires addressing structural barriers, including classism and racism. The evidence demonstrates the need for immediate action to reduce the negative impacts on communities neighboring existing facilities, and systemic changes to shift the system to one where animal production–related pollution is shared equally and minimized.

## Recommendations

*"I am a link in the chain, and the link in the chain will not break here."*—North Carolina Environmental Justice Network[78]

Everyone is needed to address environmental injustices related to IFAP—affected communities, the IFAP industry, legislators, environmental and public health agencies, scientists, journalists, lawyers, economists, and the public. Communities with firsthand experience of impacts should continue to lead efforts to recognize injustices and demand action, while the others listed above should support these communities in designing and implementing a more equitable approach to animal production. We must also shift power dynamics toward requiring the IFAP industry to demonstrate that the environmental and health effects of IFAP have been eliminated or are minimized and equally shared, rather than placing the burden of proof of environmental injustice on neighboring communities.

### Develop IFAP Regulations That Reflect Current Knowledge of Environmental Justice and Health Impacts

Legislative bodies and regulatory authorities need to engage affected communities, environmental scientists, and health experts in reviewing, revising, and developing regulations regarding air and water emissions, as well as monitoring and enforcement plans for IFAP facilities of all sizes, with a focus on protecting the environment and health of neighbors. Requirements to collect air, surface water, and groundwater monitoring data would help to understand the environmental and health impacts of this agricultural system. Consistent with APHA's policy statement, until these changes have been made, legislators should enact a moratorium on the establishment of new and expansion of existing IFAP facilities.[79]

## Strengthen and Enforce Reporting Requirements for IFAP Facilities of All Sizes

Regulatory agencies across the United States should require reporting of key characteristics of new and existing facilities of all sizes, such as IFAP locations, size, type, and waste management systems and practices, and make these data as well as any monitoring data publicly accessible.

## Increase Health Department Engagement in Environmental Justice Concerns about IFAP

Increased health department engagement would be beneficial since many regulatory agencies with jurisdiction over IFAP do not have a health focus.[80] Some health departments have environmental mapping tools that would benefit from increased availability of public data, and many conduct community health assessments that could increase their focus on environmental contributors to health and inequities. State and local health departments could work with academic partners and federal funding agencies to develop environmental justice research studies and public health practices that reduce documented harms from IFAP.

## Continue to Document Environmental Injustice Related to IFAP throughout the United States

Although sufficient evidence exists to demonstrate that IFAP represents an important injustice that requires action, continued expansion of documentation in additional geographic areas will help to further inform legislation and policies. Data should be incorporated into maps and analyses of cumulative burden of IFAP and other industries on nearby communities. Scientists and others engaging in these analyses should partner with affected communities to document impacts.[81]

## Improve Legislation Focused on Reducing Environmental Injustice Related to IFAP

Many of the above recommendations depend on fair legislation. Legislators hold the power to develop legislation that reduces and prevents continued injustices and promotes health, defined not just as the absence of disease but as the achievement of a community's full well-being and quality of life.[82] Legislators should use input from all stakeholders in their jurisdictions to inform decision-making around existing and new IFAP facilities and repeal legislation that restricts the ability of communities to call attention to injustices.

## Recognize That Urban Decisions Impact Rural Health

The current IFAP system relies on externalizing costs of environmental degradation and adverse health impacts onto communities.[83] In this context, consumer choices can be a powerful source of change. Urban communities must recognize that their health and prosperity are intertwined with that of rural communities,[84] take action to choose food that is produced using more responsible and sustainable methods, and contact policymakers to support fair legislation and healthier options for all.

In the words of the North Carolina Environmental Justice Network, "Lasting change takes time and support from everyone."[85]

**NOTES**

Epigraph: Bullard, "Dr. Robert Bullard: Father of Environmental Justice."

1. Wing, Cole, and Grant, "Environmental Injustice in North Carolina's Hog Industry"; Wilson et al., "Environmental Injustice and the Mississippi Hog Industry"; Son et al., "Distribution of Environmental Justice Metrics for Exposure to CAFOs in North Carolina, USA."

2. Kelly-Reif and Wing, "Urban-Rural Exploitation," 2016; Carrel, Young, and Tate, "Pigs in Space," 2016.

3. *Right to Harm*.

4. Fears and Dennis, "'This Is Environmental Racism.'"

5. Exchange Project, "Warren County."

6. United Church of Christ Commission for Racial Justice, "Toxic Wastes and Race in the United States."

7. Carrel, Young, and Tate, "Pigs in Space," 2016.

8. Kelly-Reif and Wing, "Urban-Rural Exploitation," 2016.

9. Kelly-Reif and Wing, "Urban-Rural Exploitation," 2016.

10. Harun and Ogneva-Himmelberger, "Distribution of Industrial Farms in the United States and Socioeconomic, Health, and Environmental Characteristics of Counties."

11. Carrel, Young, and Tate, "Pigs in Space," 2016.

12. Harun and Ogneva-Himmelberger, "Distribution of Industrial Farms in the United States and Socioeconomic, Health, and Environmental Characteristics of Counties."

13. Galarraga et al., "Environmental Injustice and Industrial Chicken Farming in Delaware," 2022.

14. United States Department of Agriculture, "USDA Census of Agriculture."

15. United States Department of Agriculture, "USDA Census of Agriculture."

16. Edwards, Bob and Ladd, "Environmental Justice, Swine Production and Farm Loss in North Carolina."

17. Slatin and Scammell, "'No Justice, No Peace' and the Right to Self-Determination."

18. Wing and Johnston, "Industrial Hog Operations in North Carolina Disproportionately Impact African-Americans, Hispanics and American Indians"; Mirabelli et al., "Race, Poverty, and Potential Exposure of Middle-School Students to Air Emissions from Confined Swine Feeding Operations"; Son et al., "Distribution of Environmental Justice Metrics for Exposure to CAFOs in North Carolina, USA"; Wing, Cole, and Grant, "Environmental Injustice in North Carolina's Hog Industry."

19. United States Department of Agriculture, "USDA Census of Agriculture."

20. Carrel, Young, and Tate, "Pigs in Space," 2016.

21. Carrel, Young, and Tate, "Pigs in Space," 2016.

22. Wilson et al., "Environmental Injustice and the Mississippi Hog Industry."

23. Khanjar et al., "Environmental Justice and the Mississippi Poultry Farming Industry."

24. Lenhardt and Ogneva-Himmelberger, "Environmental Injustice in the Spatial Distribution of Concentrated Animal Feeding Operations in Ohio."

25. Galarraga et al., "Environmental Injustice and Industrial Chicken Farming in Delaware," 2022.

26. Hall et al., "Environmental Injustice and Industrial Chicken Farming in Maryland."

27. *Right to Harm.*

28. Stuesse and Dollar, "Who Are America's Meat and Poultry Workers?"

29. Smith, "How Safe Are the Workers Who Process Our Food?"

30. *Right to Harm: A Public Health Crisis Too Big to Ignore.*

31. Guidry et al., "Connecting Environmental Justice and Community Health"; Wing et al., "Integrating Epidemiology, Education, and Organizing for Environmental Justice," 2008; Pew Commission on Industrial Farm Animal Production, "Putting Meat on the Table," 2008.

32. Casey et al., "Industrial Food Animal Production and Community Health"; Guidry et al., "Connecting Environmental Justice and Community Health"; Horton et al., "Malodor as a Trigger of Stress and Negative Mood in Neighbors of Industrial Hog Operations"; Wing and Johnston, "Industrial Hog Operations in North Carolina Disproportionately Impact African-Americans, Hispanics and American Indians."

33. Tajik et al., "Impact of Odor from Industrial Hog Operations on Daily Living Activities," 2008.

34. Donham et al., "Community Health and Socioeconomic Issues Surrounding Concentrated Animal Feeding Operations," 2007; Hamed, Johnson, and Miller, *The Impacts of Animal Feeding Operations on Rural Land Values*; Herriges, Secchi, and Babcock, "Living with Hogs in Iowa"; Weida, "Considering the Rationales for Factory Farming."

35. Herriges, Secchi, and Babcock, "Living with Hogs in Iowa."

36. Hamed, Johnson, and Miller, *The Impacts of Animal Feeding Operations on Rural Land Values*.

37. Donham et al., "Community Health and Socioeconomic Issues Surrounding Concentrated Animal Feeding Operations," 2007.

38. Wing, "Social Responsibility and Research Ethics in Community-Driven Studies of Industrialized Hog Production," 2002.

39. Donham et al., "Community Health and Socioeconomic Issues Surrounding Concentrated Animal Feeding Operations," 2007; Kelly-Reif and Wing, "Urban-Rural Exploitation," 2016.

40. Pew Commission on Industrial Farm Animal Production, "Putting Meat on the Table," 2008.

41. Donham et al., "Community Health and Socioeconomic Issues Surrounding Concentrated Animal Feeding Operations," 2007; Ashwood, Diamond, and Walker, "Property Rights and Rural Justice."

42. Ceryes and Heaney, "'Ag-Gag' Laws."

43. Fry et al., "Investigating the Role of State and Local Health Departments in Addressing Public Health Concerns Related to Industrial Food Animal Production Sites"; Fry et al., "Investigating the Role of State Permitting and Agriculture Agencies in Addressing Public Health Concerns Related to Industrial Food Animal Production"; Heinzen, "Recent Developments in the Quantification and Regulation of Air Emissions from Animal Feeding Operations."

44. Fry et al., "Investigating the Role of State Permitting and Agriculture Agencies in Addressing Public Health Concerns Related to Industrial Food Animal Production."

45. US EPA, "Clean Water Act Section 404 and Agriculture."

46. Fry et al., "Investigating the Role of State Permitting and Agriculture Agencies in Addressing Public Health Concerns Related to Industrial Food Animal Production."

47. Donham et al., "Community Health and Socioeconomic Issues Surrounding Concentrated Animal Feeding Operations," 2007.

48. Heaney et al., "Source Tracking Swine Fecal Waste in Surface Water Proximal to Swine Concentrated Animal Feeding Operations"; Mallin et al., "Industrial Swine and Poultry Production Causes Chronic Nutrient and Fecal Microbial Stream Pollution."

49. Heinzen, "Recent Developments in the Quantification and Regulation of Air Emissions from Animal Feeding Operations."

50. Fry et al., "Investigating the Role of State and Local Health Departments in Addressing Public Health Concerns Related to Industrial Food Animal Production Sites."

51. Fry et al., "Investigating the Role of State Permitting and Agriculture Agencies in Addressing Public Health Concerns Related to Industrial Food Animal Production."

52. Donham et al., "Community Health and Socioeconomic Issues Surrounding Concentrated Animal Feeding Operations," 2007.

53. Carrel, Young, and Tate, "Pigs in Space," 2016.

54. Fry et al., "Investigating the Role of State Permitting and Agriculture Agencies in Addressing Public Health Concerns Related to Industrial Food Animal Production."

55. American Public Health Association, "APHA Policy Statement 20194."

56. Fry et al., "Investigating the Role of State and Local Health Departments in Addressing Public Health Concerns Related to Industrial Food Animal Production Sites."

57. Democracy North Carolina, "July 1995—Hog Money Pollutes NC General Assembly."

58. Democracy North Carolina, "NC Hog Industry History"; "Let's Put a Foot in the Revolving Door."

59. Wing, "Social Responsibility and Research Ethics in Community-Driven Studies of Industrialized Hog Production," 2002.

60. Engleman Lado, "No More Excuses."

61. La Londe, "Who Wants to Be an Environmental Justice Advocate?"

62. La Londe, "Who Wants to Be an Environmental Justice Advocate?"; Engleman Lado, "No More Excuses."

63. Engleman Lado, "No More Excuses."

64. Engleman Lado, "No More Excuses."

65. Driscoll and Theis, "'Not in Our Water!'"; Johnston and Cushing, "Chemical Exposures, Health, and Environmental Justice in Communities Living on the Fenceline of Industry"; Tajik et al., "Impact of Odor from Industrial Hog Operations on Daily Living Activities," 2008; Wing et al., "Community Based Collaboration for Environmental Justice"; Wing et al., "Integrating Epidemiology, Education, and Organizing for Environmental Justice," 2008.

66. Slatin and Scammell, "'No Justice, No Peace' and the Right to Self-Determination."

67. Upshaw and Okun, "A Model Approach for Developing Effective Local Public Health Policies."

68. Driscoll and Theis, "'Not in Our Water!'"

69. Democracy North Carolina, "July 1995—Hog Money Pollutes NC General Assembly"; "Let's Put a Foot in the Revolving Door."

70. Owens, "Agricultural Uses and Zoning."

71. *Right to Harm.*

72. Johnston and Cushing, "Chemical Exposures, Health, and Environmental Justice in Communities Living on the Fenceline of Industry."

73. Wing et al., "Integrating Epidemiology, Education, and Organizing for Environmental Justice," 2008.

74. EARTHJUSTICE, "Re: Complaint Under Title VI of the Civil Rights Act of 1964, 42 U.S.C. § 2000d, 40 C.F.R. Part 7," 2014.

75. Southern Environmental Law Center, "Complaint under Title VI of the Civil Rights Act of 1964, 42 U.S.C. § 2000d, Regarding the North Carolina Department of Environmental Quality's Issuance of Permit Nos. AWI310035, AWI301139, AWI230466, and AWS820005," 2021; Southern Environmental Law Center, "Supplement to Complaint Number 05RNO-21-R4 Regarding the North Carolina Department of Environmental Quality's Issuance of Swine Farm Digester General Permit," 2022.

76. Sorg, "Smithfield Loses Its Third Hog Nuisance Case, Jury Awards Plaintiffs $473 Million in Damages"; Ashwood, Diamond, and Walker, "Property Rights and Rural Justice."

77. Humane Society of the United States, "An HSUS Report."

78. "EJ Summit | NCEJN."

79. American Public Health Association, "APHA Policy Statement 20194."

80. Fry et al., "Investigating the Role of State Permitting and Agriculture Agencies in Addressing Public Health Concerns Related to Industrial Food Animal Production."

81. Kelly-Reif and Wing, "Urban-Rural Exploitation," Wing, "Social Responsibility and Research Ethics in Community-Driven Studies of Industrialized Hog Production," 2002.

82. Environmental Transformation Movement of Flint, "What Are Environmental Justice & Restorative Practices?"
83. American Public Health Association, "APHA Policy Statement 20194."
84. Kelly-Reif and Wing, "Urban-Rural Exploitation," 2016.
85. North Carolina Environmental Justice Network, "CAFOs | NCEJN."

**REFERENCES**

American Public Health Association. "APHA Policy Statement 20194: Precautionary Moratorium on New and Expanding Concentrated Animal Feeding Operations." Policy Statement, November 5, 2019. https://www.apha.org/policies-and -advocacy/public-health-policy-statements/policy-database/2020/01/13 /precautionary-moratorium-on-new-and-expanding-concentrated-animal -feeding-operations

Ashwood, Loka, Danielle Diamond, and Fiona Walker. "Property Rights and Rural Justice: A Study of U.S. Right-to-Farm Laws." *Journal of Rural Studies* 67 (April 2019): 120–29. https://doi.org/10.1016/j.jrurstud.2019.02.025

Bullard, Robert. "Dr. Robert Bullard: Father of Environmental Justice." Dr Robert Bullard (blog). Accessed January 14, 2023. https://drrobertbullard.com/

Carrel, Margaret, Sean Young, and Eric Tate. "Pigs in Space: Determining the Environmental Justice Landscape of Swine Concentrated Animal Feeding Operations (CAFOs) in Iowa." *International Journal of Environmental Research and Public Health* 13, no. 9 (August 25, 2016): 849. https://doi.org/10.3390/ ijerph13090849

Casey, Joan A., Brent F. Kim, Jesper Larsen, Lance B. Price, and Keeve E. Nachman. "Industrial Food Animal Production and Community Health." *Current Environmental Health Reports* 2, no. 3 (September 2015): 259–71. https://doi.org/10.1007 /s40572-015-0061-0

Centers for Disease Control and Prevention/Agency for Toxic Substances and Disease Registry. "Environmental Justice Index (EJI) Fact Sheet." Accessed January 30, 2023. https://www.atsdr.cdc.gov/placeandhealth/eji/fact_sheet.html

Ceryes, Caitlin A., and Christopher D. Heaney. "'Ag-Gag' Laws: Evolution, Resurgence, and Public Health Implications." *NEW SOLUTIONS: A Journal of Environmental and Occupational Health Policy* 28, no. 4 (February 2019): 664–82. https:// doi.org/10.1177/1048291118808788

Democracy North Carolina. "July 1995—Hog Money Pollutes NC General Assembly." Democracy NC. Accessed January 2, 2023. https://democracync.org/research/july -1995-hog-money-pollutes-nc-general-assembly/

Democracy North Carolina. "NC Hog Industry History." Accessed January 2, 2023. https://democracync.org/reports/researchreports/Hog%20Money/nchogindustry history.html

Donham, Kelley J., Steven Wing, David Osterberg, Jan L. Flora, Carol Hodne, Kendall M. Thu, and Peter S. Thorne. "Community Health and Socioeconomic Issues Surrounding Concentrated Animal Feeding Operations." *Environmental*

*Health Perspectives* 115, no. 2 (February 2007): 317–20. https://doi.org/10.1289/ehp .8836

Driscoll, Adam, and Nicholas Theis. "'Not in Our Water!': Environmental Resistance in Rural Wisconsin." *Journal of Rural Studies* 79 (October 2020): 34–44. https://doi .org/10.1016/j.jrurstud.2020.08.018

EARTHJUSTICE. "Re: Complaint Under Title VI of the Civil Rights Act of 1964, 42 U.S.C. § 2000d, 40 C.F.R. Part 7," September 3, 2014. https://earthjustice.org/sites /default/files/files/North-Carolina-EJ-Network-et-al-Complaint-under-Title-VI. pdf

Edwards, Bob, and Anthony E. Ladd. "Environmental Justice, Swine Production and Farm Loss in North Carolina." *Sociological Spectrum* 20, no. 3 (July 2000): 263–90. https://doi.org/10.1080/027321700405054

"EJ Summit | NCEJN." Accessed January 2, 2023. https://ncejn.org/ej-summit/

Engleman Lado, Marianne. "No More Excuses: Building a New Vision of Civil Rights Enforcement in the Context of Environmental Justice." *University of Pennsylvania Journal of Law and Social Change* 22, no. 4 (2019): 281–331. https://scholarship.law .upenn.edu/jlasc/vol22/iss4/2/.

Environmental Transformation Movement of Flint. "What Are Environmental Justice & Restorative Practices?" What are Environmental Justice and Restorative Practices. Accessed January 14, 2023. https://www.etmflint.org/ej-rp-defined

Exchange Project. "Warren County—Town of Afton | Exchange Project." Exchange Project, Real People—Real Stories. Accessed January 14, 2023. https://exchange project.unc.edu/real_people/afton_overview/

Fears, Darryl, and Dennis. "'This Is Environmental Racism': How a Protest in a Black N.C. Farming Town Nearly 40 Years Ago Sparked a National Movement." *Washington Post.* Accessed January 14, 2023. https://www.washingtonpost.com /climate-environment/interactive/2021/environmental-justice-race/

Fry, Jillian P., Linnea I. Laestadius, Clare Grechis, Keeve E. Nachman, and Roni A. Neff. "Investigating the Role of State and Local Health Departments in Addressing Public Health Concerns Related to Industrial Food Animal Production Sites." *PLoS ONE* 8, no. 1 (January 30, 2013): e54720. https://doi.org/10.1371/journal.pone.0054720

Fry, Jillian P., Linnea I. Laestadius, Clare Grechis, Keeve E. Nachman, and Roni A. Neff. "Investigating the Role of State Permitting and Agriculture Agencies in Addressing Public Health Concerns Related to Industrial Food Animal Produc- tion." *PLoS ONE* 9, no. 2 (February 24, 2014): e89870. https://doi.org/10.1371 /journal.pone.0089870

Galarraga, Joseph, Niya Khanjar, Isabelle Berman, Jonanthan Hall, Camryn Edwards, Samuel Bara-Garcia, Coline Bodenreider, et al. "Environmental Injustice and Industrial Chicken Farming in Delaware." *NEW SOLUTIONS: A Journal of Environmental and Occupational Health Policy* 31, no. 4 (February 2022): 441–51. https://doi.org/10.1177/10482911211052944

Guidry, Virginia T., Sarah M. Rhodes, Courtney G. Woods, Devon J. Hall, and Jessica L. Rinsky. "Connecting Environmental Justice and Community Health:

Effects of Hog Production in North Carolina." *North Carolina Medical Journal* 79, no. 5 (September 2018): 324–28. https://doi.org/10.18043/ncm.79.5.324

Hall, Jonathan, Joseph Galarraga, Isabelle Berman, Camryn Edwards, Niya Khanjar, Lucy Kavi, Rianna Murray, Kristen Burwell-Naney, Chengsheng Jiang, and Sacoby Wilson. "Environmental Injustice and Industrial Chicken Farming in Maryland." *International Journal of Environmental Research and Public Health* 18, no. 21 (October 20, 2021): 11039. https://doi.org/10.3390/ijerph182111039

Hamed, Mubarak, Thomas Johnson, and Kathleen Miller. *The Impacts of Animal Feeding Operations on Rural Land Values.* 1999. Report presented to the Saline County Study Steering Committee, May 1999. https://www.researchgate.net /publication/258399091_The_Impacts_of_Animal_Feeding_Operations_on _Rural_Land_Values

Harun, S. M. Rafael, and Yelena Ogneva-Himmelberger. "Distribution of Industrial Farms in the United States and Socioeconomic, Health, and Environmental Characteristics of Counties." *Geography Journal* 2013 (2013): 385893. https://doi .org/10.1155/2013/385893

Heinzen, Tarah. "Recent Developments in the Quantification and Regulation of Air Emissions from Animal Feeding Operations." *Current Environmental Health Reports* 2, no. 1 (March 2015): 25–32. https://doi.org/10.1007/s40572-014-0038-4

Herriges, J. A., S. Secchi, and B. A. Babcock. "Living with Hogs in Iowa: The Impact of Livestock Facilities on Rural Residential Property Values." *Land Economics* 81, no. 4 (November 1, 2005): 530–45. https://doi.org/10.3368/le.81.4.530

Horton, Rachel Avery, Steve Wing, Stephen W. Marshall, and Kimberly A. Brownley. "Malodor as a Trigger of Stress and Negative Mood in Neighbors of Industrial Hog Operations." *American Journal of Public Health* 99, no. S3 (November 2009): S610–15. https://doi.org/10.2105/AJPH.2008.148924

Humane Society of the United States. "An HSUS Report: The Implications of Farm Animal-Based Bioenergy Production." Washington, D.C.: Humane Society of the United States, 2009.

Institute of Medicine, Committee on Environmental Justice. "1, Introduction and Executive Summary." In *Toward Environmental Justice: Research, Education, and Health Policy Needs.* Washington, D.C.: National Academies Press, 1999. https:// www.ncbi.nlm.nih.gov/books/NBK100867

Johnston, Jill, and Lara Cushing. "Chemical Exposures, Health, and Environmental Justice in Communities Living on the Fenceline of Industry." *Current Environmental Health Reports* 7, no. 1 (March 2020): 48–57. https://doi.org/10.1007/s40572 -020-00263-8

Kelly-Reif, Kaitlin, and Steve Wing. "Urban-Rural Exploitation: An Underappreciated Dimension of Environmental Injustice." *Journal of Rural Studies* 47 (October 2016): 350–58. https://doi.org/10.1016/j.jrurstud.2016.03.010

Khanjar, Niya, Jonathan Hall, Joseph Galarraga, Isabelle Berman, Camryn Edwards, Daniel Polsky, Rianna Murray, Lucy Kavi, Julie Thompson, and Sacoby Wilson. "Environmental Justice and the Mississippi Poultry Farming

Industry." *Environmental Justice* 15, no. 4 (August 1, 2022): 235–45. https://doi
.org/10.1089/env.2020.0045

La Londe, Kyle W. "Who Wants to Be an Environmental Justice Advocate? Options
for Bringing an Environmental Justice Complaint in the Wake of Alexander v.
Sandoval." *Boston College Environmental Affairs Law Review* 31, no. 1 (2004): 27–60.

Lenhardt, Julia, and Yelena Ogneva-Himmelberger. "Environmental Injustice in the
Spatial Distribution of Concentrated Animal Feeding Operations in Ohio."
*Environmental Justice* 6, no. 4 (August 2013): 133–39. https://doi.org/10.1089/env
.2013.0023

"Let's Put a Foot in the Revolving Door." *Wilmington Star News.* Accessed January 2,
2023. https://www.starnewsonline.com/story/news/2001/08/08/lets-put-a-foot
-in-the-revolving-door/30484453007/

Mirabelli, Maria C., Steve Wing, Stephen W. Marshall, and Timothy C. Wilcosky.
"Race, Poverty, and Potential Exposure of Middle-School Students to Air
Emissions from Confined Swine Feeding Operations." *Environmental Health
Perspectives* 114, no. 4 (April 2006): 591–96. https://doi.org/10.1289/ehp.8586

North Carolina Environmental Justice Network. "CAFOs | NCEJN." CAFOs.
Accessed January 15, 2023. https://ncejn.org/cafos/

North Carolina Environmental Justice Network. "Defining Environmental Justice."
Accessed January 14, 2023. https://ncejn.wordpress.com/ej-toolbox/defining
-environmental-justice/

Pew Commission on Industrial Farm Animal Production. "Putting Meat on the Table:
Industrial Farm Animal Production in America," April 29, 2008. https://www
.pewtrusts.org/en/research-and-analysis/reports/0001/01/01/putting-meat-on
-the-table

*Right to Harm: A Public Health Crisis Too Big to Ignore*, n.d. https://righttoharm.film/

Slatin, Craig, and Madeleine Kangsen Scammell. "'No Justice, No Peace' and the
Right to Self-Determination: An Interview with Gary Grant and Naeema
Muhammed of the North Carolina Environmental Justice Network." *NEW
SOLUTIONS: A Journal of Environmental and Occupational Health Policy* 24, no. 2
(August 2014): 203–29. https://doi.org/10.2190/NS.24.2.f

Smith, Sean. "How Safe Are the Workers Who Process Our Food?" *Monthly Labor
Review*, July 31, 2017. https://doi.org/10.21916/mlr.2017.19

Son, Ji-Young, Rebecca L. Muenich, Danica Schaffer-Smith, Marie Lynn Miranda,
and Michelle L. Bell. "Distribution of Environmental Justice Metrics for Exposure
to CAFOs in North Carolina, USA." *Environmental Research* 195 (April 2021):
110862. https://doi.org/10.1016/j.envres.2021.110862

Sorg. "Smithfield Loses Its Third Hog Nuisance Case, Jury Awards Plaintiffs $473
Million in Damages." *The Pulse*, August 3, 2018. https://pulse.ncpolicywatch.org
/2018/08/03/smithfield-loses-its-third-hog-nuisance-case-jury-awards-plaintiffs
-473-million-in-damages/#sthash.A2vwovLv.dpbs

Stuesse, Angela, and Nathan T. Dollar. "Who Are America's Meat and Poultry
Workers?" *Economic Policy Institute* (blog), September 24, 2020. https://www.epi
.org/blog/meat-and-poultry-worker-demographics/

Tajik, M., N. Muhammad, A. Lowman, K. Thu, S. Wing, and G. Grant. "Impact of Odor from Industrial Hog Operations on Daily Living Activities." *NEW SOLUTIONS: A Journal of Environmental and Occupational Health Policy* 18, no. 2 (August 2008): 193–205. https://doi.org/10.2190/NS.18.2.i

United Church of Christ Commission for Racial Justice. "Toxic Wastes and Race in the United States," 1987. https://www.ucc.org/wp-content/uploads/2020/12/ToxicWastesRace.pdf

United States Department of Agriculture. "Census of Agriculture." USDA National Agricultural Statistics Service Census of Agriculture. Accessed January 2, 2023. https://www.nass.usda.gov/AgCensus/

Upshaw, Vaughn Mamlin, and Melva Fager Okun. "A Model Approach for Developing Effective Local Public Health Policies: A North Carolina County Responds to Large-Scale Hog Production." *Journal of Public Health Management and Practice* 8, no. 5 (September 2002): 44–54, https://doi.org/10.1097/00124784-200209000-00006.

US Environmental Protection Agency (EPA), OP. "Learn about Environmental Justice." Overviews and Factsheets, February 13, 2015. https://www.epa.gov/environmentaljustice/learn-about-environmental-justice

Weida, William J. "Considering the Rationales for Factory Farming." Environmental Health Impacts of CAFOs: Anticipating Hazards-Searching for Solutions, 2004. https://sraproject.org/wp-content/uploads/2017/10/foundationsofsand.pdf

Wilson, Sacoby M., Frank Howell, Steve Wing, and Mark Sobsey. "Environmental Injustice and the Mississippi Hog Industry." *Environmental Health Perspectives* 110, no. Suppl 2 (April 2002): 195–201. https://doi.org/10.1289/ehp.02110s2195

Wing, S., D. Cole, and G. Grant. "Environmental Injustice in North Carolina's Hog Industry." *Environmental Health Perspectives* 108, no. 3 (March 2000): 225–31. https://doi.org/10.1289/ehp.00108225

Wing, Steve. "Social Responsibility and Research Ethics in Community-Driven Studies of Industrialized Hog Production." *Environmental Health Perspectives* 110, no. 5 (May 2002): 437–44. https://doi.org/10.1289/ehp.02110437

Wing, Steve, Gary Grant, Merle Green, and Chris Stewart. "Community Based Collaboration for Environmental Justice: South-East Halifax Environmental Reawakening." *Environment and Urbanization* 8, no. 2 (1996): 129–40.

Wing, Steve, Rachel Avery Horton, Naeema Muhammad, Gary R. Grant, Mansoureh Tajik, and Kendall Thu. "Integrating Epidemiology, Education, and Organizing for Environmental Justice: Community Health Effects of Industrial Hog Operations." *American Journal of Public Health* 98, no. 8 (August 2008): 1390–97. https://doi.org/10.2105/AJPH.2007.110486

Wing, Steve, and Jill Johnston. "Industrial Hog Operations in North Carolina Disproportionately Impact African-Americans, Hispanics and American Indians." Unpublished, August 29, 2014.

# CHAPTER 8

# Industrial Farm Animal Production and the Law

N. William Hines

## I. Introduction: Legally, What Exactly Is a CAFO?

The term "CAFO" is an acronym for a modern industrialized agricultural practice described generally in a federal statute as a "concentrated animal feeding operation." This four-word phrase entered the legal vocabulary in 1972 when Congress enacted the Clean Water Act (CWA).[1] In the CWA, Congress expressly declared that "concentrated animal feeding operations" were "Point Sources" of potential water pollution and subjected them to direct federal regulation. This chapter will explain why this early promise of active federal involvement in the regulation of CAFOs did not occur and how state and local regulation has also failed adequately to control pollution emanating from CAFOs in the places where they are most numerous, to the great detriment of neighbors.

CAFOs are a relatively recent development in American agriculture. They are the result of a nationwide shift to industrial agricultural practices in the latter years of the twentieth century. The farming trend toward feeding large concentrations of animals in tightly confined spaces started in the cattle industry. In the 1960s, large open-air cattle feedlots began popping up around the more arid parts of the country, particularly in the desert Southwest. Economies of scale produced feed-lots holding tens of thousands of cattle. The huge cattle feedlot at issue in the iconic nuisance case, *Spur Industries, Inc. v. Del E. Webb Dev Co.*,[2] provides a good example of the conflict between this type of CAFO and its close neighbors. Spur Industries was feeding 30,000 head of cattle just across the road from Sun City, a rapidly growing retirement community being built by the Webb company. The dust, noise, insects, and odor spilling over from the feedlot severely affected the quality of life experienced by Sun City residents, ultimately leading to a public nuisance lawsuit that Webb won. Nevertheless, the Arizona court ordered Webb to reimburse Spur Industries for the costs they incurred in relocating their feedlot.

In the 1970s, farmers all over the nation started to industrialize their farming practices in producing hogs, chickens, turkeys, and eggs. The big difference between these feeding operations and the open-air cattle feedlots described above was that large numbers of these animals were confined together indoors in facilities specially designed to promote feeding efficiency. The average Iowa hog CAFO, for example, annually feeds around 4,500 hogs indoors.[3] Today, this type of hog CAFO dominates the countryside in a number of US states. These year-round animal-feeding confinements enable farmers to deliver feed and water more effectively and eliminate concerns for such external factors as the local climate and unpredictable weather changes.[4]

Because most litigation over CAFOs involves the indoor feeding of confined hogs, this chapter will focus primarily on the public health and environmental problems caused by hog CAFOs. To be sure, other types of industrial agriculture can also produce serious harms to the environment and particularly to neighboring land owners. Poultry CAFOs, intensive dairy operations, and egg production generate legal actions by regulators and neighbors to correct harmful externalities, but none of these industrial agricultural practices come close to creating the level of legal activity that hog CAFOs do. Also, this chapter will pay close attention to special legislation and nuisance litigation by neighbors in Iowa and North Carolina, the nation's two leading producers of pork products.

Finally, this chapter will seek to explain why the seemingly ambitious federal regulatory initiatives of the CWA and Clean Air Act (CAA), plus expanding state environmental regulation, have failed to produce the level of legal control required to prevent modern hog CAFOs from causing damaging water and air pollution and nuisance harms that can seriously disturb the quality of rural life experienced by neighbors.

## II.   What Is the Crucial Problem Facing US Hog CAFOs?

By far the biggest problem faced by American hog CAFOs is how to dispose of the huge volume of wet animal wastes these large numbers of confined hogs produce. To grasp the scale of the problem, consider this: Iowa has a population of roughly 3 million people but annually produces over 23 million hogs. These hogs generate wet animal wastes equivalent to the human sewage that would be produced by 168 million people.[5] How to safely dispose of these potentially dangerous animal wastes is the main issue faced by hog CAFOs today.

The threats CAFOs can pose to the health, property rights, and general well-being of neighboring landowners, whether the neighbors live on farmsteads or in rural residences, are well described and documented in numerous public health and environmental studies, journalism reports of disastrous spills,[6] and recently litigated nuisance cases.[7] Liquified animal wastes leaking from CAFO waste storage structures or escaping in runoff from ground-spreading practices can occasionally pollute nearby surface waters or contaminate local groundwater aquifers.[8] By far the most common problem adversely affecting neighbors, however, is severe corruption of the ambient air shared with a nearby CAFO.[9] Air pollutants typically emitted by hog CAFOs include annoying airborne particulate matter, sulfur dioxide, ammonia, methane, antibiotic residues, and various pathogens. These unsavory emissions create a vile odor that can rise to the level that simply drives neighbors from their homes.[10] Neighbors forced to endure this odor have described it as a pungent combination of rotten eggs and concentrated battery acid.[11] In recent litigation in North Carolina, this terrible odor was described by one witness to appear as a "plume" or cloud that invaded their home with a sickening stench.[12]

Over the years, government efforts to control the possible pollutants escaping from the nation's growing number of hog CAFOs produced many new statutes and reams of administrative regulations.[13] That being so, a curious reader may wonder: With so many layers of federal, state, and local regulation of CAFOs to protect public health concerns and promote environmental quality, why is there such a heavy emphasis placed on private nuisance law in this chapter?

The answer is that public regulation may be working fairly well to protect general public health and environmental quality in most states, but such general regulations do not ensure that neighbors close to large hog CAFOs will not suffer severe nuisance harms. Particularly in states with the most hog CAFOs, and in other states aggressively competing to increase the numbers of hogs raised in their state, public regulation has proved ineffective in ensuring that neighbors of hog CAFOs can have comfortable enjoyment of their property.[14] In those states, neighbors aggrieved by the pollution escaping from a nearby hog CAFO often find that a private nuisance lawsuit against the offending CAFO is their only viable legal recourse to protect their property rights and their family's well-being.[15]

Historically, traditional nuisance law has offered reliable and effective relief from unreasonable invasions of neighbors' property rights.[16] Today, however, nuisance law itself is under attack in a few states seeking to gain a competitive edge in attracting more CAFOs. In a few states, updated right-to-farm laws already on the books are designed to exempt or otherwise insulate CAFOs from neighbors' nuisance lawsuits.[17] Further legislative efforts to weaken neighbors' rights to bring nuisance claims against CAFOs are clearly on the horizon.

## III. How to Safely and Properly Dispose of Animal Waste

In the absence of effective federal, state, or local regulation, what commonly troubles neighbors most about living next to a CAFO are the extremely unpleasant spillover effects from the prevailing method CAFO operators use for disposing of the extraordinarily large volume of wet animal wastes CAFOs regularly generate.[18] Today the standard method for managing and disposing of the huge amounts of animal wastes produced by the nation's CAFOs relies on a similar practice used to dispose of household sewage in cities during the Roman Empire two thousand years ago. In Roman times, household wastes were simply emptied into an open public sewer from which they were ultimately either dumped into a pit or discharged into the nearest waterway.[19] Until the middle of the nineteenth century, this type of primitive waste disposal method was widely used in the United States to dispose of fluid household wastes in rural America.[20] Before modern public health regulations required all rural residents with running water to install a government-certified septic system, rural residents simply ran an external pipe carrying their household wastewater downhill to a low place called a "cesspool,"[21] where it collected and gradually decomposed. I was raised on a Kansas farmstead during this era, and our household used this simple, but dirty, wastewater disposal system. We kids were frequently warned to stay away from the cesspool because it was beyond nasty.

This method for dealing with rural human wastes has not been legal anywhere in the United States for over 50 years.[22] CAFO operators, however, are still routinely allowed to employ an analogue to this crude practice to dispose of the large amounts of animal wastes they produce, adding only a final step of periodically emptying their modern cesspools by spreading or spraying the partly decomposed manure slurry on local farm fields as fertilizer.[23] As noted earlier, the big difference between the centuries-old method for dealing with household wastes in rural America and the current practice for disposing of the massive amount of animal wastes produced by hog CAFOs today is mostly a matter of scale.[24] An average-sized hog can produce up to eight times more urine and feces than does the average-sized human being.[25] The typical CAFO feeds thousands of hogs, dwarfing the waste load produced by a single human household.[26]

Here is how wet animal wastes are disposed of today by virtually every US hog CAFO. First, the animals' urine and feces are regularly hosed off with wash water and drained through a slotted floor in the confinement building. This smelly slurry of animal wastes and wash water is collected in an on-site holding tank below floor level. When this tank becomes full, its contents are flushed out and piped to an outdoor waste storage basin or impoundment some distance downhill (euphemistically called in the trade a "lagoon"), where it slowly decomposes. Because the lagoon is typically open to the air, however, the decomposition process is much slower than what takes place anaerobically in a typical rural septic tank. Also, unlike a septic tank, there is no provision made for liquids created by decomposition to drain away. To the contrary, any liquid wastes leaking from the lagoon or otherwise escaping into the local environment pose an environmental disaster for the public and for neighbors. Finally, before the lagoon overflows, the CAFO operator periodically pumps out the liquified manure and spreads it or sprays it on nearby farm fields as a natural fertilizer.

Currently, across the United States, this primitive waste disposal practice is the almost universal method for disposing of animal wastes produced by hog CAFOs.[27] It is obviously favored by CAFOs because it is the easiest and most cost-effective method for handling the disposal of such a high volume of animal wastes. It is the readily predictable impact of this conventional practice for disposing of animal wastes that make even well-managed CAFOs so objectional to nearby neighbors. A CAFO's close neighbors do not want to suffer the possible groundwater pollution or endure the regular saturation of the neighborhood air with a vile combination of particulate matter, noxious airborne chemicals and pathogens, and a pungent odor. Thus, unless a CAFO's neighbors afflicted by these negative externalities have access to some form of legal protection for their property rights, the uncontrollable side effects of this standard practice for the disposal of animal wastes can make their lives utterly miserable, particularly under unfavorable wind or other weather conditions.[28]

## IV. Why Is Federal Regulation of the Effluents and Emissions Discharged by Hog CAFOs Not Effective to Protect Neighbors?

If one were to review the lengthy sections of the federal CWA[29] and CAA,[30] as well as the voluminous regulations issued under them,[31] it would look like there is a massive amount of federal regulatory activity directly affecting CAFOs that are large enough to produce significant environmental harm. The reality on the ground, however, is quite different. Although the CWA expressly includes CAFOs in the US Environmental Protection Agency's (EPA's) responsibility to control potential "point sources" of water pollution,[32] for the most part, the EPA has delegated the direct regulation of CAFOs to state water quality control programs, and the combined federal/state regulation of CAFOs has been anything but aggressive.[33] In 2003, the EPA estimated that there were over 238,000 CAFOs operating in the United States. As of the latest report in 2018, EPA estimated that only 7,000 of the CAFOs operated with permits issued under the National Pollutant Discharge Elimination System (NPDES).

The CAA entails a similar delegation of program authority to state regulators to use the mandated State Implementation Plans to implement the national standards set forth in the act.[34] The definition of potential "stationary sources" of air pollution in the CAA does not specifically include CAFOs,[35] as the definition of "point sources" does in the CWA.[36] Thus, general federal regulation of air quality simply does not affect most of the nation's hundreds of thousands of known CAFOs. Furthermore, environmental experts claim that only a small fraction of the CAFOs in the United States are operating under any type of federal or state permit. Perhaps more disturbing, the identity and the precise location of most of the unregulated CAFOs are not even known to the EPA or to state regulators.[37]

### A. The Clean Water Act

The Clean Water Act was adopted with much fanfare in 1972 partly because it originally called for eventual attainment of a national policy of "No Discharge" of pollutants to US waters by 1985.[38] The act also set forth an intermediate goal of making all US waters "fishable and swimmable" by July 1, 1983.[39] The CWA has been amended several times over the years, and the extensive regulations promulgated under the act have been frequently revised, often as a result of legal challenges from industry groups or environmental advocates.[40] Successful suits by environmental advocates have served to tighten regulatory control over polluters,[41] but most of the changes in the CWA and its regulations resulted from victories in suits by industry groups.[42] These changes tended to reduce or delay federal requirements, weaken enforcement powers, and extend the law's many attainment deadlines.[43] Needless to say, after almost 50 years on the books, the CWA's ambitious goals have never come close to being attained, although the quality of the nation's waterways is noticeably improved.[44]

Structurally, the CWA divides all water pollution sources into two categories, "point sources" and "nonpoint sources." Point sources are defined as discrete locations from which discharges of potential water pollutants originate.[45] The CWA calls for close regulation of all point sources, initially to control them and ultimately to eliminate them.[46] New point sources are subject to the strictest regulation.[47] They are required to install the "best available" water pollution control technology before the regulations allow them to commence operation.[48] Most existing point sources were industrial or municipal and subject to increased federal regulation over the years as pollution control technology improved.[49] Not so for CAFOs. This is because the CWA requires federal regulation only of large-scale CAFOs. Medium and small CAFOs require federal regulation only when they discharge animal wastes directly into nearby bodies of water, which is rarely the case. Most of the nation's CAFOs are officially medium or small in size and therefore fall below this federal regulatory floor.

Nonpoint sources are primarily rural in nature and involve various types of open-land runoff carrying pollutants to nearby waterways.[50] In the CWA, adoption of practical strategies to control nonpoint sources was basically left for future development. Unfortunately, after almost a half-century, systematic controls over nonpoint sources have yet to emerge. Runoff from agricultural land has long been by far the largest contributor to the nation's water pollution burden from nonpoint sources.[51]

The CWA expressly designates CAFOs as "point sources"[52] of potential water pollution, and above a specified size, all CAFOs discharging animal wastes are required to secure a permit from the NPDES.[53] The regulations under the act define whether a CAFO is large, medium, or small on the basis of the number of animal units they feed at maximum capacity for at least 45 days per year.[54] For example: a CAFO feeding hogs weighing 55 pounds or more is considered a large CAFO under the regulations if it feeds over 2,500 hogs, a hog CAFO is medium-sized if it feeds 750–2,499 hogs of the requisite size, and a hog CAFO is small if it feeds 749 such hogs or fewer.[55] Only large CAFOs are required to secure NPDES permits.[56] Medium-sized CAFOs may or may not require NPEDS permits, depending on several factors relating to their location, operation, and waste disposal systems.[57] Small CAFOs are not expressly mentioned in the regulations, and therefore, generally they are not required to operate under NPDES permits unless they discharge animal wastes directly into waters of the United States or have other problematic characteristics that threaten the achievement or maintenance of local water quality standards.[58]

The EPA promulgated and published major regulations dealing with CAFOs in 1974, in 2003, and again in 2008.[59] All of these regulations were challenged in court, either by environmental organizations or by CAFO industry groups.[60] In all three instances of litigation, the resulting judicial decisions caused the EPA to withdraw or rewrite some of the proposed regulations. The most notable EPA legal setback suffered through adverse court decisions in these cases included overturning new rules that required all CAFOs, or at least all CAFOs with the "potential" or "proposing" to pollute, to operate under a NPDES permit.[61] Three other litigation losses included rejection of new rules that (1) required manure storage lagoons to withstand a 100-year, 24-hour rain event; (2) treated runoff from land on which liquefied manure was applied as a "point source" of pollution instead of exempt "agricultural stormwater runoff"; and (3) added water quality–based effluent limits (WQBELs) to CAFO permits in all cases where ordinary effluent limits were insufficient to protect local water quality standards.[62]

Thus, what appears on the surface as systematic, intense, and direct federal enforcement of the CWA against CAFOs is simply a mirage. Over the years, the EPA has engaged in a massive delegation to state water pollution control agencies of the primary regulatory authority for issuing and enforcing NPEDS permits to CAFOs within their state.[63] It has also offloaded to the states primary responsibility for regulating CAFOs not required to hold NPDES permits. Currently, 47 of the 50 states have received this delegated regulatory authority.[64] Only in Massachusetts, New Mexico, and New Hampshire are NPDES permits issued by the EPA itself through its regional offices.[65] In addition, the EPA has more or less abandoned the control of nonpoint source of water pollution to state control, and very few states exercise much regulation over them, even though they are now conceded to be the primary source of lowered water quality in the nation's lakes, rivers, streams, and coastal waters.[66]

In issuing NPDES permits, both federal and state regulators must apply EPA-promulgated CAFO effluent guidelines, best waste disposal practices, and nutrient management requirements, and any permitted discharge of pollutants must meet relevant local water quality standards.[67] Unlike the radical "No Discharge" policy of the original CWA, however, the regulations implementing effluent guidelines for CAFOs expressly consider economic practicality equally with environmental security, with the prevalent standard being "Best Conventional . . . Technology."[68] Best conventional technology for CAFOs as defined by EPA and state regulators is the lagoon storage/land spreading practice described earlier.[69] Similarly, the best available technology (BAT) for new CAFOs is limited to "best available technology economically achievable," which also translates into the conventional waste disposal practice,[70] because no higher degree of animal waste treatment has ever proved economically practical or sustainable. This is a far cry from the secondary treatment routinely required of all municipal waste treatment plants regardless of size or the tertiary treatment required of many others. In short, the EPA's effluent guidelines for CAFOs bear little resemblance to the carefully calculated, science-based effluent standards the EPA established under the CWA and aggressively applies to industries, municipalities, and other known major point sources.

One important additional federal requirement for CAFOs is that all NPDES permits must ensure that an exposed animal waste storage lagoon can withstand a 24-hour, 25-year rain event without overflowing. Plus, the regulations limit the number of days a CAFO may spread animal wastes on farm fields, depending on the climate where the facility is located.[71] Another important regulatory requirement added more recently is that state-issued NPDES permits must include detailed nutrient management plans (NMPs) for storage and land disposal of animal wastes generated by regulated CAFOs.[72] The required NMPs must reflect national best practices for storing animal feces, urine, and process water, as well as for spreading or spraying liquified animal wastes on cropland or other open land.[73] The NMPs theoretically control the maximum amounts of animal wastes that can be spread or sprayed on cropland over set periods of time, consistent with the agronomic nutrient absorption rate of the soils on which the wastes are spread.[74] Because multiple variables affect the environmental safety of spreading animal wastes as fertilizer, the NMPs lack scientific precision. Adding to this uncertainty, CAFO operators are encouraged to experiment by trial and error to determine their land's actual agronomic absorption capacity.[75] Thus, the NMPs are very different from the rigorous regulatory requirements the EPA imposes on land spreading of potential water pollutants everywhere but in the agricultural sector.

Another wrinkle in the interpretation of the NMP regulations concerns storm water runoff from lands on which CAFO wastes have been spread or sprayed as fertilizer. Such runoff can seriously pollute nearby watercourses.[76] Regulations under the CWA, however, specifically exempt "agricultural stormwater discharge" from direct regulation as point sources.[77] Under the current regulations, if a CAFO is in full compliance with its approved NMP, stormwater runoff from land fertilized with animal wastes is not regarded as the discharge of a pollutant but is treated instead as an exempt "agricultural stormwater discharge."[78] The US Court of Appeals for the Second Circuit upheld this regulatory distinction in *Waterkeepers Alliance, Inc. v. EPA.*[79]

CAFO permits issued by states to whom the EPA has delegated NPDES permitting authority must conform to national standards for CAFO effluents and for acceptable nutrient management plans promulgated by the EPA.[80] The state-issued NPDES permits must also protect federal water quality standards established for state waterways.[81] State authorities, however, are granted a good deal of discretion in managing their NPDES permitting responsibilities.[82] This includes the ability to add state-based requirements to the permits, including more exacting siting restrictions, higher construction standards for facilities, stricter operating rules, and more detailed nutrient management plan requirements.[83] All additional state regulation, however, must be at least as strict as the applicable federal requirements.[84] As a result, most states combine federal requirements with supplemental state requirements and issue a standard unified permit for operating a CAFO to all confined feeding operations within the same size category.[85]

As to CAFOs below the 1,000-animal-units minimum, state regulators are authorized to establish effluent limitations based on their "Best Professional Judgment."[86] In exercising this discretion, state regulators are instructed to consider "the cost of achieving effluent reduction, the age of the equipment and the facility, the [waste disposal] process employed, the engineering aspects of the control techniques, the process changes, and non-water quality environmental impacts."[87]

It appears states vary a great deal in how assiduously they regulate medium and small CAFOs to prevent water pollution, but one thing they seem to have in common is that in exercising their "Best Professional Judgment," they regularly approve the conventional waste disposal practices of hog CAFOs as a perfectly acceptable method for disposing of huge amounts of animal waste. They also accept this waste disposal practice as BCT, "best control technology for conventional pollutants."[88] Federal regulatory approval is granted for the lagoon/ land spreading practice unless the CAFO's waste discharges can be demonstrated to reach nearby waters directly, or through an artificial discharge point or an interconnection between underground and surface waterways, or the CAFO is sited in a particularly sensitive location.[89] If any of these conditions are present, a case-by-case analysis is required to assess the environmental risk proposed by the CAFO's proposed waste management practices.[90]

One area where the states have the primary regulatory role under the CWA is in controlling pollution of groundwater, except in cases where a discharge from a CAFO can reach US waters via a direct hydrological connection to groundwater.[91] In such a case, a NPDES permit is required.[92] Otherwise, if a proposed CAFO is located in a region where groundwater aquifers are particularly vulnerable to becoming polluted from seepage from CAFO storage lagoons or by surface runoff from lands spread with liquefied manure, the permit issued to the CAFO by a state must provide additional restrictions designed to prevent groundwater pollution.[93] A fragile limestone substratum underlies the land surface in portions of several states with large CAFO populations. This type of subsurface formation, called karst substrata by geologists, is highly susceptible to fracturing and allowing seepage from lagoons and surface runoff to flow into groundwater aquifers, polluting them for long periods of time.[94] State officials generally should not issue CAFO permits for this type of land surface, but when a rare permit is issued, state regulators should routinely subject the permitted CAFO to the strictest waste management requirements and to regular monitoring to prevent groundwater pollution.[95]

## B.  The Clean Air Act

Like the CWA, the CAA divides its regulatory authority into two categories—"stationary sources" and "indirect sources," commonly referred to as "mobile sources."[96] Unlike the CWA, which expressly identifies CAFOs as potential "point sources" of water pollution,[97] the CAA has never classified CAFOs as stationary sources of air pollution. CAFOs clearly are not mobile sources of air pollution, so they are not subject to direct regulation under the CAA. Again, like the CWA, the CAA relies heavily on state regulation and enforcement to carry out its air pollution control mission.[98] The CAA requires new stationary sources of air pollution to use the best technology available to control their emissions,[99] but unfortunately, such a stringent requirement does not apply to new CAFOs. Thus, new CAFOs are not regulated in the same way the CAA controls emissions from other stationary sources, such as new factories, electric power plants, landfills, and other significant potential sources of air pollution.[100]

Similarly, in establishing ambient air quality standards for the nation's airsheds, the EPA published limits for only six airborne pollutants (particulates, ozone, sulfur dioxide, nitrogen dioxide, carbon monoxide, and lead).[101] Notably, the list does not include ammonia or methane, which are common pollutants in the emissions from CAFOs.[102] Also, because CAFOs are not treated as stationary sources, the introduction of numerous CAFOs into an airshed with high-quality air is not affected by the CAA requirement to "prevent significant deterioration."[103] This "no degradation" policy requires all stationary sources constructing new facilities in high-quality airsheds to obtain a permit and meet an emission standard of "lowest achievable emission rate" for the pollutants they emit.[104] Being exempt from this requirement is a big advantage for CAFOs because they are generally acknowledged to emit significant air pollutants that commonly include—besides obnoxious odors and some particulate matter—methane, hydrogen sulfide, ammonia, and possibly antibiotic-resistant bacteria and other pathogens.[105]

It is this inability to apply key elements of the CAA to CAFOs that led environmental groups and public health experts to argue that emissions from CAFOs are a significant source of air quality degradation in certain specific regions around the country. For this reason, it is contended that they should be regulated as stationary sources. Treating CAFOs as stationary sources is an additional proposal to the longstanding argument that ammonia and methane should be added to the list of criteria pollutants monitored in all air sheds.[106] Every time proposals to amend the CAA to increase the regulation of CAFOs emissions are brought forward, however, strong political resistance arises from farm states' representatives that stymies any action by Congress.[107] Without such an expansion of the CAA to designate CAFOs as stationary sources of air pollution and establish air quality standards for ammonia and methane, emissions from CAFOs are almost completely unregulated by the CAA. Although the CAA requires air quality monitoring for six listed air pollutants, it is my impression that emissions from CAFOs of any of the six regulated air pollutants are so localized, they can almost never rise to a level that exceeds established air quality thresholds for a region.[108] These pollutant thresholds are set in State Implementation Plans approved by the EPA for the regulation of air quality in designated regional airsheds.[109]

Currently, the EPA regulations do not authorize a reliable monitoring methodology for measuring harmful emissions escaping from CAFOs immediately into the ambient air around them.[110] Environmental advocates petitioned the EPA to urge the agency to directly regulate emissions from CAFOs like ammonia and methane, as well as develop practical emission monitoring techniques to focus on local air pollution issues caused by CAFOs.[111] Again, because of strenuous farm state representatives in Congress, no action is expected on this front for the foreseeable future.

## V.  Why Doesn't State Regulation of CAFOs Better Protect Neighbors?

### A.  Overview

As it relates to industrialized agricultural production of food animals and eggs, in most states, regulations to prevent potential environmental harms have evolved through three stages. In the 1940s, many states started adopting public health measures to stem the tide of pollutants in state waterways and the befouling of the ambient air their citizens had to breathe. These initial regulations were adopted by state health departments. They typically sought to promote voluntary compliance by polluters because they lacked effective enforcement powers. Over time, the legal responsibility for enforcing these pollution control regulations shifted to state departments of natural resources or to state environmental protection agencies, and thereafter, enforcement of the regulations gathered strength.[112]

In the 1960s, as enforcement of pollution control regulations began to adversely affect common farming practices, a "right-to-farm" movement swept the nation. By the mid-1970s, every state had some form of right-to-farm law that sought to exempt conventional farming practices from enforcement of antipollution regulations. The early right-to-farm laws were little more than codifications of the common law's denial of the benefits of nuisance law to persons who "came to the nuisance," so they sparked little litigation.

All of this regulation predated the advent of the modern hog CAFO. Because they were a new form of industrialized agriculture, it was unclear whether the original right-to-farm laws protected hog CAFOs from nuisance suits by neighbors harmed by the manner in which animal wastes were handled by a nearby hog CAFO. This uncertainty led legislatures in several states where hog CAFOs were proliferating to adopt a second generation of right-to-farm laws expressly written to insulate CAFOs from neighbors' nuisance lawsuits. These new laws took different forms, but what they had in common was a direct effort to reduce or eliminate the threat to CAFOs of neighbors bringing and winning nuisance lawsuits against them.

## B.   General Environmental Regulation

Long before CAFOs became the dominant method in the United States for raising most types of food animals and for producing eggs, all states had adopted state-level regulatory regimes for controlling water pollution and air pollution within the state.[113] These regulations typically started out as the domain of the state health department, and what regulation occurred was focused primarily on public health concerns.[114] Early regulation of public health threats in the rural countryside was not characterized by strenuous enforcement, even against egregious polluters.[115] In the 1960s and 1970s, most states responded to the so-called environmental movement by upgrading their environmental protection laws to extend their reach beyond public health threats to broader environmental quality concerns, and they toughened their enforcement measures against violators.[116] Typically, the new laws established minimum standards for water quality in state waters and ambient air quality within state airsheds, but these statewide regulations were typically regarded as the regulatory floor.[117] Local governments were encouraged to add more demanding regulations if they needed to respond to special threats to local water quality or air quality.[118]

The advent of the federal CWA and the CAA in the early 1970s dovetailed with these reform efforts and brought the states within a nationwide system of federally established effluent and emission control requirements, along with a set of national water quality standards and ambient air quality criteria. Except for the regulatory efforts necessitated by specific inclusion of CAFOs as point sources of water pollution in the CWA discussed earlier, very little of this general state environmental regulation was directed at the types of serious health and environmental problems CAFOs could cause their immediate rural neighbors. In part, this nonregulation was the result of the fact that any water pollution or air pollution generated by a CAFO stayed very local and did not enter a waterway to violate water quality standards or was never noticed in the monitoring of a regional airshed.[119] Even large CAFOs do not occupy very much land, so the air shed surrounding them is typically more than large enough, depending on wind conditions, to make it difficult to detect airborne pollutants very far from the borders of the CAFO site. More problematic, enforcement of these types of general environmental protection laws tended to be reactionary in nature; they came into play only after some sort of environmental disaster occurred.[120] State environmental agencies typically sought to remediate known pollution problems and to punish the perpetrators,[121] not to prevent them from happening in the first place.

As CAFOs proliferated starting in the 1990s, and partly in response to the delegation to states of federal NPDES permit issuance authority, states experiencing rapid growth in CAFOs began enacting specific legislation and promulgating administrative regulations governing the siting and operation of CAFOs, including requiring detailed manure management plans.[122] Also during this era, some states amended or added to their right-to-farm laws to erect legal protections for CAFOs against neighbors' nuisance suits.[123] In this section, an effort will be made to synthesize the laws and regulations affecting CAFOs in the 10 states with the largest number of regulated animal feeding operations.[124]

The statutes and regulations focused on CAFOs in these 10 states all cover most of the same general core topics, although not necessarily in this order: (1) basic information required in an application for a CAFO permit;[125] (2) design of the CAFO buildings;[126] (3) specifications for collection of animal wastes and storage basins;[127] (4) site setbacks from neighboring properties and from environmentally sensitive areas;[128] (5) construction standards for CAFO buildings;[129] (6) operating requirements;[130] (7) manure management plan, including monitoring of waste storage basins;[131] (8) standards for open land spreading of liquified manure, including setbacks from steep slopes, neighboring properties, parks, and water courses;[132] (9) protecting ground water quality, where relevant;[133] and (10) closure requirements.[134] In addition, many states have express requirements for notifying neighbors and certain public entities within a specified distance from the proposed site when an application for a CAFO permit is filed.[135] At least one state has considered requiring more extensive treatment of collected animal wastes where the CAFO is large enough to justify the technology investment, but it has not made much progress implementing this idea.[136]

Although public regulation of CAFOs among the states may focus on the same core issues, there are significant differences from state to state in the comprehensiveness of the regulations and how aggressively they are enforced with respect to some key regulatory provisions, many of which potentially affect the quality of life of CAFO neighbors. Most common differences among states concern requirements such as the extent of serious regulation applied to medium and small CAFOs,[137] distance of site setbacks from neighbors and sensitive areas,[138] degree of monitoring air quality within CAFO buildings and at the boundaries of the site,[139] level of monitoring of the capacity and stability of storage basins,[140] policing manure management plans,[141] and enforcement of setbacks and climatic restrictions on spreading liquified manure on farm fields.[142]

Between the two states with the largest number of hogs in CAFOs, Iowa and North Carolina, Iowa stands out for having relatively weak state laws and regulations governing the approval, siting, operation, and monitoring of CAFOs. North Carolina, on the other hand, since the late 1990s, has enforced a moratorium on new hog CAFOs unless they provide advanced treatment of hog wastes they generate. Existing CAFOs, however, have been allowed to expand without close regulatory oversight. In addition, both states have experienced a great deal of pressure from the CAFO industry to amend their right-to-farm laws to nullify parts of their nuisance law enforcement with respect to CAFOs to make the state more attractive for investment in animal feeding operations.[143]

## 1.  Iowa's CAFO Regulations

In administering its regulation of CAFOs, Iowa uses an increasingly controversial "Master Matrix," which sets out a 44-point system to evaluate whether an applicant is legally entitled to receive a CAFO permit.[144] Under Iowa regulations, the strictness of regulations applied to CAFOs depends on their size.[145] CAFOs feeding 2,500 or more hogs are the most tightly regulated, medium-sized CAFOs feeding 1,250 to 2,499 hogs are less strictly regulated, and small CAFOs feeding 1,249 hogs or fewer are subject to the least regulation.[146] The Iowa Master Matrix reportedly yields approximately a 97% approval rate for first-time CAFO applicants of all sizes, and it is administered by the Iowa Department of Natural Resources (DNR) under a practice that ensures that the few failing applicants are effectively coached by its staff to be sure to succeed the next time they apply.[147]

Another problem with the administration of the Iowa Master Matrix system in practice is that the DNR handles the approval of each CAFO separately based on its ownership. So long as each CAFO is owned by a different person or entity, there is no restriction preventing several CAFOs from locating together on a small tract of land owned by one farm family.[148] Iowa hog farmers have learned how to game the Master Matrix system by proposing sequential approval for multiple lightly regulated small- or medium-sized CAFOs owned by LLCs in the names of different family members, with all the CAFOs located close together on a single-family farm. Such clusters of CAFOs are granted a series of separate permits,[149] even though the combined pollution threat these separate small lightly regulated CAFOs pose for neighbors can be much greater than the threat that would be posed by a single more tightly regulated large CAFO in the same location.

The Iowa Master Matrix system is also administered in a manner that relegates local governments to a mere advisory role. County officials can strongly recommend against granting a specific CAFO permit,[150] but DNR officials are under no compulsion to accept the advice offered by local governments. Where such disagreements occur, the DNR permit authorities can and do disregard local advice in making a decision to approve a CAFO application recommended against by the county government where the CAFO is located.[151] In 2018, county officials, frustrated by being shut out of the CAFO approval process, proposed that the Iowa legislature adopt a temporary moratorium on new CAFO permits to allow time to review and upgrade the operation of the Master Matrix system.[152] Although renewed annually, this call for a moratorium has failed to gain legislative serious support.[153]

## 2. North Carolina's CAFO Regulations

North Carolina has long been a national leader in pork production. The state's generally favorable legal climate for CAFOs was altered dramatically, however, after the catastrophic collapse of a large waste storage lagoon in 1995. This disaster released 25 million gallons of decomposing hog wastes into the nearby New River, causing massive fish kills and contaminating popular recreational waters.[154] This highly publicized calamity led the state to adopt a moratorium on the approval of new CAFOs in 1997.[155] Shortly after this moratorium was adopted, Smithfield Foods, the state's largest hog processor , whose hogs for slaughter were supplied by thousands of hog CAFOs around the state under grower contracts with Smithfield Foods, entered into an agreement with the state under which it agreed to pay for all improved systems for the disposal of hog wastes that researchers at North Carolina State found to be effective and economically feasible. This seemingly vital step to improving CAFOs' system for disposing of hog wastes was never acted upon because the economic feasibility requirement was never met to Smithfield's satisfaction.[156]

Ten years later, North Carolina enacted the Swine Farm Environmental Performance Act of 2007,[157] which officially ended the moratorium, but the act essentially banned new hog CAFOs from using the traditional waste disposal system that relied on lagoons and land spreading of liquefied wastes. The new statute required all new hog CAFOs to adopt "environmentally Superior Technologies"[158] to dispose of wastes from hog CAFOs.

North Carolina's enactment of its 2007 Swine Farm Environmental Performance Act was the first and only time a state legislature recognized the environmental and social inadequacies of the conventional waste management practices of hog CAFOs and required all new hog CAFOs to adopt more environmentally and socially responsible animal waste management technology. North Carolina followed through on this effort to upgrade hog CAFOs waste disposal practices by creating the North Carolina State Animal and Poultry Waste Management Center to support development of the needed superior animal waste management technologies.[159] The center sent out a national request for proposals to researchers to submit proposals for developing and demonstrating superior waste management technologies to meet five criteria[160] specified by the center. The center's five criteria for a superior technology were:

1. Eliminates the discharge of animal waste to surface waters and groundwaters . . . ; 2. Substantially eliminates atmospheric emissions of ammonia; 3. Substantially eliminates the emission of odor that is detectable beyond the boundaries of the . . . land on which the [CAFO] is located; 4. Substantially eliminates the release of disease-transmitting vectors and airborne pathogens; and 5. Substantially eliminates nutrient and heavy metal contamination of soil and groundwater.[161]

It would be difficult to argue that these five criteria are not exactly the results that the public generally and neighbors in particular want from hog CAFOs. For any state with many hog CAFOs, these criteria form the basis of a sound new regulatory policy.

None of the proposed technologies proved to be the "magic bullet" the center hoped to discover, but not because none of them could do the job. Rather, the legislation requiring new hog CAFOs to use environmentally superior waste disposal technology contained an overriding requirement that severely limited its force—no matter how environmentally effective a new technology might be, it could not be imposed as a requirement on a new hog CAFO unless it was determined to be technically, operationally, and economically feasible for use by North Carolina hog farmers.[162] Most of the technologically innovative solutions proposed to the center relied on some type of aerobic or anaerobic digester, which can be expensive to install and operate, and for that reason they were deemed not economically feasible to install for use by even above-average-sized North Carolina hog CAFOs. It is worth noting that neither aerobic digesters nor anaerobic digesters are a new technology. They have been in use in other waste disposal contexts for generations, often to treat household wastes generated by small rural communities. The proposals received by the center involving the use of digesters were simply adaptations of the known technology for the safe disposal of hog wastes.[163]

North Carolina research seeking better methods for managing the safe and environmentally sound disposal of hog wastes produced an entirely different type of approach called "Super Soils/Terra Blue."[164] This technology directly treated the hog wastes in real time. First the liquid wastewater was separated from the solids via a primary treatment method, and then the solids were effectively processed to convert them into commercial fertilizer. The Super Soils technology clearly worked, but it was deemed much too expensive to be practical.

As of the last report, only two very large North Carolina hog CAFOs had successfully demonstrated the effectiveness of their newly developed waste disposal technology using digesters and gained state approval to construct and operate a new hog CAFO.[165] Over time, North Carolina's "technology forcing" regulations were also weakened gradually to the point that hog CAFOs are allowed to not only add hogs to existing facilities but also activate and expand idle facilities without making any improvements to their waste management systems.[166] Slowing down or stopping approval of new CAFOs in North Carolina was roundly condemned by the CAFO industry, but it apparently only slowed but did not stop steady growth in the number of hogs confined in North Carolina's CAFOs.[167]

### 3.  Other States' CAFO Regulations

Not all the other eight states with the largest CAFO numbers have chosen to join Iowa and North Carolina in their race to the regulatory bottom. A few states have become more aggressive in their regulatory efforts to prevent CAFOs from inflicting unreasonable harm on rural neighbors. Notably, two other top hog-producing states, Missouri and Minnesota, upgraded their state laws regulating CAFOs in 2019 and 2004, respectively, by adding major protections to neighboring property owners.[168] Missouri's 2019 legislation mandated all CAFOs regardless of size must operate with a state permit, required a detailed notice to neighbors of an application to build a new CAFO or expand an existing one, and clarified that the setback rules for surface application of liquified manure applied to third parties to whom the natural fertilizer is sold or donated.[169] Minnesota amended its right-to-farm law to limit its protection for hog CAFOs against neighbors' nuisance suits to operations housing fewer than 1,000 hogs.[170]

Due to space considerations, this chapter will not go into detail about the regulatory practices of those states that appear to be conscientiously engaged in improving their regulation of CAFOs. However, it is important to note that the experiences of Iowa and North Carolina foreshadow what could happen to CAFO regulation in those states should the political climate change to emphasize the economic importance of CAFOs and the states weaken their legislative and regulatory enforcement in ways intended to attract more CAFOs.

## VI.   What Role Do Local Governments Play in the Regulation of CAFOs to Protect Neighbors?

When states began enacting legislation to regulate water pollution and air quality in the 1960s, the statutes routinely established regulatory floors for acceptable water and air quality.[171] In adopting minimum statewide standards for water and air quality, most such environmental legislation expressly contemplated that counties and cities were free, and perhaps expected, to adopt stricter quality standards as necessary to meet local needs.[172] This general policy of allowing local governments to use their home-rule authority to enact water and air quality requirements stricter than minimum state standards is still the norm in most states. Starting in the 1990s, however, a few states, competing for new CAFOs to locate in their state, have dropped this laisse-faire posture and sought to remove from local governments all such regulatory authority at it relates to CAFOs.

Iowa was the first state to make this change, and surprisingly it was the result of a 1998 judicial decision. In *Goodell v. Humboldt County*,[173] the Iowa Supreme Court considered the enforceability of a set of air quality standards adopted by the county to detect air pollutants escaping from hog CAFOs. The county ordinance set maximum limits for carbon dioxide, hydrogen sulfide, methane, carbon monoxide, and ammonia, as monitored at the boundary of the hog CAFO. In ruling these regulations were not justified under the county's home rule powers, the court adopted a controversial "implied preemption" rule,[174] based on Iowa Code 657.11, which limited CAFOs' liability for private nuisance actions.[175] A forceful dissent pointed out that the new "implied preemption" analysis was blatantly inconsistent with the court's longstanding policy of seeking to reconcile challenged county or city home rule–based regulations with state law whenever possible.[176] The dissent could also have pointed out that the Iowa Code section cited by the majority opinion, 657.11, dealt with curtailing private nuisance suits and had nothing to do with public regulation by local governments. Nevertheless, the die was cast and an ambitious county scheme to regulate the effluents and emissions from local hog CAFOs was struck down as unconstitutional.[177]

Unsure of the durability of the court's "implied preemption" approach, CAFO supporters persuaded the Iowa General Assembly to adopt an express preemption amendment to the home rule statute making clear that local governments no longer had any authority to regulate the effluents or emissions emanating from livestock CAFOs.[178] This preemptive statute was upheld by the Iowa Supreme Court in the 2004 case, *Worth County Friends of Agriculture v. Worth County*.[179] The court stated, "Our legislature intended livestock production in Iowa to be governed by statewide regulation, not local regulation."[180]

In 2017, North Carolina followed Iowa's example and adopted a similar statute preempting all local regulation of livestock CAFOs.[181] The Missouri legislature also adopted a similar statutory preemption of local regulation of hog CAFOs in 2019.[182] The Missouri statute was challenged as unconstitutional in a case before the Missouri Supreme Court.[183]

Thus, the three top states nationally in hog production have legislatively banned any local regulation of livestock CAFOs, even regulations that are clearly addressing public health concerns. This preemption is a testament to the political power of the hog industry in those states.

Whether other states with large numbers of CAFOs will follow suit with preemptive legislation remains to be seen.

## VII.   What Protection from CAFOs' Harm Does Nuisance Law Provide to Neighbors?

Perhaps there was once a time in Anglo-American history when one landowner could engage in activities on his own land that inflicted severe harm upon a neighboring landowner without concern about incurring legal liability. But if such a time ever existed, it was in the very distant past. Law students in my property rights class study *William Aldred's Case*,[184] an English nuisance law decision in 1611. In this classic case, a landowner named Thomas Benton raised hogs on his land adjacent to Aldred's rural residence.[185] Benton erected a sizable hog sty immediately across the property line from Aldred's home, causing his hogs to congregate just outside Aldred's open windows, to Aldred's great discomfort.[186] Aldred brought a nuisance suit alleging that by gathering large numbers of hogs so close to his home, Benton's new sty seriously corrupted the air in and around his land, thereby committing a nuisance by unreasonably interfering with the use and enjoyment of his property.[187] The English appellate court agreed with Aldred and affirmed a lower court nuisance judgment against Benton for £40 in damages.[188] In its opinion, the English court expressly rejected Benton's impassioned argument that anyone who chooses to live in the rural countryside "ought not to have so delicate a nose, that he cannot bear the smell of hogs."[189] This argument is still regularly made today in US farm nuisance cases, usually without any greater success than it enjoyed in England over four centuries ago.[190]

Under US constitutional law, landowners' property rights are defined almost exclusively by state law.[191] Until the development of modern industrialized agriculture, particularly CAFOs, the historic legal limitation on land use posed by nuisance law (as applied in the 400-year-old *Aldred's* case described above) was universally recognized and enforced by state courts across the United States.[192] In the past half-century, however, economically powerful agricultural interests exerted political pressure on state legislatures to protect industrialized agricultural practices that might produce nuisance lawsuits by aggrieved neighbors. This was first done in the early 1980s through enactment of generic right-to-farm laws, adopted in one form or another by all 50 states.[193] More recently, a few states seeking to gain a competitive advantage in attracting CAFOs have enacted second-generation right-to-farm statutes purporting to grant CAFOs special protections from nuisance liability to neighbors.[194] Some of these newer statutes conferring special nuisance protections on CAFOs are still undergoing constitutional challenges,[195] so the end of this story is yet to be written, but the message is clear. When state legislatures set out to promote a favored type of industrialized agriculture within their state, they are willing to enact legislation reducing or eliminating traditional property rights of neighbors protected by nuisance law. Thus far, among the 50 states, only the Iowa Supreme Court has overturned such legislation designed to protect CAFOs, ruling both a general right-to-farm law[196] and a second-generation right-to-farm statute insulating CAFOs from nuisance liability were unconstitutional takings of neighbors' property rights without just compensation.[197]

The legal maxim "use your property so as not to injure the property of another"[198] has been an important principle in Anglo-American property law for nearly a millennium.[199] This nuisance principle is the source of the crucial private property right to be free from unreasonable harm inflicted by a neighbors' intrusive use of their property.[200] Every state in the United States recognizes and enforces nuisance law in its property and tort common law,[201] and many states have codified this protection of neighbors' rights in their statutes.[202] So deeply ingrained in state law is the nuisance principle that typically the legislation codifying it is interpreted by courts to leave ample room for the common law of nuisance to continue to evolve organically.[203]

Most states recognize two types of private nuisances: nuisances *per se* and *per accidents*. A nuisance *per se* is a wrongful use of land that is a legal nuisance under all circumstance.[204] A nuisance *per accidents* is the more common type of nuisance in that it is typically a land use that is not inherently harmful but causes significant harm because of its location and the manner in which it is conducted.[205] Most state nuisance laws make clear that while a lawful business, like operation of a CAFO, may not be a nuisance *per se*, it can nevertheless be adjudged a nuisance *per accidens*, depending on the degree of harm caused and the other facts on the ground.[206] As observed earlier, in states where state and local regulation of CAFOs is weak, suing a polluting CAFO for violating nuisance law may be a neighbors' only practical recourse to try to abate or reduce the health and environmental harm that a nearby CAFO caused them. It is for this reason the continued enforcement of state nuisance law is so vital to protecting CAFO neighbors' property rights and is regarded as such an impediment to its expansion by the CAFO industry.[207]

States vary somewhat in the way they define what constitutes a nuisance and what remedies are available to a winning nuisance plaintiff. For example, the Restatement Second of Torts instructs courts to conduct a "gravity of the harm" against social "utility" balance[208] to determine whether the defendant's use of their property constitutes a nuisance to the plaintiff's land. Under the Restatement, use of one person's land is legally a nuisance to a neighboring landowner only if the gravity of the harm to the plaintiff's land exceeds the social utility of the defendant's use of their property.[209] The Restatement then sets forth several factors that courts should consider in weighing the harm against the utility, such as which use was instituted first, the character of the neighborhood, the seriousness of the harm, and how easily it can be prevented.[210] The Restatement approach to detecting a nuisance is rarely followed by state courts. The Restatement analysis is criticized as making nuisance determinations too unpredictable. It is also faulted for recognizing as a practical matter that some nuisance sources are just too big and important to the larger community to be subject to legal nuisance constraints in favor of a single private plaintiff.[211]

Many state courts adopted their nuisance jurisprudence long before the Restatement was published. Most of them do not follow the

Restatement's recommended balancing analysis to determine the existence of a nuisance. Nuisance law as administered by the Iowa courts is a good example. Long before the Restatement of Torts was promulgated, Iowa courts adopted their own legal tests to determine whether a nuisance existed.[212] They did not engage in a balancing of social utility against the gravity of the harm, but rather employed a simple three-part test: (1) which use was commenced first, (2) what is the character of the neighborhood, and (3) how severe is the harm.[213] In Iowa, nuisance cases involving hog CAFOs are typically situated in the rural countryside—where a wide variety of land uses may be appropriate—so assuming the harm done to the plaintiff is substantial, the land use that was commenced first tends to be the consistent winner.[214] Other courts apply some combination of the Restatement balance along with other specific local factors, but most states make priority of use, character of the surrounding neighborhood, and the severity of the harm the determinative factors in identifying a legal nuisance.[215] While the Restatement makes "Coming to the Nuisance"[216] (e.g., building a new rural residence too close to an existing CAFO) only one factor among many for a court to consider, right-to-farm laws and a number of courts applying common-law principles make it a determinative factor in denying a plaintiff's nuisance claim.[217]

The range of remedies available to a winning nuisance plaintiff are much the same across the states.[218] They typically include abatement of the nuisance by an injunction; a one-time award of damages for permanent loss in property value caused by the nuisance; compensatory damages for physical injuries, including medical expenses (and possibly recovery of special damages for emotional or psychological suffering); and punitive damages in cases of egregious willfulness on the part of the defendant.[219] Until the middle of the past century, most state courts granted winning nuisance plaintiffs injunctive relief on proof that the nuisance injuries were substantial.[220] This practice changed with the advent of the "Relative Hardship Balance" advocated by the Restatement (Second) of Torts.[221] Because injunctions were a form of equitable relief, the Restatement asserted that courts should not grant injunctive relief unless the remedy at law was definitely inadequate and the relative hardship balance clearly favored the plaintiff.[222] In this balancing step, the relative hardship to the defendant included the potential effect on third parties, such as employees, suppliers, and the local community's economy, along with adverse effects on the public at large.[223] Most state courts adopted this recommendation by the Restatement, and it became rare for a winning nuisance plaintiff to receive injunctive relief against polluting factories or other locally important businesses, where closing them down would impose serious economic harm on those dependent on their continuous operation.[224] As nuisance verdicts against hog CAFOs began to be awarded in the late twentieth century, this reluctance by state courts to grant injunctive relief was regularly applied to CAFOs, particularly in states actively recruiting CAFO business to bolster their farm economies.[225] When courts deny injunctive relief, they commonly give the plaintiff a one-time damages award for the permanent loss in property value suffered because of the neighboring nuisance.[226]

One consequence of modern courts' general reluctance to grant injunctive relief against a losing nuisance defendant, except in cases of extremely bad behavior, is the proliferation of permanent damages awards to winning nuisance plaintiffs in lieu of an injunction. A crucial part of this practice, however, is the understanding that when the losing defendant pays such permanent damages, the defendant is generally ruled to have acquired an easement to continue to cause the same level of harm to the neighbor in the future with impunity.[227] What this means for the winning plaintiff is that accepting permanent damages for their loss in property value caused by the nuisance entails the surrender of a valuable property right to the defendant in the form of an easement. As a result, the plaintiff must continue to suffer the same level of nuisance harm indefinitely without further legal recourse. What it means to a CAFO losing a nuisance suit, where the court awards permanent damages to the plaintiff for loss in property value, is that the losing CAFO acquires an easement to continue to inflict the same level of nuisance harm in perpetuity. Thus, through losing a nuisance suit, the CAFO in one sense wins because it acquires at a judicially determined price a court-created easement to pollute that the plaintiff might never have surrendered voluntarily.

Although critics question the constitutionality and fairness of courts routinely awarding permanent damages instead of injunctions,[228] a clear majority of recent nuisance decisions across the country have approved this judicially compelled exchange of money damages for an easement to continue polluting the plaintiff's land.[229] Like any other easement, this judicially established easement is transferable to later owners of the CAFO, and it binds whomever succeeds ownership of the neighboring servient estate.[230] The scope of the easement, however, is strictly limited to the facts of the nuisance case from which it arose.[231] If the nuisance harm increases significantly above what it was at the time of the court decision that created it, the CAFO holding the easement is vulnerable to a later suit by the aggrieved neighbor on the ground that the CAFO has violated the scope of the easement, the same as it would if the easement was created in a voluntary transfer.[232]

Besides permanent damages for loss in property value, a nuisance plaintiff is generally allowed to recover compensatory damages for personal injuries or indirect harms suffered.[233] The first category of compensatory personal damages is almost always recoverable if they can be satisfactorily proved.[234] Typically, these damages would include medical expenses for physical illness, lost wages for inability to work, and lodging and travel costs, if the plaintiffs were forced to vacate their property because of the severe nature of the pollution experienced.[235] Where special or indirect damages are allowed, they would include compensation for personal discomfort, emotional distress, mental anguish, and psychological suffering caused by continuous exposure to the CAFO nuisance.[236] It is precisely these types of subjective personal recoveries that recent statutes in North Carolina and Iowa limiting CAFOs' liability for nuisance damages are intended to prohibit or at least to cap.[237]

Theoretically, a CAFO operator inflicting wanton, malicious, or reprehensible nuisance harm on neighbors could also be liable for punitive damages intended to punish such outrageous or reckless conduct and to deter it from happening in the future.[238] Although punitive damages are often sought against CAFOs by aggrieved neighbors, courts rarely impose them for any type of nuisance harm.[239] A recent study reviewed all the punitive damages case in the United States over a 10-year period. There were slightly over 500 cases studied in which courts awarded punitive damages to plaintiffs seeking them, and only in a handful of these cases did a court award punitive damages for a nuisance.[240]

## VIII. How Do Recent Amendments to State Right-to-Farm Laws Operate to Protect CAFOs from Nuisance Suits?

One additional factor courts must often consider in resolving a neighbor's nuisance complaint against a CAFO is the possible application of a so-called right-to-farm law in the state. All 50 states have some form of right-to-farm law on the books,[241] most of them adopted during a short period between 1978 and 1983.[242] Although the specific provisions and the significance accorded to them by courts vary a good deal from state to state, the basic idea behind all right-to-farm laws is quite similar—farmers engaging in normal farming activities in areas where agriculture is the primary land use should be able to conduct conventional farming practices without fearing suit by new residential neighbors objecting to some type of minor nuisance harm.[243] In essence, the first generation of right-to-farm laws codified the common-law "coming to the nuisance" doctrine and applied it to neighbors coming into the rural neighborhood after some type of industrial agriculture had already begun operating.

Right-to-farm laws typically are either statewide in scope or they allow local governments the power to grant complete or partial immunity from nuisance suits to qualified farm operations, so long as they are engaged in conventional farming practices and are not negligent in doing so.[244] Where the decision to publicly designate "farm-friendly zones" is made by local governments, it is up to the farm operator to

convince the local government that it is in the public interest to encourage productive use of rural land by farmers who engage prudently
in conventional farming practices. If the local government agrees, basic farm activities will be legally protected within designated agricultural areas against nuisance suits by their rural neighbors who move
in later.[245] Thus, whether right-to-farm laws operate locally or statewide, neighboring landowners aggrieved by the animal waste discharges, odors, noise, dust, or other airborne contaminants emanating from a nearby CAFO generally face major legal impediments in
bringing a nuisance lawsuit. When the farm operation causing harm
was clearly initiated before the neighbor acquires their land or improves it in a way that is impaired by the CAFO's operation, the
neighbor usually cannot maintain a nuisance suit unless the CAFO
is in violation of some public regulation or is being operated in a negligent manner.[246]

Not surprisingly, CAFO operators have been quick to claim the benefits of state right-to-farm laws by seeking the special immunity from
neighbors' nuisance suits, and some have done so successfully.[247] It is
fair to observe, however, that courts are not particularly friendly to laws
that immunize any business enterprise against nuisance liability
to their neighbors. Because most right-to-farm laws typically do not
protect "negligent" farm practices and include specific timing rules regarding when their protective features take effect, including special
provisions governing major changes in the agricultural business conducted on the farm, some courts have found ways to interpret the law
so that it does not offer the protection claimed in particularly offensive nuisance cases.[248] Judicial reluctance to apply right-to-farm laws
to CAFOs led to several states enacting second-generation right-to-
farm laws that expanded legal protections against nuisance actions
afforded to CAFOs. For example, Indiana amended its right-to-farm
law in 2005 to clarify that the law applied even when farm operators
radically changed the nature of the agricultural business conducted
on their land.[249] A later case applied the revised Indiana right-to-
farm law to protect a farm owner from a neighbor's nuisance action

even when the neighbor was in residence first and the farmer changed their agricultural production from growing corn to operating a large hog CAFO.[250]

## A. Iowa's Amendments to Its Right-to-Farm Laws

The Iowa legislature enacted two different types of right-to-farm laws. The first law, enacted in 1982, was a generic right-to-farm law intended to protect all types of normal farm activities from nuisance lawsuits unless the harm complained about was the result of negligence or a violation of public law.[251] The first time this law was before the Iowa Supreme Court in 1996, the court ruled the law inapplicable because the farm activity challenged as a nuisance was initiated a year before the farm qualified for the protection of the law.[252] Two years later, the law was declared unconstitutional by the Iowa Supreme Court in *Bormann v. Board of Supervisors*.[253] In its *Bormann* decision, the Iowa Supreme Court characterized the effect of the law on neighbors' property rights as the state taking a valuable easement from the neighbors without just compensation.[254]

A second-generation Iowa right-to-farm law was enacted in 1995 for the express purpose of immunizing CAFOs from nuisance liability to their neighbors. This new right-to-farm law took the form of an amendment to Iowa's longstanding nuisance statute, Iowa Code Chapter 657. It went well beyond the negligence and illegality exceptions of the Iowa Code 352.11(1) and specifically subjected CAFOs to nuisance liability only if the pollution complained about resulted because the CAFO did not comply with applicable federal and state regulations or "failed to use existing prudent generally accepted management practices reasonable for the operation."[255] This latter phrase was a direct way of giving legislative blessing to the storage lagoon/land spreading method of handling high volumes of animal wastes currently employed by virtually every hog CAFO in Iowa.

This second-generation right-to-farm law was struck down as unconstitutional by the Iowa Supreme Court in 2004.[256] In *Gacke v. Pork*

*Xtra L.L.C.*, the Iowa Supreme Court adopted the same taking-of-an-easement reasoning propounded in *Bormann*[257] but limited that result to the loss in land value. The court rejected the CAFOs argument that the new right-to-farm law was different from the earlier law struck down in *Bormann* because the new law did not explicitly exempt negligent or illegal operation of a CAFO as did the Iowa Code 352.11(1). The court ruled that 352.11(1) and 657.11 were functionally so similar they must be considered under the same constitutional analysis.[258]

The Iowa legislature responded to the *Gacke* case in 2017 by enacting an amendment to the 1995 law to limit the money damages a winning nuisance plaintiff could collect from a CAFO defendant.[259] This latest Iowa right-to-farm law contains ambiguous language that, if interpreted broadly, could severely restrict neighbors' rights in nuisance suits against CAFOs. One possible interpretation would not only bar plaintiffs from fully recovering normal compensatory damages but, of greater concern, also prevent them from being granted injunctive relief and from being able to recover punitive damages.[260]

Among the 50 states, only the Iowa Supreme Court has unequivocally struck down right-to-farm laws protecting CAFOs as unconstitutional, and it has done it twice. In both of the *Bormann* and *Gacke* cases, the Iowa Supreme Court ruled that the legal effect of the challenged right-to-farm law was to allow the state to acquire a permanent easement against the neighbors' property that allowed a CAFO to pollute the property without any liability for the harm caused.[261] Thus, the law caused an unconstitutional taking of the neighbor's property right because the state provided no payment of just compensation to the neighbor for loss of this valuable easement.[262]

The reasoning of the Iowa Supreme Court can best be explained by analogizing the Iowa right-to-farm law to a right-to-trespass law. Suppose such a law authorized a petroleum pipeline company to run its pipeline across a farmer's land without negotiating for and acquiring an easement to do so. Such a law certainly would be struck down in every state as an unconstitutional taking of a legal easement from the farmer by the state without paying just compensation.[263]

By contrast, under conventional takings jurisprudence, without the court's characterization of the right-to-farm law as the *per se* taking an easement, such a regulatory law that caused only modest property loss to a neighboring owner would normally be upheld as a reasonable exercise of the state's police power.[264] As noted earlier, among the 50 states, only the Iowa courts apply this easement analysis to justify their holding that the result of this type of right-to-farm law on neighbors' private property is an unconstitutional taking. Other states have generally rejected the Iowa easement analysis and upheld right-to-farm laws against similar constitutional challenges, ruling instead that the loss to neighbors' land value was not an excessive diminution under *Penn Central*.[265]

A recent US Supreme Court "takings" case, *Cedar Point Nursery v. Hassid*,[266] suggests a possible argument to support the Iowa Supreme Court's constitutional "easement analysis" in the *Bormann* and *Gacke* cases. Chief Justice Roberts, writing for a 6–3 majority, cited and applied most of the Court's modern takings jurisprudence in ruling that a longstanding California farm labor regulation was invalid as a *per se* taking.[267] The California law at issue allowed representatives of a farm workers' union to "take access to" (enter) an employer's agricultural land under a restrictive time schedule for the sole purpose of recruiting potential union members.[268]

Justice Roberts made a special point of emphasizing that *per se* takings were not limited to direct physical invasions of private property.[269] Legislatively authorized regulations could also result in a *per se* taking if the practical effect on the landowner's basic property rights were the same as if a physical invasion had occurred. He cited *Kaiser Aetna v. United States*,[270] *Nollan v. California Coastal Commission*,[271] *Dolan v. City of Tigard*,[272] *Lucas v. South Carolina Coastal Council*,[273] and *Horne v. Department of Agriculture*[274] in support of this point.[275] In all of these cases except *Horne*, the Court specifically observed that the effect of the challenged regulation was for the government to take an easement in the property of the regulated party without paying any compensation.[276]

Much the same analysis could apply to the loss in a basic property right caused by a state statute exempting CAFOs from liability for causing serious harm to a neighbor's land, contrary to the private property protections otherwise afforded by the law of nuisance. The effect of such a statute immunizing CAFOs from nuisance liability to their neighbors would be to grant them an easement to pollute, very similar to the easements identified in the cases cited by the chief justice. While the right to exclude others from one's land extolled in the cases cited is the most fundamental of property rights, the right to be free from unreasonable external interference in the use and enjoyment of one's land is also a fundamental property right, universally recognized and protected for centuries by the law of nuisance. Maybe the "easement analysis" of the Iowa Supreme Court is not so unconventional after all.

There may be trouble ahead for the continued vitality of the uniquely Iowa easement analysis as applied to legislation insulating CAFOs from nuisance actions. A major nuisance suit brought by a number of neighbors against a very large Iowa CAFO is currently working its way through the Iowa courts, having already been to the Iowa Supreme Court once on an interlocutory appeal.[277] In this 2018 decision, two Iowa justices wrote a concurring opinion in which they suggested the next time the case reached the court, they were prepared to reconsider the foundations of the constitutional doctrines applied to strike down the legislative protection afforded Iowa CAFOs.[278] They posited that a fresh look at the constitutional issues was necessary because "conditions had changed"[279] since the *Bormann* and *Gacke* cases were decided.

It is not at all clear what "conditions" the justices had in mind. From the perspective of Iowa neighbors of CAFOs, "conditions" have clearly worsened. Today Iowa has more and larger hog CAFOs than ever before, while the universal manure management process is still the same lagoon storage and land spreading, a practice that continues to cause potentially noxious harms to neighbors. Meanwhile, the Iowa legislature still seems hell-bent on eliminating nuisance threats to CAFO operators from their neighbors. . . . The only thing that has changed significantly in the past two decades is the membership of the Iowa

Supreme Court. Today, there is not a single justice on the court who was there when the court decided the *Gacke* case, ratifying *Bormann's* unique "easement" analysis.

In 2022, as promised, the Iowa Supreme Court returned to the question of the constitutionality of granting Iowa CAFOs special legal protection against neighbors' nuisance actions. In *Garrison v. New Fashion Pork, LLP.*, decided by a 4–3 margin,[280] the court reversed that part of its holding in the *Gacke* case that applied the Iowa Constitution's "Inalienable Rights'" language to invalidate the statutory limits on compensatory damages established in Iowa Code 657.11.[281] More precisely, the court rejected the three-part test promulgated in *Gacke* for applying the "Inalienable Rights" provision, holding a simple "rational basis" standard of review was appropriate, and ruled it was met by the facts of the case.[282] The court's intent, announced in the *Honomichi* case, to reconsider the "easement analysis" in the *Bormann* case was thwarted in *Garrison* by the court's finding that, as the losing plaintiff below, Garrison had failed to preserve his taking claim on appeal. Nevertheless, the court tried its best to restrict the precedent of the *Bormann* case. The *Garrison* opinion argued that the *Gacke* opinion itself altered *Bormann's* holding that the legislature's taking of such an easement without just compensation was a *per se* taking. While *Bormann* was based on both the federal and state constitutions, the *Gacke* decision purported to apply only the Iowa Constitution and suggested perhaps there was no *per se* taking in the case. The *Gacke* decision did not actually reach such a conclusion about the type of taking. Rather, it ruled simply that deciding between a *per se* taking and a diminution in value regulatory taking was unnecessary because it was embracing and following the *Bormann* precedent either way. Nowhere in the *Gacke* opinion, however, did the court conduct the customary analysis to examine before and after land values to determine whether the plaintiff's property loss was an excessive diminution in value.[283]

The manner in which the *Garrison* decision dealt with the *Bormann/Gacke* precedent appears to ignore the Supremacy Clause of the US Constitution. If, as *Bormann* held, under the "taking" clause of the

US Constitution, the granting of an easement to an industrial agricultural user to pollute a neighbor's land without just compensation is a *per se* taking, applying the Iowa Constitution to the same set of nuisance facts cannot obviate the result that would be reached under the Fourteenth Amendment. State law can go further than federal law in providing citizens with greater individual constitutional rights, but it cannot curtail the rights enjoyed by all citizens under federal law. The recent *Cedar Point* case discussed earlier reinforced the idea that a state legislature cannot take away a valuable property right by destroying it through creation of an easement without providing just compensation. If it tries to do so, a *per se* taking occurs.

The *Garrison* case is a radical departure from the position the court took in the *Bormann* case and in the *Gacke* case, both of which were unanimous decisions. In those cases, the court noted its duty to give due respect to the authority of the Iowa General Assembly but also insisted that it was the court's duty to enforce citizen's constitutional rights when legislation overreached and valuable property rights were taken without just compensation. In *Bormann*, the court declared the immunity from nuisance claims the legislature attempted to confer on certain farm operations "flagrantly unconstitutional."[284] In *Garrison*, much of the rhetoric in the opinion was devoted to emphasizing that it is the job of the legislature, not the courts, to make important policy decisions. If the Iowa Supreme Court continues to chip away at the constitutional rulings in *Bormann* and *Gacke*, recent extreme amendments to the North Carolina right-to-farm law[285] may foreshadow the type of CAFO protections that the Iowa General Assembly will enact and the Iowa Supreme Court will endorse.

## B.    North Carolina Amendments to Its Right-to-Farm Law

Shortly after a large number of nuisance lawsuits were filed by CAFO neighbors against Murphy-Brown, LLC,[286] the North Carolina legislature began enacting a series of amendments to the state's right-to-farm law designed to protect hog CAFOs from neighbors' nuisance suits.[287]

The first amendment in 2013 overturned an earlier judicial ruling narrowly construing the reference in the law to "changed conditions"[288] to make clear that even a dramatic change in the type of farm product produced did not constitute a changed condition justifying a neighbor's nuisance action.[289] The 2013 amendment also adopted a new "frivolous" lawsuit punishment, allowing the awarding of attorneys' fees to the winning side when a nuisance suit was found to be without merit.[290]

CAFO expansion in North Carolina is currently in limbo due to a series of huge nuisance verdicts in the lawsuits mentioned above, which were won by neighbors against big North Carolina CAFOs.[291] What made these nuisance verdicts noteworthy was not only the 500 African American plaintiffs involved in the 26 lawsuits[292] but also the size of the compensatory damages judgments and the very large amounts of punitive damages awarded.[293]

The tens of millions of dollars in compensatory and punitive damages awarded by the North Carolina federal district court against Murphy-Brown, LLC clearly got the attention of the CAFO industry and in turn the North Carolina legislature. Shortly after the federal District Court for the Eastern District of North Carolina started hearing these highly publicized nuisance suits, the North Carolina legislature began adopting additional amendments to its right-to-farm law.[294] These latest amendments were explained on the floor of the North Carolina legislature to be needed to reduce the financial uncertainty experienced by CAFO operators stemming from the Murphy-Brown, LLC litigation.[295] This objective was achieved by further limiting CAFOs' liability in nuisance suits by their neighbors. The amendments to the right-to-farm law enacted in 2017 adversely affected neighbors' right to sue a CAFO for nuisance by severely restricting the types of compensatory damages that could be collected by winning nuisance plaintiffs. Ordinarily recoverable nuisance damages, such as personal discomfort, inconvenience, loss of enjoyment, and mental distress, were no longer available to neighbors winning nuisance suits against CAFOs.[296] The amendments also added a new "successor in interest" proviso that limited recovery in a second nuisance suit against the same CAFO to the property's fair market value, even when the second instance of nuisance harm was entirely different from the first.[297] Finally, the 2017 amendments virtually eliminated punitive damages as a remedy by restricting punitive damages awards to cases where, within the prior 3 years, the CAFO had been convicted of a crime or cited for a violation of state or federal environmental regulations.[298] The 2017 amendments were vetoed by the governor, but the veto was overridden by the legislature and the new law took effect on May 11, 2017.[299]

In 2018, barely a month after the first huge verdicts against Murphy-Brown, LLC were rendered by the US District Court for the Eastern District of North Carolina, the North Carolina legislature started adopting additional amendments to its right-to-farm law. One state senator at the time publicly announced that the latest amendments to the right-to-farm law were necessary to "fix" what was happening in the lawsuits against Murphy-Brown, LLC.[300] The new amendments limited nuisance actions against CAFOs to neighbors who live no farther away than a half-mile from the site of the feeding operation.[301] The 2018 amendments also adopted new timing rules for bringing nuisance suits against CAFOs. A CAFO cannot be sued for nuisance unless it is less than 1 year old or undergoes a "fundamental change"[302] in its operation.[303] Further, the 2018 amendments established a special statute of limitations for filing a nuisance claim against a CAFO. Nuisance claims must be filed within 1 year of the time the CAFO began operation,[304] not from when the nuisance harm from the CAFO was first experienced, which would be the normal measuring time in tort law. Perhaps most important, the 2018 amendments struck from the right-to-farm law the proviso that the law did not protect "negligent or improper" agricultural practices from nuisance actions.[305] Thus, under the latest amendments, no matter how dreadful the harms to neighbors resulting from negligent operation of a CAFO, they are no longer treated as legal nuisances in North Carolina. Finally, as noted in Section VI, the North Carolina legislature stole a page from Iowa law[306] and forbade any unit of local government from engaging in any type of health or environmental regulation of a CAFO or any nuisance abatement activity.[307]

The governor again vetoed this legislation, but the legislature over-rode the veto and the new amendments took effect in July 2018.[308] The 2017 and 2018 amendments to the North Carolina right-to-farm law are currently being challenged in state court as both unconstitutional tak-ings of private property without just compensation and a violation of the state's constitutional prohibition against "private or special" laws.[309]

## C.   The Fourth Circuit Ruling in *McKiver v. Murphy-Brown, LLC*

In late 2020, the US Court of Appeals for the Fourth Circuit finally de-cided *McKiver v. Murphy-Brown, LLC*[310]—one of the most eagerly awaited CAFO nuisance decisions in the past decade.[311] On Novem-ber 19, 2020, the court issued a 69-page opinion generally upholding the decision of the US District Court for the Eastern District of North Carolina in favor of multiple nuisance plaintiffs against a large hog CAFO, nearly all of whose hog operation was directed by Murphy-Brown, LLC.[312] In the federal diversity litigation under appeal, a dis-trict court jury awarded the nuisance plaintiffs $75,000 compensatory damages and $2.5 million punitive damages.[313] In this litigation, Murphy-Brown, LLC identified itself as "d/b/a Smithfield Hog Produc-tion Division."[314]

On appeal, the three-judge fourth circuit panel ruled two-to-one to uphold the district court decision by Senior US District Court Judge W. Earl Britt on five of the seven rulings[315] challenged by Murphy-Brown, LLC. Judge Stephanie D. Thacker wrote the majority opinion,[316] Judge J. Harvie Wilkinson III wrote a concurring opinion,[317] and Judge G. Ste-ven Agee concurred in part and dissented in part.[318]

The five lower court rulings Murphy-Brown, LLC challenged, but lost, mostly involved questions about whether the requirements for federal court jurisdiction based on diversity of citizenship were met (they were),[319] the enforceability of recently enacted state statutes of limitations on nuisance actions against CAFOs (they did not apply),[320] and the applicability of several recent legislative restrictions on nuisance actions against CAFOs adopted by the North Carolina legislature after these lawsuits against Murphy Brown, LLC had commenced (they did not apply).[321]

A key holding of the majority decision was that these new restrictions on nuisance suits against CAFOs were not intended to operate retroactively, and therefore they did not apply to the case.[322] Thus, these highly restrictive amendments to North Carolina's right-to-farm laws should not affect other pending litigation against Murphy-Brown, LLC initiated before the new restrictions were enacted. They will, however, clearly affect the viability of future nuisance litigation against CAFOs in North Carolina, unless lawsuits challenging their constitutionality succeed.[323]

The appellate court found in favor of Murphy-Brown, LLC on two main points: a claim of abuse of discretion by Judge Britt in refusing to allow testimony by an expert witness for the defense[324] and the district court's failure to separate the punitive damages phase of the trial from the compensatory damages phase.[325] The appellate court appeared to agree with the appellant's argument that the disallowance of testimony by the defense expert could possibly have been an error, but ruled it was an insufficient basis to order a new trial.[326] The district court's failure to bifurcate the jury's consideration of compensatory damages from its consideration of punitive damages was held to be serious legal error under North Carolina law—this error compelled the appellate court to remand the case to the district court for a separate hearing on the punitive damages claim.[327] There was no new hearing on punitive damages in the trial court, however, because a week after the fourth circuit opinion was released, the parties entered into a settlement agreement ending the litigation.[328] This settlement agreement was confidential, and its terms were not made public.[329]

### D. Other States' Amendments to Their Right-to-Farm Laws

Politically powerful economic interests in a few other states appear committed to further opening their state's doors to expanding types of industrialized agriculture, including hog CAFOs that pose nuisance harms to neighboring landowners.[330] Besides Iowa and North Carolina, since 1990, several other states have enacted special laws clearly intended to limit potential nuisance liability for pollution from CAFOs and other intensive agricultural activities causing serious harms to neighbors. For example, both North Dakota in 2012[331] and Missouri in 2014 amended their state constitutions to add new right-to-farm provisions.[332] Earlier, Missouri amended its right-to-farm statute in 2011 to make it more difficult for neighbors to successfully sue CAFOs and added a frivolous lawsuit clause.[333] This legislative action in Missouri followed and was obviously provoked by several years of successful nuisance suits by neighbors against Premium Standard Farms, Inc and Continental Grain Company that resulted in tens of millions of dollars in damages paid out.[334] Eventually, these nuisance suits led to a consent decree between the Missouri attorney general and the hog industry companies in which the companies agreed to install roofs over all of their waste storage basins in Missouri.[335]

In 2005, Indiana amended its right-to-farm law to define very narrowly what constituted a "significant change in . . . operation" that rendered a CAFO vulnerable to a nuisance lawsuit by an aggrieved neighbor.[336] Amazingly, this amendment was applied by a federal circuit court in a case that held the change from growing corn to operating a large hog CAFO was not a "significant change."[337] The Indiana amendment also added a "frivolous lawsuit" provision to its right-to-farm law.[338] Arkansas beefed up its right-to-farm law in 2005 to increase the protection of CAFOs.[339]

In the states adopting such laws, the courts have upheld them against various constitutional challenges, rejecting the taking analysis of Iowa's *Bormann* case.[340]

## IX. Conclusion: What Can Be Done to Protect Neighbor Nuisance Harms?

It is difficult to be optimistic about neighbors receiving greater legal protection from polluting CAFOs soon. Federal law is unlikely to change, and states with large numbers of CAFOs face a clear dilemma in choosing between their desire to reap the economic benefits of CAFO expansion and not being too permissive in their regulation of problematic CAFOs to the detriment of the public and CAFO neighbors. This ambivalence leaves private nuisance law as the primary source of legal protection against polluting CAFOs, and nuisance law itself is under attack in several states with large concentrations of CAFOs.

At the core of this problem is the general legal acceptance in the United States of allowing the external costs of CAFOs' archaic method for handling animal wastes to be imposed on the public and on neighbors. The standard storage lagoon/land spreading method routinely used by CAFOs to dispose of animal wastes may be simple and inexpensive to operate, but it would never be allowed anywhere else in the nation for the disposal of human sewage or for the disposal of industrial wastewater. In the twenty-first century, this primitive waste disposal system used by CAFOs would universally appear neither "prudent" nor "reasonable," to recite the restrictive requirements in typical right-to-farm laws. But state and federal administrative agencies and courts consistently reach a contrary conclusion in interpreting these laws.

So long as American consumers want inexpensive eggs, chicken wings, turkey, beef, bacon, ham, pork tenderloin, and sausage, however, CAFOs and their supporters have a persuasive case for keeping their waste disposal costs as low as possible. But these costs are low only because CAFOs can pass along major costs associated with their animal waste disposal systems to the public in the form of degraded waterways and lower-quality airsheds. In too many cases, these external costs are also borne heavily by CAFOs' neighbors, who must endure sickening odors causing serious private losses to their property values, health, and personal well-being.

A few states have considered at least requiring CAFO operators to install roofs over their lagoons to close them in, but such a fix only alleviates some of the nuisance problems. Roofing does not eliminate offensive odors from the buildings housing thousands of hogs or any of the problems caused neighbors by the spreading or spraying of slurry from the lagoons on nearly fields as fertilizer. It also does not affect the potential harms to neighbors associated with leaks from the covered storage lagoons into groundwater tables or overflows from waste storage basins. Lagoon covers do prevent rainwater from causing lagoon overflows, and they certainly are a step in the right direction in controlling lagoon odor.

The obvious solution to this perplexing public health and environmental safety problem is to substantially upgrade the waste disposal requirements for all CAFOs, not just new ones as North Carolina did some years ago. Although this problem often presents itself as a legal issue, the solution must almost certainly be found in advances in agricultural engineering technology. As one of the hog farmers testified in the North Carolina litigation, "In a perfect world, what is most needed is a real time waste treatment system that separates solids from liquids and fully treats them both."[341] Ideally, such a process would convert animal wastes into a product like biogas that would be of sufficient value to justify the greater cost of more effective waste disposal systems for treating animal wastes. Developments in the clean energy field for capturing the methane and carbon dioxide generated by anaerobic digestion of animal wastes and using it for commercial purposes may hold promise as the means to pay for the cost of advanced waste treatment technology. It is too early to tell. If that opportunity does not pan out, what is most needed is a technological breakthrough for treating wet animal wastes that is economically feasible for hog farmers to employ while at least benign toward the natural environment and unthreatening to CAFO neighbors. But anaerobic digesters, which many experts believe offer the desired fix, have not yet proved to be the technological "magic bullet," largely because of the high expense associated with installing and operating them.[341]

North Carolina has done by far the most work in trying to come up with a workable solution through its "technology forcing" statutory requirement that new CAFOs must employ "environmentally superior" animal waste management systems. The five criteria adopted by the state's Swine and Poultry Waste Management Center provide a blueprint for any state wishing to get serious about confronting their hog CAFO waste management issues. But since starting down this path in the mid-2000s, North Carolina has approved only two hog CAFOs large enough to justify the expense of using anaerobic digesters necessary to meet the environmentally superior requirement. Thus, North Carolina's tougher regulatory strategy can hardly be deemed a success, and there is seemingly nothing in the works to address the problems CAFOs' wastes create anywhere else in the United States.

The failure of North Carolina's experiment with requiring "environmentally superior" waste disposal systems for new CAFOs suggests an economically feasible, technologically workable fix for CAFOs' waste disposal problem is not just around the corner. But it surely is not impossible. If our nation's scientists can send a man to the Moon, decode the human genome, and plumb the deepest corners of our oceans, why cannot they be mobilized to come up with a better way for handling the mountains of animal wastes our CAFOs regularly produce? It is time for public health specialists, scientists, engineers, ecologists, environmentalists, economists, and even lawyers to start asking hard questions about our society's priorities when it comes to the harmful consequences of industrialized farming, particularly those caused by the growing numbers of large hog CAFOs. Until states like Iowa, with an exploding number of hog CAFOs, all relying on the conventional lagoon and land spreading method for disposing of the huge quantities of animal wastes, start taking more seriously the public health dangers, environmental threats, and other social harms the proliferations of hog CAFOs can produce, the threat to neighbors will only increase.

### NOTES

This chapter is adapted from the author's article, *CAFOs and the Law*, published in 107 Iowa L. Rev. Online 19 (2022).

1. The term was first used in 1972 in the federal Clean Water Act (CWA). *See* An Act to Amend the Federal Water Pollution Control Act, Pub. L. No. 92-500, § 502(14), 86 Stat. 816, 887 (1972) (codified as amended at 33 U.S.C. §§ 1151, 1251–1387).

2. 108 ARIZ. 178, 494 P.2D 700 (1972). Webb sued Spur for creating a public nuisance and won an injunction from the Arizona court, stopping the operation of the cattle feedlot. The equity court, however, applied the common-law doctrine of "coming to the nuisance" because Spur was operating the feedlot on their land before Sun City existed and ordered Webb to reimburse Spur for the costs of relocating their cattle feeding business.

3. Decision Innovation Solutions, 2020 Iowa Pork Industry Report 6 (2020), https://www.iowapork.org/wp-content/uploads/2020/08/200615-2020_Iowa-Pork -Industry-Report_State_FINAL.pdf [https://perma.cc/TT88-3U4T].

4. Decision Innovation Solutions, 2020 Iowa Pork Industry Report 6 (2020), https://www.iowapork.org/wp-content/uploads/2020/08/200615-2020_Iowa-Pork -Industry-Report_State_FINAL.pdf [https://perma.cc/TT88-3U4T].

5. *See* James Merchant & David Osterberg, *Iowans Want Action to Limit Concentrated Animal Feeding Operations and Their Harmful Effects*, DES MOINES REG. (Feb. 18, 2020, 4:46 PM), https://www.desmoinesregister.com/story/opinion /columnists/iowa-view/2020/02/18/cafos-animal-feeding-hogs-harms-iowa-have -worsened-moratorium/4794608002 [https://perma.cc/PY49-YSPG].

6. *See* CARRIE HRIBAR, UNDERSTANDING CONCENTRATED ANIMAL FEEDING OPERATIONS AND THEIR IMPACT ON COMMUNITIES 1–3 (2010), https://www.cdc.gov /nceh/ehs/docs/understanding_cafos_nalboh.pdf [https://perma.cc/YFH2-BWV2]; Barry Yeoman, *The Stink and Injustice of Life Next to an Industrial Hog Farm*, NATION (Dec. 20, 2019), https://www.thenation.com/article/aarchive/hog-farm-lawsuit -south [https://perma.cc/38HM-CVKG].

7. *See* Gacke v. Pork Xtra, L.L.C., 684 N.W.2d 168, 170–71 (Iowa 2004).

8. HRIBAR, *supra* note 6, at 3–5.

9. *See* Yeoman, *supra* note 6.

10. *See* Merchant & Osterberg, *supra* note 5.

11. *See* Weinhold v. Wolff, 555 N.W.2d 454, 459–60 (Iowa 1996).

12. *See* CORBAN ADDISON, WASTELANDS 248 (2022).

13. *See infra* notes 54–56 and accompanying text.

14. *See infra* Part V.

15. *See infra* Part VI.

16. *See infra* Part VI.

17. *See* Neil D. Hamilton, *Harvesting the Law: Personal Reflections on Thirty Years of Change in Agricultural Legislation*, 46 CREIGHTON L. REV. 563, 577–78 (2013).

18. *See, e.g.*, Weinhold v. Wolff, 555 N.W.2d 454, 459–60 (Iowa 1996) (including vivid statements of complaints by plaintiff and other neighbors about the discomfort of living in close proximity to a lagoon full of decomposing wastes from a hog CAFO); *see also* John Flesher, *Factory Farms Provide Abundant Food, but Environment Suffers*, DES MOINES REG. (Feb. 7, 2020, 10:10 AM), https://www.desmoinesregister.com /story/money/agriculture/2020/02/07/iowa-ag-factory-farming-food-environment -impacts-cafo/4682094002 [https://perma.cc/9L8P-97NY].

19. J. DONALD HUGHES, ENVIRONMENTAL PROBLEMS OF THE GREEKS AND ROMANS: ECOLOGY IN THE ANCIENT MEDITERRANEAN 177 (2014).

20. John Tibbetts, *Combined Sewer Systems: Down, Dirty, and Out of Date*, 113 ENVIRON HEALTH PERSP. A 465, A 465 (2005).

21. *Id.; see also* WEBSTER'S THIRD NEW INTERNATIONAL DICTIONARY UNABRIDGED (2002) (defining a "cesspool" as "an underground catch basin that is used where there is no sewer and into which household sewage or other liquid waste is drained to permit leaching of the liquid into the soil"). Early lagoons were also capable of collapsing and spilling their nasty contents into nearby waters and leaking their contents into adjacent soils and underground aquifers. State regulations today typically require reinforced lagoons made leakproof with some form of impermeable lining.

22. *See* N. William Hines, *Here We Go Again: A Third Legislative Attempt to Protect Polluting Iowa CAFOs from Neighbor's Nuisance Suits*, 103 IOWA L. REV. ONLINE 41, 44–45 (2018).

23. *See* N. William Hines, *Farmers, Feedlots and Federalism: The Impact of the 1972 Federal Water Pollution and Control Act Amendments on Agriculture*, 19 S.D. L. REV. 540, 549–51 (1974).

24. *See* HRIBAR, *supra* note 6, at 2–3.

25. *See* Wendee Nicole, *CAFOs and Environmental Justice: The Case of North Carolina*, 121 Env't Health Persp at A186 (2013), *supra* note 12, at A186. Iowa's human population is around 3 million, but its hog population is over 25 million. *See* Tyler Jett & Brianne Pfannenstiel, *Iowa Grows to 3.2 Million People in 2020 Census, Retains 4 Congressional Seats*, DES MOINES REG. (Apr. 27, 2021, 3:12 PM), https://www.desmoines register.com/story/news/politics/2021/04/26/iowa-us-2020-census-poulation-grows -3-2-million-retains-4-seats-congress/7381492002 [https://perma.cc/5XV8-5XCR]; Neil Hamilton, Matt Liebman, Silvia Secchi, & Chris Jones, *Iowa's Water Quality Strategy Is Not Working. Here's What Should Be Done Instead*, DES MOINES REG. (Feb. 7, 2020, 10:33 AM), https://www.desmoinesregister.com/story/opinion/columnists /iowa-view/2020/02/07/iowa-water-quality-new-strategy-needed/4546560002 [https://perma.cc/ZNN5-98TD].

26. *See* Cordon M. Smart, *The "Right to Commit Nuisance" in North Carolina: A Historical Analysis of the Right-to-Farm Act*, 94 N.C. L. REV. 2097, 2104–06 (2016).

27. Patricia M. Gilbert, *From Hogs to HABs: Impacts of Industrial Farming in the US on Nitrogen and Phosphorus and Greenhouse Gas Pollution*, 150 BIOGEOCHEMISTRY 139, 143–44 (2020).

28. *See* Hines, *supra* note 22, at 45, 48.

29. *See* An Act to Amend the Federal Water Pollution Control Act, Pub. L. No. 92-500, 86 Stat. 816 (1972) (codified as amended at 33 U.S.C. §§ 1151, 1251–1387) [hereinafter Clean Water Act ("CWA")].

30. *See* Clean Air Act Amendments of 1977, Pub. L. No. 95-95, 91 Stat. 685 (codified as amended at 42 U.S.C. §§ 7401–7671q) [hereinafter Clean Air Act ("CAA")].

31. Federal Regulations under the Clean Water Act and the Clean Air Act are found in the Code of Federal Regulations (CFR). *See* 40 C.F.R. §§ 50–149 (2021).

32. *See* 33 U.S.C. § 1362(14) (2018).

33. *See* Hines, *supra* note 22, at 46.

34. *See* 42 U.S.C. § 7411(d)(1) (2018).

35. *See id.* § 7602(z).

36. *See* 33 U.S.C. § 1362(14) (2018).

37. *See* Donnelle Eller, *Iowa Uses Satellites to Uncover 5,000 Previously Undetected Animal Confinements*, DES MOINES REG. (Sept. 19, 2017, 9:05 AM), https://www.desmoinesregister.com/story/money/agriculture/2017/09/15/iowa-discovers-thousands-more-hog-cattle-operations-state-says-most-likely-too-small-require-oversig/665956001 [https://perma.cc/ECD2-5K2K].

38. *See* 33 U.S.C. § 1251(a)(1).

39. *See* 33 U.S.C. § 1251(a)(2).

40. *See* Robert W. Adler, *The Decline and (Possible) Renewal of Aspiration in the Clean Water Act*, 88 WASH. L. REV. 759, 780–81 (2013).

41. *See id.* at 780–81, 793.

42. *See id.* at 775–79, 797.

43. *See id.* at 772, 783–87.

44. *See generally* N. William Hines, *History of the 1972 Clean Water Act: The Story behind How the 1972 Act Became the Capstone on a Decade of Extraordinary Environmental Reform*, 4 GEO. WASH. J. ENERGY & ENV'T. L. 80, 105–6 (2013).

45. *See* 33 U.S.C. § 1362(14) (2018).

46. *See id.* § 1251(a).

47. *See id.* § 1316(a)(1).

48. *Id.*

49. *See* 33 U.S.C. § 1314(b)(4).

50. Jonathan Cannon, *A Bargain for Clean Water*, 17 N.Y.U. ENV'T. L.J. 608, 610 (2008).

51. *See id.* at 610–11.

52. 33 U.S.C. § 1362(14) (2018).

53. *See* 40 C.F.R. § 122.23(d)(1) (2020).

54. *Id.* § 122.23(b).

55. *Id.*

56. *Id.* § 122.23(d), (e).

57. *Id.* § 122.23(e), (h).

58. *Id.*

59. *See* Effluent Guidelines and Standards, 39 Fed. Reg. 5704 (Feb. 14, 1974) (to be codified at 40 C.F.R. pt. 412); National Pollutant Discharge Elimination System Permit Regulation and Effluent Limitation Guidelines and Standards for Concentrated Animal Feeding Operations (CAFOs), 68 Fed. Reg. 7176 (Feb. 12, 2003) (to be codified at 40 C.F.R. pts. 9, 122, 123, 412); Revised National Pollutant Discharge Elimination System Permit Regulation and Effluent Limitations Guidelines for Concentrated Animal Feeding Operations in Response to the Waterkeeper Decision, 73 Fed. Reg. 70418 (Nov. 20, 2008) (to be codified at 40 C.F.R. pts. 9, 122, 412).

60. *See* Nat. Res. Def. Council, Inc. v. Reilly, 781 F. Supp. 806, 807–08, 811 (D.D.C. 1992); Waterkeeper All., Inc. v. EPA, 399 F.3d 486, 490–98 (2d Cir. 2005); Nat'l Pork Producers Council v. EPA, 635 F.3d 738, 741–43, 749 (5th Cir. 2011).

61. Waterkeeper All., Inc., 399 F.3d at 502–3.

62. *Id.* at 506, 520–23.

63. EPA, NPDES State Program Authority, https://www.epa.gov/npdes/npdes-state-program-authority [https://perma.cc/TPG2-H42P].

64. *Id.*

65. *Id.*

66. *See* Robin M. Rotman & Ashley A. Hollis, *Control of Nonpoint Sources Pollution Under the Clean Water Act*, Natural Resources & Environment, 8 (Fall 2022).

67. *See generally* EPA, NPDES Permit Writers' Manual for Concentrated Animal Feeding Operations (2012), https://www.epa.gov/sites/default/files/2015-10/documents/cafo_permitmanual_entire.pdf [https://perma.cc/KR9U-MSYT] (providing a comprehensive manual explaining all CAFO permitting requirements).

68. *Id.* at 13, 66, 83.

69. *Id.* at 26, 126.

70. *Id.* at 13.

71. In its 2003 rulemaking, the EPA attempted to increase this requirement to a "100-year, 24-hour rainfall event," but this change was invalidated in a court decision. *See* EPA, Concentrated Animal Feeding Operations Final Rulemaking—Q & A 1 (2008), https://www3.epa.gov/npdes/pubs/cafo_final_rule2008_qa.pdf [https://perma.cc/6RTH-PWK8].

72. *Id.*

73. *Id.*

74. *Id.* at 4.

75. *Id.*

76. *See* Waterkeeper All., Inc. v. EPA, 399 F.3d 486, 494 (2d Cir. 2005).

77. *Id.* at 496.

78. *Id.* at 507.

79. *See id.* at 522–24. Repeated excessive fertilization of farm fields, however, may vitiate this exception. See CARE v. Henry Bosma Dairy, 65 F. Supp. 3d 1129, 1133 (E, D, Wa.) 1999, aff'd 305 F. 3d 943 (9th Cir. 2002).

80. *See* 33 U.S.C. §§ 1319(a)(2), 1319(c) (2018).

81. *Id.*

82. Madhavi Kulkarni, Note, *Out of Sight, but Not Out of Mind: Reevaluating the Role of Federalism in Adequately Regulating Concentrated Animal Feeding Operations*, 44 Wm. & Mary Env't. L. & Pol'y Rev. 285, 288–89, 291–93 (2019).

83. *Id.*

84. EPA, Producers' Compliance Guide for CAFOs: Revised Clean Water Act Regulations for Concentrated Animal Feeding Operations (CAFOs) 5 (2003), https://www.epa.gov/sites/default/files/2015-06/documents/compliance-cafos.pdf [https://perma.cc/UTU5-DV3H].

85. *Id.*

86. EPA, Guide Manual on NPDES Regulations for Concentrated Animal Feeding Operations 12–14 (1995), https://www3.epa.gov/npdes/pubs/owm0266.pdf [https://perma.cc/A4FE-FN7P].

87. *Id.* at 14.

88. 40 C.F.R. § 432.47 (2020).

89. EPA, *supra* note 111–84, at 9–10.

90. *Id.* at 10.

91. *See id.* at 3; EPA, *supra* note 86, at 5.

92. *Id.* at 5–6.

93. *See* JAMES MERCHANT & DAVID OSTERBERG, THE EXPLOSION OF CAFOS IN IOWA AND ITS IMPACT ON WATER QUALITY AND PUBLIC HEALTH i–ii (2018), https://www.iowapolicyproject.org/2018docs/180125-CAFO.pdf [https://perma.cc/Y6YW-UGZ5].

94. *See id.*

95. *Id.*

96. 42 U.S.C. § 7410–11 (2018).

97. *See* 33 U.S.C. § 1362(14).

98. *See* 42 U.S.C. §§ 7411(i), 7412(l).

99. *Id.* § 7411(a)–(b).

100. *See id.* §§ 7411–7412.

101. *See id.* §§ 7408, 7409; EPA, CRITERIA AIR POLLUTANTS, https://www.epa.gov/criteria-air-pollutants [https://perma.cc/W2LG-CN84].

102. 42 U.S.C. §§ 7408, 7409; EPA, *supra* note 101.

103. *See id.* §§ 7470–7479.

104. *See id.* §§ 7501–7502.

105. *See* HRIBAR, *supra* note 6, at 2–11.

106. *See id.* at 16.

107. *See id.* at 13–15.

108. *See* 42 U.S.C. § 7401(c) (2018).

109. *Id.*

110. *See* Dustin Till, *Environmental Groups Press for Federal Regulation of Air Emissions from Animal Feeding Operations*, MARTEN L. (Apr. 27, 2011), https://web.archive.org/web/20120315164046/http://www.martenlaw.com/newsletter/20110427-afo-air-emissions-regulations [https://perma.cc/EBH3-AZC6].

111. *See* Complaint for Declaratory and Injunctive Relief at 24–26, Env't Integrity Project v. EPA, No. 1:16-cv-02203-ABJ, 2016 WL 6581149 (D.D.C. Nov. 4, 2016).

112. See N. William Hines, *Agriculture: The Unseen Foe in the War on Water Pollution*, 55 CORNELL L. REV. 740 (1970).

113. *See* N. William Hines, *Nor Any Drop to Drink: Public Regulation of Water Quality Part I: State Pollution Control Programs*, 52 IOWA L. REV. 186, 196 (1966).

114. *Id.* at 203.

115. *Id.* at 204–5. See also N. William Hines & Mark Schantz, *Improving Water Quality Regulation in Iowa*, 57 IOWA L. REV. 234 (1971).

116. *See* N. William Hines, *A Decade of Non degradation Policy in Congress and the Courts: The Erratic Pursuit of Clear Air and Clean Water*, 62 IOWA L. REV. 643, 647–49, 657 (1977).

117. *Id.* at 611–15.

118. *Id.* at 644, 665.

119. *Id.* at 698–99.

120. *Id.* at 699.

121. Hines, *supra* note 113, at 200–7.

122. *See, e.g.*, ENV'T INTEGRITY PROJECT, THREATENING IOWA'S FUTURE: IOWA'S FAILURE TO IMPLEMENT AND ENFORCE THE CLEAN WATER ACT FOR LIVESTOCK OPERATIONS 15–18 (2004), http://www.environmentalintegrity.org/pdf/publications /Report_Threatening_Iowa_Future.pdf [https://perma.cc/9JXS-KEZR].

123. During this period, the five states adopting special statutes to protect CAFOs from nuisance liability were Iowa, Oklahoma, Wyoming, Tennessee, and Kansas. More recently, North Carolina joined these states in enacting special legislation favoring CAFOs over neighbors' property rights in 2018 and 2019.

124. The 10 states whose laws are cited (in order of the number of hogs in CAFOs as reported by EPA in 2018) are Iowa, North Carolina, Minnesota, California, Texas, Nebraska, Georgia, Indiana, Arkansas, and Kansas.

125. *See, e.g.*, N.C. GEN. STAT. § 143-215.10C (2021).

126. *See, e.g.*, MO. CODE REGS. ANN. tit. 10, § 20-8.300 (2021).

127. *See, e.g.*, NEB. REV. STAT. ANN. §§ 81-1504, 81-1505 (West, Westlaw through the end of the 1st Regular Session and the end of the 1st Special Session of the 107th Legislature (2021)).

128. *See, e.g.*, 327 IND. ADMIN. CODE 19-12-3 (West, current with amendments received through the Indiana Weekly Collection, December 8, 2021).

129. *See, e.g.*, IOWA ADMIN. CODE r.567-65.105(1) (2020).

130. *See, e.g.*, MINN. R. 7020.2225 (2021).

131. *See, e.g.*, GA. COMP. R. & REGS. 40-13-8.05 (2021).

132. *See, e.g., id.* 40-13-8.06.

133. *See, e.g.*, CAL. CODE REGS. tit. 27, § 22564 (2021).

134. *See, e.g.*, MINN. R. 7020.2025 (2021).

135. *See, e.g.*, MO. ANN. STAT. § 640.715 (West, Westlaw current through the end of the 2021 First Regular and First Extraordinary Sessions of the 101st General Assembly).

136. *See* An Act to (1) Codify and Make Permanent the Swine Farm Animal Waste Management System Performance Standards That the General Assembly Enacted in 1998, (2) Provide for the Replacement of a Lagoon That Is an Imminent Hazard, (3) Assist Farmers to Voluntarily Convert to Innovative Animal Waste Management Systems, and (4) Establish the Swine Farm Methane Capture Pilot Program, 2007 N.C. SESS LAWS 523.

137. *See, e.g.*, IOWA CODE § 459.303 (2021).

138. *See, e.g.*, 29 NEB. ADMIN. CODE § 2-008.05F (2021).

139. *See, e.g.*, MINN. STAT. ANN. § 116.0713 (West, Westlaw through all legislation from the 2021 Regular Session and 1st Special Session).

140. *See, e.g.*, 327 IND. ADMIN. CODE § 19-12-4 (West, current with amendments received through the Indiana Weekly Collection, December 8, 2021).

141. *See, e.g.,* ARK. CODE R. § 138.00.22-2203.5 (LexisNexis, LEXIS through Nov. 15, 2021).

142. *See, e.g.,* IOWA CODE § 459.204 (2021).

143. *See infra* Sections VIII.A–B (detailing the Iowa and North Carolina experiences in upgrading their right-to-farm laws).

144. *See* IOWA DEP'T NAT. RES., DETAILS OF SCORING THE MASTER MATRIX (2012), https://www.iowadnr.gov/Portals/idnr/uploads/afo/afo-files/details-scoring -matrix.pdf [https://perma.cc/6W88-VFVX].

145. *See AFO Construction Permits,* IOWA DEP'T NAT. RES., https://www.iowadnr .gov/Environmental-Protection/Animal-Feeding-Operations/AFO-Construction -Permits#16368354-permitted [https://perma.cc/VS9P-WFWA].

146. *See id.*

147. *Id.; see also* Donnelle Eller, *Petition to Tighten Rules on Livestock Facilities in Iowa Fails,* DES MOINES REG. (Sept. 18, 2017, 5:17 PM), https://www .desmoinesregister.com/story/money/2017/09/18/petition-make-harder-build -livestock-facilities-iowa-fails/677775001 [https://perma.cc/K9T3-DWFZ].

148. *See Reality Check: The LLC Loophole Is Still NOT Closed,* JEFFERSON CNTY. FARMERS & NEIGHBORS, INC. (Jan. 20, 2021), https://www.jfaniowa.org/post/2020 /09/04/reality-check-the-llc-loophole-is-still-not-closed [https://perma.cc/D2FE -UPV4].

149. *Id.*

150. *See* Eller, *supra* note 147.

151. *See* Merchant & Osterberg, *supra* note 5 (reporting that Iowa now has 23 million hogs in CAFOs with the "Fecal Equivalent Population" of 168 million people, and recent polls show 80% of Iowans are concerned about the polluting impacts on nearby communities).

152. *See* Donnelle Eller, *No More Livestock Confinements Until Iowa Water Improves, Group Says,* DES MOINES REG. (Jan. 17, 2018, 11:07 AM), https://www.desmoines register.com/story/money/agriculture/2018/01/16/coalition-calls-iowa-lawmakers -support-cafo-moratorium-until-water-quality-improves/1034756001 [https://perma .cc/UY55-SN2D].

153. *See* William Petroski & Brianne Pfannenstiel, *What Ideas Did the 2018 Iowa Legislature Leave to Die?,* DES MOINES REG. (Oct. 22, 2018 5:52 PM), https://www .desmoinesregister.com/story/news/politics/2018/05/05/transgender-guns-court -classic-cars-fossils-iowa-legislature-killed-fossils/456056002 [https://perma.cc/E2F4 -W572].

154. *See* Smart, *supra* note 26, at 2109.

155. *Id.* at 2107.

156. *See* Addison, *supra* note 12, at 237.

157. *See* An Act to (1) Codify and Make Permanent the Swine Farm Animal Waste Management System Performance Standards that the General Assembly Enacted in 1998, (2) Provide for the Replacement of a Lagoon That Is an Imminent Hazard, (3) Assist Farmers to Voluntarily Convert to Innovative Animal Waste Management

Systems, and (4) Establish the Swine Farm Methane Capture Pilot Program, 2007 N.C. Sess Laws 523.

158. *Id.*

159. *See* Merchant & Osterberg, *supra* note 93, at 22–23.

160. *Id.*

161. *Id.* at 22. The Center focused on supporting what it considered the 16 most promising proposals.

162. *Id.*

163. *Id.* at 22–23.

164. *See* Addison, *supra* note 12, at 248.

165. *See* Smart, *supra* note 26, at 2107 n.68.

166. *Id.*

167. EPA statistics from 2018 show that North Carolina has 1,222 CAFOs eligible for NPDES permits, but only 14 such permits have been issued. *See* EPA, *supra* note 63.

168. *See* Mo. Code Reg. Ann. tit. 10, § 20-6.300 (2021); Minn. Stat. Ann. § 561.19 (West, Westlaw through all legislation from the 2021 Regular Session and 1st Special Session).

169. *See* 2019 MO Reg Text 498366 (NS); Mo. Code Reg. Ann. tit. 10, § 20-6.300.

170. *See* Agriculture—Loan Programs, Electronic Grain Purchase Documents, 2004 Minn. Sess. Law Serv. ch. 254 (S.F. 2428) (West), Minn. Stat. Ann. § 561.19.

171. *See* Hines, *supra* note 116, at 644–45.

172. *See id.* at 654–55, 665.

173. *See generally* Goodell v. Humboldt C'nty. 575 N.W.2d 486 (Iowa 1998) (holding "the county's authority to enact the ordinances had been preempted by the legislature").

174. *Id.* at 493, 506–7.

175. Iowa Code § 657.11 (2021).

176. *Goodell,* 575 N.W.2d at 511–13 (Snell, J., dissenting).

177. *Id.* at 507–08 (majority opinion).

178. *See* Iowa Code § 331.304A.

179. Worth Cnty. Friends of Agric. v. Worth C'nty., 688 N.W.2d 257, 264 (Iowa 2004).

180. *Id.*

181. N.C. Gen. Stat. Ann. § 153A-340 (West 2017) (repealed 2020).

182. Tom Coulter, *New CAFO Law Divides Farmers Over Future of Agriculture, Environment in Missouri,* Columbia Missourian (Aug. 7, 2019), https://www .columbiamissourian.com/news/state_news/new-cafo-law-divides-farmers-over -future-of-agriculture-environment-in-missouri/article_100544e2-b55a-11e9-896c -e384d1d22d9c.html [https://perma.cc/7B4Y-Y2XD].

183. *Id.*

184. *See generally* William Aldred's Case (1611) 77 Eng. Rep. 816; 9 Co. Rep. 57 b (holding that the plaintiff should recover damages due to defendant erecting a swine sty).

185. *Id.* at 817.

186. *Id.*

187. *Id.*

188. *Id.* at 817, 822. One might be tempted to say 40£ in damages is a petty penalty, but converted to 2020 value, 40£ would be equivalent to over $200,000 in damages today.

189. *Id.* at 817.

190. *See, e.g.*, Weinhold v. Wolff, 555 N.W.2d 454, 465–66 (Iowa 1996) (awarding $45,000 in damages to landowners neighboring a commercial hog feeding facility).

191. *See* Lucas v. S.C. Coastal Council, 505 U.S. 1003, 1030 (1992).

192. *See* DAN B. DOBBS, PAUL T. HAYDEN & ELLEN M. BUBLICK, HORNBOOK ON TORTS 733–44 (2d ed. 2016); DANIEL R. MANDELKER ET AL., PLANNING AND CONTROL OF LAND DEVELOPMENT: CASES AND MATERIALS 63–69 (8th ed. 2011).

193. *See, e.g.*, IOWA CODE § 352.11 (2021); MINN. STAT. ANN. § 561.19 (West, Westlaw through all legislation from the 2021 Regular Session and 1st Special Session); NEB. REV. STAT. ANN. § 2-4403 (West, Westlaw through the end of the 1st Regular Session and the end of the 1st Special Session of the 107th Legislature (2021)). *See also* Kitt Tovar, *Update on Right-to-Farm Legislation, Cases, and Constitutional Amendments*, IOWA ST. UNIV. CTR. FOR AGRIC. L. & TAX'N (May 28, 2019), https://www.calt.iastate.edu/article/update-right-farm-legislation-cases-and -constitutional-amendments [https://perma.cc/56V5-NYQ8].

194. *See, e.g.*, IOWA CODE § 657.11 (2021); N.C. GEN. STAT. §§ 106-701, 702 (2021).

195. *See, e.g.*, Honomichl v. Valley View Swine, 914 N.W.2d 223, 226–27, 238–39 (Iowa 2018) (challenging nuisance protections for CAFOs).

196. *See* Bormann v. Bd. of Supervisors, 584 N.W.2d 309, 314–16, 321–22 (Iowa 1998).

197. *See* Gacke v. Pork Xtra, L.L.C., 684 N.W.2d 168, 170–71 (Iowa 2004).

198. The original Latin maxim is "sic utere tuo ut alienum non lædas." William Aldred's Case (1611) 77 Eng. Rep. 816, 821; 9 Co. Rep. 57 b, 59 a.

199. *See, e.g., id.*

200. *Id.* at 821–22.

201. *See* DAN B. DOBBS, PAUL T. HAYDEN & ELLEN M. BUBLICK, THE LAW OF TORTS §399 (2d ed. June 2020 update).

202. *See, e.g.*, IOWA CODE § 657.1 (2021).

203. *See* Helmkamp v. Clark Ready Mix Co., 214 N.W.2d 126, 129–30 (Iowa 1974) (explaining that "our [nuisance] statute does not abrogate the common law").

204. David R. Gillay, *Oklahoma's Concentrated Animal Feeding Operations Act: Balancing the Interests of Landowners with the Exponential Growth of the Hog Industry*, 35 TULSA L.J. 627, 632–33 (2000).

205. *Id.*

206. *Id.* at 633.

207. *See* IOWA CODE § 657.11A(1) (2021) (statement of findings and purpose indicative of legislative intent).

208. *See* RESTATEMENT (SECOND) OF TORTS §§ 826–30 (AM. L. INST. 1979).

209. *Id.* § 826.

210. *Id.* §§ 827–28.

211. *See* John E. Bryson & Angus Macbeth, *Public Nuisance, the Restatement (Second) of Torts, and Environmental Law*, 2 ECOLOGY L.Q. 241, 269–73 (1972).

212. *See* Schlotfelt v. Vinton Farmers' Supply Co., 109 N.W.2d 695, 698–700 (Iowa 1961).

213. *See id.*

214. *See, e.g.*, Patz v. Farmegg Prods., Inc., 196 N.W.2d 557, 561 (Iowa 1972).

215. *See, e.g.*, Bove v. Donner-Hanna Coke Corp., 258 N.Y.S. 229, 231–33 (N.Y. App. Div. 1932).

216. RESTATEMENT (SECOND) OF TORTS § 827 cmt. g (AM. L. INST. 1979).

217. *See* DAN B. DOBBS, PAUL T. HAYDEN & ELLEN M. BUBLICK, TORTS AND COMPENSATION: PERSONAL ACCOUNTABILITY AND SOCIAL RESPONSIBILITY FOR INJURY 682 (7th ed. 2013); *see, e.g.*, Spur Indus., Inc. v. Del E. Webb Dev. Co., 494 P.2d 700, 707 (Ariz. 1972) ("Were Webb the only party injured, we would feel justified in holding that the doctrine of 'coming to the nuisance' would have been a bar to the relief asked by Webb").

218. *See* DAN B. DOBBS & CAPRICE L. ROBERTS, LAW OF REMEDIES: DAMAGES—EQUITY—RESTITUTION 528–44 (3d ed. 2018).

219. *See, e.g.*, Weinhold v. Wolff, 555 N.W.2d 454, 465–67 (Iowa 1996) (describing some of these remedies in detail).

220. *See, e.g.*, Boomer v. Atl. Cement Co., 257 N.E.2d 870, 874–75 (N.Y. 1970).

221. RESTATEMENT (SECOND) OF TORTS §§ 941–43 (AM. L INST. 1979).

222. *Id.* § 941.

223. *Id.* § 942.

224. *See, e.g.*, Riter v. Keokuk Electro-Metals Co., 82 N.W.2d 151, 159–62 (Iowa 1957).

225. *See, e.g.*, Gacke v. Pork Xtra, L.L.C., 684 N.W.2d 168, 171–72 (Iowa 2004) (district court below denied injunctive relief).

226. *See* Boomer v. Atl. Cement Co., 257 N.E.2d 870, 874 (N.Y. 1970) ("Where a nuisance is of such a permanent and difficult to abate character that a single recovery can be had, including the whole damage past and future resulting therefrom, there can be but one recovery.").

227. *See id.* at 874–75.

228. *See* Doug Rendleman, *Rehabilitating the Nuisance Injunction to Protect the Environment*, 75 WASH. & LEE L. REV. 1859, 1888–89 (2018).

229. *See* MANDELKER ET AL., *supra* note 214, at 71–74.

230. *Id.*

231. *Id.*

232. *See, e.g.*, Farmer v. Ky. Utils. Co., 642 S.W.2d 579, 580–81 (Ky. 1982).

233. *See* Gacke v. Pork Xtra, L.L.C., 684 N.W.2d 168, 175 (Iowa 2004).

234. *See* DOBBS & ROBERTS, *supra* note 218, at 530–31.

235. *See id.*

236. *Id.*

237. *See* IOWA CODE § 657.11A (2021); N.C. GEN. STAT. ANN. §§ 106-701, 106-702 (2021) (limiting compensatory and punitive damages).

238. *See* DOBBS & ROBERTS, *supra* note 218, at 312–29.

239. *See, e.g.*, Patz v. Farmegg Prods., Inc., 196 N.W.2d 557, 563 (Iowa 1972) (affirming a denial of special damages).

240. *See* Laura J. Hines & N. William Hines, *Constitutional Constraints on Punitive Damages: Clarity, Consistency, and the Outlier Dilemma*, 66 HASTINGS L.J. 1257, 1259, 1275 (2015).

241. *See* Kitt Kovar, *Update of Right-to-Farm Legislation, Cases, and Constitutional Amendments*, Iowa State Ctr. For Agric. Law and Tax'n (May 28, 2019).

242. *See* Jacqueline P. Hand, *Right-to-Farm Laws: Breaking New Ground in the Preservation of Farmland*, 45 U. PITT. L. REV. 289, 297–98 (1984).

243. *See* Ashwood et al., *supra* note 6, at 120–21.

244. Hand, *supra* note 242, at 309–19.

245. *See, e.g.*, Himsel v. Himsel, 122 N.E.3d 935, 938–41, 950 (Ind. Ct. App. 2019) (farmer who switched from cash crops to raising more than 4,000 hogs in a large CAFO was protected by Indiana's right-to-farm law that specifically allowed conversion from one type of agriculture to another type of agriculture).

246. *See* Steven D. Shrout, *Missouri's Right to Farm Statute's Durational Use Requirement and the Right to Farm Amendment*, 83 UMKC L. REV. 499, 517 (2014); Hand, *supra* note 242, at 314–19.

247. *See* Neil D. Hamilton, *Right-to-Farm Laws Reconsidered: Ten Reasons Why Legislative Efforts to Resolve Agricultural Nuisances May Be Ineffective*, 3 DRAKE J. AGRIC. L. 103, 108–9 (1998).

248. *See, e.g.*, Weinhold v. Wolff, 555 N.W.2d 454, 462–63 (Iowa 1996) (right-to-farm defense denied because nuisance began before CAFO qualified for statutory protection); Durham v. Britt, 451 S.E.2d 1, 3–4 (N.C. Ct. App. 1994) (change from small turkey raising operation to large hog CAFO was too great a change and denied defendant protection of the law); Mayes v. Tabor, 334 S.E.2d 489, 491 (N.C. Ct. App. 1985) ("[A]n agricultural operation that was not a nuisance when it began cannot become a nuisance due to 'changed conditions in or about the locality thereof after the same has been in operation for more than one year'"); Alpental C'mty. Club, Inc. v. Seattle Gymnastics Soc'y, 111 P. 3d 257, 261–62 (Wash. 2005) (right-to-farm law not applied because there was no evidence that defendant's forest preserve was there first).

249. *See* An Act to Amend the Indiana Code Concerning Property, 2005 IND. LEGIS. SERV. P.L. 23-2005 (West); IND. CODE ANN. § 32-30-6-9(d) (West, Westlaw current with all legislation of the 2021 First Regular Session of the 122d General Assembly effective through July 1, 2021).

250. *See* Dalzell v. Country View Fam. Farms, LLC, 517 F. App'x 518, 518–20 (7th Cir. 2013) (mem.).

251. Bormann v. Bd. of Supervisors, 584 N.W.2d 309, 313–14 (Iowa 1998).

252. *See* Weinhold v. Wolff, 555 N.W.2d 454, 462–63 (Iowa 1996).

253. Bormann, 584 N.W.2d at 311, 321–22.

254. *Id.* at 311, 313.

255. Gacke v. Pork Xtra, L.L.C., 684 N.W.2d 168, 173 (Iowa 2004).

256. *See id.* at 171.

257. *See id.* at 172–74.

258. *Id.* at 173.

259. *See* IOWA CODE § 657.11A (2021).

260. *See* Hines, *supra* note 22, at 55–59, 63–64; David Bennett, *Right to Farm Laws Being Tweaked across Nation*, FARM PROGRESS (Aug. 7, 2013), https://www .farmprogress.com/government/right-farm-laws-being-tweaked-across-nation [https://perma.cc/RH92-GHRC].

261. *See* Hines, *supra* note 22, at 55.

262. *Id.*

263. *See* Lucas v. S.C. Coastal Council, 505 U.S. 1003, 1019, 1027 (1992).

264. *See* Penn Cent. Transp. Co. v. City of New York, 438 U.S. 104, 105 (1978) (taking occurs only if the diminution in the property value is excessive); *see also* Jeffry R. Gittins, Comment, Bormann *Revisited: Using the* Penn Central *Test to Determine the Constitutionality of Right-to-Farm Statutes*, 2006 B.Y.U. L. Rev. 1381, 1403–7.

265. *See Penn Cent. Transp. Co.*, 438 U.S. at 131.

266. *See generally* Cedar Point Nursery v. Hassid, 141 S. Ct. 2063 (2021) (takings clause case decided June 23, 2021).

267. *Id.* at 2078–80.

268. *Id.* at 2070–71.

269. *Id.* at 2072–73.

270. Kaiser Aetna v. United States, 444 U.S. 164 (1979).

271. Nollan v. Cal. Coastal Comm'n, 483 U.S. 825 (1987).

272. Dolan v. City of Tigard, 512 U.S. 374 (1994).

273. Lucas v. S.C. Coastal Council, 505 U.S. 1003 (1992).

274. Horne v. Dep't of Agric., 135 S. Ct. 2419 (2015).

275. Cedar Point Nursery v. Hassid, 141 S. Ct. 2063, 2072–74 (2021).

276. *Id.*

277. *See* Honomichl v. Valley View Swine, LLC, 914 N.W.2d 223 (Iowa 2018).

278. *Id.* at 239–40 (Waterman, J., concurring).

279. *Id.*

280. 977 N.W. 2d 67 (2022).

281. *Id.* at 77.

282. *Id.* at 78.

283. Gacke v. Pork Extra, LLC, 684 N.W. 2d 168, `172 ( Iowa 2004).

284. Bormann at 322.

285. *See supra* Section V.B.2.

286. Addison, *supra* note 12 tells the complete story of these nuisance cases

287. *See* Smart, *supra* note 26, at 2124–34.

288. *See* Durham v. Britt, 451 S.E.2d 1, 3–4 (N.C. Ct. App. 1994).

289. *See* Smart, *supra* note 26, at 2129–31.

290. *See id.* at 2131–32; N.C. GEN. STAT. § 106-701(f) (2021).

291. *See* Yeoman, *supra* note 6.

292. *Id.*

293. *Id.* ("The jury awarded the 10 plaintiffs $50.75 million combined, though the award was reduced to $3.25 million because of a state cap on punitive damages.")

294. Lisa Sorg, *Neutering Nuisance Laws in North Carolina*, NC POL'Y WATCH (Nov. 15, 2017), https://ncpolicywatch.com/2017/11/15/neutering-nuisance-laws -north-carolina [https://perma.cc/PNJ2-3397].

295. *See* Yeoman, *supra* note 6.

296. *See* N.C. GEN. STAT. § 106-702 (2021) (determining damages strictly on loss in fair market value of the affected property).

297. *Id.* § 106-702(b).

298. *Id.* § 106-702(a1).

299. Erica Hellerstein, *Despite Governor Cooper's Veto, HB 467—The Hog-Farm-Protection Bill—Is Now Law*, INDY WEEK (May 17, 2017, 7:00 AM), https://indyweek .com/news/despite-governor-cooper-s-veto-hb-467-the-hog-farm-protection-bill-is -now-law [https://perma.cc/KX6G-6KAX].

300. *See* Yeoman, *supra* note 6.

301. *See* N.C. GEN. STAT. § 106-701(a)(2) (2021).

302. *Id.* §§ 106-701(a)(3), (a1). Recall that North Carolina's 2013 right-to-farm amendments had already eliminated almost every relevant change in a farming operation from being treated as a "fundamental change." *See supra* notes 304–6 and accompanying text.

303. *See* N.C. GEN. STAT. § 106-701(a)(3), (a1) (2021).

304. *Id.*

305. *See* 2018 N.C. SESS LAWS 113 (deleting N.C. GEN. STAT. § 106-701(a2)).

306. *See* IOWA CODE § 331.304A (2021). This code section was ruled constitutional by the Iowa Supreme Court in Worth Cnty. Friends of Agric. v. Worth Cnty., 688 N.W.2d 257, 265 (Iowa 2004).

307. IOWA CODE § 331.304A.

308. Ashley Pollard, Note, *This Little Piggy Caused a Nuisance: Analyzing North Carolina's 2018 Amendment to Its Right-to-Farm Act*, 14 LIBERTY U. L. REV. 569, 582–83 (2020).

309. *See* Complaint at 16–22, Rural Empowerment Ass'n for Cmty. Help v. North Carolina, No. 19-CVS-008198, 2019 WL 3456702 (N.C. Super. June 19, 2019).

310. McKiver v. Murphy-Brown, LLC, 980 F.3d 937, 977 (4th Cir. 2020).

311. *See* Addison, *supra* note 12, at 361.

312. *Id.* at 946.

313. *Id.*

314. *Id.* at 937.

315. *Id.* at 976–77.

316. *Id.* at 946, 965–66 (emphasizing the defendants knew they were causing severe harms to the plaintiffs but continued business as usual, justifying the punitive damages).

317. *Id.* at 977, 979–82 (Wilkinson, J., concurring) (eloquently describing the serious health and environmental dangers the operation of ever larger CAFOs pose to the confined animals, to workers in the facilities, to neighbors, and to the public at large).

318. *Id.* at 984 (Agee, J., concurring in part and dissenting in part) (finding he would have denied plaintiffs any punitive damages).

319. *Id.* at 950–52 (majority opinion). To qualify for federal diversity jurisdiction, the plaintiffs deliberately did not sue Kinlaw Farms, LLC, the North Carolina CAFO from which the nuisance damages to plaintiffs emanated. *Id.* The Court ruled Kinlaw Farms, LLC was not a necessary party in the case because the hogs involved were all owned by Murphy-Brown, LLC, who also completely controlled the operation of the hog CAFO, including its manure management practices, under the terms of its contract with Kinlaw Farms, LLC. *Id.*

320. *Id.* at 952–54.

321. *Id.* at 954–58.

322. *Id.* at 958.

323. In new litigation against Murphy-Brown, LLC, initiated in 2020, the plaintiffs are claiming trespass and negligence harms against the offending CAFOs to avoid the force of the new legislation restricting nuisance suits against CAFOs. In an initial procedural ruling, the federal district court agreed to allow this litigation to go forward. *See* Gary Baise, *Smithfield Loses Another Right-to-Farm Legal Battle Over CAFOs*, FARM FUTURES (Apr. 6, 2021), https://www.farmprogress.com/commentary /smithfield-loses-another-right-farm-legal-battle-over-cafos [https://perma.cc /BUQ2-EC5V].

324. *McKiver*, 980 F.3d at 961–63.

325. *Id.* at 965–77.

326. *Id.* at 962.

327. *Id.* at 965, 976–77.

328. *See* Gary D. Robertson, *Court Upholds Hog Verdict; Smithfield Announces Settlement*, AP NEWS (Nov. 19, 2020), https://apnews.com/article/north-carolina -courts-4b2f1db4c21e03653851e81b81996410 [https://perma.cc/L2EC-ZEMF].

329. *See* Addison, *supra* note 12, at 377.

330. *See* Ross H. Pifer, *Right to Farm Statutes and the Changing State of Modern Agriculture*, 46 CREIGHTON L. REV. 707, 709–11, 719 (2013).

331. *See* Blake Nicholson, *Voters Make North Dakota First State in Nation to Protect Right to Farm in Constitution*, STAR TRIBUNE (Nov. 8, 2012, 1:07 PM), https://www .startribune.com/north-dakota-voters-add-farmer-protection-to-constitution /177921891 [https://perma.cc/4DKZ-FHDU].

332. The Missouri Amendment was upheld against a constitutional challenge in Shoemyer v. Missouri Secretary of State, 464 S.W.3d 171 (Mo. 2015).

333. *See* S. 187, 96th Gen. Assemb., 1st Reg. Sess. (Mo. 2011); MO. ANN. STAT. § 537.296 (West, Westlaw current through the end of the 2021 First Regular and First Extraordinary Sessions of the 101st General Assembly).

334. *See, e.g.,* Citizens Legal Environmental Action Network, Inc v. Premium Standard Farms, Inc., 2000 WL 220464 (W.D. Mo. 2000).

335. *See* Addison, *supra* note 12, at 243.

336. *See* An Act to Amend the Indiana Code Concerning Property, 2005 Ind. Legis. Serv. P.L. 23-2005 (West); IND. CODE ANN. § 32-30-6-9(d)(1) (West, Westlaw current with all legislation of the 2021 First Regular Session of the 122d General Assembly effective through July 1, 2021).

337. *See* Dalzell v. Country View Fam. Farms, LLC, 517 F. App'x 518, 518–20 (7th Cir. 2013) (mem.).

338. *See* IND. CODE ANN. § 32-30-6-9.5 (West, Westlaw current with all legislation of the 2021 First Regular Session of the 122nd General Assembly effective through July 1, 2021).

339. *See* H.B. 2918, 85th Gen. Assembly., Reg. Sess. (Ark. 2005); ARK. CODE ANN. § 2-4-107 (2021).

340. *See* Moon v. N. Idaho Farmers Ass'n, 96 P.3d 637, 645 (Idaho 2004); Labrayere v. Bohr Farms, LLC, 458 S.W.3d 319, 327–31 (Mo. 2015); Himsel v. Himsel, 122 N.E.3d 935, 946–48 (Ind. Ct. App. 2019).

341. Technological solutions to attaining a higher level of treatment of wet hog wastes is discussed elsewhere in this book.

# CHAPTER 9

# Packing Plant Worker Health Effects

Impact of COVID-19

Debbie Berkowitz and James A. Merchant

From Upton Sinclair's *The Jungle*[1] published in 1906 to the 2019 report by Human Rights Watch, "When We're Dead and Buried Our Bones Will Keep Hurting,"[2] the continuous hazardous working conditions facing workers in meat and poultry slaughter and processing plants have been well documented. Sinclair singled out the breakneck line speeds as the key source of worker misery over 100 years ago. Meatpacking workers still face dangerous working conditions that now result in injury rates three times the national average, exceptionally high numbers of amputations and lacerations, and extraordinarily high rates of repetitive trauma disorders. Declared "essential workers" who worked throughout the pandemic, meatpacking workers and their communities suffered disproportionally high rates of COVID-19 infections, illnesses, and deaths. Congressional reports documented the meat industry's failure to protect workers during the pandemic, underscoring how the meat and poultry industry not only failed to implement effective mitigation measures but actually fought to avoid protecting workers.[3] As a result, meatpacking plants witnessed some of the worst outbreaks in the country, endangering not only workers but also their families and their local communities—resulting in preventable widespread illness and death.[4] Government studies found that the overwhelming majority of meatpacking workers infected with the coronavirus were racial and ethnic minorities.[5]

## A Vertically Integrated Industry Where Just a Few Corporations Dominate

Today, the meat and poultry industry is highly concentrated and dominated by a handful of billion-dollar corporations.[6] Two corporations dominate much of the industry in the United States: JBS/Pilgrim's Pride, a Brazilian-owned company, is the largest meatpacker in the world with $270 billion in revenue in 2020,[7] and Tyson Foods is the second largest meatpacker in the world and the largest poultry company in the United States, with $43.2 billion in revenue in 2020.[8] JBS/Pilgrim's Pride, Tyson Foods, Smithfield Foods (a Chinese-owned company), Cargill, and National Beef Packing (a majority-owned Brazilian company) represent over 80% of the beef market and 60% of the market for pork in the United States.[9] The top five chicken processors are Tyson Foods and JBS/Pilgrim's Pride, with almost 40% of the market; Sanderson (now Cargill); Perdue; and Koch.[10] On an annual basis, meatpacking workers process 33.6 million cattle, nearly 600,000 calves, 130 million hogs, and over 2 million sheep and lambs. Poultry plant workers process over 9.3 billion chickens and 228 million turkeys into 50 billion pounds of chicken and turkey products. In the United States, meat and poultry slaughtering and processing is an over $172 billion industry.[11,12] A good deal of all US meat production is exported. In 2020, 26% of all US pork production was exported.[13]

## A Vulnerable, Immigrant, People of Color Workforce

Almost 500,000 workers nationwide are employed in the meat and poultry slaughter and processing industry. The plants are located primarily in rural areas and employ between several hundred to a few thousand workers in each plant. Nationally, the American Community

Survey (ACS), an annual survey administered by the US Census Bureau, provides the best ethnographic information on the meat- and poultry-processing workforce. The workforce is nearly two-thirds male with a mean age of 41. It is overwhelmingly made up of people of color (35% white, 22% Black, 35% Latino, and 9% other people of color). Nearly two-thirds are foreign born, mainly from Mexico and Latin America, and nearly two-thirds speak Spanish. Many are refugees, and dozens of languages are spoken in most plants. Of foreign-born workers, over 70% are noncitizens. Median wage and salary income is $30,500–$35,000 for meatpacking workers but only $26,449 for poultry plant workers, reflecting this largely southern nonunion workforce. Nearly 9% have incomes below the poverty line and only 15.5% have health insurance.[14,15] University of North Carolina's Angela Stuesse and Nathan Dollar write that "America's food chain workers have long lived with the economic, social, and health effects of neoliberalism, white supremacy, patriarchy, and xenophobia. These intersecting ills have set the table for the COVID-19 pandemic to dramatically and disproportionally infect meat and poultry workers across the country and around the world."[16]

### Workplace Dangers, Impacts on Worker Health and Safety

The meat- and poultry-processing industry ranks as one of the harshest work environments in the United States.[17] In meat and poultry plants across the country, workers stand side-by-side on both sides of long conveyor belts, in cold, damp, dangerously loud conditions while working with knives and scissors. They make the same forceful cuts or movements thousands of times a day as they slaughter, skin, disassemble, debone, and package cattle, hogs, and poultry into the products consumers buy in the supermarket. Many poultry worker handles dozens of birds per minute.[18] Annual employee turnover in these plants averages 60% but can run as high as 150%.[19]

The meat and poultry industry was already unsafe when the COVID-19 pandemic began.[20,21,22] Data from the Bureau of Labor Statistics (BLS) released in late 2021, based on the industry's self-reported case numbers, reveal that meat and poultry plant workers sustain serious injuries and illnesses that result in lost time or restricted duty at rates more than triple the average for all private industry.[23] Four government agencies— the Occupational Safety and Health Administration (OSHA),[24] the National Institute of Occupational Safety and Health (NIOSH),[25] the Government Accountability Office (GAO),[26] and the US Department of Agriculture (USDA)[27]—as well as academic research[28] have found that these statistics are all undercounts—the true rates are much higher for meat and poultry plants. For example, in the 2014 USDA final rule establishing a new poultry inspection system (a rule that did not increase line speeds in the poultry industry), the USDA concluded that "poultry processors' injury and illness logs often do not reflect the full extent of work-related conditions experienced by poultry workers" and further recognized that "systematic underreporting of work-related injuries and illnesses could make it difficult to accurately assess the extent to which poultry workers suffer from work related injuries and musculo-skeletal diseases and disorders."[29] NIOSH published two Health Hazard Evaluations in 2012 and 2015 documenting high rates of carpal tunnel syndrome among production workers in poultry plants but found that the companies had self-reported only a handful of such cases on their OSHA recordkeeping forms.[30,31] And OSHA has cited meat and poultry plants for their failure to report injuries.[32,33,34] Even given underreporting, the BLS self-reported industry data show that poultry workers face amputation rates that are 5 times the average for all industries, and meatpacking workers suffer amputations at rates 14 times the average for all industries.[35]

The rapid, forceful, and repetitive physical movements required on meat and poultry lines, over sustained periods of time, often lead to chronic painful musculoskeletal disorders. A survey of 200 poultry plant workers in North Carolina found that 28% reported at least one work-related injury or illness in the previous 12 months, and 46% reported musculoskeletal symptoms (including legs, feet, back, neck, and upper extremities) within the preceding 30 days.[36] A study of African American women poultry plant workers reported two to three times as many upper extremity and neck symptoms, such as hand, wrist, and neck pain, as a matched group of nonpoultry women workers. Symptoms of carpal tunnel syndrome (numbness, tingling, and pain of the palm and wrist) were twice as frequent in these poultry workers as those of the nonpoultry workers.[37] An additional study of this same group of African American women poultry workers found a positive association between symptoms of musculoskeletal disorders and cumulative exposure to job tasks with repetitive, forceful movements and extreme, awkward upper extremity postures. The authors recommended that "it would be prudent to slow the speed of the lines while working to reduce postural load and force."[38]

A 2012 study of Latino poultry plant workers (cutting, eviscerating, washing, trimming, deboning) reported that the prevalence of carpal tunnel syndrome was two and a half times higher in poultry workers when compared to Latino manual nonpoultry workers.[39] In 2014 and 2015 Health Hazard Evaluations, NIOSH found alarmingly high rates of carpal tunnel syndrome among production workers in two chicken-processing plants—rates from 34% to 42% of plant workers, respectively. Fully 41% of the participants worked in jobs that had levels of hand activity and force above the American Conference of Governmental Industrial Hygienists' threshold limit values (TLVs).[40,41] According to the most recent BLS data, meatpacking workers suffer rates of carpal tunnel syndrome requiring time off work that are more than five times higher than the average for all other private industries.[42]

Epidemiological studies also reveal that the fast line speeds and pace of work in meatpacking plants also lead to other serious injuries—such as lacerations.[43,44] One study concluded, "Rushing was identified as the cause of nearly 50% of injuries" and that "self-reported incidence rate of severe injury was more than twice official industry estimates."[45] The use of OSHA-required metal mesh sleeves and gloves in meatpacking plants has been found to significantly reduce risk of injury.[46]

Conditions inside meatpacking facilities expose workers to other serious health and safety hazards: high noise levels; hazardous chemicals used as antimicrobials, refrigerants, and to sanitize plants; unguarded equipment; and slippery floors.[47] High production line speeds increase meat and poultry workers' exposure to all of these hazards.

Respiratory and eye complaints have been documented from exposure to high levels of chlorinated cleaning compounds, a primary finding of a joint NIOSH, OSHA, USDA, and several state health department study in 1995.[48] NIOSH Health Hazard Evaluations (HHEs) found poultry processing plant workers to have significantly higher rates of respiratory symptoms in areas with high exposures to chlorine-related compounds. Implementation of engineering and ventilation controls reduced both exposures and symptoms.[49,50] Additional studies have found that high levels of organic dust and endotoxin in poultry hanging rooms have resulted in significant increases in respiratory symptoms and decreases in lung function.[51,52] Other studies have documented increases in the prevalence of both respiratory illnesses and skin diseases.[53,54] Peracetic acid (PAA) is now widely used in the poultry and meat industry as an antimicrobial. PAA is a highly corrosive toxic chemical that is irritating to eyes and skin, causing severe rashes, burns, and destruction of the eye tissue among exposed workers. In poultry plants, the chicken product is dipped and sprayed with PAA many times during both the slaughter and processing of the birds.[55] Few plants have enclosed systems to limit worker exposure to PAA.

Many meat and poultry plants have on-site workplace clinics where workers are required to visit to obtain care for work-related injuries and illnesses. Multiple investigations by OSHA have found that meat and poultry plant clinics endanger injured workers by delaying appropriate medical treatment and continue unsafe work exposures, rather than resulting in mitigation of hazards to prevent further injuries and illnesses.[56,57,58] Workers who sought help in plant clinics for musculoskeletal disorders as well as emergencies such as frostbite or head injuries have been sent back to work rather than sent to a doctor.[59,60] If workers sought the doctor's care on their own, they risked retaliatory actions by the company.[61,62] OSHA investigations have found clinic staff operating without supervision and working outside their scope of practice, resulting in worse medical outcomes for injured workers.[63,64] A recent OSHA investigation in a meatpacking plant in Oklahoma described findings about the plant's on-site clinic, which is typical of what OSHA found in clinics in other plants:

> OSHA's inspection revealed that staff with inadequate credentials appear to treat conditions without a diagnosis, without scheduling employees for follow-up visits with the First Aid clinic, and not referring to a healthcare provider with the necessary expertise—even when employees ask for a referral. Some workers who sought care from private healthcare providers were informed that they must seek care at Seaboard Foods (the nation's fourth largest pork producer) for work-related conditions in order to have insurance cover it. Thus, if Seaboard Farms does not refer, the worker either continues to work with chronic pain or quits and may still have chronic pain and ongoing disability.[65]

When a worker is not approved to see a doctor and only receives first aid treatment by the company's clinic, their injury or illness does not have to be recorded on the company's official log of injuries and illnesses, per OSHA regulations. A recent study of meatpacking workers in Nebraska found that workers were intimidated to not report work-related injuries or illnesses for fear of losing their jobs. "Workers lack of trust in the health office was multifactorial and centered on fear of job loss, inadequate support for their health and safety needs, and language barriers." With misleading low recordable injury rates, the industry claims it is safer than it really is.[66,67]

Most meatpacking companies provide no paid or unpaid sick leave to workers. Throughout the industry, employers have adopted punitive leave systems whereby a worker who is injured or ill and must miss work, even for a work-related injury, is punished with points. If the worker accumulates too many points, they are fired. The lack of sick leave creates a culture in meat and poultry plants that incentivizes sick and injured workers to come back to work or lose their job.[68]

And in February 2023, the Department of Labor announced they had found over 100 children illegally employed in hazardous jobs in 13 meat-processing facilities in eight states (including plants owned by JBS,

Tyson Foods, and Cargill). The children, some as young as 13, were employed by a subcontractor (Packers Sanitation Services Inc., PSSI) and found to be working the overnight shift in big meat plants "with hazardous chemicals and cleaning meat processing equipment including back saws, brisket saws and head splitters. Investigators learned at least three minors suffered injuries while working" in the plants.[69]

## Meatpacking Plants and the Wildfire Spread of COVID-19

From the very beginning of the pandemic, in early March 2020, COVID-19 infections and deaths raced through meat and poultry plants across the United States. Meatpacking plants witnessed alarming infection rates of between 20% and 50% of plant workers during just the first months of the pandemic. At a Tyson Food hog-processing plant in Waterloo, Iowa, which produces pork for export to China, COVID-19 began spreading in March 2020 and infected over 1,000 workers, leaving 5 workers dead by early May.[70,71] A wrongful death lawsuit, filed by family members of workers who died, uncovered that plant managers had a betting pool on how many workers would get infected, while at the same time telling interpreters to downplay the threat of infection in the plant to keep workers on the line.[72,73,74] After being fired by Tyson Foods, these managers are suing to recover lost incentive payments claimed because they did meet Tyson quotas.[75] In a Smithfield hog slaughter plant in Sioux Falls, South Dakota, over 1,600 workers (42% of the workforce) were infected and 4 workers died in the first few months of the pandemic.[76,77] In a JBS beef plant in Cactus, Texas, an executive received an April 2020 email from a doctor in a nearby hospital: "100% of all COVID-19 patients we have in the hospital are either direct employees or family member[s] of your employees" and warned that "your employees will get sick and may die if this factory continues to be open."[78] In a large Tyson's beef packinghouse in Dakota City, Nebraska, 18 workers lost their lives to COVID-19 and 1,973 employees were infected (an infection rate of approximately 46%).[79] In a rural Eastern Shore of Maryland poultry-processing plant, hundreds of workers were infected and several died in the first few pandemic weeks, resulting in Salisbury, Maryland, becoming one of the nation's emerging hot spots for COVID-19 infections.[80] In a Foster Farms poultry plant in Livingston, California, where by mid-August 2020 there were over 360 infections, nearly a third of the plant's employees were infected and eight workers died.[81,82] More workers in meat and poultry plants died from COVID-19 during the first 12 months of the pandemic than from all other work-related causes in the past 15 years.[83,84]

When COVID-19 spread through the meat and poultry plants, it was the workers' unions, their children, and community groups who sounded the alarm about the spread of COVID-19 in the plants and fearlessly fought for better protections. In some plants, the rising case numbers early in the pandemic led to days of community protests demanding better protection for workers.[85,86,87,88,89,90,91,92]

The full extent of coronavirus infections and deaths in the meatpacking industry will never be known. The meat industry never published their own data on how many of their workers tested positive and died from COVID-19. The federal government did not require meat and poultry companies to report their test data or outbreaks. Some, but not all states, collected data from limited COVID-19 testing on workers in meat plants, but almost all the big meatpacking states did not make that data public. States with some of the largest numbers of meat and poultry plants, such as Texas, Iowa, Arkansas, Missouri, South Dakota, Georgia, Mississippi, Alabama, and eventually Nebraska, did not make any plantwide outbreak or case numbers public.[93,94,95]

The few meatpacking plants that made their data publicly available drastically underreported the true numbers. In October 2021, the House Select Subcommittee on the Coronavirus released initial findings from its investigation on the COVID-19 outbreaks in the meatpacking industry during the first 12 months of the pandemic and found that five big meatpacking corporations publicly underreported the number of cases among their workers by two-thirds:

> Newly obtained documents from five of the largest meatpacking conglomerates, which represent over 80 percent of the market for beef and

over 60 percent of the market for pork in the United States (and approximately 40% of the poultry industry)—JBS USA Food Company which includes Pilgrim's Pride (JBS), Tyson Foods, Inc. (Tyson), Smithfield Foods (Smithfield), Cargill Meat Solutions Corporation (Cargill), and National Beef Packing Company, LLC (National Beef)—reveal that coronavirus infections and deaths among their meatpacking workers were substantially higher than previously estimated. While publicly available data already indicated high volumes of coronavirus infections and deaths at these companies, data from JBS, Tyson, Smithfield, Cargill, and National Beef obtained by the Select Subcommittee now show that:

- Across [just] these five companies' respective workforces, at least 59,000 meatpacking workers were infected with the coronavirus during the first year of the pandemic—almost triple the 22,700 infections previously estimated by publicly available data.
- At least 269 meatpacking workers lost their lives in [just] these five companies to the coronavirus between approximately March 1, 2020, and February 1, 2021—over three times higher than what was previously estimated.[96]

These newly revealed infection and death data reflect infections and deaths for only about half of the meat and poultry industry. The Black, Latino, and immigrant workers, who make up most workers in meatpacking plants, were disproportionately impacted by the devastating spread of COVID-19. The Centers for Disease Control and Prevention (CDC) estimated that 87% of all infections occurred among racial and ethnic minorities in the meat industry.[97]

The COVID-19 infections among meatpacking and poultry plant workers, during the first year of the pandemic, became vectors for significant community spread and contributed to the rapid spread of COVID-19 throughout the United States.[98] The *Proceeding of the National Academy of Sciences* published a study reviewing COVID-19 data during just the first few months of the pandemic (through July 21, 2020) that estimated the "total excess COVID cases and deaths associated with proximity to livestock plants to be 236,000 to 310,000 cases (6–8% of all total US cases), and 4,300 to 5,200 deaths (a stunning 3–4% of all US deaths) respectively." "Our results indicate a strong positive relationship between livestock processing plants and local community transmission of COVID-19."[99] The USDA's Economic Research Services (ERC) published a working paper regarding COVID-19–related deaths and illnesses. During the first 4 months of the pandemic, communities near meatpacking plants were compared to other communities dependent on a different single industry. The study concluded that, by mid-April 2020, COVID-19 cases in meatpacking-dependent rural counties rose by nearly 10 times that in rural counties dependent on another single manufacturing industry.[100]

## More Than a Failure to Protect Workers from COVID-19: The Industry Actively Endangered Workers

The wildfire spread of COVID-19 infections, illness, and death in meat and poultry plants and their surrounding communities was a direct result of a failure by the industry to implement effective mitigation measures.[101,102,103] While other large "essential" businesses (e.g., auto manufacturing, supermarkets) retooled and reconfigured their workplaces at the beginning of the pandemic to incorporate mitigation measures, such as social distancing and mask use, the meat industry kept things the same, with workers congregating together on the production lines and in common spaces.[104] The industry was slow to provide masks, incentivized sick workers to come back to work, and fought hard to keep plants with hundreds of workers exposed and sick from closing down. The meatpacking industry was well aware of the risks to workers from COVID-19, having been warned over a decade before by the federal government that it must prepare for a pandemic by stockpiling masks and creating plans to implement social distancing. It did not prepare.[105] Faced with widespread infections, illness, hospitalizations, and death among their workers in the first year of the pandemic, the evidence is clear that the industry did not implement effective mitigation measures.[106] A congressional investigation, as well as extensive news reports, found that the industry launched "an aggressive campaign" to lobby federal officials to try to prevent local and state health departments from shutting down their facilities, regardless of the unsafe conditions. According to the House Select Subcommittee Report, the meatpacking industry actively endangered their workers during the pandemic by spreading "baseless fears" of meat shortages. It sought help from government officials to force meatpacking workers to continue working despite known health risks that "ultimately contributing to tens of thousands of worker infections and hundreds of worker deaths." Numerous reports found there were no meat shortages. The subcommittee report underscored the "shameful conduct of corporate executives pursuing profit at any cost during a crisis."[107]

Workers were crowded together in the meat and poultry industry throughout the pandemic. When 100 different meat and poultry plants were asked by the CDC, after the first few months of the pandemic, to list the protective measures that they implemented to mitigate the spread of COVID-19 infections among the workers in their plants, not one meatpacking or poultry plant reported social distancing on its lines.[108]

When OSHA issued new guidance at the beginning of March 2020,[109] recommending using masks to mitigate the spread of the disease, even though there were already widespread outbreaks in their plants, meat companies were slow to provide masks to workers.[110] Congressional investigators found that in April 2020, on a meat industry call (held prior to a call with the then secretary of agriculture), the CEO of Smithfield reminded the group of other meatpacking CEOs "that they should use the opportunity to lobby Secretary Perdue not to secure more PPE for workers, but to leverage the Trump officials to spread the message that workers must continue reporting to work."[111] In some plants, workers were told to use their hair nets as face masks.[112] At a pork plant in Iowa, for example, local officials and workers said that employees were using bandannas and sleep eyewear as facial coverings, while others had no facial coverings at all. "A memorandum from the CDC and Texas health authorities to a meat plant in Texas, on May 2, 2020, informed the company that many employees at the plant were working with masks 'saturated' from sweat or other fluids and that lines where workers were not socially distanced were separated by only flimsy 'plastic bags on frames.' This plant saw over 1,900 workers contract the coronavirus—49.8% of the plant's workforce—and at least 5 employees died of the coronavirus between March 1, 2020, and February 1, 2021."[113]

As the number of COVID-19 illnesses soared in the meatpacking industry and workers became too sick to work with many in the hospital, the biggest meatpacking companies incentivized sick workers to come back to work, regardless of whether they were infectious. CDC COVID-19 guidance to businesses,[114] from February 2020, recommended that sick workers should be removed from the plants and quarantined, but much of the meat and poultry industry implemented policies that incentivized sick workers to come back to work. These industry policies, some of which lasted well into the first year of the pandemic, provided a $500–$600 bonus to meat workers who worked every day in a month.[115,116] For some companies, workers could not miss a day in 3 months to qualify for a bonus.[117] If workers missed one day, the bonus was denied. For meat and poultry workers whose pay is as low as $13.60 an hour, this was a big incentive to come back to work, even if sick. The companies called these bonuses "hazard pay" or "responsibility bonuses." Further, companies also tried to pressure workers to come back to work. JBS sent letters to all the employees in an Iowa packing plant, where COVID-19 was spreading and a worker had already died, warning of consequences for excessive absenteeism. These policies added fuel to the wildfire spread of COVID-19 through the meat and poultry plants and in the communities in which they reside.[118,119,120]

As COVID-19 spread in the meat plants, instead of implementing social distancing, masks, identification and quarantining of sick workers, and other CDC recommendations, the industry told workers it was protecting them from COVID-19 by hanging plastic sheeting between workers standing shoulder to shoulder on production lines. For the most part, the sheeting was hung on the sides of workers, not in front of their faces. The CDC, however, as early as April 2020, informed the industry these sheets alone would not mitigate the spread of COVID-19 in meat plants and that there is no evidence that these plastic sheets would do anything to protect workers.[121] The evidence is clear that plastic barriers and partitions do nothing to block exposure to virus-laden aerosols that are a major source of exposure to COVID-19, yet this was the industry's response to COVID-19 in their plants.[122] Research also suggests that barriers could make things even worse by impeding ventilation. In many plants, workers cut holes in the barriers so they could breathe better, and in some plants, they got in the way of workers' ability to do their jobs.[123,124,125,126]

When some tried to blame the spread of COVID-19 on the high numbers of immigrant workers in the plants, the CDC conducted a study confirming that it was workplace exposure and congregate work settings that led to the high number of COVID-19 infections in meatpacking plants. The study showed that the conditions in meatpacking plants themselves were the key vectors for the spread of COVID-19 among workers. The CDC found that the poultry workers who worked in fixed positions that involved close proximity to others (e.g., cutup, packaging, receiving) got sick at higher rates than others.[127] It had nothing to do with where they lived or where they were born. Further, a study in a meatpacking plant in Germany during the first few months of the pandemic confirmed that the workplace was the main vector for the spread of infection. Sharing accommodations or transportation was not identified as a risk factor for infection. That study also confirmed that the highest infection rates were among employees in the meat-processing and slaughtering areas: "These results highlight the importance of implementing preventative measures targeting meat processing plants. Face masks, distancing, staggering breaks, increased hygiene and regular testing for SARS-CoV2 helped limit this outbreak, as the plant remained open throughout the outbreak."[120,129]

## Political Influence Used to Obstruct Public Health Measures

Many local health departments around the country tried to close meat-packing plants with widespread outbreaks. While other workplaces closed, such as supermarkets,[130] when a few workers got sick, the meat industry fought back against local health departments that insisted on closing plants with widespread outbreaks. For example, as the House Subcommittee Report found, as late as May 22, 2020—well after the efficacy and necessity of coronavirus precautions such as testing, social distancing, and personal protective equipment were widely recommended—an executive at Koch Foods told a meatpacking industry lobbyist that temperature screening was "all we should be doing." The lobbyist agreed, saying, "Now to get rid of those pesky health departments!" The House report documents how the industry enlisted the assistance of the Trump administration at the highest levels to intimidate local health departments to make sure plants would stay open or, if they had been closed, to make sure they would open immediately—despite no social distancing and the lack of other measures to protect workers.[131,132,133,134,135]

An early example is from March 26, 2020, when the Weld County Health Department in Colorado launched an investigation into the outbreak of COVID-19 at the JBS meatpacking plant in Greeley, Colorado. The county found that almost 200 of JBS employees or their family members had COVID-19. The County Health Department informed the JBS plant to implement protective measure or they would shut them down. By that first week of April, three infected workers had died. The County Health Department informed JBS it must space workers 6 feet apart and make sure sick workers were kept out of the workplace. They also informed JBS to notify any employee who was exposed to a co-worker who had tested positive that the employee be allowed to self-isolate for 14 days. When conditions did not improve, the Weld County Health Department and the Colorado State Health Department issued a closure order to JBS. On the day the closure order was sent, according to news reports and confirmed by the House Select Subcommittee

Committee on the Coronavirus, JBS reached out to the White House, seeking its help and intervention. The next day, the Trump administration's CDC director Robert Redfield himself called the director of Colorado's health department regarding the Greeley plant and the closure order. In an email to the Weld County health director, the state health department director summarized the call: "JBS was in touch with VP (Pence) who had Director Redfield call me." Redfield wanted the local and state health authorities to send "asymptomatic people back to work even if we suspect exposure but they have no symptoms." Shortly after this interference from Washington, the plant was reopened with few mitigation measures and with some exposed workers—who were infectious but asymptomatic—remaining on the job. As a direct result, COVID-19 continued to spread in the plant, sickening hundreds and killing an additional five workers by mid-May. A month later, the director of the Weld County Health Department, Dr. Mark Wallace, who had been in that job for 20 years, resigned.[136,137,138,139]

At the same time, the industry trade association, the North American Meat Institute (NAMI), was lobbying the White House for an Executive Order (EO) that would prevent public health agencies from interfering with the operations of meat and poultry plants—so they could keep their plants operating regardless of the costs in sickness and death. The House Select Committee found that on April 11, the CEOs of Tyson Foods and Smithfield conceived of the idea, with Tyson Foods creating and circulating a draft order on April 13.[140] On April 28, 2020, the Trump administration did issue an Eo at the industry's request, but it was far different from what the meat industry had asked for. The EO did not require meatpacking plants to remain open, but the administration acted as though it did.[141] The industry continued to use its influence with the USDA to help fight against local health departments seeking to protect communities.[142,143,144,145] As the committee report documented, well into the summer of 2020, "meatpacking companies and the political appointees at USDA were regularly attempting to stifle attempts by state and local authorities in order to force the plants to stay open despite the coronavirus risk."[146]

Yet, the meat industry knew how to protect workers and mitigate the spread of COVID-19 in their plants, and it knew they could do it. Documents uncovered in a wrongful death lawsuit filed in 2022 showed that Tyson moved swiftly at its plants in China to implement "extensive protocols, including a mask requirement and reduced production in place by mid-February 2020, more than a month before cases showed up in U.S. plants."[147] The US meat industry not only failed to protect workers and implement the necessary measures to mitigate the spread of COVID-19 in their plants during the first 17 months of the pandemic but demonstrated a reckless disregard for the lives of their workers, their families, and others in workforce communities.[148]

During the late summer and fall of 2021, 17 months after COVID-19 had spread like wildfire in the plants, with workers continuing to work shoulder to shoulder and as vaccines were becoming widely available, a few meat companies did implement the protective requirement that workers get vaccinated.[149] This was done in advance of an expected OSHA standard that would require protective measures such as vaccines or testing in large employers.[150] The OSHA standard was overturned by the US Supreme Court in January 2023, and the vaccine requirements have since ended in some meatpacking companies.[151,152,153]

### Failure of Government Agencies to Protect Workers during the Pandemic

Federal worker safety protections, enacted in 1970 with the passage of the Occupational Safety and Health Act (OSHAct), are very weak. The OSHAct created the Occupational Safety and Health Administration that has been chronically underfunded since it was created in 1971. In 2019, funding was so low that it would take OSHA 162 years to inspect every workplace under its jurisdiction just once.[154,155]

The evidence is clear that not only did the meat industry fail to protect workers, but so did government agencies. Federal OSHA, under direction from Trump administration political appointees, in an unprecedented move, abdicated nearly all responsibility during the first year of the pandemic to ensure that companies would implement measures to mitigate the spread of COVID-19.[156] Although petitioned on March 6, 2020, by a coalition of unions to write an Emergency Standard on COVID-19 that would require basic protections in the workplace, OSHA refused.[157] The agency also severely cut back on enforcement.[158,159] By January 2021, OSHA had received over 13,000 COVID-19 complaints from workers worried about dangerous conditions in their workplaces during the first year of the pandemic. Nearly all of these complaints were simply closed by federal OSHA with no inspection.[160,161,162] Repeatedly, meat and poultry workers and their families filed complaints with OSHA, letting OSHA know that there was no social distancing in the plants, that sick workers were incentivized to come back to work, that sick workers were kept on the lines, that there was no ability for workers to wash their hands, and that masks were wet with fluids and not replaced. OSHA still refused to conduct inspections. For example, on April 3, 2020, OSHA received a complaint that workers were in danger at the JBS meat plant in Grand Island, Nebraska. The complaint read in part, "The company has had a number of positive cases of COVID-19 and is not practicing social distancing and other protective measures. This includes, but is not limited to, the site is still allowing large gathering for lunch (300 persons)." OSHA did not inspect. Three weeks later, there was an outbreak at this plant with hundreds of infections.[163,164,165]

Unlike with many other labor and consumer protection statutes, workers have no private right of action to sue their employer for violations of the OSHAct, including when their employer illegally retaliates against them for raising health and safety concerns. Workers have only an administrative remedy, to file a complaint and request an OSHA inspection.[166] If OSHA decides not to inspect or not to cite the company for a violation, workers are left on their own.[167]

Not only do workers have a limited ability to enforce their safety rights, but they also have a very limited ability to hold employers accountable when they get injured, become ill, or die from work-related incidents. In almost all cases, when a worker suffers from a work-related injury or illness or dies from a work-related cause, their exclusive remedy is workers' compensation. In 49 states and the District of Columbia, almost all private-sector employers must carry some type of workers' compensation insurance. The bedrock principle, upon which every state workers' compensation system was founded, is the no-fault principle: employers assume responsibility for providing insurance to cover medical treatment, rehabilitation, partial reimbursement for lost wages, and death benefits for injured workers (or those killed on the job), and in turn, workers are barred from suing their employer, even when the employer is negligent.[168,169]

Because of changes in state workers' compensation laws over the past 30 years, workers now need attorneys to file claims, while benefits have been reduced and covered injuries further restricted in most states. This has made it more difficult for low-wage workers, such as meat and poultry workers, to access benefits from workers' compensation. One study of more than 4,000 low-wage workers found that among those experiencing a serious injury on the job, fewer than 1 in 9 (8%) filed for workers' compensation.[170] In addition to weak workers' compensation laws, meat and poultry workers face real fears of retaliation for reporting injuries.[171]

During 2020, when tens of thousands of meatpacking workers were sick with COVID-19, few filed workers' compensation case. For those who did file, meatpacking companies denied most claims, arguing that the cases (despite documented outbreaks in their plants) were not work related. For example, in Minnesota, over 933 meatpacking workers filed workers' compensation claims during the first year of the pandemic. All were denied. Because so few meat and poultry workers received workers' compensation for their COVID-related illnesses, it was big news when a meatpacking worker was finally awarded workers' compensation. A JBS employee in Texas, who was sick with COVID-19 and missed 3 weeks of work, filed a claim that was at first, like other claims, denied by JBS's insurer. A worker legal advocacy organization, representing the worker, challenged the denial and brought in a George Washington University epidemiologist, who had studied work-related illnesses and injuries in meatpacking plants, to refute the company's denial. The judge hearing the case awarded the worker damages. For the vast majority of workers without resources to bring in experts, the industry is able to walk away from claims.[172]

In addition to OSHA's failures during the first year of the pandemic, the USDA's political appointees intervened with public health agencies on behalf of meatpacking companies with massive outbreaks seeking to allow the plants to operate while endangering workers and their communities. Further, USDA implemented policies allowing dozens of chicken plants to increase their line speeds during the first year of the pandemic, an action that contributed to crowding in poultry plants. The USDA's directives flew in the face of the CDC's primary recommendation to the industry on how to mitigate the spread of COVID-19 in their plants: social distancing. To achieve social distancing on production lines, CDC had notified the meat and poultry industry that "changes in production practices (e.g., line speed reductions) may be necessary in order to maintain appropriate distancing among employees."[173]

Equally egregious, CDC and NIOSH's investigations and guidance to the meat industry during the first year of the pandemic were compromised by political pressure from the meat industry.[174] The House Select Subcommittee's investigations found that Trump administration political appointees, on behalf of the meatpacking industry, altered or otherwise interfered in a series of coronavirus guidance documents, including the CDC's worker protection guidance for meatpacking plants.[175] The subcommittee's final report details over four single-space pages how foreign-owned Smithfield Corporation was successful at having the former CDC director, Dr. Robert Redfield, water down not only the specific CDC mitigation recommendations to the company but the final CDC worker protection guidance for all meatpacking plants. A career CDC employee later told House investigators that the agency watered down their worker protection guidance to meatpacking plants based on Smithfield's requests and edits and that these revisions harmed the recommendations "by undermining the whole recommendation."[176]

## Conclusions

The $170 billion US meatpacking industry relies heavily on a workforce that is predominantly made up of Black, Latino, and immigrant workers. Working conditions are among the harshest in industry, yet health and safety protection measures are often limited or absent.

Meatpacking corporations were negligent in their failure to mitigate coronavirus infections and deaths in their plants during the first year of the pandemic. Instead of protecting workers, as other large industries did, the meat industry ran a public relations and lobbying campaign intended to devolve these corporations of any responsibility to protect workers. A local packing plant town public official summarized the lack of responsibility by the industry well: "Those deaths were needless, absolutely needless. That was just poor policy, poor implementation, bad defensive moves by a corporate greed kind of approach."[177]

## Recommendations

### General

NIOSH should recommend, and OSHA should promulgate, a comprehensive vertical standard that applies to both meat and poultry plants with at least these several provisions:

- Regulate line speeds and pace of work in plants so it does not contribute to acute and chronic worker injuries.
- Implement ergonomic designs to decrease repetitive motion and awkward posture injuries.
- Proscribe the use of improved floor drainage, closed systems, and ventilation exhaust systems to control exposure to antimicrobials such as PAA and other highly concentrated respiratory irritants.
- Require that all plant on-site medical/first aid offices employ staff operating with licensure, working within their scope of

practice, clinically supervised by a medically qualified health professional, and following protocols emphasizing early referrals for medical treatment by physicians. All onsite medical programs must employ staff that provide linguistically appropriate services for the workers under their care.

- Require medical surveillance programs that include testing to detect infectious agents and report outbreaks (two or more cases within a 14-day period) to OSHA and local health departments.
- Require that all information, training, and education for employees be provided in a language workers understand.

The USDA should:

- Establish a binding policy to not intervene when local and state public health agencies seek to mitigate the spread of infectious agents in meat and poultry plants through requiring mitigation measures such as masks, social distancing, and shutting plants for a time to mitigate community spread.
- Must prohibit allowing increases in line speeds in meat and poultry plants that result in increased pace of work and/or increased crowding of workers.

### Epidemic and Pandemic

NIOSH and CDC should recommend, and OSHA should promulgate, a supplemental standard for COVID-19 and for other airborne and infectious disease outbreaks, with several provisions that cover meatpacking plants:

- Provision for increased microbiological testing as dictated by the outbreak, medical, and public health advisories, together with proscribed reporting to workers and public health authorities of all cases.
- As appropriate, require and incentivize a schedule of vaccination.

- Provision for a definition of an outbreak with specifications for reporting to workers, OSHA and public health agencies, medical removal of cases, quarantining of sick workers, and provision of paid sick leave.
- Provision for upgraded NIOSH-approved respirators and appropriate personal protective equipment.
- Provision for increased social distancing on production lines that may require reduction of line speeds.
- Provision for enhanced sanitation measures.
- Provision for congregation limits, increased ventilation of break-rooms and locker rooms, and use of germicidal ultraviolet light.
- Provisions requiring enhanced communication (orally and in writing) with workers, their representatives, and trusted community partners that provides up-to-date information about the nature of any outbreak, provisions to control the outbreak, and advisories to workers for their benefit and that of their family and community members.

The USDA should:

- Accede to and support CDC- and OSHA-recommended health and safety provisions to decrease microbiological spread, including prohibition of increased line speeds.
- Promote collaboration between USDA and CDC for meat and poultry infectious agent testing under the supervision of a licensed veterinarian and a plant medical surveillance program to optimize control of a plant outbreak.

**NOTES**

1. Sinclair U. *The Jungle*. 1906. New York: Doubleday.
2. Human Rights Watch. "When we're dead and buried, our bones will keep hurting": Workers' rights under threat in US meat and poultry plants. September 4, 2019. https://www.hrw.org/report/2019/09/04/when-were-dead-and-buried-our-bones-will-keep-hurting/workers-rights-under-threat
3. US House Select Subcommittee on the Coronavirus Crisis Staff Report. "Now to get rid of those pesky health departments": How the Trump administration

helped the meat industry block pandemic worker protections. May 12, 2022. https://coronavirus-democrats-oversight.house.gov/sites/democrats.coronavirus .house.gov/files/2022.5.12%20-%20SSCC%20report%20Meatpacking%20FINAL.pdf

4. Taylor CA, Boulos C, Almond D. Livestock plants and COVID-19 transmission. *Economic Sci.* 2020;117(50):31706–31715. https://www.pnas.org/doi/full/10.1073/pnas .2010115117

5. Centers for Disease Control and Prevention. Morbidity and mortality weekly report July 10,2020; update: COVID-19 among workers in meat and poultry processing facilities, April–May 2020. https://www.cdc.gov/mmwr/volumes/69/wr/mm6927e2.htm

6. Deese, B, Fazili, S, Ramamurti, B. Addressing concentration in the meat-processing industry to lower food prices for American families. The White House, September 8, 2021. https://www.whitehouse.gov/briefing-room/blog/2021/09/08 /addressing-concentration-in-the-meat-processing-industry-to-lower-food-prices-for -american-families/

7. McCarthy, R. JBS SA shows quarter 4 growth meat+poultry. March 2021. https://www.meatpoultry.com/articles/24733-jbs-sa-shows-q4-growth

8. *Wall Street Journal.* Markets: Tyson Foods Inc. https://www.wsj.com/market -data/quotes/TSN/financials/annual/income-statement

9. US House Select Subcommittee on the Coronavirus Crisis Staff. Staff memo on "Coronavirus infections and deaths among meatpacking workers at top five companies were nearly three times higher than previous estimates." October 27, 2021. https://docs.house.gov/meetings/VC/VC00/20211027/114179/HHRG-117-VC00 -20211027-SD003.pdf

10. Souza, K. Tyson Foods maintains its top ranking in poultry production. Talk Business and Politics, March 2019. https://talkbusiness.net/2019/03/tyson-foods -maintains-its-top-ranking-in-poultry-production/.

11. North American Meat Institute. The meat and poultry industry, basic statistics. The market works. 2023. https://meatinstitute.org

12. Fortune Business Insights.com. The U.S. meat market is projected to grow from $172.94 billion in 2021 to $215.76 billion by 2028, exhibiting a CAGR of 3.21% in forecast period, 2021–2028. April 2024. https://www.fortunebusinessinsights.com/u -s-meat-market-105342

13. Mintert J. Exports more important to pork than beef or chicken. Purdue University. September 22, 2021. https://ag.purdue.edu/commercialag/home/resource /2021/09/exports-more-important-to-pork-than-beef-or-chicken/

14. Stuesse A, Dollar NT. Who are America's meat and poultry workers? Economic Policy Institute. September 24, 2020. https://www.epi.org/blog/meat-and -poultry-worker-demographics/

15. Fremstad S, Rho HJ, Brown H. Meatpacking workers are a diverse group who need better protections. CEPR. April 29, 2020. https://cepr.net/meatpacking -workers-are-a-diverse-group-who-need-better-protections/

16. Stuesse A, Dollar NT. Who are America's meat and poultry workers? Economic Policy Institute. September 24, 2020. https://www.epi.org/blog/meat-and -poultry-worker-demographics/

17. US Government Accountability Office. Workplace safety and health: better outreach, collaboration, and information needed to help protect workers at meat and poultry plants. 2017. https://www.gao.gov/assets/gao-18-12.pdf

18. OXFAM America. Lives on the line: the high cost of chicken. 2015. https://www.oxfamamerica.org/livesontheline/2015

19. Alonzo A. Why poultry employees leave or stay. August 9, 2018. https://www.wattagnet.com/articles/34821-why-poultry-employees-leave-or-stay?v=preview

20. Southern Poverty Law Center. Unsafe at these speeds. March 1, 2013. https://www.splcenter.org/20130228/unsafe-these-speeds

21. Nevin RL, Bernt J, Hodgson M. Association of poultry processing industry exposures with reports of occupational finger amputations. *J Occup Environ Med.* 2017;59(10):159–163.

22. Leibler JH, Perry MJ. Self-reported occupational injuries among industrial beef slaughterhouse workers in the Midwestern United States. *J Occup Environ Hyg.* 2017;14(1):23–30.

23. US Bureau of Labor Statistics. Injuries, illness, and fatalities. Table 1. Incidence rates of nonfatal occupational injuries and illnesses by industry and case types, 2020. November 3, 2021. https://www.bls.gov/web/osh/summ1_00.htm

24. Barnes CB, Ainsworth B, Denigan-Macauley M, et al. Workplace safety and health: Additional data needed to address continued hazards in the meat and poultry industry. US Government Accountability Office, 2016. GAO 16–337, https://www.gao.gov/assets/gao-16-337.pdf

25. Musolin K, Ramsey JG, Wassell JT, Hard DL, Mueller C. Evaluation of carpal tunnel syndrome and other musculoskeletal disorders among employees at a poultry processing plant. National Institute for Occupational Safety and Health, Centers for Disease Control and Prevention, US Department of Health and Human Services, 2014. HHE report 2012-0125-3204. www.cdc.gov/niosh/hhe/reports/pdfs/2012-0125-3204.pdf

26. US Government Accountability Office. Workplace safety and health: additional data needed to address continued hazards in the meat and poultry industry. April 25, 2016. https://www.gao.gov/products/GAO-16-337

27. Food Safety and Inspection Service, United States Department of Agriculture. Modernization of poultry slaughter inspection rule. August 2024. https://www.regulations.gov/document/FSIS-2011-0012-2263

28. Leibler JH, Perry MJ. Self-reported occupational injuries among industrial beef slaughterhouse workers in the Midwestern United States. *J Occup Environ Hyg.* 2017;14(1):23–30.

29. Food Safety and Inspection Service, United States Department of Agriculture. Modernization of poultry slaughter inspection rule. August 2024. https://www.regulations.gov/document/FSIS-2011-0012-2263

30. Musolin K, Ramsey JG, Wassell JT, Hard DL, Mueller C. Evaluation of carpal tunnel syndrome and other musculoskeletal disorders among employees at a poultry processing plant. National Institute for Occupational Safety and Health, Centers for Disease Control and Prevention, US Department of Health and Human Services,

2014. HHE report 2012-0125-3204. https://www.cdc.gov/niosh/hhe/reports/pdfs /2012-0125-3204.pdf

31. Ramsey JG, Musolin K, Mueller C. Evaluation of carpal tunnel syndrome and other musculoskeletal disorders among employees at a poultry processing plant (Report No. 2014- 0040-3232). National Institute of Occupational Safety and Health. March 2015. https://www.cdc.gov/niosh/hhe/reports/pdfs/2014-0040-3232.pdf

32. Occupational Safety and Health Administration, US Department of Labor, Citation to Wayne Farms, Inspection Nr. 975114.015, 2014. https://www.osha.gov /ords/imis/establishment.violation_detail?id=975114.015&citation_id=03001

33. US Government Accountability Office. Workplace safety and health: additional data needed to address continued hazards in the meat and poultry industry. April 25, 2016. https://www.gao.gov/products/GAO-16-337

34. McVan, M. OSHA Cites Seaboard Foods pork plant for failing to document worker injuries and illnesses. Investigate Midwest. June 2022. https://investigate midwest.org/2022/06/08/osha-cites-seaboard-foods-pork-plant-for-failing-to -document-worker-injuries-and-illnesses/

35. US Bureau of Labor Statistics. Injuries, illness, and fatalities. Table R5. Incidence rates for nonfatal occupational injuries and illnesses involving days away from work per 10,000 full-time workers by industry and selected natures of injury or illness, private industry, 2020. November 3, 2021. https://www.bls.gov/web/osh/cd _r5.htm

36. Quandt SA, , Grzywaca JG, Marin A, et al. Illnesses and injuries reported by Latino poultry workers in western North Carolina. *Am J Ind Med.* 2006;49:343–351.

37. Lipscomb H, Epling CA, Pompeii LA, Dement JM. Musculoskeletal symptoms among poultry processing workers and a community comparison group: Black women in low-wage jobs in the rural South. *Am J Ind Med.* 2007;50(5):327–338.

38. Lipscomb H, Kucera K, Epling C, Dement J. Upper extremity musculoskeletal symptoms and disorders among a cohort of women employed in poultry processing. *Am J Ind Med.* 2007; 51(1):24–36.

39. Cartwright MS, et al. The prevalence of carpal tunnel syndrome in Latino poultry processing workers and other Latino manual workers. *J Occup Environ Med.* 2012;54:198–201.

40. Musolin K, Ramsey JG, Wassell JT, Hard DL, Mueller, C. Evaluation of musculoskeletal disorders and traumatic injuries among employees at a poultry processing plant (Report No. 2012-0125-3204). National Institute for Occupational Safety and Health, Health Hazard Evaluation. 2014. https://www.cdc.gov/niosh/hhe /reports/pdfs/2012-0125-3204.pdf

41. Ramsey JG, Musolin K, Mueller C. Evaluation of carpal tunnel syndrome and other musculoskeletal disorders among employees at a poultry processing plant (Report No. 2014- 0040-3232). National Institute of Occupational Safety and Health. March 2015. https://www.cdc.gov/niosh/hhe/reports/pdfs/2014-0040-3232.pdf

42. US Bureau of Labor Statistics. Injuries, Illness, and Fatalities. Table R5. Incidence rates for nonfatal occupational injuries and illnesses involving days away from work per 10,000 full-time workers by industry and selected natures of injury or

illness, private industry, 2020. November 3, 2021. https://www.bls.gov/web/osh/cd
_r5.htm

43. Kyeremateng-Amoah E, Nowell J, et al. Laceration injuries and infections among workers in poultry processing and pork meatpacking industries. *Am J Ind Med.* 2014;57:669–682.

44. Lander L, Sorock G. A case crossover study of laceration injuries in pork processing. *Occup Environ Med.* 2012;69:410416.

45. Leibler JH, Perry MJ. Self-reported occupational injuries among industrial beef slaughterhouse workers in the Midwestern United States. *J Occup Environ Hyg.* 2017;14(1):23–30.

46. Leibler JH, Perry MJ. Self-reported occupational injuries among industrial beef slaughterhouse workers in the Midwestern United States. *J Occup Environ Hyg.* 2017;14(1):23–30.

47. US Department of Labor, Occupational Safety and Health Administration. Safety and health topics webpage: poultry processing. https://www.osha.gov/poultry -processing

48. Sanderson WT, Weber A, Echt A. Case reports: epidemic eye and upper respiratory irritation in poultry processing plants. *Appl Occup Environ Hyg.* 1995;10(1):43–49.

49. NIOSH. Hazard evaluation and technical assistance report: Bil-Mar Foods, Inc. Storm Lake, IA: US Department of Health and Human Services, Public Health Service, Centers for Disease Control and Prevention, National Institute for Occupational Safety and Health; 2003. NIOSH HETA Report No. 2002-0257-2916.

50. NIOSH. Hazard evaluation and technical assistance report: Sar Le Foods. Storm Lake, IA: US Department of Health and Human Services, Public Health Service, Centers for Disease Control and Prevention, National Institute for Occupational Safety and Health; 2006. NIOSH HETA Report No. 2006-0153-3022.

51. Donham KJ, Cumro D, Reynolds SJ, Merchant JA. Dose-response relationships between occupational aerosol exposures and cross-shift declines in lung function in poultry workers: recommendations for exposure limits. *J Occup Environ Med.* 2000;42(3):260–269.

52. NIOSH. Hazard evaluation and technical assistance report: Oscar Mayer Foods. Madison, WI: US Department of Health and Human Services, Public Health Service, Centers for Disease Control and Prevention, National Institute for Occupational Safety and Health; 1996. NIOSH HETA Report No. 96-021 302638.

53. Quandt SA, et al. Illnesses and injuries reported by Latino poultry workers in western North Carolina. *Am J Ind Med.* 2006;49:343–351.

54. Mirabelli MC, Chatterjee AB, Arcury TA, et al. Poultry processing work and respiratory health of Latino men and women in North Carolina. *J Occup Environ Med.* 2012;54(2):177–183.

55. US Government Accountability Office. Workplace safety and health: better outreach, collaboration, and information needed to help protect workers at meat and poultry plants. 2017. https://www.gao.gov/assets/gao-18-12.pdf

56. Tustin AW, Fagan KM, Hodgson MJ. What are a consulting physician's responsibilities when reviewing and approving medical protocols of a company's on-site clinic? *J Occup Environ Med.* 2018;60(7):321–323.

57. United States Department of Labor. OSHA cites Pilgrim's Pride for medical mismanagement, fall, machine guarding and other safety, health hazards; proposes $78K in fines chicken producer faces 14 serious violations. News release. OSHA; July 27, 2016. https://www.osha.gov/news/newsreleases/region4/07272016

58. Berkowitz D, Goff AD, Fagan KM, Gerrek, ML. Do clinics in meat and poultry plants endanger workers. *AMA J Ethics.* 2023;25(4):E278–286.

59. Berkowitz D. What the label on your Thanksgiving turkey won't tell you. *Washington Post.* November 23, 2016. https://www.washingtonpost.com/opinions /what-the-label-on-your-thanksgiving-turkey-wont-tell-you/2016/11/23/977fe740 -b0e1-11e6-8616-52b15787addo_story.html

60. US Department of Labor. OSHA inspects Selbyville poultry processor after worker suffers finger amputation: investigation finds musculoskeletal stressors, other safety hazards. News release; December 12, 2016. https://www.osha.gov/news /newsreleases/region3/12122016

61. US Government Accountability Office. Workplace safety and health: additional data needed to address continued hazards in the meat and poultry industry. April 25, 2016. https://www.gao.gov/products/GAO-16-337

62. United States Department of Labor. Alabama's Wayne Farms poultry plant cited for exposing workers to musculoskeletal, other repeat, serious safety and health hazards OSHA proposes more than $102K in fines for serious, repeat violations. News release. OSHA. October 29, 2014. https://www.osha.gov/news /newsreleases/region4/10292014

63. US Department of Labor. OSHA inspects Selbyville poultry processor after worker suffers finger amputation: investigation finds musculoskeletal stressors, other safety hazards. News release; December 12, 2016. https://www.osha.gov/news /newsreleases/region3/12122016

64. US Government Accountability Office. Workplace safety and health: better outreach, collaboration, and information needed to help protect workers at meat and poultry plants. 2017. https://www.gao.gov/assets/gao-18-12.pdf

65. Kirby SA; Occupational Safety and Health Administration. Letter to Rick Sappington, Seaboard Foods, LLC. US Department of Labor; December 1, 2021. Accessed May 19, 2022. https://www.dol.gov/sites/dolgov/files/OPA/news%20 releases/OSHA20262021%20-%20Medical%20Managment%20HAL%201534564.pdf

66. Ramos AK, Carvajal-Suarez M, Trinidad N, et al. Health and well-being of Hispanic/Latino meatpacking workers in Nebraska: an application of the health belief model. *Workplace Health Saf.* 2021;69(12):564–572.

67. US Department of Labor. OSHA injury and illness recordkeeping and reporting requirements. https://www.osha.gov/recordkeeping/

68. Dineen K. Meat processing workers and COVID-19 pandemic: the subrogation of people, public health, and ethics to profits and a path forward. *St Louis Univ J Health Law Policy.* 2020; 14(1). https://scholarship.law.slu.edu/jhlp/vol14/iss1/4

69. Wage and Hour Division, US Department of Labor. More than 100 children illegally employed in hazardous jobs, federal investigation finds. News release. February 2023. https://www.dol.gov/newsroom/releases/whd/whd20230217-1

70. Foley, R. Another worker at Tyson Food's Waterloo plant dies after long battle with COVID 19. *Des Moines Register.* May 2020 https://www.desmoinesregister.com/story/news/2020/05/25/fifth-tyson-foods-waterloo-iowa-employee-jose-ayala-dies-coronavirus/5257056002/

71. Birch, T. As Coronavirus spikes in Black Hawk County, local officials blast Tyson Foods for not closing its Waterloo plant. *Des Moines Register.* April 2020. https://www.desmoinesregister.com/story/news/health/2020/04/17/tyson-foods-black-hawk-county-govonor-kim-reynolds/5151840002/

72. Kauffman, C. Lawsuit: Tyson managers bet money on how many workers would contract COVID-19. *Des Moines Register.* November 2020. https://www.desmoinesregister.com/story/money/agriculture/2020/11/19/lawsuit-tyson-iowa-plant-managers-made-bets-on-workers-getting-covid/3775558001

73. Grabell, M, Yeung B. The battle for Waterloo: As COVID-19 ravaged this Iowa city, officials discovered meatpacking executives were the ones in charge. ProPublica. December 2020. https://features.propublica.org/waterloo-meatpacking/as-covid-19-ravaged-this-iowa-city-officials-discovered-meatpacking-executives-were-the-ones-in-charge/

74. Weiner-Bronner, D. Managers at Tyson meat plant had betting pool on how many workers would get COVID. CNN Business. November 2020. https://www.cnn.com/2020/11/19/business/tyson-coronavirus-lawsuit/index.html

75. Foster, K. Fired managers at Tyson Waterloo sue for lost bonuses. KOEL AM 950. November 2022. https://koel.com/fired-managers-at-tyson-waterloo-sue-for-lost-bonuses/

76. Kuber, M. How COVID-19 tore through Smithfield's meatpacking plant in 17 days. *Sioux Falls Argus Leader.* April 2021. https://www.argusleader.com/story/news/2021/04/08/timeline-of-smithfields-sioux-falls-south-dakota-meatpacking-plant-covid-19-outbreak-in-2020/7124095002/

77. Burns, K. New report reveals COVID-19 infections, deaths at meatpacking plants much higher than reported. KELO South Dakota. October 2021. https://www.keloland.com/news/healthbeat/coronavirus/new-report-reveals-covid-19-infections-deaths-at-meatpacking-plants-much-higher-than-reported/

78. US House Select Subcommittee on the Coronavirus Crisis Staff Report. "Now to get rid of those pesky health departments": How the Trump administration helped the meat industry block pandemic worker protections. May 12, 2022. https://coronavirus-democrats-oversight.house.gov/sites/democrats.coronavirus.house.gov/files/2022.5.12%20-%20SSCC%20report%20Meatpacking%20FINAL.pdf

79. US House Select Subcommittee on the Coronavirus Crisis Staff. Staff memo on "Coronavirus infections and deaths among meatpacking workers at top five companies were nearly three times higher than previous estimates." October 27, 2021. https://docs.house.gov/meetings/VC/VC00/20211027/114179/HHRG-117-VC00-20211027-SD003.pdf

80. Dance, S. Coronavirus has killed 5 poultry plant workers and infected more than 200 other employees in Maryland's Eastern Shore. *Baltimore Sun*. June 2020. https://www.baltimoresun.com/coronavirus/bs-md-chicken-plant-cases-20200611 -ck65omlurrd63anpoqiibitblm-story.html

81. Statement regarding COVID-19 outbreak at Foster Farms facility in Livingston. Department of Public Health, Merced County CA press release. August 2020. https://www.countyofmerced.com/DocumentCenter/View/25497/MCDPH-Foster -Farms-Statement--82720?bidId=

82. US House Select Subcommittee on the Coronavirus Crisis Staff Report. "Now to get rid of those pesky health departments": How the Trump administration helped the meat industry block pandemic worker protections. May 12, 2022. https://coronavirus-democrats-oversight.house.gov/sites/democrats.coronavirus .house.gov/files/2022.5.12%20-%20SSCC%20report%20Meatpacking%20FINAL.pdf

83. US Bureau of Labor Statistics. Injuries, illnesses and fatalities. Census of fatal occupational injuries. Fatal occupational injuries by industry and event or exposure 2005–2020. https://www.bls.gov/iif/fatal-injuries-tables.htm

84. Testimony of Debbie Berkowitz, National Employment Law Project, on Health and Safety Protections for Meatpacking, Poultry and Agriculture Workers before the House Committee on Appropriations, Subcommittee on Labor, Health and Human Services. March 2, 2021.

85. Keith, T. Union reports 9th COVID -19 death at Colorado meatpacking plant. KKTV, Colorado Springs. May 2020. https://www.kktv.com/content/news /Union-reports-8th-COVID-19-death-at-Colorado-meatpacking-plant-570582201. html

86. Poultry industry's delayed COVID-19 response is killing America's essential workers: Protect them now. Press release issued by the Retail, Wholesale and Department Store Union, USA. April 2020. https://www.iuf.org/wp-content/uploads /attachments/RWDSUPressRelease.pdf

87. Keefe J, Bolton M. When chickens devoured cows: The collapse of national bargaining in the red meat industry and union rebuilding in the meat and poultry industry. October 29, 2012. http://dx.doi.org/10.2139/ssrn.2168241

88. Huber, M. Smithfield Workers asked for safety from COVID_19: Their company offered cash. *Sioux Falls Argus Leader*, April 2020. https://www.argusleader .com/story/news/2020/04/09/smithfield-foods-workers-criticize-conditions -coronavirus-covid-19/5124387002/

89. National Public Radio. The Children of Smithfield. Radio interview. August 2020. https://www.npr.org/2020/08/11/901217452/the-children-of-smithfield

90. Trujillo, T. Protesters take a second stand at the Smithfield Foods meat factory. KLKN TV, Nebraska. May 2020 https://www.klkntv.com/protesters-take-a -second-stand-at-the-smithfield-foods-meat-factory/

91. Andrei, MA, Honig, E. Pandemic and protest in a meatpacking town: When COVID-19 spread rapidly through slaughterhouses, most workers stayed quiet: But their kids did not. Food and Environment Reporting Network, August 2020. https://thefern.org/2020/08/pandemic-and-protest-in-a-meatpacking-town/

92. Jordan, M, Dickerson C. Poultry worker's death highlights spread of coronavirus in meat plants. *New York Times*. April 2020 https://www.nytimes.com /2020/04/09/us/coronavirus-chicken-meat-processing-plants-immigrants.html

93. US House Select Subcommittee on the Coronavirus Crisis. Hybrid hearing on "How the meatpacking industry failed the workers who feed America." October 27, 2021. https://coronavirus.house.gov/subcommittee-activity/hearings /hybrid-hearing-how-meatpacking-industry-failed-workers-who-feed

94. Douglas, L. A year later it is still impossible to tell how many food workers are contracting COVID-19. Mother Jones. April 2021. https://www.motherjones.com /food/2021/04/a-year-later-conditions-for-many-food-workers-at-high-risk-of-covid -19-remain-the-same/

95. Douglas, L. FERN'S Covid-19 mapping project concludes. Food and Environment Reporting Network. September 2021. https://thefern.org/blog_posts/ferns -covid-19-mapping-project-concludes/

96. US House Select Subcommittee on the Coronavirus Crisis Staff Report. "Now to get rid of those pesky health departments": How the Trump administration helped the meat industry block pandemic worker protections. May 12, 2022. https://coronavirus-democrats-oversight.house.gov/sites/democrats.coronavirus .house.gov/files/2022.5.12%20-%20SSCC%20report%20Meatpacking%20FINAL .pdf

97. Centers for Disease Control and Prevention. Morbidity and mortality weekly report July 10, 2020; update: COVID-19 among workers in meat and poultry processing facilities. April-May 2020. https://www.cdc.gov/mmwr/volumes/69/wr/mm6927e2. htm

98. Kaplan S, Butler D, Eilperin J, et.al. How genetic science helped expose a coronavirus outbreak in Iowa. *Washington Post*. September 202. https://www .washingtonpost.com/graphics/2020/national/genetic-science-coronavirus-outbreak -iowa/

99. Taylor CA, Boulos C, Almond D. Livestock plants and COVID-19 transmission. *Economic Sci.* 2020;117(50):31706–31715. https://www.pnas.org/doi/full/10.1073 /pnas.2010115117

100. Krumel T, Goodrich C; US Department of Agriculture, Economic Research Service. COVID-19 working paper: Meatpacking working conditions and the spread of COVID 19. September 2021. https://www.ers.usda.gov/publications/pub-details /?pubid=102205

101. US House Select Subcommittee on the Coronavirus Crisis. Hybrid hearing on "How the meatpacking industry failed the workers who feed America." October 27, 2021. https://coronavirus.house.gov/subcommittee-activity/hearings/hybrid -hearing-how-meatpacking-industry-failed-workers-who-feed

102. Hearing Before the House Committee on Appropriations, Subcommittee on Labor and Health and Human Services, Education and Related Industries. Health and Safety Protections for Meatpacking, Poultry and Agriculture Workers, March 2, 2021. https://www.congress.gov/event/117th-congress/house-event /111253?s=1&r=1

103. Schlosser E. The essentials: How we're killing the people who feed us. *The Atlantic*. May 2020. https://www.theatlantic.com/ideas/archive/2020/05/essentials-meatpeacking-coronavirus/611437/

104. Wayland M. How GM, other automakers, plan to reopen plants during coronavirus pandemic. CNN. April 2020. https://www.cnbc.com/2020/04/25/how-gm-others-plan-to-reopen-us-plants-during-coronavirus-pandemic.html

105. Grabell M. The plot to keep meatpacking plants open during COVID-19. ProPublica. May 2022. https://www.propublica.org/article/documents-covid-meatpacking-tyson-smithfield-trump

106. Telford T, Kindy K. As they rushed to maintain U.S. meat supply, big processors saw plants become Covid-19-hot spots: Worker illness spikes. *Washington Post*. April 2020 https://www.washingtonpost.com/business/2020/04/25/meat-workers-safety-jbs-smithfield-tyson/

107. US House Select Subcommittee on the Coronavirus Crisis Staff Report. "Now to get rid of those pesky health departments": How the Trump administration helped the meat industry block pandemic worker protections. May 12, 2022. https://coronavirus-democrats-oversight.house.gov/sites/democrats.coronavirus.house.gov/files/2022.5.12%20-%20SSCC%20report%20Meatpacking%20FINAL.pdf

108. Waltenburg MA, Victoroff T, Rose CE, et al. Update: COVID-19 among workers in meat and poultry processing facilities—United States, April–May 2020. *MMWR Morb Mortal Wkly Rep*. 2020;69:887–892. https://www.cdc.gov/mmwr/volumes/69/wr/mm6927e2.htm

109. Occupational Safety and Health Administration, US Department of Labor. Guidance on Preparing Workplaces for COVID-19. March 2020. https://www.osha.gov/sites/default/files/publications/OSHA3990.pdf

110. Telford T, Kindy K. As they rushed to maintain U.S. meat supply, big processors saw plants become Covid-19-hot spots, worker illness spikes. *Washington Post*. April 2020. https://www.washingtonpost.com/business/2020/04/25/meat-workers-safety-jbs-smithfield-tyson/

111. US House Select Subcommittee on the Coronavirus Crisis Staff Report. "Now to get rid of those pesky health departments": How the Trump administration helped the meat industry block pandemic worker protections. May 12, 2022. https://coronavirus-democrats-oversight.house.gov/sites/democrats.coronavirus.house.gov/files/2022.5.12%20-%20SSCC%20report%20Meatpacking%20FINAL.pdf

112. Perez M. Please do something: As COVID-19 swept through Wisconsin food plants, companies, government failed to protect workers. *Milwaukee Journal Sentinel*. July 2020. https://www.jsonline.com/story/news/2020/07/31/wisconsin-food-plants-failed-protect-workers-covid-19-smithfield-birds-eye-diversified-meats-calumet/5334812002/

113. House Select Subcommittee on the Coronavirus Crisis Staff. Staff memo on "Coronavirus infections and deaths among meatpacking workers at top five companies were nearly three times higher than previous estimates." October 27, 2021. https://docs.house.gov/meetings/VC/VC00/20211027/114179/HHRG-117-VC00-20211027-SD003.pdf

114. Centers for Disease Control and Prevention. Interim guidance for business and employers to plan and respond to 2019 coronavirus disease (COVID-2019). February 2020. https://stacks.cdc.gov/view/cdc/85488

115. Tyson Foods doubles bonuses. Tyson Foods press release. April 19, 2020. https://www.tysonfoods.com/news/news-releases/2020/4/tyson-foods-doubles-bonuses-increases-health-benefits-and-protections

116. Mosendz P, Wardman P, Mulvaney L. How meat plants were allowed to become coronavirus hot spots. *Bloomberg Business Week*. June 18, 2020. https://www.bloomberg.com/news/features/2020-06-18/how-meat-plants-were-allowed-to-become-coronavirus-hot-spots

117. Kauffman C. Law suit: Tyson managers at Iowa plant bet money on how many workers would contract COVID-19. *Des Moines Register*. November 2020. https://www.desmoinesregister.com/story/money/agriculture/2020/11/19/lawsuit-tyson-iowa-plant-managers-made-bets-on-workers-getting-covid/3775558001/

118. Paschall O. COVID-19 pounded Arkansas poultry workers as government and industry looked on. Facing South. August 2020. https://www.facingsouth.org/2020/08/covid-19-pounded-arkansas-poultry-workersgovernment-and-industry-looked

119. Huber, M. Smithfield workers asked for safety from COVID-19: Their company offered cash. *Sioux Falls Argus Leader*. April 2020. https://www.argusleader.com/story/news/2020/04/09/smithfield-foods-workerscriticize-conditions-coronavirus-covid-19/5124387002/

120. Jett T. Iowa JBS meatpacking employees warned of excessive absenteeism as pandemic continues. *Des Moines Register*. June 2020. https://www.desmoinesregister.com/story/money/business/2020/06/17/covid-19- iowa-letter-warns-meatpacking-workers-excess-absences/3202317001/

121. US Department of Health and Human Services, Centers for Disease Control and Prevention. Memorandum on "Strategies to reduce COVID-19 transmission at the JBS Greeley Beef Plant," April 20, 2020. https://www.documentcloud.org/documents/6987094-JBS-CDC-Strategies-Other-Release

122. Parker-Pope T. Those anti-Covid plastic barriers probably don't help and may make things worse. *New York Times*. August 19, 2021. https://www.nytimes.com/2021/08/19/well/live/coronavirus-restaurants-classrooms-salons.html

123. Parker-Pope T. Those anti-Covid plastic barriers probably don't help and may make things worse. *New York Times*. August 19, 2021. https://www.nytimes.com/2021/08/19/well/live/coronavirus-restaurants-classrooms-salons.html

124. Morawska L, Milton DK. It is time to address airborne transmission of COVID-19. *Clin Infect Dis.* 2020;71(9):2311–2313. https://academic.oup.com/cid/article/doi/10.1093/cid/ciaa939/5867798

125. Prather KA, Wang CC, Schooley RT. Reducing transmission of SARS-CoV-2. *Science.* 2020; 368(6498):1422–1424.

126. Prather KA, Marr LC, Schooley RT, McDiarmid MA, Wilson ME, Milton DK. Airborne transmission of SARS-CoV-2. *Science.* 2020;370(6514):303–304.

127. Rubenstein B, Campbell S, Alysha M. Centers for Disease Control and Prevention. Factors that may affect SARS-CoV-2-transmission among foreign born

and U.S-born poultry facility workers—Maryland 2020. *Morbidity and Mortality Weekly Report.* 69(50):1906–1910. https://stacks.cdc.gov/view/cdc/100100

128. Brown, HC. Foreign born workers were blamed for spreading COVID-19 in meatpacking plants: Their behavior was not the issue, new research suggest. The Counter. December 2020. https://thecounter.org/new-research-cdc-meatpacking-plant-workers-covid-19/

129. Finci I, Siebenbaum R, Richtzenhain J, et al. Risk factors associated with an outbreak of COVID-19 in a meat processing plant in southern Germany, April to June 2020. *Euro Surveill.* 2022;27(13):pii=2100354. https://doi.org/10.2807/1560-7917.ES.2022.27.13.2100354

130. Alim T. Trader Joes on 14th Street NW in DC temporarily closes due to Covid 19. WTOP News, DC. April 8, 2020. https://wtop.com/coronavirus/2020/04/trader-joes-on-14th-street-nw-in-dc-temporarily-closes-due-to-covid-19/

131. US House Select Subcommittee on the Coronavirus Crisis Staff Report. "Now to get rid of those pesky health departments": How the Trump administration helped the meat industry block pandemic worker protections. May 12, 2022. https://coronavirus-democrats-oversight.house.gov/sites/democrats.coronavirus.house.gov/files/2022.5.12%20-%20SSCC%20report%20Meatpacking%20FINAL.pdf

132. Kravitz D, Gee G, McVan M, Calderon I. The feds told Illinois to leave Rochelle Foods alone: Then a second Covid-19 outbreak hit. USA Today. January 2021. https://www.usatoday.com/story/news/investigations/2021/01/18/trump-admin-told-illinois-keep-rochellefoods-open-covid-19-hit/4196577001/

133. Jansen S. Merced County official: Feds tried to "intimidate" staff into keeping Foster Farms open. *Merced Sun-Star.* October 2020. https://www.mercedsunstar.com/news/coronavirus/article246153690.html

134. Samuel S. A Utah meat plant is staying open even after 287 workers got coronavirus. VOX. June 2020. https://www.vox.com/future-perfect/2020/6/11/21286840/meat-plant-covid-19-utah-coronavirus

135. Chadde S, Bagenstose K, Axon R. A week before Trump's order protecting meat plants, industry sent draft language to feds. *USA Today.* September 14, 2020. https://www.usatoday.com/story/news=2020/09/14/covid-19-meat-plants-sought-feds-protection-local-healthdepts/5797051002/

136. Navarro N. Weld County warned JBS about its work while sick culture a week before shutting them down. CPR News. April 17, 2020. https://www.cpr.org/2020/04/17/weld-county-warned-jbs-about-its-work-while-sick-culture-a-week-before-shutting-them-down/

137. Klemko R, Kindy K. He fled Congo to work in a US meat plant: Then he—and hundreds of his coworkers—got the coronavirus. *Washington Post.* August 2020. https://www.washingtonpost.com/national/he-fled-the-congo-to-work-in-a-us-meat-plant-then-he--and-hundreds-of-his-co-workers--got-the-coronavirus/2020/08/06/11e7e13e-c526-11ea-8ffe-372be8d82298_story.html

138. Smith M, Exclusive: Health official quits after being pushed to reopen Colorado County and hot spot meat plant. Market Watch. May 2020. https://www

.marketwatch.com/story/health-chief-quits-after-coronavirus-crisis-at-colorado
-meatpacking-plant-2020-05-11

139. US House Select Subcommittee on the Coronavirus Crisis Staff Report. "Now to get rid of those pesky health departments": How the Trump administration helped the meat industry block pandemic worker protections. May 12, 2022. https://coronavirus-democrats-oversight.house.gov/sites/democrats.coronavirus .house.gov/files/2022.5.12%20-%20SSCC%20report%20Meatpacking%20FINAL .pdf

140. US House Select Subcommittee on the Coronavirus Crisis Staff Report. "Now to get rid of those pesky health departments": How the Trump administration helped the meat industry block pandemic worker protections. May 12, 2022. https://coronavirus-democrats-oversight.house.gov/sites/democrats.coronavirus .house.gov/files/2022.5.12%20-%20SSCC%20report%20Meatpacking%20FINAL .pdf

141. Hemel, D. No, Trump did not order meat processing plants to reopen. *Washington Post.* May 4, 2020. https://www.washingtonpost.com/outlook/2020/05 /04/trump-meat-processing-order/

142. The USDA, meatpacking industry collaborated to undermine COVID-19 response, FOIA docs show. September 15, 2020. Public Citizen press release. https://www.citizen.org/news/usda-meatpacking-industry-collaborated-to -undermine-covid-19-response-foia-docs-show/

143. Vladeck S. (professor of law at University of Texas School of Law). Twitter, April 28, 2020. https://twitter.com/steve_vladeck/status/1255313648177885184

144. Gremillion, T. What does the Defense Production Act have to do with food. Food Safety News. May 2020. https://www.foodsafetynews.com/2020/05/what-does -the-defense-production-act-have-to-do-with-food/

145. Covid-19 outbreak: Large Foster Farms processing plant ordered to shut down: It's time to hit the reset button. April 2020. CBS News. https://www.cbsnews .com/sanfrancisco/news/covid-19-outbreak-large-foster-farms-chicken-processing -plant-ordered-to-shutdown-its-time-to-hit-the-reset-button/

146. US House Select Subcommittee on the Coronavirus Crisis Staff Report. "Now to get rid of those pesky health departments": how the Trump administration helped the meat industry block pandemic worker protections. May 12, 2022. https://coronavirus-democrats-oversight.house.gov/sites/democrats.coronavirus .house.gov/files/2022.5.12%20-%20SSCC%20report%20Meatpacking%20FINAL.pdf

147. Grabell M. The plot to keep meatpacking plants open during COVID-19. ProPublica. May 2022. https://www.propublica.org/article/documents-covid -meatpacking-tyson-smithfield-trump

148. Grabell M. The plot to keep meatpacking plants open during COVID-19. ProPublica. May 2022. https://www.propublica.org/article/documents-covid -meatpacking-tyson-smithfield-trump

149. Tyson Foods to require Covid-19 vaccinations for its U.S. workforce. Tyson Foods news release. August 2021. https://www.tysonfoods.com/n ews/news -releases/2021/8/tyson-foods-require-covid-19-vaccinations-its-us-workforce

150. Wiseman, P. Small agency, big job: Biden tasks OSHA with vaccine mandate. AP News. September 2021. https://apnews.com/article/joe-biden-business-health -coronavirus-pandemic-henry-mcmaster-f33acd986ad5045e48088a832c6f9903

151. Tyson Foods to Require Covid-19 Vaccinations for its U.S. Workforce. Tyson Foods news release. August 2021. https://www.tysonfoods.com/news/news -releases/2021/8/tyson-foods-require-covid-19-vaccinations-its-us-workforce

152. Polansek, T. Tyson ends Covid-19 vaccine mandate for employees. Reuters. November 2022. https://www.reuters.com/business/healthcare-pharmaceuticals /tyson-foods-ends-covid-19-vaccine-mandate-employees-2022-11-16/

153. Stohr G. Supreme Court blocks Biden's shot or test rule for workers. Bloomberg. January 2022. https://www.bloomberg.com/news/articles/2022-01-13 /supreme-court-halts-osha-rule-that-covered-80-million-workers

154. Department of Labor. Public Law 91-596. The OSH Act of 1970. https://www .osha.gov/laws-regs/oshact/completeoshact

155. American Federation of Labor and Congress of Industrial Organizations. Death on the job: The toll of neglect, 2021. April 2022. https://aflcio.org/sites/default /files/2022-04/2214_DOTJ_Final_42622_nobug.pdf

156. Modessit N. OSHA's comprehensive failure to protect workers during the Covid-19 pandemic. *Dickinson Law Review*. 2021;126(1). https://ideas.dickinsonlaw .psu.edu/dlr/vol126/iss1/7/

157. OSHA denies AFL-CIO petition calling for an emergency temporary standard on infectious diseases. Safety and Health Magazine. June 2020. https:// www.safetyandhealthmagazine.com/articles/19945-osha-denies-afl-cio-petition calling-for-an-emergency-standard-on-infectious-diseases

158. Berkowitz D. The cost of a weakened OSHA. April 28, 2020. National Employment Law Project. https://www.nelp.org/publication/worker-safety-crisis -cost-weakened-osha/

159. U.S. Department of Labor Office of Inspector General. Covid-19: OSHA's enforcement activities did not sufficiently protect workers from pandemic health hazards. Report to the Occupational Safety and Health Administration. October 2022. https://www.oig.dol.gov/public/reports/oa/2023/19-23-001-10-105.pdf

160. Department of Labor Occupational Safety and Health Administration. COVID-19 response summary. https://www.osha.gov/enforcement/covid-19 -data#complaints_referrals

161. Department of Labor Occupational Safety and Health Administration. COVID-19 complaint data previous reports. https://www.osha.gov/foia/archived -covid-19-data

162. Grabell M, Yeung B, Jameel M. Millions of essential workers are being left out of COVID-19 workplace safety protections, thanks to OSHA. ProPublica. April 2020. https://www.propublica.org/article/millions-of-essential-workers-are -being-left-out-of-covid-19-workplace-safety-protections-thanks-to-osha

163. Duffy E. 237 Coronavirus cases now tied to JBS beef plant. April 2020. *The Grand Island Independent*. https://theindependent.com/news/237-coronavirus-cases -now-tied-to-jbs-beef-plant/article_49820822-83ea-11ea-933d-c3c188ac00fc.html

164. Flener, M. Exclusive: OSHA never visited Missouri poultry facility after COVID-19 complaints. KMBC 9 News. August 2020. https://www.kmbc.com/article/exclusive-osha-never-visited-missouri-poultry-facility-after-covid-19-complaints/33660429

165. Testimony of Debbie Berkowitz, National Employment Law Project, on Health and Safety Protections for Meatpacking, Poultry and Agriculture Workers before the House Committee on Appropriations, Subcommittee on Labor, Health and Human Services. March 2, 2021.

166. Testimony of Debbie Berkowitz, National Employment Law Project, on Health and Safety Protections for Meatpacking, Poultry and Agriculture Workers before the House Committee on Appropriations, Subcommittee on Labor, Health and Human Services. March 2, 2021.

167. New York Times Editorial Board. "You're on your own," essential workers are being told. *New York Times*. April 20, 2020. https://www.nytimes.com/2020/04/20/opinion/osha-coronavirus.html?action=click&module=RelatedLinks&pgtype=Article

168. US Department of Labor. Does the workers' compensation system fulfill its obligations to injured workers? 2016. https://www.dol.gov/sites/dolgov/files/OASP/files/WorkersCompensationSystemReport.pdf

169. Texas Department of Insurance. Workers' compensation insurance guide. January 25, 2022. https://www.tdi.texas.gov/pubs/consumer/cb030.html

170. Bernhardt A, Milkmen R, Theodore N. Broken laws, unprotected workers. September 2009. https://www.nelp.org/publication/broken-laws-unprotected-workers-violations-of-employment-and-labor-laws-in-americas-cities/

171. Ramos AK, Carvajal-Suarez M, Trinidad N, et al. Health and well-being of Hispanic/Latino meatpacking workers in Nebraska: An application of the health belief model. *Workplace Health Saf.* 2021;69(12):564–572.

172. Niepow, D. A Texas meatpacking worker has won a COVID-19 worker's comp claim: Is Minnesota next? Twin Cities Business Magazine. May 2021. https://tcbmag.com/a-texas-meatpacking-worker-has-won-a-covid-19-workers-comp-claim-is-minnesota-next/

173. Centers for Disease Control and Prevention. Meat and poultry processing workers and employers: Interim guidance from CDC and the Occupational Safety and Health Administration (OSHA). April 2020. https://stacks.cdc.gov/view/cdc/87280

174. US House Select Subcommittee on the Coronavirus Crisis Staff Report. "Now to get rid of those pesky health departments": How the Trump administration helped the meat industry block pandemic worker protections. May 12, 2022. https://coronavirus-democrats-oversight.house.gov/sites/democrats.coronavirus.house.gov/files/2022.5.12%20-%20SSCC%20report%20Meatpacking%20FINAL.pdf

175. US House Select Subcommittee on the Coronavirus Crisis Staff Report. "Now to get rid of those pesky health departments": How the Trump administration helped the meat industry block pandemic worker protections. May 12, 2022.

176. US House Select Subcommittee on the Coronavirus Crisis Staff Report. "Now to get rid of those pesky health departments": How the Trump administration

helped the meat industry block pandemic worker protections. May 12, 2022. https://coronavirus-democrats-oversight.house.gov/sites/democrats.coronavirus .house.gov/files/2022.5.12%20-%20SSCC%20report%20Meatpacking%20FINAL.pdf

177. Grabell, M, Yeung B. The battle for Waterloo: As COVID-19 ravaged this Iowa City, officials discovered meatpacking executives were the ones in charge. ProPublica. December 2020. https://features.propublica.org/waterloo-meatpacking/as-covid-19 -ravaged-this-iowa-city-officials-discovered-meatpacking-executives-were-the-ones -in-charge/

# CHAPTER 10

# Superior Technologies

Viney P. Aneja, Matias Vanotti, Ariel A. Szogi,
and Gudigopuram Reddy

Animal agriculture is essential to global food, nutrition, and economic security. Raising farm animals has become an integral part of agriculture in the United States. However, there is a shift in animal agriculture in the United States, where family-owned production systems have given way to large corporately owned and managed operations. This transformation, most prominent in poultry and swine production, has resulted in environmental and air quality challenges (Nina et al., 2021). In the United States, large poultry-operated farms are concentrated in southeastern states. In contrast, large swine farms are located in a few states, such as Iowa, North Carolina, Missouri, and Minnesota. These poultry and swine operations are housed in high-density confined spaces called concentrated animal feeding operations (CAFOs). Beef and dairy cattle are commonly raised in similar circumstances.

CAFOs refer to animals raised in large facilities where they are confined and fed for 45 days or more per year. The US Department of Agriculture (USDA) has defined a CAFO as an animal operation having over 1,000 animal units (animal unit equals 1,000 lbs of live weight) in a confined facility (Copeland, 2010). The US Environemental Protection Agency (USEPA, 2014) defines CAFOs as containing >1,000 head of beef cattle, 2,500 swine with >25 kg weight, or 10,000 swine with <25 kg weight and 125,000 chickens (Copeland, 2010). Not only are CAFOs classified by the type and number of animal units, but they are not permitted to discharge waste/wastewater directly into the water supply or come into contact with the water bodies.

CAFO facilities produce enormous amounts of waste (i.e., manure, a mixture of feces, urine, discarded bedding, and spilled feed). For example, swine barns commonly have a slotted floor that permits the passage of excreted waste into a pit. Waste can be transferred from the pit to a lagoon or above-ground storage tank in some operations. Lagoons may be aerobic (shallow) or anaerobic (deep). Some hog farm operations spray excess supernatant from lagoons to nearby fields grown with Bgrass; likewise, the effluents from the lagoon and other CAFO types can be applied to fields managed for corn and other crops. These management waste practices can impact the environment (air, water, and soil) and human health because they produce a large amount of waste in a concentrated, small area of land that can generate noxious air pollutants, particulates, suspended dust, pathogens, and odorous compounds (Aneja et al., 2008d; Aneja et al., 2009; USEPA, 2014). Land application of waste coupled with extreme weather can degrade surface and groundwater quality (Mallin, 2000; Hooda et al., 2000). Therefore, effective manure management practices and treatment technologies are required to mitigate or reduce environmental impacts.

## Background

### Overview of Animal Waste Treatment Lagoon and Spray Technology in North Carolina

Animal waste treatment lagoons are ubiquitous in eastern North Carolina, where CAFO hog production is typical. These lagoons are built for the biological treatment of wastewater and consist of an excavated pit with an earthen embankment or levee (USDA, 2009). The liquid manure is transferred from the barn to the lagoon, where it is held for storage and stabilization to reduce environmental pollution potential (USDA, 2019). Seepage can occur in treatment lagoons but is minimized when manure solids accumulate in the bottom and sides of the structure. However, manure sealing is ineffective in soils with low clay content. Therefore, as part of the design, state regulations require using clay or synthetic liners to avoid polluting surface and groundwater with lagoon seepage (USDA, 2008). Originally designed as a total disposal system, anaerobic lagoons are a pretreatment in a complete manure management system. The manure management system includes the land disposal of anaerobic lagoon effluents in spray fields because North Carolina's annual rainfall surplus generates a net excess of lagoon liquid effluents.

Anaerobic lagoons depend on physical, chemical, and biological processes for processing organic wastes into more stable by-products. However, biological processes play the most significant role in the anaerobic decomposition of liquid manure (Hamilton et al., 2006). The growth and maintenance of anaerobic biological processes in treatment lagoons depend on temperature, pH, organic load, microbial communities, and anaerobic conditions. An essential aspect of treatment lagoons is that their liquid volume is drawn down by land-applying effluents during the crop season, but lagoons never become fully emptied. A minimum operating liquid level keeps biological degradation processes active in anaerobic lagoons (USDA, 2019). Specific lagoon design standards provide lagoon sizing with sufficient volume for sludge accumulation and treatment, plus volume for liquid manure storage and rainfall storage produced during the period between drawdown events (ASABE, 2011).

Lagoon systems have several advantages compared to land disposal of unstabilized animal waste. Treatment lagoons reduce labor and operating costs for removing manure from barns by allowing regular flushing and emptying of the liquid manure collected in pits under slotted floors into the treatment lagoon. The lagoon liquid is recycled into the barn to repeat the flushing of the pits. Treatment lagoons allow long storage times and flexibility in the disposal of effluents when scant vegetative growth limits land application during the cold season.

Anaerobic lagoon processes degrade liquid manure wastes with high loads of organic matter in the absence of oxygen. These processes can more efficiently decompose organic matter on a per-unit volume basis than aerobic ones (Hamilton et al., 2006). However, the environmental risks associated with lagoons compromised by leakage and weather-caused overflow call into question their viability in a total manure management system. As a result of the anaerobic microbial decomposition of organic manure, lagoon effluents have an appreciable loss of nutrient value to fresh animal manure.

The microbial degradation of manure in the treatment lagoon transforms large organic compounds into smaller, volatile organic compounds and manure proteins and urea into ammonia gas. Ammonia ($NH_3$), reduced sulfur (e.g., $H_2S$), and volatile organic compounds (VOCs) contribute to emissions of offensive odors from the lagoon (Aneja et al., 2000; Blunden et al., 2008; Blunden and Aneja, 2008; Rumsey and Aneja 2014; Rumsey et al., 2014). Land application of effluents from improperly designed or managed treatment lagoons can further extend the emission zone of offensive odors and ammonia.

Anaerobic lagoon design standards require the removal of solids before sludge fills up the treatment volume through agitation or dredging to maintain lagoon treatment performance (Owusu-Twum and Sharara, 2020). However, the cost of removing sludge can become an economic challenge for the producers if sludge dredging is frequently needed because of undersized lagoon designs. The cost of sludge removal can be burdensome because of limited cropland areas for application near animal production and the hauling costs associated with transporting the material to distant fields.

## Emissions from Hog CAFOs

Manure collection, storage, and land application are components of animal manure management systems, and the pollutants are released in each of these management steps. CAFOs generate noxious air pollutants such as ammonia ($NH_3$), hydrogen sulfide ($H_2S$), VOCs, organic acids, particulate matter, and other gases (Aneja et al., 2000; Baek et al., 2004b; Aneja et al., 2008d; Aneja et al., 2009; Heinzen, 2015). Manure also contains hormones, antibiotics, heavy metals, nutrients, solids, pathogens, and particulate dust (Scanes, 2018). The air around CAFOs can be contaminated with high concentrations of particulates or suspended dust, of which one-third is respirable ($PM_{2.5}$ and $PM_{10}$). Casey et al. (2006) described in detail the measurements of air emission methods and emission rate calculations from different animal facilities in different states.

Recent studies have used a mass balance approach to estimate $NH_3$ emission rates from liquid swine manure and have found that swine houses represent a more significant source than previously thought (Doorn et al., 2002). Based on a review of published data, the loss of $NH_3$ from swine houses was estimated to be around 15% of the total N excreted (Westerman et al., 2000). This study (Westerman et al., 2000) also used a mass balance approach to estimate $NH_3$-N emissions from different components of advanced manure treatment and lagoon spray technologies, as well as N excretion rates, based on swine population and feed data. Normalizing emissions by N excretion rate, percentage reductions in $NH_3$-N emissions are determined for water-holding structures, barns, and the whole farm for each Environmentally Superior Technology (EST) facility from their estimated values for the appropriate Lagoon and Sprayfield Technology (LST) farm. Griffing et al. (2004) used the mass balance method to estimate that approximately 80% of $NH_3$ loss was due to volatilization from liquid waste storage systems.

Animal urine is the primary source of ammonia ($NH_3$) in hog production. Ammonia is generated during protein decomposition in excreta during storage in animal houses. Ammonia emissions occur during manure storage, transportation, and land application. Also, $NH_3$ emission has been observed in manure composting facilities where concentrations were higher in the summer and winter months and higher during the day than at night (Zhao et al., 2016). Aneja et al. (2000) measured ammonia fluxes seasonally from a 2.5-ha hog waste storage lagoon in North Carolina. They found higher summer fluxes (mean $NH_3$ flux $4,017 \pm 987$ µg N m$^{-2}$ m$^{-1}$) followed by a decrease in spring, then fall followed by winter as $1,706 \pm 552$ µg N m$^{-2}$ m$^{-1}$, $844 \pm 401$ µg N m$^{-2}$ m$^{-1}$, and $305 \pm 154$ µg N m$^{-2}$ m$^{-1}$, respectively. Szogi and Vanotti (2007) found that 80% of annual nitrogen loss was as $NH_3$ volatilization after anaerobic decomposition in lagoons.

Nitrous oxide ($N_2O$) is a significant greenhouse gas and has 298 times more global warming potential than $CO_2$ over 100 years (Ren et al., 2017). N-containing substances in the manure are converted to ammonium ($NH_4$) during the manure decomposition process. In aerobic conditions, $NH_4$ is oxidized to nitrate ($NO_3$), which can then undergo reduction to NO$^-$ $N_2O$ and $N_2$ if anaerobic conditions exist. Nitrous oxide is generated during anaerobic and manure application and in partially aerobic soil that has received swine manure slurry (Onema et al., 2005). Eighty-five selected publications and their meta-analytical results showed that animal manure has significantly increased $N_2O$ emissions by 17.7% (Shakoor and Mehmood, 2021), while Vac et al. (2013) concluded ~37% of global $N_2O$ emissions are from application and storage of animal manure.

Hydrogen sulfide ($H_2S$): Hydrogen sulfide is a toxic gas with a characteristic odor. It is produced in all anaerobic manure storage systems such as underground storage tanks and outside earthen manure-holding lagoons. $H_2S$ results from sulfur-containing proteins present in manure. Liu et al. (2014) measured $H_2S$ emitting from deep pits, recharge pits, and lagoons receiving wastewater from farrowing, gestation, and finishing houses. They found that farrowing houses showed the highest emission rates of $H_2S$ (2.5 kg yr$^{-1}$pig$^{-1}$) than other houses. Rumsey and Aneja (2014) measured $H_2S$ seasonally from swine lagoons at CAFOs and found that $H_2S$ fluxes were higher in summer ($3.81 \pm 3.24$ µg m$^{-2}$ m$^{-1}$) and lowest in winter ($0.08 \pm 0.09$ µg m$^{-2}$ m$^{-1}$).

Methane (CH4): The emissions of $CH_4$ occur when liquid manure is collected in underground pits in animal confinement operations in an anaerobic digester. During this period, $CH_4$ and $CO_2$ emissions occur due to the organic matter decomposition. The rate of $CH_4$ emissions depends on the type of manure (percentage of volatile solids) and retention time in storage pits, tanks, or lagoons. Estimating methane ($CH_4$) emission rates in field conditions is difficult due to expensive equipment, environmental variables (wind speed, wind direction, temperature, pH), and seasonality. Therefore, highly variable rates may be observed between farms. Methane emission rates from deep swine pits have been measured at $5.5 \pm 1.1$ kg $CH_4$ per finished pig (Liu et al., 2013), 0.24 to 63 mg $m^{-2}$ $min^{-1}$ (Park et al., 2006), and 15 mg $m^{-2}$ $min^{-1}$ (Zhan et al., 2001). An inventory of 15 different digestates showed an average residual gas formation of $CH_4$ of 5 $m^3$ $ton^{-1}$ (range 1–10 $m^3$ $CH_4$ $ton^{-1}$ digestate) for central manure systems (Climate Policy Watcher, January 9, 2022, drawn from Van Lier et al., 2008). Methane fluxes from an anaerobic swine lagoon ranged from 1 to 500 kg $ha^{-1}$ $d^{-1}$ and the average flux for the year was 52.3 kg of $CH_4$ $ha^{-1}$ $d^{-1}$ (Sharpe and Harper, 1999).

Odors: Odor generation is a complex process that depends on feed types, manure storage method and length of storage, manure temperature, pH, and bacterial species. Bacterial species and communities act on manure and produce an extensive range of volatile organic compounds, which are responsible for odors emitting from storage pits or lagoons (Aneja et al., 2000; Blunden et al., 2008; Rumsey and Aneja, 2014).

## Impact of Manure on the Environment

### Air Pollution

Air pollutants that escape into the atmosphere from animal houses, manure handling methods, manure storage, and land applications impact the environment (soil, water, and air) and human life. Ammonia ($NH_3$) that is released has a mean life of about 14–36 hours, depending on weather conditions. It reacts rapidly with acidic agents such as sulfuric acid, nitric acid, and hydrochloric acid to form fine-particulate ammonium salts (i.e., $PM_{2.5}$) (Renard et al., 2004; Wiegand et al., 2022). These ammonium salts are the main components of smog aerosols, causing visisbility problems. These particulates linger in the atmosphere for days and can be transported hundreds of miles. Also, these fine particulates will lead to respiratory problems in humans. Ammonia is deposited by dry (wind drift) or wet (precipitation) mechanisms. When ammonia is deposited on soils, consequences include soil acidification, nitrification, ammonium ($NH_4$) adsorption to the clay particles, and subsequent erosion along with soil particles. Nitrate from nitrification is soluble and contaminates ground water through leaching processes. Ammonia is also an important contributor to surface water eutrophication (Whitall et al., 2003).

Nitrous oxide ($N_2O$) is a potent greenhouse gas and essentially an inert gas in the atmosphere and has no significant sinks at the Earth's surface and may be transported to the stratosphere (Muller, 2021). Nitrous oxide has a Global Warming Potential (GWP) of 298 times that of $CO_2$ for a 100-year time scale. $NO_x$ compounds, including $N_2O$, are destroying agents of ozone in the stratosphere, and constitute the third most important long-lived greenhouse gas after $CO_2$ and $CH_4$ (Muller, 2021). Oxides of nitrogen ($NO_x$) pollution impact visibility and cause acid rain, reducing soil pH, solubilizing aluminum and other minerals, and reducing the availability of Ca and Mg to growing plants.

Methane ($CH_4$) is a potent greenhouse gas with a 100-year GWP 28–34 times that of $CO_2$. Measured over 20 years, that ratio grows to 84–86 times. Methane is oxidized in the presence of water vapor to $CO_2$.

When hydrogen sulfide ($H_2S$) is released into the atmosphere, it dissipates into the air and may form sulfur dioxide ($SO_2$) and sulfuric acid ($H_2SO_4$) (Seinfeld and Pandis, 1998). It has a short half-life of 18 hours, after which it may enter the soil as $H_2SO_4$ dissolved in rainwater, thereby reducing soil pH and increasing soil acidification.

*Manure Impact on Water Quality*
When animal manure is applied to crops beyond crop nutrient requirements and soil adsorption capacity, nutrients accumulate and then run off into the stream network, causing eutrophication. Therefore, if nutrient applications are not aligned with crop needs, then degraded

water quality results. If manure is applied aligned with crop N requirements, phosphorus and other components may be in excess, along with manure pathogens (Mallin and McIver, 2018). Because of the imbalance of N and P in animal manure (N:P < 4:1) relative to crop needs (N:P = 8:1), land application of lagoon effluents at optimal N rates for crop growth results in the accumulation of P in soils and insufficient use of plant nutrients by crops (Szogi et al., 2015). Phosphorus enrichment contributes to eutrophication in P-sensitive ecosystems and has been linked to *Pfiesteria* outbreaks in North Carolina waters (Burkholder et al., 2007). Elevated nitrate in well waters has been known to cause methemoglobinemia or blue-baby syndrome (Johnson and Bonrud, 1988). USEPA found that 29 states have identified animal feeding operations (AFOs) contributing to water quality impairment (Copeland, 2010). In 1995, 22 million gallons of liquid swine waste entered North Carolina's Neuse River and its estuary due to a waste lagoon rupture (Aneja et al., 2001b). Similarly, major CAFO accidents have occurred in Iowa, Maryland, and Missouri (Thu and Durrenberger, 1998; Mallin, 2000). Miralha et al. (2022) have monitored CAFOs in 16 states across the United States for N and P levels relating to water quality. When manure was land applied, high levels of N and P were found in watersheds where clusters of CAFOs were present. The United States Geological Survey (USGS) has conducted studies on animal manure's impact on water quality in southern US states, and their reports indicated significant levels of nutrients, pathogens, and pharmaceutical chemicals contaminating streams and rivers. Apart from land application of waste, pollutants also enter the groundwater through leakage from poorly constructed manure-holding lagoons. These open lagoons are prone to overflow during unexpected high rainfall or hurricane events.

Veterinary pharmaceuticals (Boxall et al., 2004) and hormones (Kjaer et al., 2007; Shappell et al., 2007) have also been found in animal manure. Once manure is applied to agricultural fields, these compounds can persist in soils for days to years. Shappell et al. (2007) found that estradiol (hormone) equivalents in a manure pit (washed manure from farrowing swine facility) ranged from 843 to 858 pM, whereas in lagoon wastewater, levels ranged from 6.4 to 11.5 pM (37 pM = 10 ng). Kjaer et al. (2007) found that 17 beta-estradiol (E2) and its degradation product estrone (E1) were 68.1±2.5 ng/L, respectively, and they were found in leachates from the root zone to the tile drainage system after 3 months of field application of swine manure. There are at least 17 classes of antimicrobials approved for use in animals raised in the United States to control diseases (Anderson et al., 2003). The use of antimicrobials in animal production is a significant concern because of the potential for developing antimicrobial resistance. Ibekwe et al. (2016) reported that *Escherichia coli* bacteria in swine wastewater were highly resistant to tetracycline, erythromycin, ampicillin, and streptomycin.

## Manure Processing Technologies

Treatment methods are designed to improve manure management in-house systems to meet on-farm nutrient reduction goals and to reduce pollution from manure nutrients before land application.

### Binders, Scrubbers, and Covers for Ammonia Emissions

Binders like zeolites, sphagnum moss, and commercial additives such as Alliance (Environ Chem; Monsanto) have reduced $NH_3$ emissions in pig slurries by 20–30% (Herber et al., 2002). Diet modifications such as increasing fiber or reducing N (crude protein) in the feed can lead to less N content in manure (Cahn et al., 1998). About a 28–79% reduction of N in manure has been achieved by supplementing with amino acids and reducing crude protein in the diet (Cahn et al., 1998; Otto et al., 2003, Clark et al., 2005). Treating air exhausted from CAFOs with scrubbers (acid solutions), biofilters (having nitrifying films), or gas-permeable membranes reduces $NH_3$ emissions to the surrounding environment (Szogi et al., 2014b; Ndegwa et al., 2008; Moore, 2014).

Reduction of ammonia emissions from hog waste lagoons occurs when using impermeable covers such as floating film (2-mm-thick polyethylene film and/or 0.5-mm-thick reinforced UV-light stabilized opaque polyethylene) or tarpaulins (Funk et al., 2004) by 99.7%, 99.5%, and 100%, respectively (Miner et al., 2003).

## Solids Liquid Separation Technologies

Solids separation techniques that have been implemented in animal wastewater include gravity sedimentation (Metcalf and Eddy, 2003), centrifugation, screening, screw press filtration, belt process filtration (Burton, 2007), and bag filtration (Sharrer et al., 2009; Reddy et al., 2013). However, these mechanical solid separation methods do not remove colloidal particles and dissolved solids unless some chemical coagulants and flocculants are used for further treatment. Common coagulants include alum ($Al_2 (SO_4)_3$, $18H_2O$), ferric chloride ($FeCl_3$), ferric sulfate (Fe $(SO_4)_3$), and hydrated lime (Ca (OH)). In wastewater treatment, one of these coagulants was used in combination with a flocculant such as polyacrylamides (Reddy et al., 2013; Vanotti and Hunt, 1999). Ferric chloride as a coagulant and Hyperfloc CE 854 as a flocculant have reduced solids by 91–95% from liquid swine manure by using a geotextile bag (Reddy et al., 2013). After solids are separated from liquid manure, solids can be subjected to pelletization, giving advantages in dust-free and easy transportation. Solids separated from liquid manure may also be used for composting and in boilers for heating, producing energy, and biochar.

## Composting

Composting is an aerobic process where organic chemicals are decomposed by micro-organisms with favorable pH, temperature, moisture, and nutrient conditions. A commercial and viable composting facility is operated in eastern North Carolina using a mixture of swine manure sludge, a polymer, and carbon-rich materials such as cotton gin waste, wood, and peanut hulls. Stabilization of pathogens occurs by maintaining temperatures at 130°F. After adequate time to allow composting, a commercial compost product is distributed to retailers (Sharara and Spearman, 2020).

## Thermochemical Processes

Thermochemical methods such as incineration, pyrolysis, and gasification are used for biosolid conversion to energy. In these methods, biosolids are subjected to high temperatures ranging from 400–600°C to convert biosolids into gases, hydrocarbon fuels, and charcoal or ash residues. Pyrolysis may hold the most potential for this because it produces value-added biochar (Ro et al., 2010) and is used as a soil amendment for carbon sequestration and improving soil fertility (Cantrell et al., 2012). Solids separation from liquid manure followed by pyrolysis can be economically prohibitive. Hydrothermal carbonization can pyrolyze wet manure directly at lower temperatures (180–350°C) (Libra et al., 2011). This technology saves input energy and produces a usable end product as hydrochar.

## Nitrification/Denitrification

Removal of N by nitrification/denitrification in aerobic/anaerobic conditions can be effective in reducing N concentrations. However, removing N efficiently at high rates requires control of pH, $O_2$, temperature, nitrifying bacteria, and organic carbon at favorable levels. Cold temperatures slow nitrification, and to circumvent this problem, a high-performance nitrifying sludge (HPNS) has been introduced for treating swine wastewater (Vanotti et al., 2013). Using this system enabled the removal of >95% $NH_3$ from swine wastewater containing 1,000–2,700 mg $NH_3$ $L^{-1}$ (Vanotti et al., 2009a). Nitrification/denitrification systems using continuous-flow intermittent aeration (Hu et al., 2003) and sequencing batch reactor (Zhang et al., 2006) removed N by 80% and 97.5%, respectively.

## Constructed Wetlands and Zeolites

Another technology uses constructed wetlands to remove or reduce nutrients in wastewater. Reddy et al. (2001) reported a reduction of >70% N and 30–45% P by treating lagoon swine wastewater through constructed wetlands while not accounting for a loss of N through ammonia volatilization (<12% of total N introduced into wetlands) (Poach et al., 2004). Reddy et al. (2013) developed a technology to treat swine wastewater directly by flushing from houses through a series of treatment stages such as geotextile bag (solids removal), zeolite bed (adsorption of $PO_4$), and constructed wetlands. This system removed solids, N, and P by >95%, 92%, and 88%, respectively. The advantage of this system was effluent water from constructed wetlands can be used to flush manure on floors in swine houses and thereby save fresh water. Zeolite-adsorbed nutrients can be used as fertilizers for horticulture, solids recovered in geotextile bags can be used for composting or producing energy, and and it is cost-effective. However, this technology is limited to operations with <2,500 swine.

## Phosphorus Recovery

In animal manures, the presence of bicarbonate is an interference in the production of high-grade phosphates. Vanotti et al. (2005) used a biological (microbial) acidification with nitrifiers to destroy the bicarbonate and produce high-grade phosphates from swine wastewater using an alkaline-earth metal. Another method used is chemical acidification: it adds mineral or organic acids to acidify the manure before the P precipitation step with lime (Quick Wash process developed for P extraction from poultry manure, swine lagoon sludges, and municipal solids; Szogi et al., 2014a).

## Ammonia Recovery with Gas-Permeable Membranes

The gas-permeable membrane process (Vanotti and Szogi, 2015) is used for removing and recovering nitrogen from several types of liquid manures; it includes the passage of gaseous ammonia ($NH_3$) through a microporous hydrophobic membrane and subsequent capture and concentration in an acidic stripping solution. Gas-permeable membranes have effectively recovered more than 97% of $NH_4^+$ from swine wastewater (García-González and Vanotti, 2015; Dube et al., 2016). The membrane manifolds are submerged and the $NH_3$ is removed from the liquid manure before it escapes into the air. The concept was tested using digested and raw swine and dairy manures containing a wide range of $NH_4$-N concentrations (140 to 5,000 mg N $L^{-1}$). Using the same stripping solution in 10 consecutive batches treating raw swine manure, the recovered N was concentrated in a clear solution containing 50,000 mg N $L^{-1}$ (Vanotti and Szogi, 2015). By coupling the ammonia recovery technology with anaerobic digestion, the methane yield increased up to 28% (González-García et al., 2021).

## Background for Developing Environmental Superior Technologies to Solve Hog Manure Issues in North Carolina

In the United States, North Carolina represents a state and region in which pork production activity has received national and international attention over the past two decades due, in part, to the rapid growth of this industry during the late 1980s to mid-1990s. Subsequent attention was directed to environmental, social, and political issues related to this growth, as well as research and policy initiatives to develop "advanced manure treatment technologies" to address these issues.

The need to develop environmentally superior and sustainable solutions for the management of animal waste is vital for the future of animal farms in North Carolina, the United States, and the world. The EST process was initiated in July 2000 through a government–industry–university framework whereby the state attorney general entered into an agreement with then one of the world's largest pork-producing companies, Smithfield Foods, Inc., to identify EST through research coordinated by North Carolina State University (Agreement, 2000) (Williams, 2009). EST is defined as any technology or combination of technologies that is permittable by the appropriate governmental agencies; is determined to be technically, operationally, and economically feasible; and meets the following environmental performance standards:

1. Eliminate the discharge of animal waste to surface waters and groundwater through direct discharge, seepage, or runoff.
2. Substantially eliminate atmospheric emissions of ammonia.
3. Substantially eliminate the emission of odor that is detectable beyond the boundaries of the parcel or tract of land on which the swine farm is located.
4. Substantially eliminate the release of disease-transmitting vectors and airborne pathogens.
5. Substantially eliminate nutrient and heavy metal contamination of soil and groundwater.

In addition to the environmental standards, economic and operational feasibility criteria must be considered (Williams, 2009).

## North Carolina Engineered Environmental Superior Technologies to Treat Hog Manure

Six selected ESTs had the potential to meet the environmental performance criteria with minor technological modifications or improvements and in combination with other technologies (Williams, 2009). These six technologies are described below in the following format: name of the farm where the potential EST was used, type of technology, and brand name where applicable (Aneja et al., 2008b).

(1) Barham farm: in-ground ambient temperature anaerobic digester/energy recovery/greenhouse vegetable production system
(2) BOC #93 farm: upflow biofiltration system—EKOKAN
(3) Carrolls farm: aerobic blanket system—ISSUESABS
(4) Corbett #1 farm: solids separation/gasification for energy and ash recovery centralized system—BEST

(5) Corbett #2 farm: solid separation/reciprocating water technology—ReCip

(6) Vestal farm: Recycling of Nutrient, Energy and Water System—ISSUES-RENEW

These potential ESTs were evaluated during two seasons (cool and warm), and the results were compared and contrasted with data from two conventional LST swine farms (Moore farm and Stokes farm) (Aneja et al., 2008a). Two other potential ESTs qualified as unconditional ESTs relative to $NH_3$ emissions reductions (Aneja et al., 2008c): Red Hill Farm and Goshen Ridge Farm—Super Soils Systems.

A brief description of each of the potential ESTs that have been evaluated is provided here (Aneja et al., 2008b). Williams (2005, 2006) contains more detailed information, including site plans, design schematics, and projected operational characteristics.

**Barham Farm.** Barham Farm is located near Zebulon, North Carolina, in Johnston County. This potential EST has an in-ground ambient digester composed of a covered anaerobic waste lagoon. The primary lagoon was covered by an impermeable layer of 40-mm-thick high-density polypropylene that prevented gaseous methane and other gases and odor from escaping into the atmosphere during the digestion process. Methane gas that is produced during the digestive process was extracted and burned into a biogas generator to produce electricity. The heat from the generator was captured and used to produce hot water that was used by the farm in its production activities. Effluent from the digester (covered lagoon) flowed into a storage pond with a surface area of 4,459 m$^2$. This storage pond was formerly part of the primary anaerobic lagoon before the digester was built. A portion of this effluent was further treated via biofilters, the purpose of which was to convert $NH_4$ to nitrate in the effluent. This nitrified effluent was then used to flush out the swine production facilities, and the excess effluent was channeled into the larger overflow pond with a surface area of 19,398 m$^2$. A heavy polymer baffle separated the overflow and storage ponds. The overflow pond was used to store rainwater and overspills from the storage pond. Water from the overflow pond was also pumped into a nitrification biofiltration system, where the nutrients in the treated effluent were used to fertilize vegetables grown in greenhouses adjacent to the swine production facility.

**BOC #93 Farm.** BOC #93 farm: up-flow biofiltration system— EKOKAN is located near Bladenboro, North Carolina, in Bladen County. The EKOKAN waste treatment system consisted of solids/liquid separation and biofiltration of the liquid with up-flow aerated biological filters. Five finishing barns were connected to the waste treatment system, and the barn pits were emptied automatically in sequence. Wastewater from the barn pits was released to a solid separation unit. Coarse solids were separated from the wastewater using a screen separator (TR separator). After the solids/liquid separation process, the liquid was pumped to a 40,000-gallon equalization tank. The liquid flowed from the equalization tank by gravity and passed through first- and second-stage aerated biofilters connected in series (two sets). Wastewater flowed upward through the biofilters, and the air was supplied at the bottom of each biofilter with blowers. The biofilter tanks were covered, and air and any excess foam from the aerated treatment were routed through polyvinyl chloride pipes to exit points over an anaerobic lagoon. The biofilters were backwashed periodically to remove excess biosolids. Treated effluent from the biofilters flowed by gravity to a storage basin, with a portion of the treated effluent being recycled to the solid's separation basin, from which it was pumped to the equalization tank, which had a surface area of 28.3 m$^2$. Water was pumped from the storage basin to the barns to refill the pits. At this site, the anaerobic lagoon received manure from 10 barns and was partitioned using plastic curtains into three sections, with one section much larger than the other two. The larger section received manure from five barns not connected to the EKOKAN treatment system. One of the smaller sections received any overflow from the solid's separation basin. The separated solids and backwashed biosolids were removed from the biofilters. This was known as the biosolids lagoon and had a surface area of 3,229.2 m$^2$. The other small section received the treated effluent from the biofilters. This was known as the treated effluent lagoon and had a surface area of 1,614.6 m$^2$.

**Carrolls** is located near Warsaw, North Carolina, in Duplin County. The waste stream in the proposed EST flows from the houses to a primary anaerobic lagoon equipped with the Aerobic Blanket System (ABS). This is known as the ABS lagoon and has a surface area of 3,304.8 m$^2$. The ABS consists of a fine mist of treated swine waste that is applied every 15 minutes to the surface of the anaerobic lagoon. The treated swine waste arises from an aeration treatment that takes place in an adjoining water-holding structure (aerobic digester). Waste from the anaerobic lagoon flows into an aerobic digester (IESS aeration system). This is referred to as the west side of the aerated lagoon and has a surface area of 5,068.8 m$^2$. This portion of the basin is sectioned off with a plastic barrier. The aerated waste eventually flows into the sectioned-off portion of the aeration treatment basin. This is known as the eastside of the aerated lagoon and has a surface area of 6,010.2 m$^2$. The waste is then used to flush the animal houses and supplies the treated water for the ABS. Only waste from finishing houses 5–13 flowed into the ABS-equipped anaerobic lagoon. Waste from the remaining farrow and weaning houses flowed into a separate lagoon.

**Corbett #1 Farm.** Corbett #1 farm is located near Rose Hill, North Carolina, in Duplin County. Manure flushed from the barns flows first to a collection pit, then to an above-ground feed tank, and then to a screw-press separator on a raised platform. The separator has a screen with 0.25-mm openings. The liquid that flows through the screw-press separator screen flows to a second feed tank, which has a surface area of 27.1 m$^2$, and then to two tangential-flow gravity settling tanks sited parallel to each other. Each tangential-flow settling system consists of a 2.2-m diameter tank with a cone bottom followed by a 1.2-m diameter sludge thickening tank, also with a cone bottom. Tangential flow in the first tank causes solids to concentrate in the center of the tank and settle down to the bottom. This settled slurry is then pumped to the second tank for sludge thickening. For approximately 10 minutes every hour, the settled slurry from the second tangential-flow settling tank is pumped back to the tank that feeds the screw-press separator, where the settled slurry is combined with the flushed manure that is being pumped to the screw-press separator. The treated waste and any overflow go to a stabilization and treatment pond, which has an area of 8,291.9 m².

**Corbett #2 Farm:** Solid separation/reciprocating water technology—ReCip. Corbett #2 farm is located near Rose Hill, North Carolina, in Duplin County. The ReCip encompasses two cells, or treatment basins, filled with media (proprietary technology) that would alternately drain and fill on a cyclic basis. The draining and filling cycles created aerobic, anaerobic, and anoxic conditions within the cells, providing both biotic and abiotic treatment processes to promote nitrification and denitrification. The treatment process was preceded by a solid's separation step. The solid waste and the treated liquid waste went into individual lagoons, which had surface areas of 2,601 m² and 2,717 m², respectively.

**Vestal Farm:** Recycling of Nutrient, Energy and Water System—ISSUES-RENEW. Vestal Farm is located near Kenansville, North Carolina, in Duplin County. The RENEW system uses a mesophilic digester as well as aeration and wastewater filtering and disinfection systems. This technology also incorporated a microturbine generator. For this system, the waste first flows from the pig barns to equalization and concentrator tanks, which serve to produce a thickened liquid. This liquid then flows to a mesophilic digester. The digester, which operates at a temperature of 95°F, produces biogas, which is used to fuel the microturbine generator. The generator produces electricity, which is sold and used on the electric power grid. The waste stream then flows to a polishing storage basin, which has a surface area of 22,636 m², and then to an aerobic digester, also called a nitrification pond, which has a surface area of 1,880.6 m². A portion of the waste stream then flows back to the polishing storage basin, where it is used to flush the pig barns and is sprayed on cropland if necessary. The remaining portion of the waste stream flows through a filtration system. The filtration system consists of sand carbon filters and reverse osmosis. The water is then disinfected using ozonation and ultraviolet light. Filtered and disinfected water is then returned to the pig barns, where it is used as drinking water for the pigs.

Red Hill Farm

Red Hill Farm is located near Ayden, North Caroliona, in Pitt County. The EST at Red Hill Farm was provided by "Environmental Technologies." This EST is described as a "closed-loop" system, and its primary objective is to treat the liquid fraction of the waste in such a way that it can be used both for flushing the hog barns and for hog drinking water. This could eliminate the need for the traditional hog waste lagoon. A flush system is used for removing the manure from the barns, which, prior to installation of the treatment system, flushed the waste into a lagoon. The first step in the closed-loop process is the collection of the waste in an "equalization" or buffering tank. The waste in the tank is continuously pumped to an inclined separator, where the solids are collected and further treated. The liquid collected from the separator is injected with a polymer flocculant and sanitizer/disinfectant and pumped into a settling tank where flocculated solids collect at the bottom over a period of approximately 4 hours. Most of the liquid fraction from the settling tank is returned to the hog barns for reuse as flush water. When the flush tanks are full, however, excess water is pumped to a tertiary treatment system. This system provides filtration and aeration and is housed in a septic tank. The treated water is blended with well water to achieve a dissolved-solids content that is consistent with human drinking water standards for use as hog drinking water. Solids from the settling tanks are combined with the solids from the inclined separator for further treatment.

Goshen Ridge Farm—Super Soils Systems

It was the first on-farm system certified by the state of North Carolina as an EST due to its efficacy in reducing ammonia emissions, excess ni-

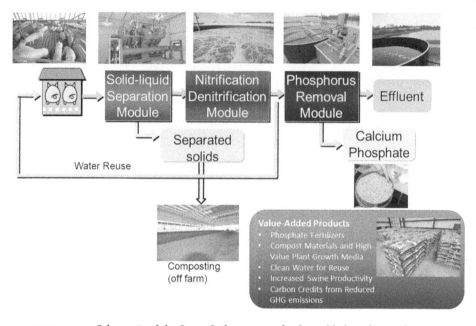

FIGURE 10.1. Schematic of the Super Soil system and value-added products. The on-farm system used three modules: the first to separate organic solids from the liquid manure, the second to remove the ammonia and odors, and the third to separate phosphorus and disinfect the effluent. A closed loop recycled treated water to recharge the barn pits. The organic solids were further processed off-farm in a centralized composting facility. *Source*: USDA.

trogen and phosphorus, pathogens, odors, and heavy metals (Williams, 2009).

The on-farm technology uses liquid–solid separation, nitrification/ denitrification, and soluble phosphorus removal processes linked together into a practical system (Fig. 10.1). It was developed by the USDA and is covered by US patents 6,893,567 and 7,674,379 (Vanotti et al., 2005; Vanotti, 2010) that are now available for public use.

The on-farm system was demonstrated at full scale on three North Carolina swine farms sequentially between 2003 and 2013 by Super Soil Systems USA (Terra Blue, Inc. after 2010) of Clinton, North Carolina, and the treatment system was referenced as the "Super Soils" system. The first-generation on-farm system was demonstrated at Goshen Ridge Farm, a 4,360-head feeder-to-finish swine farm in Duplin County,

North Carolina. The second-generation system was demonstrated at B&B Tyndall Farm, a 5,145-head feeder-to-finish swine farm in Sampson County, North Carolina (Vanotti et al., 2010). The third-generation system was demonstrated at Jernigan Farm in Wayne County, North Carolina, and treated the entire waste stream from two swine production operations: a 1,200-sow farrow-to-feeder operation and a 12,960-head feeder-to-finish operation.

The on-farm system that treated the liquid waste stream used solid–liquid separation and nitrogen and phosphorus removal processes that replaced traditional anaerobic lagoons with a system that produces a clean, deodorized, and disinfected effluent (Fig. 10.1). Treated water was reused in the barns.

Solid–liquid separation upfront in a treatment train allows recovery of the organic compounds that can be used for the manufacture of compost materials, peat substitutes, biochars, and so on. The Super Soils project was completed with composting of the separated manure solids, which was done in a centralized facility in Sampson County, North Carolina (Vanotti et al., 2006; Aneja et al., 2008c), that processed dewatered solids from the three full-scale projects. The composting process used a mixture of manure and cotton gin residue and produced class A composts and value-added organic products for use in horticultural markets. The Super Soils compost system also met the environmental standards of an EST, together with the other three technologies that also processed separated swine solids in centralized facilities using high-solids anaerobic digestion or gasification processes (Williams, 2009).

## Super Soils Technology Description

The liquid treatment begins with the separation of the solid and liquid portions of the waste stream. Solids separation is accomplished using polyacrylamide, a flocculating agent. The liquid portion of the waste stream goes to a nitrogen module, where the liquid flows between tanks in a circulating loop undergoing denitrification as a result of anaerobic activity in one tank and nitrification through the use of concentrated nitrifying bacteria in the second tank under aerobic conditions. Nitrogen is removed from the waste stream during this stage of the process. The liquid then flows to a settling tank, where phosphorus is removed through the addition of calcium hydroxide and a dewatering bag system. Calcium phosphate, which has value as a fertilizer, precipitates out during this process, providing a value-added product. During phosphorus removal, the pH of the liquid is raised to 9.5–10.5 using lime, which precipitates the soluble P and disinfects the effluent. Roughly 80% of the liquid is recycled through the hog houses, while 20% is used to irrigate crop fields.

### First-Generation Super Soils System: Meeting of EST Standards

The first-generation version of the Super Soils technology was first pilot tested for 2 years at the North Carolina State University's Lake Wheeler Rd. Swine Unit (Vanotti et al., 2001). Subsequently, the same system was scaled up (125:1) for performance verification of EST. It was installed and demonstrated at full scale for 2 years on Goshen Ridge farm, a 4,360-head swine finishing operation in Duplin County, North Carolina (Vanotti et al., 2007; Vanotti and Szogi, 2008). The manure was collected under the barns using slatted floors and a pit-recharge system. With the new treatment system, the flow of raw wastewater into the lagoons was discontinued; instead, all the raw wastewater was sent to the treatment plant (Fig. 10.2). The barn pits were flushed once a week as before, but the flushed manure (barns 1–6) was diverted into a homogenization tank that mixed the manure before the solid–liquid separation step. The separated liquid moved into the nitrogen module that contained polymer-immobilized nitrifiers. The nitrified wastewater was continually recycled into the DN (denitrification) tank using a modified Ludzack–Ettinger (MLE) configuration. In the DN tank, suspended denitrifying bacteria used soluble manure carbon and volatile odorous compounds in the separated manure to transform oxidized nitrogen into $N_2$ gas. In the third step of the system—the phosphorus

FIGURE 10.2. First-generation on-farm system using solid–liquid separation, nitrogen, and phosphorus modules treating all the animal waste from a 4,360-head swine finishing farm in Duplin County, North Carolina. *Source:* USDA.

treatment/disinfection module—the soluble P was recovered as a calcium phosphate solid, and pathogens were substantially reduced by the alkaline environment (pH 10.5). A portion of the water after ammonia treatment was used to recharge the barn pits for flushing. The first-generation system removed from the wastewater 97.6% of the suspended solids, 99.7% of biochemical oxygen demand, 98.5% of total Kjeldahl nitrogen (TKN), 98.7% of ammonia ($NH_4^+$-N), 95.0% of total P, 98.7% of copper, 99.0% of zinc, and 97.9% of malodorous aromatic compounds and produced a sanitized effluent with a reduction in the number of pathogenic bacteria to nondetectable levels (Vanotti et al., 2007). According to Aneja et al. (2008b), the $NH_3$ emissions for this first-generation wastewater treatment plant were reduced by 94.4% for the warm season and by 99.0% for the cool season with respect to a conventional lagoon system. In addition, the system transformed the old lagoon into an aerobic reservoir within a year and significantly reduced lagoon odor (Loughrin et al., 2006). Recommendations were also made to evaluate an improved, redesigned second-generation version of the wastewater treatment system. Therefore, a lower-cost, second-generation treatment system was designed and demonstrated full scale on B&B Tyndall farm, a 5,145-head finishing swine operation in North Carolina.

## Second- and Third-Generation Systems: Cost Improvements While Meeting EST Standards

The second-generation system (Fig. 10.3 and Table 10.1) provided improvements while meeting EST standards (Vanotti et al., 2009a). Data in Table 10.1 show the key contributions of each component of the technology toward the total efficiency of the system. Solid–liquid separation with polymers was effective in separating suspended solids, oxygen-demanding organic compounds, and organic nutrients and heavy metals by capturing the suspended particles. This efficient removal of suspended solids early in the treatment train is a significant departure from treatment typically used in municipal wastewater systems because it recovers most of the organic carbon and organic nutrient compounds contained in the liquid manure, therefore enabling the conservation and generation of value-added products. The system recovered most (97% and 95%, respectively) of the organic phosphorus and nitrogen contained in the flushed manure that left the farm and the swine production farm and were incorporated into compost products. The third generation was designed to further reduce the cost of manure treatment by economies of scale by installation on a larger farm and to test adaptation of the system to farms using the flushing approach that results in very diluted manure (compared to pit-recharge systems). The adaptation consisted of a preconcentration of the diluted manure before polymer application. The project sponsor was North Carolina's Clean Water Management Trust Fund.

V. P. ANEJA, M. VANOTTI, A. A. SZOGI, AND G. REDDY

FIGURE 10.3. Aerial picture of the second-generation on-farm system using solid–liquid separation, nitrogen, and phosphorus modules treating all the animal waste from a 5,145-head swine finishing farm in Sampson County, North Carolina. *Source*: USDA.

The third-generation technology was demonstrated full scale on a 2,575,444-lb. steady-state live weight (SSLW) farrow-to-finish farm that produced 30,450 hogs per year in Wayne County, North Carolina. The treatment system was operated by the farmer. The treatment system was contained in tanks and replaced two anaerobic lagoons (Fig. 10.4). The system treated the waste stream from two operations: (1) a 1,200-sow farrow-to-feeder operation (sow farm) that used a flushing system and generated 37,136 gallons of manure per day (total suspended solids [TSS] = 1.3 g/L) and (2) a 12,960 feeder-to-finish operation (finishing farm) that used a pit-recharge system and generated 41,286 gallons of manure per day (TSS = 10.1 g/L). A decanting tank was added in this project to the flushing system waste stream (sow farm) to preconcentrate the manure in a very diluted stream before solid–liquid separation with flocculants. Highly efficient treatment performance was obtained with both high hydraulic loads typical of flushing systems and high strength wastewater typical of the pit-recharge systems

Table 10.1 Second-Generation USDA Technology Using Solid-Liquid Separation, Nitrogen, and Phosphorus Modules for the Treatment of Swine Manure (Super Soils System) and Performance by Treatment Step and Overall System Efficiency (Vanotti et al., 2009a, 2018)

| Water Quality Parameter[a] | Raw Flushed Swine Manure (system influent) mg L$^{-1b}$ | After Solid–Liquid Separation Treatment | After Ammonia Treatment | After Phosphorus Treatment (system effluent) | System Efficiency, %[c] |
|---|---|---|---|---|---|
| | | Treatment Step, mg L$^{-1b}$ | | | |
| TSS | 11,754 ± 6,417 | 1,254 ± 1,015 | 227 ± 199 | 325 ± 215 | 97.2[b] |
| VSS | 8,926 ± 5103 | 891 ± 756 | 154 ± 129 | 142 ± 105 | 98.4 |
| TS | 30,065 ± 12,475 | 14,244 ± 5,104 | 9,824 ± 2,312 | 10,008 ± 2,495 | 67.7 |
| VS | 17,799 ± 8,725 | 5,322 ± 2,893 | 1,818 ± 827 | 1,738 ± 1,046 | 90.2 |
| COD | 22,204 ± 14,363 | 8,196 ± 5286 | 1,058 ± 541 | 821 ± 405 | 96.3 |
| Soluble COD | 7,338 ± 6,012 | 6,073 ± 4098 | 862 ± 393 | 684 ± 308 | 90.6 |
| BOD$_5$ | 7,364 ± 6,313 | 3,185 ± 2,692 | 62 ± 88 | 41 ± 61 | 99.4 |
| TKN | 2,054 ± 778 | 1,466 ± 600 | 138 ± 166 | 87 ± 130 | 95.7 |
| NH$_4$-N | 1,290 ± 615 | 1,213 ± 451 | 124 ± 171 | 45 ± 92 | 96.5 |
| Oxidized N | 1.4 ± 4.6 | 0.2 ± 1.5 | 221 ± 179 | 162 ± 144 | — |
| Organic N | 739 ± 447 | 230 ± 290 | 33 ± 38 | 36 ± 51 | 95.1 |
| Total N | 2055 | 1466 | 359 | 249 | 87.9 |
| TP | 492 ± 272 | 151 ± 79 | 83 ± 30 | 33 ± 23 | 93.3 |
| Soluble P | 94 ± 63 | 82 ± 42 | 76 ± 29 | 19 ± 17 | 79.8 |
| Organic P | 380 ± 259 | 62 ± 63 | 11 ± 12 | 12 ± 14 | 96.8 |
| Ca | 417 ± 196 | 106 ± 58 | 39 ± 18 | 90 ± 95 | 78.4 |
| Mg | 219 ± 110 | 44 ± 30 | 16 ± 7 | 12 ± 5 | 94.5 |
| Zn | 25.4 ± 12.6 | 2.9 ± 2.8 | 0.4 ± 0.4 | 0.3 ± 0.3 | 98.8 |
| Cu | 16.8 ± 11.1 | 2.0 ± 2.4 | 0.2 ± 0.1 | 0.2 ± 0.1 | 98.8 |
| Fe | 39.9 ± 21.3 | 4.81 ± 4.55 | 0.49 ± 0.40 | 0.39 ± 0.35 | 99.0 |
| S | 128 ± 60 | 49 ± 19 | 34 ± 8 | 31 ± 8 | 75.8 |
| Alkalinity | 7,027 ± 2,175 | 5,469 ± 1505 | 1,422 ± 1,013 | 1,580 ± 835 | 77.5 |
| ORP, mV | −64 ± 72 | 6 ± 135 | 202 ± 177 | ND | — |
| pH | 7.80 ± 0.35 | 7.78 ± 0.23 | 7.98 ± 0.50 | 9.72 ± 0.69 | — |
| EC, mS cm$^{-1}$ | 14.97 ± 4.36 | 14.09 ± 4.08 | 7.25 ± 1.91 | 6.58 ± 1.57 | 56.0 |
| Odor compounds[d] ng/mL | 71,269 ± 14,733 | 63,642 ± 12,366 | 40 ± 17 | 44 ± 11 | 99.9 |
| Total fecal coliforms (log$_{10}$/mL)[e] | 4.11 ± 0.19 | 3.47 ± 0.16 | 0.84 ± 0.23 | 0.17 ± 0.18 | 99.99 |

Note: Data are means ± standard deviations of 122 samples during 2 years of continuous operation.

[a] BOD$_5$, 5-day biochemical oxygen demand; COD, chemical oxygen demand; EC, electrical conductivity; ND, not determined; ORP, oxidation reduction potential; TKN, total Kjeldahl nitrogen; TP, total phosphorus; TS, total solids; TSS, total suspended solids; VSS, volatile suspended solids; Oxidized-N = NO$_3$-N + NO$_2$-N (nitrate plus nitrite); Total N = TKN + Oxidized-N.

[b] Units are mg/L except for ORP (mV), EC (mS cm$^{-1}$), pH, odor compounds, and pathogens. ORP values are standard hydrogen electrode (Eh).

[c] System efficiency (concentration reduction) = [(Influent Conc.−Effluent Conc.) / Influent Conc.] * 100.

[d] Odor compounds are the sum of concentrations of five malodorous compounds contained in the liquid (phenol, p-cresol, p-ethylphenol, indole, and skatole) that are characteristic of swine manure. Values are means ± standard errors of 15 monthly determinations.

[e] Total fecal coliforms values are means ± standard errors of log$_{10}$ colony-forming units (cfu) per milliliter for duplicate samples of six monthly determinations.

FIGURE 10.4. Third-generation swine waste treatment system that replaced the lagoon treatment using solid–liquid separation, nitrogen, and phosphorus modules. The system provided treatment to all the manure from a 1,200-sow farrow-to-feeder farm that used a flushing system and a 12,960-head feeder-to-finish farm that used a pit-recharge system. *Source*: USDA.

(Vanotti et al., 2013): (1) Solids separation: The decanting tank was effective to concentrate the diluted manure in the flushing waste stream. It reduced the total manure volume processed by the solid separator press by 25,860 gal/day, and it increased polymer use efficiency 5.4 times (from 52 to 279 g/g). This is one of the major advances of this project: it increased solid separator press capacity and lowered operating expenses. (2) Water quality: On a mass basis, the system removed 98.6% of the TSS, 98.1% of the chemical oxygen demand, 99.3% of the TKN, 96.7% of the total N, 100% of ammonia, 91.9% of total phosphorus, 95.4% of copper, and 97.0% of zinc. (3) Pathogens: Due to the high pH in the phosphorus module, the system was effective in killing pathogens. It met the new Swine Waste Management System Performance Standards (15A NCAC 02T, 2010) for pathogens (fecal coliforms <7,000 MPN/100 mL) (< 3.84 $\log_{10}$). (4) Odors: The treatment system removed 100% of odorous compounds in the liquid, including skatole, phenol, total cresol, indole, and volatile fatty acids (acetate, propionate, isobutyric).

## Climate Change Impact with the Super Soils System

Although the climate impact (greenhouse gas [GHG] emission) of manure processing technologies is very important now, it was not an environmental standard that ESTs needed to comply with in 2000 as part of the AG Agreement process (ESTs addressed only the elimination of pathogens, ammonia emissions, odor, heavy metals, phosphorus, and discharge to surface and groundwater). However, they can also be very effective in reducing GHG emissions. Using protocols adopted through the United Nations Framework Convention on Climate Change (UNFCCC), Vanotti et al. (2008) estimated a 96.9% reduction in GHG emissions by replacement of the traditional lagoon-spray field technology with the cleaner, aerobic Super Soils technology (on-farm liquid treatment plus composting). The GHG emissions reductions due to the installation of this technology in a 6,000-head swine farm in North Carolina were 6,732 tonnes of $CO_2$-eq per year. This represents an additional economic benefit of $26,930 per year from carbon offsets (Vanotti et al., 2008).

## Animal Productivity and Health Improvement with Super Soils System

The reuse of cleaner, sanitized water to refill barn pits reduced ammonia concentration in the air and improved the growing environment. It replaced the dirtier lagoon liquid charged with ammonia used for the same task under traditional lagoon management. The enhanced animal productivity was demonstrated by comparing five production cycles before conversion to the new system (traditional lagoon management) and five production cycles after conversion to the new technology. Since the recycled wastewater was mostly ammonia-free, ambient ammonia levels in the barns dropped an average of 75%. As a result, animal health and productivity were enhanced (Vanotti, 2010). Daily weight gain increased by 6.1%, and feed conversion improved by 5.1%. Animal mortality decreased by 47%, and cull weight was reduced by 80%. The farmer sold an average of 5,265 pigs per growing cycle, which resulted in a 1,138,247-lb. net gain per cycle. Using the second-generation system instead of the lagoon system, the farmer sold 61,996 pounds more hogs—a 5.8% increase—per growing cycle. Additional economic benefits from improvements in animal productivity and health amount to $91,920 per year ($120.15/1,000 lbs. live animal weight/year).

## Sistrates System in Brazil Using AD Coupled with Super Soils System N and P Modules

The new generation of the Super Soils System (Vanotti et al., 2005, 2010) has been commercialized in Santa Catarina, Brazil, with the Swine Farming Effluent Treatment System (Sistrates) (Embrapa, 2020). It is a combination of biological and chemical processes to jointly remove carbon, nitrogen, and phosphorus, generating reusable water, electricity, and phosphorus fertilizer. Another advantage is that the process can be applied in a modular and supplementary way, according to treatment needs and conditions in the property.

### Anaerobic Digestion

Anaerobic digestion (AD) is a method for converting biomass into bioenergy. Livestock manure is a commonly used biomass material for the production of bioenergy.

Many livestock (hog and cattle) manure treatment systems rely on open lagoons where the $CH_4$, $CO_2$, $NH_3$ (ammonia), and other gases, such as reduced sulfur compounds, and VOCs are emitted into the atmosphere. When these open systems are covered, gaseous emissions are reduced, which results in the effluent leaving the anaerobic digester, known as digestate, with a modified chemical content (e.g., total solids, carbon, ammonia, ammonium [$NH_4^+$], and pH), relative to waste from a conventional open lagoon system. The digestate contains more ammonium ($NH_4^+$) due to a reduction in ammonia emissions from the anaerobic digester (i.e., covered lagoon) to the atmosphere and has less degradable biomass carbon than the substrate in an open lagoon, resulting in changes in GHG and $NH_3$ emissions (Clemens et al., 2006).

The production of biogas through AD of livestock manure is a complex process. It involves a variety of physiological and biochemical metabolic pathways, the essence of which is the material and energy metabolism of micro-organisms under anaerobic conditions.

## Best Management Practices

Sound animal manure management practices are essential to reap economic and health benefits while reducing adverse environmental effects. Best management practices must be followed in each animal waste system step, such as reducing gas emissions in animal houses, handling and storing of manure, land application, and protecting or reducing the potential of surface and groundwater contamination. Several methods have been used to reduce greenhouse gas emissions in animal houses. In handling and storing manure in lagoons or pits, best management practices have been developed by state and extension services that may help operators during events such as big storms and excess rainfall. However, CAFOs must be prepared to tackle these situations to avoid liquid manure contaminating surface waters by installing terraces or diversion channels or using vegetation strips. The *Agricultural Waste Management Field Handbook* (AWMFH) was developed by the US Department of Agriculture–Natural Resources Conservation Service (USDA-NRCS), allowing producers to follow guidelines to plan, organize, and integrate into their overall farm operations. Animal waste management (subset of the AWMFH) is a tool for animal feeding operations whereby producers can estimate manure production, storage size, and treatment facilities. Each state has also developed National Pollutant Discharge Elimination System (NPDES) regulations and nutrients budget plans for CAFO operations.

## Recommendations and Policy

Animal manure is a traditional and valuable source of nutrients that can reduce or eliminate commercial fertilizer use, providing organic carbon to enhance soil health. However, significant concerns about the impact of land-applied manure nutrients on soil and air resources in North Carolina arose during the late 1980s to mid-1990s due to the swine industry's rapid growth, resulting in the concentration of CAFOs within relatively small geographic areas (Williams, 2001;2009). Along with the industry's expansion, federal and state governments' environmental policies under the Clean Water Act supported required compliance with land application of treated wastewater or manure solids based on realistic crop yield expectations and nutrient loading rates through comprehensive nutrient management plans (CNMPs). These regulatory measures remain appropriate to manage manure effectively to protect the nation's water quality. However, their enforcement in North Carolina counties with high CAFO concentrations is ineffective in protecting water resources. A nutrient assessment and geographic distribution of animal manure revealed that several counties had enough animal manure to exceed by over a 100% the nitrogen and phosphorus requirements of all nonlegume agronomic crops and forages (Zublena and Barker, 1992). Information derived from this assessment served extension practitioners to educate producers on strategies to reduce environmental pollution due to land application of manure nutrients above cropland needs. These strategies included dispersing livestock operations to avoid localized nutrient saturation in soils, integrating manure into existing commercial fertilizer operations, or transporting manure long distances to solve distribution problems of manure nutrients. None of these were attractive to pork producers and industry because of the high production costs for producing organic and inorganic fertilizer blends, feed and manure long-distance transportation costs, and no government policy for incentivizing these strategies.

With the urgent need to address alternatives to lagoon treatment and land application of swine manure, the North Carolina attorney general started the "Environmentally Superior Technology" (EST) research initiative in 2000. The EST initiative propelled a more comprehensive policy as a strategy to reduce CAFOs' environmental impacts. Therefore, EST performance standards included impacts of animal waste to surface and groundwater, emission of ammonia and odor, the release of disease-transmitting pathogens, and heavy metal contamination of soil and groundwater. As a result of North Carolina's EST development, a statewide volunteer Lagoon Conversion Program (LCP), enacted through North Carolina Law 2007-523, assisted farmers financially in installing EST systems. This law included an indefinite extension of the moratorium for building lagoon and spray field systems in new farms and established a swine farm methane-capture pilot program. The outcome of the EST research initiative was recognized worldwide for its impact on engineering, air quality, animal science, food safety, and climate change (Vanotti et al., 2009b). The new animal waste management methods developed under the EST protect the environment and allow manure management to switch to a current recycling view of manure handling within the food chain's circular economy. The Farm Bill provides financial and technical assistance to America's agricultural producers, addressing natural resource concerns and delivering environmental benefits, such as improved water and air quality through the Environmental Quality Incentives Program (EQIP) and Conservation Innovation Grants (CIG) (USDA, 2018). These cost-share and matching requirement programs award competitive grants to develop and implement new tools, technologies, and strategies in soil, water, and air conservation efforts. These programs could help implement proven ESTs or its components, contributing to greenhouse gas reductions and improved water quality.

The following recommendations are proposed, based on the collective experience with the EST and current trends in animal production concentration, for environmentally safe technologies to handle excess manure produced in CAFOs:

- Seek public policies and government programs to incentivize building new systems, like the Super Soils EST, to create US manufacturing jobs for wastewater treatment equipment, construction, installation, and service maintenance, providing economic opportunities in rural communities (Gereffi et al., 2008).
- Implement affordable treatment technologies for reducing manure nitrogen and phosphorus loads to enable CAFOs to meet required CNMPs when land is limited for manure application. Include P recovery technologies in CNMPs to help maintain the sustainability of confined animal production while conserving phosphorus, a finite resource.
- Establish an initiative or process for other technologies to be viable ESTs that may result from engineering improvements and demonstrated economic feasibility. This initiative could also include technologies not part of the EST initiative.
- Identify potential public policies, government incentives, and markets related to trading manure by-products. Trading green energy production (biogas production) and environmental credits (carbon and nutrient credits) could compensate farmers for utilizing technologies providing improvements and environmental benefits over current lagoon-based waste treatment systems.
- Address the excess greenhouse gases, ammonia, and odors released into the environment from CAFOs to significantly reduce the impact on the surrounding community's health and well-being (Williams et al., 2003; Wing et al., 2008). Adopting technologies that eliminate the off-site impact of manure ammonia and malodor on poor and disadvantaged rural communities repeatedly exposed to ammonia and odor from nearby would reduce the hefty costs on public health.

- Promote manure treatment technologies that can increase animal productivity by improving the CAFOs' respiratory environment. The Super Soils EST demonstrated that when excess nitrogen is removed, it offsets the negative effect of excess ammonia gas on animal health, and confined swine can gain 5% more weight with 5% less feed.
- Many CAFOs are located in environmentally sensitive areas, magnifying the negative impact of ammonia emissions and nitrogen deposition, such as on or adjacent to wetlands. The opportunity to generate sustainable biogas as a clean energy source promises immediate and sustainable environmental benefits to nutrient-sensitive ecosystems. However, the widespread adoption of lagoon coverings would require the inclusion of a technology to significantly reduce or capture ammonia in wastewater to generate sustainable biogas efficiently without detrimental ammonia side effects and clean water for recycling into the swine house or crop irrigation.

## Acknowledgments

We thank Dr. C. Mike Williams for all his management and research efforts to help us understand the animal waste management technologies. We also thank Mr. M. Shehzaib Ali for providing assistance in the word processing of the manuscript.

### REFERENCES

Anderson AD, Nelson JM, Rossiter S, Angulo FJ. Public health consequences of use of antimicrobial agents in food animals in the United States. Microbial Drug Resist. 2003;9:373–379.

Aneja VP, Arya SP, Kim DS, Rumsey IC, Arkinson HL, Semunegus H, . . . Williams CM. (2008a). Characterizing ammonia emissions from swine farms in eastern North Carolina: Part 1—Conventional lagoon and spray technology for waste treatment. J Air Waste Mgmt Assoc. 2008a; 58(9):1130–1144.

Aneja VP, Arya SP, Rumsey IC, et al. Characterizing ammonia emissions from swine farms in eastern North Carolina: part 2—potential environmentally superior technologies for waste treatment. J Air Waste Mgmt Assoc. 2008b;58(9):1145–1157.

Aneja VP, Arya SP, Rumsey IC, Kim D-S, Bajwa KS, Williams CM. Charactering ammonia emissions from swine farms in eastern North Carolina: reduction of emissions from water-holding structures at two candidate superior technologies for waste treatment. Atmos Environ. 2008c;42:3291–3300.

Aneja VP, Bunton BJ, Walker JT, Malik BP. Measurements and Analysis of of atmospheric ammonia emissions from anaerobic lagoons. Atmos Environ. 2001a;35(11):1949–1958.

Aneja VP, Chauhan JP, Walker JT. Characterization of atmospheric ammonia emissions from swine waste storage and treatment lagoons. J Geophys Res. 2000;105(D9):11535–11545.

Aneja VP, Roelle PA, Murray GC, Southerland J, Erisman JW, Fowler D, Asman WAH, and Patni N. Atmospheric nitrogen compounds II: emissions, transport, transformation, deposition and assessment. Atmos. Environ. 2001b;35(11): 1903–1911.

Aneja VP, Schlesinger WH, Erisman JW. Effects of agriculture upon the air quality and climate: research, policy, and regulations. Environ Sci Technol. 2009;43(12): 4234–4240.

Aneja VP, Schlesinger WH, Erisman JW. (2008d). Farming pollution. Nat Geosci. 2008d;1:409–411.

ASABE. Design of anaerobic lagoons for animal waste management. ANSI/ASAE EP403.4 FEB2011 (R2020). American National Standard; 2011.

Baek BH, Aneja VP. Measurement and analysis of the relationship between ammonia, acid gases, and fine particles in eastern North Carolina. J Air Waste Manage Assoc. 2004a;54:623–633.

Baek BH, Aneja VP, Tong Q. Chemical coupling between ammonia, acid gases, and fine particles. Environ Pollut. 2004b;129:89–98.

Blunden J, Aneja VP. Characterizing ammonia and hydrogen sulfide emissions from a swine waste treatment lagoon in North Carolina. Atmos Environ. 2008;42(14):3277–3290.

Blunden J, Aneja VP, Overton JH. Modeling hydrogen sulfide emissions across the gas–liquid interface of an anaerobic swine waste treatment storage system. Atmos Environ. 2008;42(22):5602–5611.

Boxall ABA, Fogg LA, Blackwell PA, Kay P, Pemberton EJ, Croxford A. Veterinary medicines in the environment. Rev Environ Contam Toxicol. 2004;180:1–91.

Burkholder J, Libra B, Weyer P, et al. Impacts of waste from concentrated animal feeding operations on water quality. Environ Health Perspect. 2007;11(2):308–312.

Burton C. The potential contribution of separation technologies to the management of livestock manure. Livest Sci. 2007;112(3):208–216.

Cahn TT, Sutton A, Aarnink AJA, Verstergen MWA, Sharma JW, Baker JW. Dietary protein effects, nitrogen excretion and ammonia emission from slurry of growing finishing pigs. Livestock Prod Sci. 1998;56:181–191.

Cantrell KB, Hunt PG, Uchimiya M, Novak JM, Ro KS. Impact of pyrolysis temperature and manure source on physicochemical characteristics of biochar. Bioresour. Technol. 2012;107: 419–428.

Casey KD, Bicudi JR, Schmidt DR, et al. Air quality and emissions from livestock and poultry production/waste management systems. In: Rice JM, Caldwell DF, Humenick FJ, eds. Animal Agriculture and the Environment. National Center for Manure and Animal waste Management White Papers. St. Joseph, MI: ASABE; 2006:1–40.

Clark OG, Moehn S, Edeogu I, Price J, Leonard J. Manipulation of dietaryprotein and non-starch polysaccharide to control swine manure emissions. J Environ Qual. 2005;34:1461–1466.

Copeland C. Animal Waste and Water Quality: EPA Regulation of Concentrated Animal Feeding Operations (CAFOs). Washington, D.C.: Congressional Research Service Report for Congress; 2010. Order Code RL 31851.

Domingoa NGG, Balasubramaniana S, Thakrar SK, et al. Air quality–related health damages of food. Proc Natl Acad Sci U S A. 2021118(20):e2013637118.

Doorn MRJ, Natschke DF, Thorneloe SA, Southerland J. Development of an emission factor for ammonia emissions from U.S. swine farms based on field tests and application of a mass balance method. Atmos Environ. 2002;36:5619–5625.

Dube PJ, Vanotti MB, Szogi AA, García-González MC. Enhancing recovery of ammonia from swine manure anaerobic digester effluent using gas-permeable membrane technology. Waste Manage. 2016;49:372–377.

Embrapa. Technology generates energy, fertilizer and water from pig manure. 2020. https://www.embrapa.br/en/busca-de-noticias/-/noticia/52090750/technology -generates-energy-fertilizer-and-water-from-pig-manure

Funk TL, Hussey R, Zhang Y, Ellis M. Synthetic covers for emissions control from earthen embarked swine lagoons, part 1: positive pressure lagoon cover. Appl Eng Agr. 2004;20(2):233–238.

García-González MC, Vanotti MB. Recovery of ammonia from swine manure using gas-permeable membranes: effect of waste strength and pH. Waste Manage. 2015;38:455–461.

Gereffi G, Dubay K, Lowe M. Manufacturing climate solutions. Carbon-Reducing Tech nologies and US Jobs. 2008.

González-García I, Riaño B, Molinuevo-Salces B, Vanotti MB, García-González MC. Improved anaerobic digestion of swine manure by simultaneous ammonia recovery using gas-permeable membranes. Water Res. 2021;190:116789.

Griffing E, Overcash M, Kim S. Environmental analysis of swine waste processing technologies using the life-cycle method. Report No. 350. Raleigh, NC: Water Resources Research Institute of the University of North Carolina; 2004.

Hamilton DW, Fathepure B, Fulhage CD, Clarkson W, Lalman J. Treatment lagoons for animal agriculture. 2006:547.

Heinzen T. Quantification and regulation of air emissions from animal feeding operations. Curr Environ Health Rep. 2015;2:25–32.

Herber LT, Quin NJ, Kendall DC. Effects of manure removal strategies on odor and gas emissions from swine finishing. Trans Am Soc Agr Eng. 2002;4753(6). doi:10.13031/2013.9383

Hooda PS, Edwards AC, Anderson HA, Miller A. A review of water quality concerns in livestock farming areas. Sci Total Environ. 2000;250:143–167.

Hu Z, Mota CR, and Cheng J. Optimization of nitrogen removal from anaerobically pretreated swine wastewater in intermittent aeration tanks. In: Animal, Agricultural and Food Processing Wastes. 2003;IX: 1. American Society of Agricultural and Biological Engineers.

Ibekwe AM, Murinda SE, DeRoy C, Reddy GB. Potential pathogens, antimicrobial patterns, and genotypic diversity of Escherichia coli isolated in constructed wetlands treating swine wastewater. FEMS Microbiol Ecol. 2016;92:fiw006.

Johnson CJ, Bonrud P. Methemoglobinemia: is it coming back to haunt us? Health Environ Digest. 1988;1(12):3–4.

Kjaer J, Olsen P, Bach K, Bariebo HC. Leaching of estrogenic hormones from manure-treated structured soils. Environ Sci Technol. 2007;41(11):3911–3917.

Libra JA, Ro KS, Kammann C, Funke A, Berge ND, Neubauer Y, Titirici M-M, et al. Hydrothermal carbonization of biomass residuals: a comparative review of the chemistry, processes and applications of wet and dry pyrolysis. Biofuels. 2011;2(1): 71–106.

Liu J, Power W, Murphy J, Maghirang R. Ammonia and hydrogen sulfide emissions from swine production facilities in Northern America: a meta-analysis. J Anim Sci. 2014;92(4): 1656–1665.

Liu Z, Powers W, Liu H. Greenhouse gas emissions from swine operations: evaluation of the Inter-Governmental Panel on Climate Change Approaches through meta-analysis. J Anim Sci. 2013;91(8):4017–4032.

Loughrin JH, Szogi AA, Vanotti MB. Reduction of malodorous compounds from a treated swine anaerobic lagoon. J. Environ. Qual. 2006;35:194–199.

Mallin MA. Impacts of industrial scale swine and poultry production on rivers and estuaries. Am Sci. 2000;88:26–37.

Mallin MA, McIver MR. Season matters when sampling streams for swine CAFO waste pollution impacts. J Water Health. 2018;16.1.

Metcalf E, Eddy E. Wastewater Engineering: Treatment, Disposal, and Reuse. New York: McGraw-Hill; 2003.

Miner JR, Humenik FJ, Rice JM, et al. Evaluation of a permeable, 5 cm thick polyethylene foam lagoon cover. Trans Am Soc Agr Eng. 2003;46(5):1421–1426.

Miralha L, Siddique S, Muenich RL. The special organization of CAFOs and its relationship to water quality in the United States. J Hydrol. 2022;613(pt A):128301.

Moore PA Jr. Animal containment facility ventilation system. 2014. US patent 8, 663, 551.

Muller R. Impact of the rise in atmosphere nitrous oxide on stratospheric ozone. Ambio. 2021;50(1):35–39.

Ndegwa PM, Hristov AN, Arogo J, Sheffield RE. A review of ammonia emission mitigation techniques for concentrated animal feeding operations. Biosyst. Eng. 2008;100(4):453–469.

Onema O, Wrage N, Velthof GL, Groenigen JW, Dolfing J, Kurman PJ. Trends in global nitrous oxide emissions from animal production systems. Nutrient Cycling Agrosyst. 2005;72:51–56.

Otto ER, Yokoyama M, Hengemuehle S, Bermuth RD, Von Kempen T, Van Trottier NL. Ammonia volatile fatty acids, phenolics, and odor offensiveness in manure from growing pigs fed diets reduced in protein concentration. J Anim Sci. 2003;81:1754–1763.

Owusu-Twum MY, Sharara MA. Sludge management in anaerobic swine lagoons: a review. J Environ Manage. 2020;271:110949.

Park KH, Thompson AG, Marinier M, Clark K, Wagner RC. Greenhouse gas emissions from stored liquid swine manure in cold climate. Atmos Environ. 2006;40(4):618–627.

Poach PE, Hunt PG, Reddy GB, et al. Ammonia volatilization from marsh-pond-marsh constructed wetlands treating swine wastewater. J Environ Qual. 2004;33(3):844–851.

Reddy GB, Forbes D, Phillips R, Cyrus JS, Porter J. Demonstration of technology to treat swine waste using geotextile bag, zeolite bed and constructed wetlands. Ecol Eng. 2013;57:353–360.

Reddy GB, Hunt PG, Phillips R, Stone K, Grubbs A. Treatment of swine wastewater in marsh-pond-marsh constructed wetlands. Water Sci Technol. 2001;44(11–12): 545–550.

Ren F, Zhang X, Liu J, Sun N, Wu L, Li Z, Xu M. A synthetic analysis of greenhouse gas emissions from manure amended agricultural soils in China. Sci. Rep. 2017;7(1):8123.

Renard JJ, Calidonna SE, Henley M. Fate of ammonia in the atmosphere: a review for applicability to hazardous releases. J Hazard Mater. 2004;108(1–2):29–60.

Ro KS, Vanotti MB, Szogi AA, Loughrin JH, Millner PD. High-rate solid-liquid separation coupled with nitrogen and phosphorous treatment of swine manure: effect on ammonia emission. Front Sustain Food Syst. 2018;2:62.

Rumsey IC, Aneja VP, Lonneman WA. Characterizing reduced sulfur compounds emissions from a swine concentrated animal feeding operation. Atmos Environ. 2014;94:458–466.

Rumsey IC, Aneja VP. Measurement and modeling of hydrogen sulfide lagoon emissions from a swine concentrated animal feeding operation. Environ. Sci. Tech. 2014;48:1609–1617.

Scanes CG. Impact of agricultural animals on the environment. In: Scanes CG, Toukhsati SR, eds. Animals and Human Society. Academic Press. 2018; 427–449.

Seinfeld JH, Pandis SN. Atmospheric Chemistry and Physics. New York: John Wiley; 1998.

Shakoor A, Mehmood T. Nitrous oxide emission from agricultural soils: application of animal manure or biochar: a global meta-analysis. J Environ Manage. 2021; 285:112170.

Shappell NW, Billey LO, Forbes D, et al. Estrogenic activity and steroid hormones in swine wastewater through a lagoon constructed wetland systems. Environ Sci Technol. 2007;41(2):444–450.

Sharara M, Spearman B. Composting turns swine lagoon sludge to landscaping products. November 12, 2020. https://animalwaste.ces.ncsu.edu/2020/11/composting-turns-swine-lagoon-sludge-to-landscaping-products/.

Sharpe RR, Harper LA. Methane emissions from an anaerobic swine lagoon. Atmos Environ. 1999;33(22):3627–3633.

Sharrer MJ, Rishel KL, Summerfelt RS. Evaluation of geotextile filtration applying coagulant and flocculant amendments for aquaculture biosolids dewatering and phosphorus removal. Aquacult Eng. 2009;40(10):1–10.

Szogi AA, Vanotti MB, Hunt PG. Process for removing and recovering phosphorus from animal waste. 2014a. US patent 8,673,046 B1. US Patent and Trademark Office.

Szogi AA, Vanotti MB, Rothrock MJ Jr. Gaseous ammonia removal system. 2014b. US Patent 8, 906,332.

Szogi AA, Vanotti MB. Abatement of ammonia emissions from swine lagoons using polymer-enhanced solid-liquid separation. Appl Eng Agr. 2007;23(6): 837–845.

Szogi AA, Vanotti MB, Ro KS. Methods for treatment of animal manures to reduce nutrient pollution prior to soil application. Curr Pollut Rep. 2015;1(1):47–56.

Thu KM, Durrenberger EP. Pigs, Profits, and Rural Communities. New York: Albany State University of New York Press; 1998.

US Department of Agriculture (USDA). Agricultural Waste Management Field Handbook Part 651 Appendix 10D. Washington, D.C.: USDA; 2008.

US Department of Agriculture (USDA). Agricultural management system component design. In: Agricultural Waste Management Field Handbook Part 651. Washington, D.C.: USDA; 2009.

US Department of Agriculture (USDA). Farmers' guide to 2018 USDA Farm Bill Programs. https://www.fsa.usda.gov/Assets/USDA-FSA-Public/usdafiles/Farm -Bill/pdf/farmbill-2018-brochure.pdf

US Department of Agriculture (USDA). Quarterly hogs and pigs report. Washington, D.C.: USDA; 2016. http://USDA.mannlib.cornell.edu/MannUSDA/view Document Info.doi.1086

US Department of Agriculture (USDA). Waste treatment lagoon. Conservation Standard Code 359. Washington, D.C.: USDA; 2019.

US Environment Protection Agency (USEPA). Managing Manure Nutrients at Concentrated Animal Feeding Operations. EPA-821-B-04-009. Washington, D.C.: USEPA; 2014.

Vac SC, Popita GE, Frunzeti N, Popovici A. Evaluation of greenhouse gas emission from animal manure using the enclosed chamber method for gas fluxes. Nol Bot Horti Agrobot. 2013;41:576–581.

Van Lier JB, Mahmoud N, Zeeman G. Anaerobic wastewater treatment. 2008. In Biological wastewater treatment: principles, modelling and design, edited by M. Henze et al., 415–457. London: IWA Publishing.

Vanotti MB. Producer benefits using Terra Blue treatment technology: increased pig productivity, expansion, and carbon credits. In: Proceedings of the National Poultry and Animal Waste Management Symposium. NCSU (CD-ROM). Greensboro, NC, 2010.

Vanotti M, Hunt P, Rice M, Kunz A, Loughrin, J. Evaluation of generation 3 treatment technology for swine waste: a North Carolina's Clean Water Management

Trust Fund project. Final Environmental Performance Report for the Director, NCSU Animal and Poultry Waste Management Center. 2013. http://www.cals .ncsu.edu/waste_mgt/smithfield_projects/CWMTF-Report.pdf

Vanotti MB, Rice JM, Hunt PG, et al. Evaluation of polymer solids separation, nitrification-denitrification and soluble phosphorus removal system for treating swine manure. In: Proceedings of the International Symposium Addressing Animal Production and Environmental Issues, Raleigh, NC. (CD-ROM). 2001.

Vanotti MB, Millner PD, Szogi AA, Campbell CR, Fetterman LM. Aerobic composting of swine manure solids mixed with cotton gin trash. ASABE Paper #064061. 2006. https://www.ars.usda.gov/ARSUserFiles/60820000/Manuscripts/2006/Man729.pdf

Vanotti MB, Ro KS, Szogi AA, Loughrin JH, Millner PD. High-rate solid-liquid separation coupled with nitrogen and phosphorus treatment of swine manure: effect on water quality. Front Sustain Food Syst. 2018;2:49.

Vanotti M, Szogi AA. Evaluation of environmental superior technology contingent determination—second generation super soil technology. Final Report for NC Department of Justice—Office of the Attorney General Environmental Enhancement Fund Program. 2007. http://www.cals.ncsu.edu/waste_mgt/smithfield _projects/supersoils2ndgeneration/pdfs/technical_report.pdf

Vanotti MB, Szogi AA. Systems and methods for reducing ammonia emissions from liquid effluents and for recovering ammonia. 2015. U.S. Patent 9,005,333 B1. U.S. Patent and Trademark Office.

Vanotti, MB, Szogi AA. Water quality improvements of CAFO wastewater after advanced treatment. J. Environ. Qual. 2008;37: S86–S96.

Vanotti M, Szogi M, Bernal MP, Martinez J. Livestock waste treatment systems of the future: a challenge to environmental quality, food safety, and sustainability. OECD Workshop. Biores Technol. 2009b;100(22):5371.

Vanotti MB, Szogi AA, Ducey TF. High performance nitrifying sludge for high ammonium concentration and low temperature wastewater treatment. 2013. US patent 8,445,253 B2. US Patent and Trademark Office.

Vanotti, MB, Szogi AA, Fetterman L. Wastewater treatment system with simultaneous separation of phosphorus sludge and manure solids. 2010. U.S. Patent No. 7,674,379.

Vanotti MB, Szogi AA, Hunt PG, Millner PD, Humenik FJ. Development of environmentally superior treatment system to replace anaerobic swine waste lagoons in the USA. Biores Technol. 2007;98(17):3184–3194.

Vanotti MB, Szogi AA, Millner PD, Loughrin JH. Development of a second-generation environmentally superior technology for treatment of swine manure in the USA. Biores Technol. 2009a;100(22):5406–5416.

Vanotti MB, Szogi AA, Vives CA. Greenhouse gas emission reduction and environmental quality improvement from implementation of aerobic waste treatment systems in swine farms. Waste Manage. 2008;28:759–766.

Wang Y, Wen Y, Zhang S, Zheng G, Zheng H, Chang X, Huang C, Wang S, Wu Y, Hao J. Vehicular ammonia emissions significantly contribute to urban PM2. 5 pollution in two Chinese megacities. Environ. Sci. Tech. 2023;57(7):2698–2705.

Westerman PW, Bicudo JR, Kantardjieff A. Upflow biological aerated filters for the treatment of flushed swine manure. Biores Technol. 2000;74:181–190.

Whitall D, Hendrickson B, Paerl H. Importance of atmospherically deposited nitrogen to the annual nitrogen budget of the Neuse River estuary, North Carolina. Environ Int. 2003;29:393–399.

Wiegand R, Battye W, Bray C, Aneja VP. Ammonia and fine particulate matter (PM2.5) pollution in intensive agricultural regions of North Carolina: satellite analysis and integrated ground-based measurements. Atmosphere. 2022;13(5):821.

Williams CM. Development of environmentally superior technologies in the US and policy. Biores Technol. 2009;100:5512–5518.

Williams CM. Technologies to address air quality issues impacting animal agriculture. Water Sci Technol. 2001;44:233–236.

Williams CM. Development of environmentally superior technologies. Phase III report for technology determination per agreements between the Attorney General of North Carolina and Smithfield Foods, Premium Standard Farms, and Frontline Farmers. 2006. http://www.cals.ncsu.edu/waste_mgt/smithfield _projects/phase3report06/phase3report.htm

Williams CM. Development of environmentally superior technologies: phase 2 report—technology determinations per agreements between the attorney general of North Carolina and Smithfield Foods, Premium Standard Farms, and Frontline Farmers; North Carolina State University; College of Agriculture and Life Sciences: Raleigh, NC, 2005. https://p2infohouse.org/ref/37/36451.pdf

Williams CM, Murray BC, Van Houtven GL, Deerhake ME, Dodd RC, Lowry MMI, Yao C, Miles AM, Bowman EJ, Bruhn MC, Game JL. Benefits of adopting environmentally superior swine waste management technologies in North Carolina: an environmental and economic assessment. Final report. 2003. RTI International. Research Triangle Park, NC.

Wing S, Horton RA, Marshall SW, et al. Air pollution and odor in communities near industrial swine operations. Environ Health Perspect. 2008;116(10):1362–1368.

Zhan JA, Dispirito AA, Do YS, Brooks BE, Cooper EE, Hatfield JL. Correlation of human olfactory responses to air born concentrations of malodorous volatile organic compounds emitted from swine effluent. J Environ Qual. 2001;30: 624–634.

Zhang Z, Zhu J, Li W. A two-step fed SBR for treating swine manure. Process Biochem. 2006;41(4):892–900.

Zhao L, Hadlocon LJS, Manuzon RB, Darr MJ, Keener HM, Heber AJ, Ni J. Ammonia concentrations and emission rates at a commercial poultry manure composting facility. Biosyst. Eng. 2016;150:69–78.

Zublena JP, Barker JC. Nutrient assessment and distribution of animal manure. Better Crop. Summer 1992:28–31.

# CHAPTER 11

# Toward Sustainable Agriculture

John E. Ikerd

The public health risks posed by industrial animal agriculture have been clearly documented in the preceding chapters. However, government regulation to mitigate these risks remains inadequate or nonexistent. The pollution of air and water with chemical and biological wastes is treated as an environmental problem rather than a threat to public health. The health threats of antibiotic-resistant bacteria spawned and spread by industrial animal agriculture operations have been widely acknowledged among global scientists. In the United States, however, responsible use of antibiotics in animal agriculture depends on voluntary compliance with suggested guidelines. The threats to farm workers are perhaps the most clearly documented of all health risks associated with industrial animal agriculture. However, government regulations protecting the health and safety of workers in concentrated animal feeding operations or CAFOs are essentially nonexistent.

Massive public relations campaigns appear to have persuaded the general public that any public health threats associated with industrial agriculture are minimal. Legislators and regulators have been pressured into treating CAFOs as if they were simply a modern-day version of traditional family farming. Family farmers would not do anything that threatens the health of their families or neighbors. As a last resort, defenders claim that today's industrial animal agricultural operations are at least more environmentally responsible than the family farming operations they displaced. The public has also been led to believe there are no economically viable or socially acceptable alternatives to industrial systems of agricultural production.

There are, however, economically viable alternatives to industrial agriculture that are more ecologically sound and socially responsible and pose far fewer public health threats. These alternatives have been growing in popularity over the past 40 years but have not yet gained sufficient market share to gain widespread public attention. These alternatives may be called organic, holistic, biodynamic, ecological, natural, practical, regenerative, resilient, permaculture, agroecology, or some other name that is clearly nonindustrial. Animal agriculture alternatives include free-range, grass-based, pastured, hormone and antibiotic-free, or some other nonindustrial distinction. These alternative systems are capable of evolving into agrifood systems that provide both domestic and global food security.[1]

## The Sustainable Agriculture Movement

All of these ecologically, socially, and economically viable alternatives to industrial agriculture fit under the conceptual umbrella of sustainable agriculture. Sustainable agriculture is not a new concept. It is rooted in the work of early advocates of organic, biodynamic, and other systems of "permanent" agriculture during the early 1900s. The organic food movement was boosted when Rachel Carson's book, *Silent Spring*, ignited the modern environmental movement in the early 1960s. The book focused on the environmental consequences of an increasingly chemically dependent agriculture. The environmental movement gained momentum during the 1970s and 1980s as information documenting the environmental and public health threats of industrial agriculture became more widely available. Sustainable agriculture emerged as a significant public issue in the late 1980s.

A group of organic farming advocates began pleading for support from the US Department of Agriculture (USDA) during the early 1980s. A group of conventional farmers, caught in the cost-price squeeze of the 1980s, also began pressuring the government to help bring down their costs of fertilizer, pesticides, and other purchased inputs. Rural advocacy organizations also had been calling on the USDA for more money to help rural communities cope with the dramatic loss of family farms during the farm financial crisis of the 1980s. These three groups eventually joined forces, and the result was the USDA Low Input Sustainable Agriculture program, or LISA.

The LISA program was authorized by Congress in the 1985 farm bill but was not funded until 1988.[2] The enabling legislation defined sustainable agriculture as "an integrated system of plant and animal production practices having a site-specific application that will over the long-term: satisfy human food and fiber needs; enhance environmental quality and the natural resource base upon which the agriculture economy depends; make the most efficient use of nonrenewable resources and on-farm resources and integrate, where appropriate, natural biological cycles and controls; sustain the economic viability of farm operations; and enhance the quality of life for farmers and society as a whole" (US Code Title 7, Section 3103).[3]

This official definition of sustainable agriculture includes the multiple economic, ecological, and social dimensions generally accepted as essential for sustainability. Sustainable agriculture also is identified as "an integrated system of plant and animal production practices"—rather than random collections of sustainable practices. A diversity of farm enterprises and site-specific, farm-specific farming practices and applications must be integrated to create sustainable whole farm systems.

Defenders of industrial agriculture were quick to label the LISA program as a threat to traditional family farming. They attempted to link LISA to the organic farming movement–which they associated with *back-to-earthers, tree-huggers, hippies, or commune-ists*—certainly not farmers. At that time, organic was the "O-word." The word "sustainable" was selected primarily to avoid references to organic in the rulemaking process. To the organic farming pioneers, however, there was no distinction between sustainable and organic agriculture: real organic farming was sustainable. Even the "low-input" part of LISA was ridiculed by opponents, likely to protect the interest of corporate suppliers of agricultural inputs. It was sometimes called Low Intelligence Subsistence Farming, suggesting that LISA meant going back to the so-called primitive farming methods of homesteaders and the indigenous farmers before them.

With growing environmental and sustainability concerns among consumers, retail sales of organic foods grew at 20% to 25% per year during the 1990s and early 2000s—even at premium retail prices.[4] Organic food sales began moving from natural food stores into mainstream supermarkets as the "O-word" became the economic "Opportunity word." In 1992, the LISA program was renamed Sustainable Agriculture Research and Education to blunt earlier criticism and to gain support from traditional family farmers. Fencerow-to-fencerow cultivation during the 1970s and 1980s had resulted in soil erosion reminiscent of the 1930s. A resurgence of public concerns about soil erosion strengthened support for the USDA LISA 1990s. Even many conventional farmers were becoming concerned about the long-run sustainability of agricultural productivity.

Sustainable agriculture also benefited from its identification with the global sustainability movement. In 1987, the World Commission on Environment and Development released the Brundtland Report, *Our Common Future*, which defined "sustainable development [as] development that meets the needs of the present without compromising the ability of future generations to meet their own needs."[5] This was to become the most widely accepted definition of sustainability among those who took the question of sustainability seriously.

There is growing public pressure, globally and domestically, for a postindustrial paradigm or model of development. The inevitable ecological degradation and socioeconomic inequalities of industrial development not only threaten the well-being of billions of people in the world today but also threaten the future of human life on Earth. A postindustrial agriculture, a sustainable agriculture, must provide the foundation for sustainable development. Sustainable agriculture must meet the needs of the present without compromising the ability of future generations to meet their own needs.

## Pseudo-sustainability

Growing public support for sustainable agriculture eventually forced the defenders of industrial agriculture to retreat and regroup. They grudgingly accepted organic farming as a means of responding to a growing "niche market"—but not as a logical alternative to conventional farming. In return, organic farmers were expected to refrain from claims that organic foods are safer or more nutritious or that organic farms are more sustainable. The industrial agrifood establishment also supported the USDA standards for organic production. They knew if the organic food market continued to grow and remained profitable, they could capture the market and eventually redefine organic standards to accommodate industrial farming methods.

If advocates of industrial agriculture could not stop the sustainable agriculture movement, they would co-opt it. Industrial farmers embraced conservation tillage and no-till farming systems because new chemical and mechanical technologies allowed them to cultivate more land and make more profits than they could with conventional tillage. Farmers changed production practices whenever they found opportunities to increase productivity and profitability or take advantage of government incentives for conservation and environmental protection. While denying any lack of sustainability, industrial producers were quick to exploit the profitable niche markets created by environmentally conscious consumers. They also saw an opportunity to enhance their public image by proclaiming their commitment to sustainability.

Industrial farmers adopted the same strategies as others in the corporate world. Many corporate claims of social responsibility and environmental stewardship are nothing more than "greenwashing."

"Greenwashing conveys false impressions or misleading claims that a company's products are more environmentally sound."[6] Public relations firms were hired to polish the environmental image of industrial agriculture with claims of sustainability. Anything related in any way to protecting the environment or conserving natural resources was labeled as sustainable. Virtually every corporate website, including those of agribusinesses and major agricultural organizations, now proclaims a commitment to sustainability. The ecological and social consequences of their business strategies tell a very different story.

The defenders of industrial agriculture have largely avoided addressing public health threats by limiting their pseudo-sustainability initiatives to changing specific farming methods and practices rather than changing farming systems. They focus on reducing soil erosion or reducing chemical and biological pollution but only support those practices that can be integrated into their large-scale, industrial farming operations. They defend CAFOs as a means of facilitating more effective manure management. They know they cannot actually create ecologically sound and socially responsible farming systems without abandoning their current industrial systems of farming.

Industrial agriculture advocates claim their current systems of farming are supported by "sound science." In 2019, the international EAT-Lancet Commission released a landmark study proposing a global strategy for "healthy diets from sustainable food systems."[7] The study claimed to be "the first attempt to set universal scientific targets for the food system that meet the needs of all people as well as the planet."[8] The Commission acknowledged that the current global agrifood system is not sustainable: "Food systems have the potential to nurture human health and support environmental sustainability; however, they are currently threatening both."[9] Since its release, the report has become the blueprint for responses to growing public concerns for sustainability by both for-profit and nonprofit organizations.

The Commission's proposed strategy for future food production is referred to as "sustainable intensification." Sustainable intensification relies on the development and implementation of new, sophisticated production technologies that would allow industrial farming systems of the future to produce more while using less, polluting less, and wasting less. To meet global food needs, these resource-efficient, biotech, infotech systems of production would need to replace today's subsistence farms and other small-scale, low-tech family farming operations. The primary means proposed for reducing reliance on nonrenewable resources and reducing waste and pollution is to increase productivity and economic efficiency.

The EAT-Lancet report acknowledges that "food systems affect society, culture, economy, and animal welfare,"[10] but the Commission made no attempt to address these critical dimensions of sustainability. Regarding sustainable animal agriculture, they relied on producing more meat, milk, and eggs more efficiently to mitigate environmental impacts. No consideration was given to the logical implications for the health or welfare of farm animals. Food animals are already being overcrowded, force-fed, physically mutilated, and stressed beyond humane limits in efforts to maximize economic efficiency and productivity.[11] Sustainable intensification implies even more of the same inhumane treatment.

The Commission recognized that "sharing space for biodiversity in production landscapes is necessary to secure biodiversity's contribution to food production, including pollination, pest control, carbon capture, and regulating water quality."[12] Their only significant proposal, however, was to require 10% of "production landscapes" be designated for "sharing space" for biodiversity and conservation. Presumably, this means 90% of tillable lands would be managed as specialized, mechanized industrial farming systems. The EAT-Lancet report suggests that farmers of the future should just "do industrial better."

Sustainable intensification would require new agricultural *technologies* but would still rely on today's unsustainable industrial farming *systems*. A 2008 report by the Pew Commission on Industrial Farm Animal Production concluded, "Tweaking the current monoculture confinement operations . . . will be very useful in the short term, but as energy, water, and climate resources undergo dramatic changes, it is the Commission's judgment that US agricultural production will need to transition to much more biologically diverse systems, organized into biological synergies that exchange energy, improve soil quality, and conserve water and other resources."[13]

Regardless of their efficiency, industrial agricultural systems are extractive and exploitative production systems that deplete and permanently damage the natural and human resources they ultimately must depend on for their productivity. Sustainable intensification might slow the process of resource depletion and degradation, but the capability of industrial agriculture to provide global food security eventually would be lost. The spread of intensive industrial agriculture to all parts of the world, as recommended by the EAT-Lancet Commission, might actually exacerbate global food insecurity and accelerate global resource degradation and depletion.

The Commission acknowledged the failure of industrial agrifood systems to provide nutritional food security. "Although global food production of calories has kept pace with population growth, more than 820 million people have insufficient food and many more consume low-quality diets that cause micronutrient deficiencies and contribute to a substantial rise in the incidence of diet-related obesity and diet-related non-communicable diseases, including coronary heart disease, stroke, and diabetes."[14] There is nothing to indicate how increasing production would solve current problems of hunger and malnutrition when more than enough food for everyone is already being produced.

The EAT-Lancet Commission's strategies for sustainable food consumption relied primarily on consumer information and education. Their proposed diets would limit or exclude red meats and rely heavily on alternative sources of protein, fruits, and vegetables.[15] There is no mention of the public health threats associated with the industrial production of alternative sources of protein, fruits, and vegetables. Alternative farming systems that do not create the dietary or other public health threats associated with industrial animal agriculture were summarily dismissed as "not scalable" and thus not feasible.

The proposed solutions to problems of sustainability all boil down to using the same industrial systems of agricultural production that are being used today but simply using them more efficiently. This strategy, at best, might delay the ultimate collapse of the food system, but industrial agriculture, quite simply, is not sustainable.

## Authentic Sustainability

Pseudo-sustainability may be a buzzword, but sustainability is a real word that has a definite meaning. According to Merriam-Webster, sustainability refers to "methods of harvesting or using a resource so that the resource is not depleted or permanently damaged."[16] If something is sustainable, it is lasting, enduring, nondepleting—permanent. When used in reference to sustainable agriculture and sustainable development, sustainable refers to methods of production that meet the needs of the present without depleting or permanently damaging the resources that will be essential to meet the needs of the future. Sustainable agriculture is specifically, but not exclusively, about meeting the present and future needs of people—of humanity.

The organic farming pioneers understood the meaning of authentic sustainability. The publisher of *Organic Gardening*, J. I. Rodale, wrote, "The *organiculturist* farmer must realize that in him is placed a sacred trust, the task of producing food that will impart health to the people who consume it. As a patriotic duty, he assumes an obligation to preserve the fertility of the soil, a precious heritage that he must pass on, undefiled and even enriched, to subsequent generations."[17] Sir Albert Howard began his classic 1940 book, *An Agricultural Testament*, with the assertion, "The maintenance of the fertility of the soil is the first condition of any permanent system of agriculture," which is the foundation of any permanent society.[18]

As these organic pioneers understood, everything of use to humans, including everything of economic value, ultimately is derived from the earth—from energy, air, water, minerals, and the other biological organisms of the earth. Beyond self-sufficiency, individuals must realize the usefulness of the earth through relationships with other humans—through society. Economies are created by societies as means of meeting their needs through impersonal transactions, rather than the personal relationships of friendships, families, and communities. Thus, everything of use to humanity is derived from the earth by way of society. The ecological, social, and economic dimensions of authentic sustainability are logically derived from the nature of our relationships with each other and with the earth.

Sustainable agricultural systems must be ecologically sound: they must not diminish or permanently damage the resources of the earth— air, soil, water, natural ecosystems. They must be socially responsible: they must not only meet the basic food and fiber needs of society but also do so without diminishing or permanently damaging the productivity or the quality of life of farmers or society as a whole. Finally, sustainable agricultural systems must be economically viable: they must generate sufficient economic revenue to meet basic needs that cannot be met through direct ecological and social relationships. This includes meeting the income needs of farm families as well as being affordable to consumers.

As suggested previously, agricultural sustainability refers to farming systems rather than specific farming enterprises, methods, or practices. The sustainability of a farm depends as much or more on how various enterprises, methods, and practices are arranged or managed than on the enterprises, methods, and practices employed on the farm. Sustainability is an "emergent property," meaning it is a characteristic of the "farm as a whole" rather than a collection of enterprises, methods, and practices. A new whole emerges from each new arrangement.

Sustainable farming systems must be regenerative. They must continually renew and regenerate the productivity of resources, which are inevitably diminished in the process of production. Sustainable farms must be managed for resilience. They must be able to withstand, respond, and adjust to the inevitable shocks and changes in the ecological, political, and economic environment in which farms must function. Sustainable farms must also be managed to make efficient use of their resources; they must be resourceful. Sustainable farming systems must be regenerative, resilient, and resourceful. When farms are managed sustainably, they have the ability to meet the needs of the present without degrading or permanently damaging their productive resources and thus without diminishing opportunities for the future.

Sustainable farming is consistent with the initial USDA definition of sustainable agriculture. Industrial farming systems are not. Sustainable farms are "integrated systems of plant and animal production practices having a site-specific application." Industrial farms are specialized systems that rely on specific crop or livestock species and often include only specific phases of plant or animal production. Industrial farming systems are designed to function efficiently under a wide range of climatic and other geographic conditions. Commercial fertilizers and pesticides, irrigation, greenhouses, and hydroponics are all attempts to remove the site specificity of crop production. Large-scale confinement animal feeding operations or CAFOs are attempts to make livestock and poultry production feasible everywhere, at all times of the year—without regard to place or season.

Sustainable farming systems "will over the long-term: satisfy human food and fiber needs; enhance environmental quality and the natural resource base upon which the agriculture economy depends."[19] Industrial farming systems only provide food for those who can afford to pay global market prices. They only provide safe, nutritious food for those who can afford premium prices. Sustainable farming systems "make the most efficient use of nonrenewable resources and on-farm resources and integrate, where appropriate, natural biological cycles and controls."[20] Industrial farming systems depend on fossil energy and commercial fertilizers that deplete as well as pollute streams and groundwater. They rely on commercial pesticides that taint the food supply and threaten the health of farmers, farm workers, and residents of rural communities.

Sustainable farming systems also "sustain the economic viability of farm operations; and enhance the quality of life for farmers and society as a whole."[21] Industrial farming systems inevitably result in larger farms, meaning fewer farming operations and fewer farm owners and farm managers—fewer quality employment opportunities. Industrial routinization and mechanization also result in fewer, lower-skilled, and lower-paying farm workers. The pollution of air and water with agricultural wastes and loss of employment opportunities diminish the economic and social quality of life in rural communities.[22]

A comprehensive assessment of the negative *economic* external or unpaid costs of US food production, including environmental and public health costs, was funded by the Rockefeller Foundation. The study concluded, "In 2019, American consumers spent an estimated $1.1 trillion on food. . . . That price tag does not include the cost of healthcare for the millions who fall ill with diet-related diseases. Nor does $1.1 trillion include the present and future costs of the food system's contributions to water and air pollution, reduced biodiversity, or greenhouse gas emissions, which cause climate change. Take those costs into account and it becomes clear the true cost of the U.S. food system is at least three times as big—$3.2 trillion per year."[23] The *noneconomic* or purely human costs of preventable illness, premature death, social and political divisiveness, and mental stress are far greater.

## Agroecology: The Science of Sustainable Agriculture

Contrary to the claims of its early critics, sustainable agriculture is a science-based approach to farming. Agroecology is sometimes referred to as the science of sustainable agriculture because it applies the science of ecology to agriculture.[24] Ecology is the study of the relationships of living organisms, including humans, with the other elements of their natural and social environments. There is a common phrase in ecology that relates directly to agroecology: "You can't do just one thing." The relationships in agroecosystems, such as those in the soil and among plants, animals, and people on farms, are incredibly complex. And everything is related, in one way or another, to everything else. Any one thing a farmer may do affects everything else on the farm—some in small ways and others in important ways. When farmers do one thing, they need to be aware of all of the other things that may be affected. The unintended consequences may be large or small and may appear either quickly or at some time in the distant future.

Agroecology also respects the fact that the natural ecosystems upon which sustainable individual farming systems depend are inherently different or unique. Sometimes the differences are insignificant and sometimes they are critical to the performance of the farm as a whole. A set of specific farming methods and practices that are successful for one farmer on one farm may or may not work for another farmer or another farm—even though nature functions by the same principles on every farm. Agroecological farming systems are defined by principles rather than specific farming methods or practices. Agroecology respects the *ecology of place*.

Agroecology also respects the *social ecology of place*. Agroecology views humans as members of the earth's integrally connected ecological community. The farmer is a member of a farm's agroecosystem, and the relationship between a specific farm and its farmer is critical to the farm's success or failure. This makes it difficult, if not impossible, to do traditional agricultural research relevant to agroecological farming systems. What works for one farmer might not work for another, even on the same farm.

Equally important, agroecology recognizes that farms are inherently interconnected with the specific communities and societies within which they function. Farmers who rely on local markets are obviously dependent on people in their communities to buy their products. Less appreciated, the quality of life of farmers and farm families is critically affected by their personal relationships with others in their communities—their customers, neighbors, and people they meet in town through churches, schools, or participation in public service. These relationships may critically affect the farmer's sense of acceptance, belonging, and self-esteem. Personal relationships affect the quality of farm life, which also may affect the economic success or failure of the farm.

All authentically sustainable farming systems fit under the conceptual umbrella of agroecology. Organic, biodynamic, ecological, biological, restorative, regenerative, resilient, holistic, and permanent are different management systems, but they all respect the scientific principles of ecology. As indicated previously, the EAT-Lancet report dismissed agroecology, along with other alternatives to sustainable intensification, as not being "scalable" and thus incapable of providing global food security.[25] However, numerous highly credible global studies have shown that agroecological farming systems are capable of producing enough healthful food for a growing global population without compromising their ecological, social, or economic integrity.[26]

## Sustainable Animal Agriculture

The EAT-Lancet Commission identified animal agriculture as a major source of both environmental degradation and public health risks. Animal agriculture reportedly is "the second largest contributor to human-made greenhouse gas (GHG) emissions after fossil fuels and is a leading cause of deforestation, water and air pollution, and biodiversity loss."[27] The Commission identified red meat as a major source of diet-related health risks as well as environmental degradation. They wrote, "Despite this limitation, in a meta-analysis of prospective studies, consumption of processed red meat (beef, pork, or lamb) was associated with increased risk of death from any cause and cardiovascular disease; unprocessed red meat was also weakly associated with cardiovascular disease mortality. In other meta-analyses, consumption of red meat was associated with increased risk of stroke and type 2 diabetes."[28]

In response, the Commission called for a "substantial [global] dietary shift, including a greater than 50% reduction in global consumption of unhealthy foods, such as red meat and sugar, and a greater than 100% increase in consumption of healthy foods, such as nuts, fruits, vegetables, and legumes." [29] They wrote, "A healthy diet should optimize health, defined broadly by WHO as being a state of complete physical, mental, and social wellbeing, and not just absence of disease."[30] However, the proposed strategies included nothing to improve the physical, mental, or social well-being of consumers left to the mercy of corporately controlled global food systems. The Commission acknowledged that dietary changes would need to be different for different parts of the world. However, it is doubtful whether consumers in many parts of the world could afford to pay the costs or would even willingly accept the strict dietary requirements of the EAT-Lancet diet.[31]

Animal products are an important source of protein in the diets of people in many parts of the world. Animal agriculture also is an essential component of agroecological farming systems in many parts of the world. In healthy natural ecosystems, different species of biological organisms consume the secretions, embryos, or dead carcasses of other once-living species, turning redundancy and wastes into life-giving sustenance. Species diversity, including plants and animals, also adds resilience to ecosystems, increasing their ability to endure shocks and disruptions—such as climate change.

The diversity of living organisms needed to sustain life and sustenance in one geographical and cultural ecosystem may be quite different from the diversity needed in another. Thus, the role of animal agriculture may be quite different, and of greater or lesser importance, in different sustainable agroecosystems—but nonetheless essential. In most healthy ecosystems of the world, animals play a vital role in cycles by which solar energy is sequestered, cycled, and recycled by animals and plants, regenerating the diversity of life essential for efficiency, resilience, and sustainability.

Agroecology was the natural farming system of choice for the global Food Sovereignty Movement. Food Sovereignty is defined as "the right of peoples to healthy and culturally appropriate food produced through ecologically sound and sustainable methods, and their right to define their own food and agriculture systems."[32] Adherence to the principles of agroecology ensures that ecologically sound and sustainable farming methods are used to produce healthy and culturally appropriate foods and protects the rights of people to define their own food and farming systems that respect the natural and social ecology of place.

Diets in food-sovereign communities are not dictated by global markets or government experts. Instead, diets reflect the food preferences of the people and the sustainable capacity of the agroecosystems upon which specific communities depend for their food. The proportions of animal and vegetable products in diets reflect the correspondence of people's food preferences with nature's capacity to produce. The physical, social, and mental health of people in food-sovereign communities reflects the health of the soils, plants, animals, and natural agroecosystem they choose to depend on for their food. Food-sovereign communities are sustainable agrifood system communities.

## Public Health Benefits of Sustainable Agriculture

Nowhere are the differences between pseudo-sustainability and authentic sustainability more glaring or more critical than concerning the impacts of industrial agriculture on public health. The public health threats posed by industrial agriculture are inherent consequences of industrial agricultural systems of agricultural production. The focus of pseudo-sustainability is an attempt to mitigate threats inherent in industrial systems. Sustainable agricultural systems do not create unnecessary risks to public health and thus pose few if any threats to be mitigated.

Environmental pollution is a public health issue because it involves threats to human health as well as the health of natural ecosystems. Water and air pollution are not simply environmental problems that threaten biological diversity or the economic viability of resource-based enterprises, such as fishing, water sports, or tourism. Agricultural pollution threatens not only the health of people who live in farming areas but also the health of people in urban areas who depend on sources of drinking water polluted with agricultural wastes. Most air and water quality threats associated with agriculture are a consequence of the inevitable concentration of potentially toxic chemical and biological pollutants in industrial agriculture operations.

All of the chemicals in the agricultural herbicides, fertilizers, and medications for farm animals are present in the natural environment in quantities that nature can accommodate or assimilate. In fact, many of these elements may be essential for ecosystem health. However, when these chemicals are concentrated into fertilizers, pesticides, and medications, they become potentially toxic to humans. When fertilizers, pesticides, and medications are applied in the large quantities associated with intensive cropping operations and concentrated animal feeding operations, they exceed nature's capacity for utilization, assimilation, or neutralization. Chemical elements that were once harmless become threats to public health.

CAFOs provide a prime example of industrial agriculture's proclivity to transform otherwise benign or potentially valuable productive resources into toxic substances that threaten public health. Livestock manure is a valuable and sometimes essential component of diversified agroecological farming systems that integrate crop and livestock enterprises. Manure applied in the right amounts at the right time is a valuable resource. Healthy agroecosystems also need to have some quantities of agricultural waste to provide food for natural ecosystems. However, in most CAFOs, it is not economically feasible to return manure to the fields where the feed crops were grown or other croplands that are deficient in fertility. The application of manure from CAFOs often exceeds the nutrient needs of crops and nature's ability to absorb or neutralize the excess. Many farmers also apply commercial fertilizers in addition to animal manure because the nutrient content and availability of manure are less precisely measurable. These practices result in potentially toxic levels of pollution that threaten both natural ecosystems and human health.

Potentially toxic levels of ammonia, hydrogen sulfide, methane, and particulate pollutants in the air inside and surrounding CAFOs also is a consequence of the concentration of large numbers of animals in confined spaces. Some of these pollutants are a result of the anaerobic decomposition of manure in pits or large storage structures associated with CAFOs. The health threats associated with dust-borne particulates and pungent odors that create illness due to mental stress are related to levels of concentration of animals in CAFOs. Manure that is dispersed and decomposes under the aerobic conditions of agroecological farming systems does not create toxic compounds that threaten public health.

The same is true for antibiotics and other medications used in animal agriculture. The routine inclusion of medications in the feed rations in CAFOs is a natural consequence of concentrating too many animals in too small spaces. Animals in crowded conditions are at greater risk of biological and viral infections than are animals that have space to move freely and maintain a comfortable distance from others. The routine feeding of antibiotics in stressful living environments provides ideal breeding grounds for organisms to develop antibiotic resistance. In the confined conditions of CAFOs, it is also easy for workers to carry antibiotic bacteria and diseases into the surrounding community. The biosecurity measures common in CAFOs are more about protecting animals than protecting people and are unnecessary on sustainable farms.

Farms that are managed as sustainable agroecosystems simply do not rely on high concentrations of chemical fertilizers and pesticides that make industrial agriculture possible. They rely on diverse crop rotations and integrated crop and livestock systems to maintain soil fertility and manage pests. Agroecological farms do not concentrate large numbers of animals in confined spaces but limit animal numbers to those needed to sustain diverse, integrated whole-farm systems—ecologically, socially, and economically. Sustainable farmers rely on healthy animal diets and comfortable, humane living environments, rather than routine medication, to keep their animals healthy. They do not create environments conducive to antibiotic resistance or community spread of animal diseases. Sustainable agriculture addresses the environmentally related public health threats associated with industrial agriculture by simply not creating them.

The negative economic and societal impacts of industrial agriculture on rural communities also is an inherent consequence of concentrating total agricultural production among fewer, larger farming operations. The continued expansion of industrial agriculture in a community eventually results in the displacement of any remaining independent family farmers and the demise of local businesses they support. With local farmers increasingly under the control of large agrifood corporations, local communities lose control over local natural and human resources and local economies. They lose the ability to protect their communities from economic extraction and exploitation. Sustainable agriculture, on the other hand, creates more, rather than fewer, quality farm and nonfarm employment opportunities in rural areas. Sustainable farmers are good neighbors and community members as well as responsible stewards of the land.

The industrialization of American agriculture has clearly been associated with the loss of rural doctors, the closing of rural hospitals, and declining access to rural physical and mental health care in general. The impacts of loss of health care services have been magnified by stresses associated with unemployment, disruption of social relationships, and loss of cultural identity. The threat to rural health is in an underappreciated dimension of the threat to the quality of rural life caused by industrial agriculture—industrial animal agriculture in particular. On the other hand, healthy plants and animals and healthy farms provide the foundation for healthy rural communities.

## Conclusion and Recommendations

Industrial agricultural systems of production persist only because their social, environmental, and public health threats are either undervalued or ignored in US farm policies and government regulation of agrifood systems.[33] As suggested previously, the defenders of industrial agriculture avoid addressing public health threats by labeling sustainability as an environmental or resource conservation issue. The government agencies that administer environmental and resource conservation programs are not equipped to address the public health concerns associated with industrial agriculture. They do not have a mandate to do so and do not have personnel who are adequately trained to do so.

Some county-level public health departments have been willing to risk corporate lawsuits in their attempts to protect the health of their constituents from industrial animal agriculture.[34] Most local officials, however, lack the confidence or courage to confront the industrial agricultural establishment by attempting to regulate agriculture. Many states have "right-to-farm" laws that explicitly prevent local government officials from any form of regulation of agriculture—including public health regulations. It seems unlikely that the negative public health consequences of agriculture will be addressed by the government until public pressure forces governments to regulate industrial agriculture as any other industry that poses similar threats to public health.

Agricultural workers should be protected at least as well as workers in other industries. People who live near CAFOs and other industrial agricultural operations should be protected at least as well as those who live near manufacturing plants with similar potentially toxic emissions. And the manure produced in CAFOs should go through treatment processes at least similar to the sewage treatment required of municipalities that produce similar quantities of potentially toxic biological wastes. The arguments by defenders of industrial agriculture that such regulations would cause dramatic increases in retail food prices and that only industrial agriculture is capable of meeting global food needs are simply not true.

A 2016 study by an International Panel of Experts on Sustainability-Food (IPES) reviewed and cited more than 350 sources in support of its indictment of industrial agriculture and its call for fundamental change. They concluded, "Today's food and farming systems have succeeded in supplying large volumes of foods to global markets, but are generating negative outcomes on multiple fronts: widespread degradation of land, water, and ecosystems; high GHG emissions; biodiversity losses; persistent hunger and micro-nutrient deficiencies alongside the rapid rise of obesity and diet-related diseases; and livelihood stresses for farmers around the world."[35]

They concluded, "What is required is a fundamentally different model of agriculture based on diversifying farms and farming landscapes, replacing chemical inputs, optimizing biodiversity and stimulating interactions between different species, as part of holistic strategies to build long-term fertility, healthy agroecosystems, and secure livelihoods. Data shows that these systems can compete with industrial agriculture in terms of total outputs, performing particularly strongly under environmental stress, and delivering production increases in the places where additional food is desperately needed. Diversified agroecological systems can also pave the way for diverse diets and improved health."[36]

Olivier De Schutter, leader of the IPES panel of experts, stated, "It is not a lack of evidence holding back the agroecological alternative. The way food systems are currently structured allows value to accrue to a limited number of actors, reinforcing their economic and political power, and thus their ability to influence the governance of food systems. Simply tweaking industrial agriculture will not provide long-term solutions to the multiple problems it generates. We must change the way we set political priorities."[37]

Numerous policy proposals have been developed to turn the principles of agroecology into workable, effective farm and food policies. Among these, *Regenerative Farming and the Green New Deal* was released in January 2020.[38] Among its specific proposals are (1) over time, phase out government-subsidized crop insurance programs for single crops and all commodity-based programs unless accompanied by supply management programs; (2) replace the current crop insurance programs with a whole-farm net revenue insurance program that shares risks of family farms transitioning to regenerative, sustainable farming systems; (3) support existing programs that prepare farmers to transition from monoculture farming practices to soil building, carbon sequestering, and regenerative farming systems; (4) train existing US soil health experts to help farmers develop and implement regenerative whole farm plans; and (5) grow the agricultural research and development budget to improve resilience and regenerative capacity of family farms. There is no shortage of proposals for transformative change in farm policy, only the political will.

The scientific and technical knowledge necessary to transition to an agroecological sustainable agriculture is further advanced today than was the scientific and technical knowledge of industrial agriculture during the 1960s and 1970s. It is time for another transformation in agricultural policies from supporting industrial agricultural operations to supporting sustainable family farms. There is no more important

responsibility of national, state, or local governments than protecting public health—including protecting the public from health threats
posed by industrial animal agriculture.

**NOTES**

1. International Panel of Experts on Sustainability-Food (IPES), From Uniformity to Diversity, "A paradigm shift from industrial agriculture to diversified
agroecological systems," June 2016, https://ipes-food.org/_img/upload/files
/UniformityToDiversity_FULL.pdf.

2. Sustainable Agriculture Research and Education, "History of SARE," https://
www.sare.org/about/history-of-sare.

3. Sustainable Agriculture Research and Education, "History of SARE."

4. Carolyn Dimitri and Catherine Greene, "Recent Growth Patterns in the U.S.
Organic Foods Market," *Economic Research Service*, USDA AIB-777, 1, https://www.ers
.usda.gov/webdocs/publications/42455/13377_aib777c_1_.pdf?v=0.

5. International Institute for Sustainable Development, "Sustainable Development," https://www.iisd.org/mission-and-goals/sustainable-development.

6. Will Kenton, "Greenwashing," *Investopedia*, March 22, 2022, https://www
.investopedia.com/terms/g/greenwashing.asp.

7. EAT Lancet Commission, "Food in the Anthropocene: The EAT-Lancet
Commission on Healthy Diets from Sustainable Food Systems, Executive Summary,"
February 2019, https://www.researchgate.net/publication/330443133_Food_in_the
_Anthropocene_the_EAT-Lancet_Commission_on_healthy_diets_from_sustainable
_food_systems.

8. EAT-Lancet, "Food in Anthropocene," 5.

9. EAT-Lancet, "Food in Anthropocene," 3.

10. EAT-Lancet, "Food in Anthropocene," 6.

11. Pew Commission on Industrial Farm Animal Production, "Putting Meat on
the Table," A Project of the Pew Charitable Trusts and Johns Hopkins Bloomberg
School of Public Health, 2008, 33–34, https://www.pewtrusts.org/-/media/legacy
/uploadedfiles/phg/content_level_pages/reports/pcifapfinalpdf.pdf.

12. EAT-Lancet, "Food in Anthropocene," 36.

13. Pew Commission, "Putting Meat on the Table," 55.

14. EAT-Lancet, "Food in Anthropocene," 1.

15. R. Ramsing, K. Chang, Z. Hendrickson, Z. Xu, M. Friel, and E. Calves, "The
Role of Community-Based Efforts in Promoting Sustainable Diets," *Journal of
Agriculture, Food Systems, and Community Development* 10, no. 2 (2021): 373–397.

16. Merriam Webster, "Sustainability," https://www.merriam-webster.com
/dictionary/sustainable.

17. J. I. Rodale, "The Organiculturist's Creed," in *The Organic Front* (Emmaus,
PA: Rodale Press, 1948), https://www.amazon.com/organic-front-J-I-Rodale/dp
/B0007DMGV6.

18. Sir Albert Howard, *An Agricultural Testament* (Oxford: Oxford University Press, 1940), also in "Small Farms Library," http://journeytoforever.org/farm_library /howardAT/ATtoc.html.

19. Sustainable Agriculture Research and Education, History of SARE.

20. Sustainable Agriculture Research and Education, History of SARE.

21. Sustainable Agriculture Research and Education, History of SARE.

22. Pew Commission, "Industrial Farm Animal Production," 51.

23. The Rockefeller Fund, "True Cost of Food," July 2021, https://www .rockefellerfoundation.org/wp-content/uploads/2021/07/True-Cost-of-Food-Full -Report-Final.pdf .

24. Miguel Altieri, "Agroecology: Principles and Strategies for Designing Sustainable Farming Systems," University of California, http://www.agroeco.org/doc /new_docs/Agroeco_principles.pdf.

25. EAT-Lancet, "Food in Anthropocene," 15.

26. IPES, "Uniformity to Diversity."

27. Climate Nexus, "Animal Agriculture's Impact on Climate Change," https:// climatenexus.org/climate-issues/food/animal-agricultures-impact-on-climate -change/.

28. EAT Lancet, "Food in Anthropocene," 9.

29. EAT Lancet, "Food in Anthropocene," 7.

30. EAT Lancet, "Food in Anthropocene," 7.

31. Sam Bloch, "World Health Organization Drops its High-Profile Sponsorship of the EAT-Lancet Diet," *The Counter*, April 12, 2019, https://thecounter.org/world -health-organization-drops-its-high-profile-endorsement-of-the-eat-lancet-diet/.

32. Nyelini Forum on Food Sovereignty, "Declaration of Nyeleni," February 27, 2007, https://nyeleni.org/IMG/pdf/DeclNyeleni-en.pdf.

33. John Ikerd, "Farm and Food Policies for a Sustainable Future," *Business Entrepreneurship & Tax Law Review* 6 (2022), https://scholarship.law.missouri.edu /betr/vol6/iss1/6.

34. William C. Ellis, "Pig in a Poke: Missouri Draws Tenuous Line between Public Health and Zoning Ordinances," Borron v. Farrenkopf, *Missouri Environmental Law & Policy Review* 8 (2001): 29, https://scholarship.law.missouri.edu/jesl/vol8/iss1/4.

35. IPES, "Uniformity to Diversity," 3.

36. IPES, Uniformity to Diversity," 3.

37. Olivier De Schutter, quoted in, Andrea Germanos, "'Overwhelming' Evidence Shows Path Is Clear: It's Time to Ditch Industrial Agriculture for Good," *Common Dreams*, June 2, 2016, http://www.commondreams.org/news/2016/06/02 /overwhelming-evidence-shows-path-clear-its-time-ditch-industrial-agriculture-good ?utm_campaign=shareaholic&utm_medium=facebook&utm_source=socialnetwork.

38. Mackenzie Feldman, John Ikerd, Seth Watkins, Charlie Mitchell, Johnny Bowman, Cella Rose Ostrander, "Regenerative Agriculture and the Green New Deal," Data for Progress, January 17, 2020, https://www.dataforprogress.org/memos /regenerative-agriculture-and-the-green-new-deal.

# CHAPTER 12

# Still a Jungle Out There

Advocacy to Mitigate Environmental and
Public Health Impacts of Industrial Meat

Tom Philpott

The US meat industry began taking on its modern industrialized form
in the late nineteenth century, with the rise of refrigerated rail cars that
could haul freshly slaughtered beef and pork over long distances. Cheap
access to lucrative East Coast markets inspired meat traders to expand
slaughterhouses at the edge of budding heartland metropolises like
Chicago and Cincinnati. The meatpacking industry quickly emerged as
one of the Gilded Age's most lucrative ventures. By 1900, a vast Armour
meatpacking plant in Chicago's stockyards counted as the world's largest factory of any kind. But the mass killing and disassembling of cattle
and hogs did more than mint gaudy fortunes for a few and deliver plentiful meat to the burgeoning urban middle classes. It also created a
new kind of occupation: the labor required to break down cattle and
hog carcasses as they glided past, dangling from an overhead trolley.
(Henry Ford observed Chicago's meatpacking workers in action, each
performing a single task on "the chain," and later applied the system
to streamline automobile assembly.[1]) Moreover, the resulting concentration of blood and guts—as well as manure buildup in the stockyards—
greatly expanded and intensified "barnyard" odors that had been distributed widely across rural and even urban areas in milder form. And it

opened new opportunities for bacterial pathogens to reach consumers. From the start, the handful of firms that arose to dominate the meat industry proved more effective at churning out profits for their owners than they did at providing fair conditions for its workforce, keeping its meat safe to eat, or keeping its waste out of neighbors' water and air. And advocacy efforts to limit these harms began almost immediately.

Scandals like the infamous "embalmed beef" affair, involving potentially tainted meat supplied to the US military during its conquests in the Caribbean in 1898, resonated with public suspicion about the hygienic state of the carnivorous bounty that was suddenly available. In 1904, meanwhile, after years of labor organizing, the Amalgamated Meat Cutters Union, representing the 50,000-strong largely immigrant workforce in Chicago's stockyards and slaughterhouses, called a strike to demand a living wage. The dominant meatpacking firms used scab labor to crush the uprising, but their victory proved pyrrhic.

The ill-fated strike drew the attention of an obscure New York City–based socialist writer, who soon alighted upon Chicago to document conditions on the kill floor and in the lives of impoverished workers. Upton Sinclair's hoped-for resulting novel, *The Jungle* (1906),[2] would galvanize public solidarity with meatpacking workers. Instead, his vivid descriptions of what (literally) went into the nation's sausage caused an uproar around a different issue.

> There was never the least attention paid to what was cut up for sausage; there would come all the way back from Europe old sausage that had been rejected, and that was moldy and white—it would be dosed with borax and glycerine, and dumped into the hoppers, and made over again for home consumption. There would be meat that had tumbled out on the floor, in the dirt and sawdust, where the workers had tramped and spit uncounted billions of consumption germs. There would be meat stored in great piles in rooms; and the water from leaky roofs would drip over it, and thousands of rats would race about on it. It was too dark in these storage places to see well, but a man could run his hand over these piles of meat and sweep off handfuls of the dried dung of rats. These rats were

nuisances, and the packers would put poisoned bread out for them; they would die, and then rats, bread, and meat would go into the hoppers together. This is no fairy story and no joke; the meat would be shoveled into carts, and the man who did the shoveling would not trouble to lift out a rat even when he saw one—there were things that went into the sausage in comparison with which a poisoned rat was a tidbit. There was no place for the men to wash their hands before they ate their dinner, and so they made a practice of washing them in the water that was to be ladled into the sausage.[3]

An instant sensation, *The Jungle* inspired fierce denials from the meat industry. "Scrupulous cleanliness is ordered and enforced," insisted meat baron J. Ogden Armour in response to Sinclair's depiction. "These dispensers of 'literature' . . . [do] real harm . . . practically to the entire public. . . . It is an injustice to every man, woman, or child who eats meat, utterly without justification, it plants in their minds a suspicion of the wholesomeness of their daily food."[4] Even so, *The Jungle* drew the attention of President Theodore Roosevelt, who had already cast a wary eye at the growing power of the Big Five packers, known collectively as the "beef trust." As a "Rough Rider" during the 1898 Spanish–American War, Roosevelt himself had publicly complained that the canned meat supplied to troops by Armour and Swift was "disagreeable-looking and nasty" and declared it overall a "bad ration."[5] (He also blamed the meat trust and the railroads for running his ranch in Dakota Territory out of business in the late 1870s.[6])

Suspicious of Sinclair's socialist leanings, Roosevelt dispatched US Department of Agriculture (USDA) officials to investigate whether things were quite so dire behind the closed doors of Chicago's slaughterhouses. The USDA's report essentially backed Armour's nothing-to-see-here view, concluding that *The Jungle* had wildly exaggerated the industry's hygiene problems. Skeptical because he saw the USDA as too chummy with the meatpackers to deliver a frank assessment, the president then sent two trusted advisers to Chicago to investigate further. Their resulting Neill–Reynolds Report confirmed the veracity of Sinclair's gross-out descriptions. "In a word, we saw meat shoveled from filthy wooden floors, piled on tables rarely washed, pushed from room to room in rotten box carts, in all of which processes it was in the way of gathering dirt, splinters, floor filth, and the expectoration of tuberculous and other diseases," the inspectors found. They also echoed Sinclair's findings on labor conditions, decrying the "feverish pace they [workers] are forced to maintain," which must "inevitably affect their health."[7]

After delivering the startling Neill–Reynolds findings to Congress, Roosevelt found an opening to ram home two landmark bills that had been languishing for years, stymied by Meat Trust lobbying. Just four months after *The Jungle*'s publication, the president signed the Pure Food and Drug Act of 1906, which prohibited the "manufacture, sale, or transportation of adulterated or misbranded or poisonous or deleterious foods, drugs or medicines, and liquors," and the Federal Meat Inspection Act, which boosted requirements for sanitary conditions in packing houses and mandated federal inspection of meat destined to cross state lines. *The Jungle* is widely credited with breaking the impasse. On its twenty-first century website, the US Food and Drug Administration hails the book for delivering the "final precipitating force behind both a meat inspection law and a comprehensive food and drug law."[8]

Sinclair's novel stands as the first—and perhaps still the most successful—major act of advocacy to rein in the harms of industrial meat production. The author himself complained that the reforms his book helped trigger did not go deeper—particularly with regard to workers. "I had objected to Roosevelt that he was giving all his attention to the subject of meat-inspection, and none to the subject of labor-inspection. His answer was that he had power to remedy the former evils, but no power to remedy the latter," he wrote in 1919. "*The Jungle* caused the whitewashing of some packing-house walls . . . but it left the wage-slaves in those huge brick packing-boxes exactly where they were before."[9]

The book's publication and reception reveal a set of forces that remains relevant today: after having its harms exposed, the industry fights hard to deny those harms and maintain its practices, and the government requires forceful prodding before it will act against the industry's interests (if it acts at all). In the nearly 120 years since *The Jungle*, the conventional meat industry has grown ever larger, more consolidated, and more influential in Washington, D.C.—and its conduct continues to menace surrounding communities, overall public health, the environment, and workers, as this book's previous chapters show. And organized, collective efforts to rein in and mitigate these harms— my definition of advocacy—has evolved too, as I'll show in this chapter.

What follows is a brief overview of current strategies and avenues for advancing toward less harmful ways of raising animals and managing land.

### Precursor to Advocacy: Sunlight

Just as sausage requires a raw material—animal flesh—advocacy needs source material, too: exposure, revelation, a peek behind slaughterhouse doors, a whiff of the manure lagoon outside a factory-scale animal facility, a bacterial analysis of the water trickling from one into a stream. Many early twentieth-century urban consumers who lived far from the heartland's great stockyards had an inkling that something was off about the meat products that had suddenly become so cheap and available. But it was not until Upton Sinclair described what it was like to work at a meatpacking plant that they *knew* what was going on— and could pressure politicians to change it. What advocacy for change requires, then, is a view from the front lines: from people directly exposed to CAFO-tainted air or drinking water, say, or from a scientist analyzing said air or water.

### Investigative Reporting

The kind of from-the-ground reportage pioneered by Sinclair and his fellow "muckrakers" remains relevant. In the twenty-first century, US journalists have produced a succession of nonfiction books in the *Jungle* tradition. In his 2001 *Fast Food Nation*, Eric Schlosser documented how meatpacking firms cut corners on food safety while endangering workers' lives and limbs. Michael Pollan's *Omnivore's Dilemma* (2006) delivered the view from a vast Kansas feedlot, where corn-heavy rations damage cows' livers and weaponize the *Escherichia coli* in their guts into a strain particularly harmful to people. (These corn-heavy diets often lead feedlot operators to add antibiotics to feed to counter the ill effects on cow health, meaning that in addition to being more virulent, their *E. coli* often also resists antibiotics.) Ted Genoways' *The Chain* (2014)[10] spotlighted the severe hardships the meatpacking industry imposes on its largely immigrant workforce by focusing on gruesome events at a pork factory in Minnesota. Chris Leonard's *The Meat Racket* (2014)[11] took readers to rural Arkansas to expose the industry's systemic exploitation of debt-strapped poultry farmers. Barry Estabrook's *Pig Tales* (2015)[12] brought attention to the tortured lives of hogs under factory regimentation. Maryn McKenna's *Big Chicken* (2017)[13] teased out how the meat industry came to rely on routine antibiotic use to make animals grow faster and boost profits—and how that practice helps drive a deadly crisis in antibiotic resistance in human medicine. In my own *Perilous Bounty* (2020),[14] I visited farm fields in Iowa to show how an agriculture system geared to producing cheap feed for industrial meat production triggers devastating soil erosion and water pollution. For his 2022 book *Wastelands: The True Story of Farm Country on Trial*,[15] novelist and former trial attorney Corban Addison used in-depth reporting and narrative skill to recount the efforts of Black residents of rural North Carolina to fight for access to clean air and water amid intensive hog production.

In addition, print and online media outlets have produced a steady stream of investigative content on industrial food animal production (IFAP) over the past 20 years. In virtually every region of the United States with large concentrations of intensive livestock production, journalists in local and national media have documented the burdens placed on communities.

A *Charlotte Observer* and Raleigh *News & Observer* joint project called Big Poultry (2022–2023), on North Carolina's fast-growing concentration of chicken concentrated animal feeding operations (CAFOs), exemplifies excellent local reporting on the industry. The newspaper devoted a team of five reporters, and more than a dozen articles, to exposing the ecological and social costs of raising 1 billion chickens, clustered in a few largely low-income areas of the state, with minimal regulatory oversight.[16] As the business model for newspapers erodes, such deep-dive local reporting becomes more and more rare.

Meanwhile, the remaining national newspapers have run superb investigative work on the industry over the years. Examples include Charles Duhigg's 2009 *New York Times* story "Health Ills Abound as Farm Runoff Fouls Wells," which showed piecemeal state and local regulation allows how manure runoff from industrial dairy operations routinely seeps into groundwater in rural Wisconsin.[17] For the *Washington Post*, investigative reporter Kimberly Kindy has done invaluable work over the years documenting how lax workplace safety oversight has made meatpacking workers and even federal inspectors vulnerable to injury, as in her 2013 piece "At chicken plants, chemicals blamed for health ailments are poised to proliferate."[18] But neither the *Post* nor the *Times* devotes a full-time reporter to the beat, and so coverage is sporadic.

Nonprofit enterprises like the Food and Environment Reporting Network (FERN)[19] and Investigate Midwest (previously The Midwest Center for Investigative Reporting)[20] remain steady sources of high-quality IFAP coverage, as do regional nonprofit newsrooms like Southerly, which "serves communities in the South who face environmental injustice and are most at-risk of the effects of climate change" and often focuses on CAFO pollution and slaughterhouse working conditions.[21] These operations often partner with large national media outlets like the *New York Times Magazine* and *The Atlantic*, increasing their reach.

Despite the patchy state of media coverage of IFAP, it is worth noting that the meat industry's failure to protect workers during the COVID-19 pandemic inspired an extraordinary outpouring of exposés, in both national and local publications, revealing how meatpacking executives leveraged influence over state and federal regulators to keep workers toiling at close quarters even as the virus spread within plants and into surrounding communities.[22] Perhaps more important of all, Leah Douglas, then of FERN (now a correspondent for Reuters), helped keep attention on the issue by maintaining a running count of workers known to have tested positive for COVID-19 and died of it—a tally she kept through September 2, 2021.[23] The work of Douglas and other reporters in turn inspired the US House Select Subcommittee on the Coronavirus Crisis to investigate the matter. The resulting report, released in October 2021, found that that in plants run by the five biggest US meatpacking firms—JBS, Tyson, Smithfield, Cargill, and National Beef Packing Company—at least 59,000 workers tested positive for the virus during the first year of the pandemic, at least 269 died, and the carnage "was likely much worse than these figures suggest" because of "incomplete data."[24] It added, "Instead of addressing the clear indications that workers were contracting the coronavirus at alarming rates due to conditions in meatpacking facilities, meatpacking companies prioritized profits and production over worker safety, continuing to employ practices that led to crowded facilities in which the virus spread easily."

### Nongovernmental Organizations

In other instances, researchers from nongovernmental organizations (NGOs) provide the raw material for advocacy. Partially inspired by Schlosser's *Fast Food Nation*, Human Rights Watch—which normally scrutinizes government and corporate abuses in developing nations—turned its attention to the US meatpacking industry, interviewing dozens of workers in Nebraska, North Carolina, and Arkansas, as well as industry executives and government overseers. Its resulting 2004 report, "Blood, Sweat, and Fear," found "systematic human rights violations embedded in meat and poultry industry employment."[25] Fifteen years later, months before the COVID-19 pandemic's onset, the global human rights advocacy group came out with a second damning report on US meatpacking, this one called "When We're Dead and Buried, Our Bones Will Keep Hurting: Workers' Rights under Threat in US Meat and Poultry Plants" (2019). It found little had changed in the decade and a half since its previous report. Again, the researchers documented "alarmingly high rates of serious injury and chronic illness among workers at chicken, hog, and cattle slaughtering and processing plants, as well as business practices that endanger workers and obscure the reality of workplace hazards."[26]

Meanwhile, a broad network of NGOs focus consistently on the injustices and depredations of IFAP. Examples include the Institute for Agriculture and Trade Policy, Environmental Integrity Project, Center for Food Safety, Friends of the Earth, Food and Water Watch, Government Accountability Project, Green Latinos, Sierra Club, and Water Keeper Alliance.

## Academic Research

Academic research has emerged as a key source of knowledge on the impacts of industrial farm animal production—one that can be amplified by journalists and NGOs. In 2002, Dr. Marion Nestle, a nutrition and public health researcher at New York University, published the groundbreaking book *Food Politics* (2007),[27] which demonstrated how the food industry, including its meat sector, invests a portion of its profit in lobbying and campaign finance to resist oversight and limit regulation. The Pew Commission on Industrial Farm Animal Production represents another major example. A two-year effort funded by a grant from The Pew Charitable Trusts to the Johns Hopkins Bloomberg School of Public Health, the commission brought together university researchers, farmers, and rural residents with the charge of developing consensus recommendations for addressing the public health, environmental, rural community, and animal welfare problems created by IFAP. The project resulted in the 2008 report, "Putting Meat on The Table: Industrial Farm Animal Production in America," called for a ban on routine farm antibiotic use and for confinement operations to be "regulated as rigorously as other industrial operations, and that a new system of laws and regulations for dealing with farm waste replace the inflexible, patchwork, and broken systems that exist today," among other fundamental reforms.[28] The commission also generated nine technical reports by academic researchers on various aspects of IFAP, including the widely cited paper "Industrial Farm Animal Production, Antimicrobial Resistance and Human Health."[29] As a journalist covering the harms of industrial agriculture when the commission published its work, I found that the reports provided clear, citable evidence of industrial livestock farming's harms, pushing back against a flood of industry spin.

A third example of academic research connecting to the larger world is the work of Steve Wing (1952–2016), an epidemiologist at the University of North Carolina at Chapel Hill who worked with communities to document the harms of living near massive hog operations, which are heavily concentrated in low-income, largely African American counties of eastern North Carolina. Wing helped found and publish research from the Community Health Effects of Industrial Livestock Operations study, which gauged acute symptoms being experienced by people who lived near CAFOs while instruments on a trailer nearby monitored livestock-related air pollution. The results found that increases in livestock-generated air pollution correlated with jumps in respiratory irritation and blood pressure, as well as a loss in overall quality of life.[30] Wing championed a community-centered approach to research and often credited community members as coauthors on published papers. Wing died of cancer in 2016, but his legacy lives on. The Community Health Effects of Industrial Livestock Operations projects research "loomed large" as evidence in successful nuisance lawsuits filed by community members against the hog industry, NC Health News reported in 2021.[31] And his former graduate students Sacoby Wilson and Christopher Heaney, now professors at the University of Maryland and Johns Hopkins, respectively, continue to conduct and publish research in collaboration with communities in close proximity to concentrated livestock farming.

## Worker and Community Organizations

From the meatpacking industry's origins in the late nineteenth century, labor unionism has played a crucial role in generating pressure for fair pay and safe working conditions on the slaughterhouse floor. After the Amalgamated Meat Cutters Union's strike collapsed in 1904, the union lost its standing in the Midwest's vast packing houses. As a result, poverty-level wages prevailed. But when the United States entered World War I in 1917, demand for meat ramped up. To attract and retain workers in a fast-growing industry deemed crucial to the war effort, the US government intervened by negotiating an agreement with the big meatpackers that allowed workers to freely join unions. The pact also established a process for unsettled labor disputes to be adjudicated by a government administrator. As a result, union membership surged. By 1950, 90% of the industry's 165,400 workers belonged to a union, a 1952 US Department of Labor study found.[32] The benefits they won in bargaining included "three weeks' vacation, generally after 1.5 years service, as well as 8 paid holidays, uncommon in most industries," the report concluded. Workers also enjoyed paid sick leave and severance pay in the case of plant closures. Union membership paid dividends. Average hourly wages roughly equaled those of auto workers—meaning that by the middle of the twentieth century, US meatpacking workers had attained middle-class lifestyles, fully participating in the post–World War II economic boom.[33]

By the 1980s, two forces intersected to undermine those gains. One was the crushing of the 1985–1986 strike at Hormel's vast pork-packing plant in Austin, Minnesota, which the company won by employing scab labor. The defeat reverberated throughout the industry, triggering an erosion of union membership and giving management the upper hand in future negotiations. The second was the dramatic expansion of chicken production, which tended to be located in the antiunion states of the Deep South and Mississippi Delta regions. With labor unionism on the decline, the meatpacking industry managed to speed up its kill lines—making work more hazardous, boosting profitability—while exerting downward pressure on wages.[34] As of 2022, meatpacking workers earned 35% less per hour on average compared to durable-goods manufacturing workers.[35]

But labor organizing has not ended. The coronavirus pandemic kindled a revival in the public profile of the United Food and Commercial Workers, which still represents 60% of US pork workers and 70% of beef workers. In the right-to-work states of the South, the nonunion "worker center" movement has arisen to fill some of the organizing void. Defined by the think-tank Economic Policy Institute as "community-based and community-led organizations that engage in a combination of service, advocacy, and organizing to provide support to low-wage workers,"[36] many worker centers in the meatpacking space take a behind-the-scenes approach, pressuring government agencies like the Occupational Safety and Health Administration (OSHA) and the Department of Agriculture to ramp up slaughterhouse worker safety regulation through letter-writing campaigns and public comments in the rulemaking process. Under cofounder Magaly Licolli and inspired by the Florida tomato-picker advocacy group the Coalition of Immokloee Workers,[37] Arkansas-based Venceremos takes a more public-facing approach. The group held street demonstrations outside of Tyson plants during the COVID-19 pandemic to demand more protections from the virus. And Licolli regularly talks to journalists and links them to poultry workers, helping amplify their voices to the public. Aided by Licolli, the journalist Alice Driver spent 2 years in Arkansas poultry country during the pandemic, documenting the lives of workers under enormous strain. Driver's reportage resulted in two blockbuster articles in the prestigious the *New York Review of Books* and a book, *The Life and Death of the American Worker*, forthcoming in 2024.[38]

Such community organizations play a dual role in advocacy to rein in the harms of industrial farm agriculture. They directly organize community members and workers to demand better living and working conditions. And they also amplify their voices, by linking people affected by IFAP to journalists and academic researchers. In the hog-intensive counties of eastern North Carolina, the North Carolina Environmental Justice Network (NCEJN) describes itself as a "grassroots, people of color-led coalition of community organizations and their supporters who work with low-income communities and people of color on issues of climate, environmental, racial, and social injustice." The group holds regular meetings to hear residents' concerns and educate them about emerging research around IFAP pollution as well as legislative developments in Raleigh and Washington, D.C., and occasionally mobilizes them to attend political protests in those political capitals. Working in coalition with environmental groups like Waterkeepers Alliance and NC Riverkeepers, NCEJN also helps journalists meet and develop trust with community members, facilitating the reporting and publication of exposés from North Carolina hog country that center the people most affected by IFAP. One notable recent example of NCEJN's function as a resource for journalists is the work of Jamie Berger. In 2022, after years of working on the ground in North Carolina hog country with community residents she met through NCEJN, Berger authored an excellent piece in the widely read policy site *Vox* called "How Black North Carolinians Pay the Price for the World's Cheap Bacon"[39] and wrote and produced a powerful documentary with director Shawn Bannon called *The Smell of Money*, which chronicles the legal battle mounted by several NCEJN members to claim their right to live without regularly being bombarded by airborne hog manure.

NCEJN and Venceremos are just two of many NGOs working at the state and national levels to expose and address the environmental, social, and public health impacts of IFAP. Other major ones include Food & Water Watch, Environmental Working Group, the Public Justice Foundation, the Institute for Agriculture and Trade Policy, Environmental Integrity Project, Center for Food Safety, Friends of the Earth, the Government Accountability Project, GreenLatinos, the Sierra Club, and the Water Keepers Alliance.

### From Exposure to Action: Avenues for Advocacy

Books, documentaries, and investigative articles do not generate change all on their own (*The Jungle* perhaps counting as the closest thing to an exception). Exposure of injustice and environmental harm must do more than trouble the conscious. Changing the status quo requires action—and organization. What follows is a brief rundown of various forms advocacy takes in the effort to mitigate the harms of industrial farm animal production.

## Regulation

Advocacy around regulation of IFAP can take two forms: (1) urging government agencies to strengthen and enforce existing rules and (2) urging them to adopt new ones.

Farm Action, led by veteran antimonopoly advocates Joe Maxwell and Angela Huffman, has made a priority of pushing the US Department of Agriculture to enforce the Packers and Stockyards (P&S) Act of 1921, enacted by Congress after a blistering 1919 report from the newly hatched Federal Trade Commission (FTC) report finding severe market concentration, which gave rise to "collusive manipulation by the big packers" to drive the price of meat up or down to suit their interests. The FTC report also found that the packers used their market heft to concentrate livestock production in a few big meatpacking centers, squeezing out would-be producers in other areas.[40] The P&S Act charged the USDA with protecting livestock and poultry producers from the monopoly power of packers. It resulted in material changes to the market structure. In 1918, the country's five largest beef meatpacking companies controlled 55% of the meat market. By 1976, the market share of the four largest companies had been reduced to 25%, a 2022 Farm Action report found.[41] But in the 1980s, a deregulatory fervor took hold in Washington, which included a renewed appetite to let corporations merge as they pleased. As a result, consolidation returned with a vengeance, as has the geographical concentration of slaughter infrastructure the FTC denounced a century ago. In 2021, against intense industry lobbying and after years of pressure from Farm Action and other groups, the USDA released a proposal that would update and reinvigorate the P&S Act. As of February 2023, the

USDA had yet to finalize the new rules, and Farm Action was vowing to "keep USDA officials' feet to the fire using every tool at our disposal."[42]

As for new regulations, a classic example is the effort to push the federal Food and Drug Administration (FDA) to limit use of antibiotics in livestock production. Concern that routinely feeding farm animals low doses of the same antibiotics crucial to human medicine would contribute to the rise of antibiotic-resistant pathogens dates to the 1950s, when the practice started. The FDA chose not to regulate the novel practice. By 1977, a significant body of research had accrued pointing to trouble, and the FDA proposed a rule that would have effectively banned tetracycline and penicillin from animal feed and required veterinarian prescriptions for all other antibiotics used on the farm. Before they could be implemented, US Rep. Jamie Whitten (D-Miss.), who chaired the House Appropriations Subcommittee on Agriculture and Rural Development, threatened to slash the FDA's funding if it moved ahead with the regulations.[43] Whitten's intervention worked, and for the next three-plus decades, the FDA continued allowing antibiotics to be used on farms without restriction. In the intervening years, on-farm antibiotic consumption surged, an increasingly deadly resistance crisis in human medicine emerged, and scientific evidence linking the two accrued apace. Finally, under pressure from public health groups and reports like the Pew Commission's 2008 technical paper on the topic, the FDA rolled out rules. But the agency took a voluntary approach to curtailing antibiotic use. Meat producers were given until the end of 2016 to wean themselves from routine use of antibiotics used in human medicine. At that point, the agency warned, it would consider banning certain antibiotics if its light-handed approach did not "yield satisfactory results." However, the plan also handed industry a gaping loophole: while it suggested livestock producers should no longer use medically important antibiotics as growth promoters, it left companies free to use them to "prevent" disease. Total US on-farm antibiotic use dropped 40% between 2015 and 2017, but most of the drop was concentrated in the poultry industry. Overall on-farm US use began creeping back up in 2018, and as of 2023, the pork and beef industries have continued using the crucial drugs at pre-2011 levels.[44]

## The Courts

The courts, through tort law, are another avenue for advocacy. The most relevant recent example emerges from the hog-dense counties of eastern North Carolina mentioned earlier in this chapter. In 2014, around 500 residents, many of involved with the North Carolina Environmental Justice network, launched 26 nuisance lawsuits against pork producer Murphy-Brown, a subsidiary of Smithfield Foods, the world's largest pork company. Guided by attorney Mona Lisa Wallace and her firm, the suits—relying on testimony from plaintiffs as well as academic research—claimed the industry's air and water pollution undermined plaintiffs' health and the value of their homes. Five of the lawsuits went to trial, and jurors unanimously sided with the residents in each one, initially awarding them a total of $549,902,400, later slashed to $97,880,000 due to a state cap on punitive damages—a reduction mandated by industry-friendly North Carolina state legislators. After Smithfield appealed, a federal appeals court sided with the plaintiffs, forcing the company into a settlement on all remaining cases for an undisclosed amount.[45] Residents say that Smithfield, which reported an annual profit of $1.043 billion in 2021, has not changed its practices in the wake of its legal setbacks. "That makes me feel good that we won," plaintiff René Miller told journalist/filmmaker Berger in 2022. "But because we won, that don't stop them from spraying [hog manure] on my house. So, it's still going on. I don't go out my front door, and I stay in the house, keep the window closed. I still smell it."[46]

Another recent example involves the large dairy operations in Washington's Yakima Valley. In 2013, a local NGO, the Community Association for Restoration of the Environment, along with the D.C.-based Center for Food Safety, sued large milking operations, charging that the storage and spreading of excessive amounts of manure constituted "solid waste" and should be regulated by the US Environmental Protection

Agency (EPA) under the Resource Conservation and Recovery Act. In a landmark 2015 decision, the US District Court of Eastern Washington ruled in favor of the plaintiffs. As a result, the EPA required the affected dairies to "monitor groundwater, test soil to prevent manure spreading on land with elevated levels of nutrients, and line their waste lagoons to prevent leaks," the water-issues newsite *Circle of Blue* reported in 2022. "Among other measures to prevent water contamination, farms are prohibited from spreading manure on frozen ground."[47] Affected communities in other regions could potentially find relief by suing for relief under the Resource Conservation and Recovery Act. "This could be replicated anywhere," Amy van Sauna, senior attorney for the Center for Food Safety, told *Circle of Blue*.[48] "You need the data to show the polluter, in this case the dairy, is contributing to the problem. That's groundwater testing. In the Yakima Valley the problem had been going on so long. With community advocacy, the EPA finally came in and did a big study and determined that, in fact, it was the dairies that caused groundwater pollution."

## Legislation

The meat industry maintains one of Washington's most powerful lobbying forces, devoting a portion of its annual profits to invest in lobbying and campaign donations. A 2021 report from the nonprofit advocacy group Feed the Truth, using data from the money-in-politics watchdog Maplight, found that as of 2020, 5 meat industry trade groups counted among the nation's 20 largest: the National Pork Producers Council, the American Meat Institute, the National Cattleman's Beef Association, the Livestock Marketing Association, and the US Poultry & Egg Association. Together, they spent more than $26 million on lobbying and $8.5 million on campaign donations between 2007 and 2020. In 2019, 12 of the 19 lobbyists representing the National Pork Producers Council previously worked for the federal government or Congress.[49] Anne McMillan, who lobbies for the National Pork Producers' Council (NPPC), a swine industry lobbying organization on behalf of employer,[50] the D.C. powerhouse political-influence outfit Invariant, provides a telling example. In 2009–2010, she worked as a senior policy adviser to Nancy Pelosi (D-Ca.). From 2010 to 2014, she worked as deputy chief of staff to Tom Vilsack—then the USDA chief for Barack Obama, now serving the same role for President Joe Biden.

Partially as a result of its lobbying might and bipartisan appeal in Washington, the meat industry tends to be relatively lightly regulated. But that has not stopped some politicians from trying to push through legislation to rein in its abuses. Sen. Cory Booker (D.-N.J.) has in recent years filed several bills, with cosponsors in both chambers of Congress, that would do just that.

In 2019, Booker rolled out the Farm System Reform Act, which proposed an immediate moratorium on new large-scale CAFOs, as well as a halt to the expansion of existing CAFOs over a certain size. And it allotted $100 billion over 10 years to a voluntary buyout program for CAFO owners who want to exit the business. The fund would also offer transition assistance to operators who want to take up "agriculture activities such as raising pasture-based livestock, growing specialty crops, or organic commodity production."

In 2021, after reintroducing the Farm System Reform Act, Booker introduced the Protecting America's Meatpacking Workers Act, which would direct the OSHA to come up with an industrywide protocol for protecting workers from repetitive stress injuries after evaluating the hazards of each job on the line, with worker participation in the process. And it would establish remedies for hazards, including "rest breaks, equipment and workstation redesign, work pace reductions, or job rotation to less forceful or repetitive jobs." (Back in 2001, management-side labor lawyer Eugene Scalia, whose father then served on the Supreme Court, led a lobbying push that crushed a previous OSHA effort to roll out just such a suite of rules, known as an "ergonomic standard.")[51]

Neither has gained traction in Congress, but Booker has not stopped pushing. In 2023, he reintroduced both bills,[52] cosponsored by high-profile Sens. Bernie Sanders (I.-Vt) and Elizabeth Warren (D.-Mass.). US Rep. Ro Khanna D. (Ca) rolled out companion versions in the US House.

On the state level, perhaps the most important legislative success has been California's move to ban eggs from hens raised in battery cages, as well as the practice of housing breeding pigs in cramped gestation crates. Appealing to voters' concern for animal welfare, the Humane Society of the United States and a handful of other animal welfare organizations promoted Proposition 8, the Prevention of Farm Animal Cruelty Act. The measure did not specifically ban battery cages or gestation crates but mandated that sows and hens have sufficient space to fully turn around. Voters passed it by a margin of two to one in 2008. Two years later, the California Assembly passed AB 1437, which broadened the standards to include not just farm operations in California but also the production of any eggs and pork sold in the state. The passage of AB 1437 made the state's anticage push a major lever point for national change—California represents the largest domestic market in the United States, and neither eggs nor pork figure heavily in its agricultural output. In 2018, the state's voters doubled down, passing Proposition 12 by a wide margin. It increased the average amount of space each hen and sow must be allotted.[53] The US egg industry responded by rapidly moving away from battery cages, boosting cage-free production from just 6% of total output in 2014 to around 30% in 2020.[54] The pork industry, however, fought back. The National Pork Producers Council and the American Farm Bureau Federation sued to nullify Prop 12 influence on out-of-state producers, arguing that it violates the "dormant interstate-commerce clause," a legal doctrine not found in the Constitution. In 2021, the US Court of Appeals for the Ninth Circuit rejected the plaintiffs' complaint. In March 2022, the US Supreme Court decided to review the case, reversing its previous decision not to.[55] The probusiness, antiregulation recent bent of the Court raised speculation it would rule against California's voters and enshrine the pork industry's right to confine sows in tight cages. In a surprise 5–4 decision in May 2023, the Court rejected the pork industry's plea to overturn Proposition 12. "While the Constitution addresses many weighty issues, the type of pork chops California merchants may sell is not on the list," wrote Justice Neil Gorsuch in his majority opinion.[56]

### Public Persuasion Campaigns and Meat Alternatives

Alongside blunt instruments like regulation, legislation, and lawsuits, many advocates have focused on a softer approach: mitigating IFAP's harms by convincing consumers to eat less meat. It should be said that such efforts must be global to be successful. As domestic per capita US meat consumption has leveled off in recent years, the industry increasingly relies on exports. As of 2023, nearly a third of US-grown pork goes to foreign markets, as does nearly 16% of chicken and 13% of beef.[57] That means that when US residents eat less meat, the industry can easily shift the excess overseas, keeping factory-scale operations in North Carolina, Iowa, Arkansas, and other large production states humming along.

That said, campaigns that raise awareness of alternatives to meat-centered diets make a difference. The Meatless Monday concept, launched in 2003 by advertising executive and public health advocate Sid Lerner (1930–2021), stands as one of the most high-profile. Inspired by successful food-rationing efforts during World Wars I and II, it simply urges people to forgo meat every Monday—an act that not only cuts adherents' meat consumption by one-seventh but also gives them an occasion to think about the origin of the meat they consume during the week's other 6 days. From the start, the campaign focused on institutional settings like school, office, and hospital cafeterias. By 2010, through a partnership with the Johns Hopkins School of Public Health, the Baltimore public school cafeterias had gone meat-free on Mondays, as had college campuses ranging from Northern Kentucky University to the University of California–Davis to Yale University, NPR reported.[58] It has a global scope and now boasts ongoing efforts in more than 40 countries.[59]

In 2012, a mid-level USDA employee endorsed Meatless Monday in an internal staff newsletter, informing peers that "one simple way to reduce your environmental impact while dining at our cafeterias is to participate" is to forgo meat on Mondays. The item leaked to meat industry officials and friendly congressional members, and they immediately lashed out against it. Senators Jerry Moran (R-Kansas), Chuck Grassley (R-Iowa), and John Thune (R-S.D.) issued condemnations, and the president of the National Cattlemen's Beef Association declared that the USDA functionary's pro–Meatless Monday stance "should be condemned by anyone who believes agriculture is fundamental to sustaining life on this planet." The USDA quickly under then and current Secretary Tom Vilsack backtracked, stating that the department "does not endorse Meatless Monday," that the statement had been posted without "proper clearance," and that it had been "removed." (Between his stints in the Obama and Biden agriculture departments, Vilsack worked as a dairy industry executive, his salary paid by the USDA-collected checkoff program.)[60]

The incident demonstrated the industry's power to influence public policy: the spectacle of a major federal department trembling publicly before the very industry it is supposed to oversee. But it also suggested the power of campaigns like Meatless Monday: an entrenched industry does not stage a public tantrum over such a minor slight, if it is confident in the product it is selling to the public.

Another consumer-directed avenue for reducing meat consumption is the promotion of substitutes. Plant-based meat analogues like tofu, tempeh, and seitan have existed in societies with religious restrictions against carnivory for centuries or longer and have gained popularity in the United States in recent decades, as have hamburger-like patties made from legumes. But in the 2010s, venture capital investors began funding startup companies claiming that their particular patent-protected methods for processing legumes delivered substitutes that could not be distinguished from meat—or even surpassed meat in flavor and overall culinary experience. Two Silicon Valley–funded companies, Beyond Meat and Impossible Foods, embodied the trend. Impossible Foods' 2017 sustainability report exemplified their ambitions. The company aimed "to supply people with all the delicious, nutritious and affordable meat they want," the report claimed, insisting on calling its own product, a meatless substance made mainly from soy-protein isolate, "meat." It added, "We want to replace a prehistoric means of food production with one that can sustainably feed 10 billion people by 2050." Accordingly, Impossible and Beyond sales surged in 2019 and 2020. Perhaps spooked by the trend, major meat conglomerates including Tyson, Smithfield, Perdue, and Hormel all rushed to roll out their own plant-based meat analogues.[61]

By 2023, however, their appeal had "fizzled," their sales had dropped, their market valuations had plummeted, and their workforces had shrunk, *Bloomberg* reported, in an article headlined "Fake Meat Was Supposed to Save the World. It Became Just Another Fad."[62] US per capita meat consumption, meanwhile, held steady. Silicon Valley's vow to "disrupt" meat production had come up short.

The episode yields several lessons. One is that the flavor and mouthfeel of cooked animal flesh may be more difficult to replicate with processed beans than some technologists might hope. Another is that even if perfect analogues could be achieved, consumers might not readily discard animal meat—foodways are deeply embedded in culture and emotion, and not readily given to instant transformation by some hotly marketed novelty.

### Toward a Better Future

But the failure of high-tech analogues does not mean Americans cannot thrive while eating less meat. As recently as 1960, Americans devoured 167 pounds of meat per capita annually. Within a decade, consumption had hit 193.3 pounds—a 16% jump. By 2022, we were up to around 225 pounds—more than a half-pound per person daily.[63] That jump represents a dramatic expansion and intensification of animal production, as well as significant hardship imposed on meatpacking workers, communities in CAFO country, and the environment. The rapid rise of cheap and ubiquitous meat also reminds us that within living memory, we made do with one-third less meat than we have access to now. Meanwhile, it seems unlikely that some technical breakthrough will allow us to maintain current consumption levels while magically eliminating these downsides.

The other advocacy methods described in this chapter have not worked magic, either. It should be emphasized that none of them, in isolation, offer anything like a silver bullet for improving our meat production system. Rather, they work best in combination. For example, the unfinished fight for justice in eastern North Carolina's hog-heavy African American communities has resulted in legal verdicts that can help boost the case for regulating CAFO pollution, and the work of groups like Venceremos has raised the profile of meatpacking workers toiling under unbearable conditions, putting pressure on the OSHA to impose rules that would prevent routine repetitive-stress injuries. Both help make the case—and broaden constituencies for—Sen. Booker's transformative food system legislation. Passing it would open space for producers who take care of the environment and respect workers and surrounding communities— likely leading to less, and more expensive, meat. Projects like Meatless Monday would then be well positioned to show Americans that replacing some meat with whole foods like beans, grains, and vegetables can be delicious, not punishing. And high-tech meat-like products might find a niche in diets as well. On the other hand, failure to advocate for change means accepting an increasingly disastrous status quo.

### NOTES

1. Diane Charlton, "Meatpacking: A Consolidated Industry," Montana State University Department of Agricultural Economics, January 25, 2021, https://ageconmt .com/meatpacking-a-consolidated-industry/

2. Upton Sinclair, *The Jungle* (New York: Doubleday, Page & Co, 1906).

3. Sinclair, *The Jungle*.

4. Upton Sinclair, "Follow up to 'The Jungle'—'The Condemned-Meat Industry: A Reply to Mr. J. Ogden Armour,'" Undercover Reporting, https://undercover.hosting .nyu.edu/s/undercover-reporting/item/12142

5. "Roosevelt on Army Beef," *New York Times*, March 26, 1899, https://timesmachine .nytimes.com/timesmachine/1899/03/26/102531710.pdf?pdf_redirect=true&ip=0

6. Roger L. Di Silvestro, *Theodore Roosevelt in the Badlands* (London: Bloomberg Publishing, 2011).

7. "Condemnation: The Neill-Reynolds Report," https://82558588.weebly.com/the -neill-reynolds-report.html

8. Food and Drug Administration, "Part I: The 1906 Food and Drugs Act and Its Enforcement," https://www.fda.gov/about-fda/changes-science-law-and-regulatory-authorities/part-i-1906-food-and-drugs-act-and-its-enforcement

9. Arvind Dilawar, "America's Most Famous Novel about Bad Meat Was Actually about Immigrant Labor Abuses," Talk Poverty, January 10, 2019, https://talkpoverty.org/2019/01/10/sinclair-jungle-immigrant-narrative/index.html

10. Ted Genoways, The Chain (New York: Harper, 2014).

11. Chris Leonard, The Meat Racket (New York: Simon and Schuster, 2014).

12. Barry Estabrook, Pig Tales (New York: WW Norton, 2014).

13. Maryn McKenna, Big Chicken (Washington, DC: National Geographic, 2017).

14. Tom Philpott, Perilous Bounty (London: Bloomsbury Publishing, 2020).

15. Corban Addison, Wastelands: The True Story of Farm Country on Trial (New York: Vintage Books, 2023).

16. Gavin Off, Ames Alexander, and Adam Wagner, "Big Poultry: Five Takeaways from Investigating North Carolina's Secretive Ag Industry," Charlotte Observer, December 8, 2023, https://www.charlotteobserver.com/news/state/north-carolina/article269733696.html

17. Charles Duhigg, "Health Ills Abound as Farm Runoff Fouls Wells," New York Times, September 17, 2009, https://www.nytimes.com/2009/09/18/us/18dairy.html

18. Kimberly Kinde, "At Chicken Plants, Chemicals Blamed for Health Ailments Poised to Proliferate," Washington Post, April 25, 2013, https://www.washingtonpost.com/politics/at-chicken-plants-chemicals-blamed-for-health-ailments-are-poised-to-proliferate/2013/04/25/d2a65ec8-97b1-11e2-97cd-3d8c1afe4f0f_story.html

19. Landing page for Food and Environment Reporting Network, https://thefern.org/what-we-do/

20. Landing page for Investigate Midwest, https://investigatemidwest.org/about/

21. Landing page for Southerly Magazine, https://southerlymag.org/about/

22. Some notable examples: Michael Grabell, "The Plot to Keep Meatpacking Plants Open during COVID-19," Propublica, May 13, 2022; Talor Telford and Kimberly Kindy, "As They Rushed to Maintain U.S. Meat Supply, Big Processors Saw Plants Become Covid-19 Hot Spots, Worker Illnesses Spike," Washington Post, April 25, 2020; Easter Honing and Ted Genoways, "The Workers Are Being Sacrificed: As Cases Mounted, Meatpacker JBS Kept People on Crowded Factory Floors," Mother Jones, May 1, 2020.

23. Leah Douglas, "Mapping Covid Outbreaks in the Food System," Food and Environment Reporting Network, April 22, 2020, https://thefern.org/2020/04/mapping-covid-19-in-meat-and-food-processing-plants/

24. Staff Report, "NOW TO GET RID OF THOSE PESKY HEALTH DEPART-MENTS! How the Trump Administration Helped the Meatpacking Industry Block Pandemic Protection for Workers," Select House Subcommittee on Response to the Coronavirus Crisis, May 2022, https://coronavirus.house.gov/sites/democrats.coronavirus.house.gov/files/2021.10.27%20Meatpacking%20Report.Final_.pdf

25. Lance Compa, "Blood, Sweat and Fear, Workers Rights in U.S. Meat and Poultry Plants," Human Rights Watch, 2004, https://www.hrw.org/sites/default/files/reports/usa0105.pdf

26. "When We're Dead and Buried, Our Bones Will Keep Hurting: Workers' Rights Under Threat in US Meat and Poultry Plants," Human Right Watch, September 4, 2019, https://www.hrw.org/report/2019/09/04/when-were-dead-and-buried -our-bones-will-keep-hurting/workers-rights-under-threat

27. Marion Nestle, *Food Politics* (Berkeley: University California Press, 2007).

28. Pew Commission on Industrial Farm Animal Production, "Putting Meat on the Table: Industrial Farm Animal Production in America," April 29, 2008, https://www .pewtrusts.org/en/research-and-analysis/reports/0001/01/01/putting-meat-on-the -table

29. The Pew Charitable Trusts, "Industrial Farm Animal Production, Antimicrobial Resistance and Human Health," January 30, 2008, https://www.pewtrusts.org /en/research-and-analysis/reports/2008/01/30/industrial-farm-animal-production -antimicrobial-resistance-and-human-health

30. Virginia T. Guidry, "In Memoriam: Steve Wing," Environmental Health Perspectives, January 2017, https://www.ncbi.nlm.nih.gov/pmc/articles/PMC5226689/

31. Melba Newsome, "Decades of Legal Battles over Pollution by Industrial Hog Farms Haven't Changed Much for Eastern NC Residents Burdened by Environmental Racism," NC Health News, October 29, 2021,"https://www.northcarolinahealthnews .org/2021/10/29/legal-battles-over-pollution-from-hog-waste-environmental-racism -havent-changed-much/

32. US Department of Labor, "Collective Bargaining in the Meat-Packing Industry," Bulletin No. 1063, 1952, https://fraser.stlouisfed.org/files/docs/publications/bls/bls _1063_1952.pdf

33. The 1952 Department of Labor paper reports puts 1950 meatpacking worker average hourly wages at $1.57. Autoworkers earned on average $1.61 at the time, according to US Department of Labor, "Wage Structure Motor Vehicles and Parts, 1950: Hourly Earnings and Supplementary Wage Practices Bulletin No. 1015," https://fraser.stlouisfed.org/title/wage-structure-motor-vehicles-parts-1950-hourly -earnings-supplementary-wage-practices-4443

34. See Ted Genoways, "The Spam Factory's Dirty Secret: First, Hormel Gutted the Union. Then It Sped Up the Line. And When the Pig-Brain Machine Made Workers Sick, They Got Canned," *Mother Jones*, July/August 2011, https://www .motherjones.com/politics/2011/06/hormel-spam-pig-brains-disease/. See also Genoways, *The Chain*.

35. Meatpacking worker wages: https://www.bls.gov/oes/current/oes513022.htm. Durable-goods manufacturing wages: https://www.bls.gov/news.release/empsit.t24.htm

36. Janice Fine, "Worker Centers: Organizing Communities at the Edge of the Dream," Economic Policy Institute, December 13, 2005, https://www.epi.org /publication/bp159/

37. Tom Philpott, "Tomato Pickers Won Better Protections: Can Their Strategy Work for Poultry?," Mother Jones, May 1, 2022, https://www.motherjones.com/food /2022/05/tomato-workers-wendys-poultry-coalition-imokalee-workers-labor/

38. Alice Driver author page, *New York Review*, December 2022, https://www .nybooks.com/contributors/alice-driver/

39. Jamie Berger, "How Black North Carolinians Pay the Price for the World's Cheap Bacon," Vox, April 1, 2022, https://www.vox.com/future-perfect/23003487/north-carolina-hog-pork-bacon-farms-environmental-racism-black-residents-pollution-meat-industry

40. Federal Trade Commission, "Meat Packing Industry, Summary and Part 1," June 24, 1919, https://babel.hathitrust.org/cgi/pt?id=pst.000008113016&view=1up&seq=78

41. Sarah Carden, "The Fall of Antitrust and Rise of Corporate Power: Impacts of Concentration on Farmers and Ranchers," Farm Action, March 1, 2022, https://farmaction.us/wp-content/uploads/2022/04/The-Fall-of-Antitrust-the-Rise-of-Corporate-Power.pdf

42. Farm Action, "Dear USDA: Issue the Packers and Stockyard Rules, Now!," Farm Action, April 7, 2022, https://farmaction.us/2022/04/07/dear-usda-issue-the-packers-and-stockyards-rules-now/

43. Maryn McKenna, "How Congress Ignored Science and Fueled Antibiotic Resistance," WIRED, September 19, 2017, https://www.wired.com/story/big-chicken/

44. Kenny Torella, "Big Meat Just Can't Quit Antibiotics, VOX, December 15, 2023, https://www.vox.com/future-perfect/2023/1/8/23542789/big-meat-antibiotics-resistance-fda

45. Berger, "How Black North Carolinians Pay the Price for the World's Cheap Bacon."

46. Berger, "How Black North Carolinians Pay the Price for the World's Cheap Bacon."

47. Keith Schneider, "Remedies for Harmful Algal Blooms Are Available in Law and Practice," Circle Blue, September 27, 2022, https://www.circleofblue.org/2022/world/remedies-for-harmful-algal-blooms-are-available-in-law-and-practice/

48. Circle of Blue landing page, https://www.circleofblue.org/

49. Feed The Truth report, "Draining the Big Food Swamp, Feed The Truth, February 2021, https://web.archive.org/web/20210304202218/https://feedthetruth.org/wp-content/uploads/sites/91/FTT-DrainingTheSwamp-ExecSummary-FINAL.pdf

50. Open Secrets, "Lobbyist Activities: Anne MacMillan, Open Secrets, 2022, httpswww.opensecrets.org/federal-lobbying/lobbyists/summary?cycle=2022&id=Y0000049782L

51. Tom Philpott, "How Labor Secretary Scalia Played Chicken with Meatpacking Workers' Lives," Mother Jones, September-October 2022, https://www.motherjones.com/food/2020/07/labor-eugene-scalia-meatpacking-osha-stress-carpal-tunnel-coronavirus-covid/

52. Senator Cory Booker, "Booker Introduces Package of Bills to Reform U.S. Food System," official Senator Cory Booker webpage, February 2, 2023, https://www.booker.senate.gov/news/press/booker-introduces-package-of-bills-to-reform-us-food-system

53. Kenny Torella, "The Fight over Cage-Free Eggs and Bacon in California, Explained," Vox, August 10, 2021, https://www.vox.com/future-perfect/22576044

/prop-12-california-eggs-pork-bacon-veal-animal-welfare-law-gestation-crates
-battery-cages

54. Kenny Torella, "The Biggest Animal Welfare Successes in the Past 6 Years, in One Chart," Vox, March 23, 2021,https://www.vox.com/future-perfect/22331708/eggs -cages-chickens-hens-meat-poultry

55. Pig Progress, "Prop 12—US Supreme Court ruling expected by February 2023," Pig Progress, March 11, 2022, https://www.pigprogress.net/the-industrymarkets /market-trends-analysis-the-industrymarkets-2/prop-12-us-supreme-court-ruling -expected-by-february-2023/

56. Justin Marceau and Doug Kysar, "The Supreme Court's Ruling on Prop 12 Is a Win against Factory Farming: But the Pigs' Lives Will Still Suck," Vox, May 12, 2023, https://www.vox.com/future-perfect/23721488/prop-12-scotus-pork-pigs-factory -farming-california-bacon

57. "Meat Handling Guidelines," The American Meat Institute, May 2023, https://www.meatinstitute.org/index.php?ht=d/sp/i/47465/pid/47465

58. Allison Aubrey, "Campaign Aims to Make Meatless Monday Hip," National Public Radio, *Morning Edition*, August 9, 2010, https://www.npr.org/2010/08/09 /129025298/campaign-aims-to-make-meatless-mondays-hip

59. Meatless Monday, "The Monday Campaigns, 9 Seasonal Meatless Recipes," https://www.mondaycampaigns.org/meatless-monday/about#:~:text=Meatless%20 Monday%20is%20a%20global,Center%20for%20a%20Livable%20Future

60. Caray Spivak, "Ex-agriculture Secretary Tom Vilsack Is the Top Paid Executive at Dairy Management," *Milwaukee Journal*, January 7, 2020, "https://www.jsonline .com/story/news/special-reports/dairy-crisis/2019/12/02/former-secretary -agriculture-tom-vilsack-top-paid-dairy-management-exec/4265818002/

61. David Yaffey-Bellany, "The New Makers of Plant-Based Meat? Big Meat Companies," *New York Times*, October 14, 2019, https://www.nytimes.com/2019/10 /14/business/the-new-makers-of-plant-based-meat-big-meat-companies.html

62. Denna Shanker, "Fake Meat Was Supposed to Save the World: It Became Just Another Fad," *Businessweek*, January 19, 2023, https://www.bloomberg.com/news /features/2023-01-19/beyond-meat-bynd-impossible-foods-burgers-are-just-another -food-fad

63. National Chicken Council, "Per Capita Consumption of Poultry and Livestock, 1965 to Forecast 2022, in Pounds," National Council, December 2021, https://www .nationalchickencouncil.org/about-the-industry/statistics/per-capita-consumption -of-poultry-and-livestock-1965-to-estimated-2012-in-pounds/

academic research, related to IFAP: as
advocacy initiative, 367–68, 370; suppression by IFAP, xiv–xxi, 176
advocacy initiatives, against IFAP, 359–85;
academic research, 367–68, 370; of com-
munities/community organizations, 151,
154–55, 178–81, 360, 369–71, 374–75, 381;
investigative journalism, xxi, 359–66,
370, 371; of labor unions, 360, 369–70;
legislation, 375–77, 381; meat consumption reduction campaigns, 378–80;
mitigation initiatives, 371–81; of NGOs,
366–67, 370–71; regulatory, 372–74; tort
law-based, 374–75
African swine fever, 129
Agency for Toxic Substances and Diseases
Registry, 56–57
ag-gag laws, 70, 156, 176
Agge, G. Steven, 235
agribusiness corporations, 1, 5; federal
subsidies, 13, 143–46, 157, 159; global/
foreign ownership, 142, 144, 145, 258;
market power, 13, 143–50, 157–58;
monopolistic and oligopolistic practices, 12–13, 143, 145–46, 257, 360,
372–73. *See also* industrial food animal
production (IFAP)
Agricultural Foreign Investment Disclosure
Act, 145
*Agricultural Testament, An* (Howard), 344
*Agricultural Waste Management Field
Handbook* (USDA-NRCS), 324
agroecology, 347–49
agro-industrial complex, xiii, xx–xxi, 175
air pollution/airborne emissions, from
CAFOs, 12, 14, 19, 46–104, 294, 297–300;
components, 50, 80–81, 352; dispersion
models, 52, 53, 81–82, 88; neighbor and

rural community exposures, 47, 50–54,
56–66, 67–68, 173–74, 196–97; occupational exposures, xvii–xviii, 47–50, 51, 54,
55–56, 57, 61, 67–68, 69; policy recommendations, 68–71, 182–83; regional and
global exposures, 54–55, 68; regulations
and regulatory failures, 36, 199; regulations and regulatory failures (federal),
69, 91, 176, 196, 200, 206–8; regulations
and regulatory failures (local governments), 70–71, 210, 217–19; regulations
and regulatory failures (states), 69–70,
91, 208–11; sampling, monitoring, and
documentation, xx, 52–54, 80, 176, 208,
210; stationary sources, 206–8; wet and
dry depositions, 19, 47, 54–55. *See also*
Clean Air Act; odors, IFAP-related
alfalfa, 17, 34, 35
algal blooms, 21–22
allergens and allergies, 47, 57, 64, 82, 83–84,
87, 88
Altmaier, R., 52, 53
Amalgamated Meat Cutters Union, 361
American Community Survey, 257–58
American Conference of Governmental
Industrial Hygienists, 260
American Farm Bureau Federation, 159,
377
American Meat Institute, 375
American Public Health Association
(APHA), 93, 177, 183
American Society of Agronomy, 10
ammonia, emission from CAFOs, 8, 19,
54–55, 207–8, 297–98, 352; adverse
human health effects, 46–47, 49, 55, 57,
60, 66–67, 68, 80–81, 84, 88, 90–91, 196,
197–98, 207, 301, 352; adverse livestock
health effects, 322–23, 328; emission

COVID-19 pandemic, impact on meatpacking workers, 256–93; government's failure to protect workers, 271–77; meat industry's endangerment of workers, 266–76, 365–66, 370; policy recommendations, 276–78; political influences in, 177, 267, 270–73, 275, 293n177
COVID-19 pandemic, impact on meat production, 106
crop insurance programs, 144–45
crop production, 4, 9–11, 142; for animal feeds, 12, 16, 33–34; for ethanol, 30, 33–34, 256; irrigation use, 34, 35, 105–6; as monoculture, 34; recoupling with livestock production, 35–36; as water pollution cause, 16–29, 30, 33–34
crop rotation: corn-soybean, 17–18, 19, 34; grass, 12
Curry, Susan, xvii–xviii
CWA. See Clean Water Act

dairy cattle: diseases, 116–17, 123–24; inventories, 146–47, 159n2
dairy cattle CAFOs, 11, 56, 64, 69, 88, 107, 172–73, 195, 294
dairy industry, 144, 146–47; political influence, 379
dairy-producing communities, 151
dairy products. See milk and dairy products
deer, 106, 112
diet, human, 67, 341, 343, 347, 349–51, 355; diseases associated with, 343, 347, 348, 355; for reduced meat consumption, 378–80
dispersion models, 52, 53, 81–82, 88
dissolved oxygen (DO), 21
Dollar, Nathan, 258
Donham, Kelly, xviii
Douglas, Leah, 366
Duffy, Mike, 13
Duhigg, Charles, 365
dusts: as CAFO airborne pollutants, 47, 49, 50, 55, 56, 80, 82–83, 195, 226, 298, 352; meat processing workers' exposures, 261

EAT-Lancet Commission report, 341–42, 348–49
Ebola viruses, 125

Economic Policy Institute, 370
economies of scale, 106–7, 185
efficiencies of production, 13, 16–17, 19–20, 34
eggs: from battery-raised hens, 377; incubators, 2–3; nutritional value, 5; *Salmonella* contamination, 114
encephalitis viruses: Japanese, 125; tick-borne, 123
endotoxins, 46–47, 50, 52, 54, 56, 57, 60–63, 66, 261
energy production: animal waste-based, 181, 239, 307, 323–24, 327; corn-based ethanol, 12, 29, 30, 34; fossil fuel-based, 35, 346, 349
Enterobacteriaceae, 113, 121
environmental injustice, IFAP-perpetrated, 157, 166–93; community actions against, 178–81; definitions, 167–69; policy recommendations, 182–85; structural barriers in, 175–78, 182
environmental justice movement, 167–68
Environmentally Superior Technologies (ESTs), 298, 307–24
environmental movement, 337
Environmental Protection Agency, 56–57, 69, 91, 92–93, 168, 176, 200, 294–95; CAFO airborne emissions regulatory responsibility, 207–8, 374–75; CAFO effluent regulatory responsibility, 200, 202–5; Hypoxia Task Force, 23
Environmental Quality Incentive Program, 326
Environmental Working Group, 12, 13
EPA. See Environmental Protection Agency
*Escherichia coli*, xix, 47, 109, 110–12, 113, 120–21, 303, 364
European Union, 67, 113, 118, 129, 158
eutrophication, 20–39, 301–2; Baltic Sea, 28–29; Black Sea, 27–28; Chesapeake Bay, 25–27, 25–28; Gulf of Mexico, 19–20, 21, 22, 23, 32; Lake Erie, 21–24, 33
Evans, Alice C., 115
export markets, 94, 147, 257, 263, 378

Fair Labor Standards Act, 69
Far East scarlet-like fever, 112

Farm Action, 372–73
Farm Bill, 326, 338
Farm Bureau, 151
farm debt, 143–44
farm labor legislation, 229
farms: consolidation, 34, 141–50, 159; family farms, 13, 141, 147, 153, 336–37; number of, 141
Farm Service Agency, 145
farm size, 141, 146, 147; large, 144, 147–48, 347; scale, 148, 159n3; small and mid-sized, 13, 97, 141, 146, 147, 149, 151, 157, 158, 169–70
Farm System Reform Act, 376
farm workers, impacts of IFAP on, 148–49, 336, 346–47; airborne pollutant exposures, 47–50, 51, 54, 55–56, 57, 61, 67–68, 69; environmental injustice issue, 173; health and safety protections from, 69
*Fast Food Nation* (Schlosser), 363–64, 366
fecal microbial source (MST) tracking, 82–83
Federal Farm Loan Act, 143
federal government, regulatory authority: air pollution, 69, 91, 176, 196, 200; manure/animal waste treatment, 200–208; water pollution, 176, 200–206, 210. *See also specific federal government agencies*
Federal Meat Inspection Act, 362
Federal Trade Commission, 372
feed: additives, 3, 5, 7, 11; airborne emissions, 47, 80–81; conversion rates, 6, 322; cost, 4; crop production of, 12, 16, 17, 18, 29, 30, 33–34, 35, 142, 144–45; slaughterhouse wastes in, 4–5; subsidization programs, 144–45
feeder cattle, 29
feedlots, 11, 34, 46, 152, 194–95, 364
fertilizers, 307; commercial/chemical, 10, 11, 16, 17, 18–19, 20, 23, 142, 145, 216, 346, 351–52, 353; as water pollutant, 20, 21, 22, 30. *See also* manure/animal waste lagoons and spray practices; nitrogen/nitrogen fertilizers
fish and fisheries, impact of IFAP on, xix, 26–27, 28, 117, 214, 351
flies, 80, 92, 93, 95, 150

food, consumer costs, 34, 38, 181–82, 238, 347, 349–50
Food and Drug Administration (FDA), 362, 373
Food and Environment Reporting Network (FERN), 365, 366
foodborne illnesses: bacterial, 14, 105–18, 119, 120, 128–29; policy recommendations, 128–30; viral, 125, 127–29
*Food Politics* (Nestle), 367
food production, 1; economic and noneconomic costs, 347; historical changes, 1–2; sustainable intensification, 341–44; during WW II, 4
Food Safety and Inspection Service, 111–12
food security/insecurity, 129–30, 337, 343, 348–49
Food Sovereignty Movement, 350–51
foot and mouth disease virus, 126
*Forages* (Hughes), 10
Ford, Henry, 359
fossil fuels, 35, 37, 346, 349
Foster Farms, 264

gases: from CAFOs, 47–48, 49–52, 54, 55, 297–98; greenhouse, 37, 54, 55, 67, 68, 299, 301, 322, 324, 326, 327, 347, 349
Geisinger Clinic, 64–65
genomic sequencing, 119
George Washington University, 274–75
Getah virus, 126
Global Warming Potential (GWP), 54, 301, 322
glucans, 47
goats, 62–63, 65; zoonotic diseases, 112, 113, 114, 115, 117, 126, 127
Goldschmidt, Walter, 147–48
Gorsuch, Neil, 377
Government Accountability Office, 145, 259
Grassley, Chuck, 379
grass/pasture-based livestock production, 9–11, 12, 34–36, 337, 376
Gray, Gregory C., 105–40
greenwashing practice, 340–41
grower agreements, 7, 214; integrator contracts, 80, 93–96
Guidry, Virginia T., 166–93

Harkin, Tom, ix–xi, xvi–xvii
Harl, Neil, 12–13
Harreld, Bruce, xvii
Hatcher, Sarah, 166–93
health, definition, 79, 98, 349
health care, rural, 354
health impacts, of IFAP, 14, 347; antibiotic resistance, 14, 49, 105, 110, 116–17, 118–21, 128–29, 207, 336, 353, 364, 373; behavioral health, 79, 84–86, 98, 99, 173–74; in meatpacking workers, 258–93; in minority and low-income communities, 166–67, 173–75, 177, 182; physiological health, 79, 86–88, 93, 99, 173–74. See also respiratory conditions; zoonoses
Heaney, Christopher D., 79–104, 368
heavy metals, 298, 308, 313–14, 318, 322, 326
hemolytic uremic syndrome, 111–12
hemorrhagic fever viruses: Alkhurma, 127; Crimean-Congo, 123, 126
Hendra virus, 125
hepatitis E virus, 125, 127
herbicides, 11, 351–52
Herring, Elsie, 175
Hines, N. William, 194–255
hog CAFOs, 6–8, 16, 34, 294–95; airborne emissions and odors, xvii–xviii, 46, 52, 55–62, 69, 81, 82–83, 86–88, 89, 90, 91–92, 195, 196–98, 297–300; animal welfare issues, 7–8, 158–59, 364, 377; community opposition, 151; environmental injustice issue, 169–73; fecal contamination markers, 82–83; geographic distribution, 107, 108, 124; in minority and low-income communities, 169–73, 179, 327, 364, 368, 371, 381; nuisance lawsuits against, 93–96, 195–200, 209, 211, 212, 217, 218–40, 368, 371, 381; occupational exposures, 47–50, 51, 54, 55–56, 57, 61, 67–68, 69; property rights and values impact, 152, 197; quality of life impact, 89, 90, 91–96; regulations and regulatory failures, 195–240; regulations and regulatory failures (federal), 196, 197, 200–208; regulations and regulatory failures (local governments), 197, 217–18; regulations and regulatory

failures (states), 197, 208–17, 374; waste disposal issue, xix–xx, 28, 36, 196–98 18; waste processing technologies, 303–24, 303–27, 325–27; zoonotic diseases, 105, 106
hog industry, 142; corporate consolidation, 146–47, 149; integrator contracts, 93–96; market crash (1998), 143; political influence, 218
hogs: antibiotic use and resistance, 119–20, 121, 129; inventories, 24, 146–47, 159n2, 242n25; pasture farrowing system, 36; zoonotic diseases, xvii, 105, 106, 112, 113, 114, 115, 117, 121–22, 124–26, 129
Hormel, 369, 380
hormones, 298, 302–3
Horner, J., 97–98
horses, 65; zoonotic diseases, 117, 125, 127
Huffman, Angela, 372
Humane Methods of Slaughter Act, 156
Humane Society of the United States, 377
Human Rights Watch, 256, 366–67
hydrochar, 305
hydrochloric acid, 300
hydrogen sulfide, 81, 297–98, 299, 352; community exposures, 46–47, 50–51, 57, 62, 63–64, 86, 87–88; exposure limits, 70, 90–91; occupational exposures, 46–47, 49; quality of life effects, 91–92; regional and global exposures, 54; sampling, 52, 53–54

IFAP. See industrial food animal production (IFAP) industry
Ikerd, John, 173, 336–58
Imlay, Aimee, 141–65
immigrants, 148–49, 173, 257–58, 265, 269, 276, 360, 364
Impossible Foods, 379–80
income equality/inequality, 148, 149, 157, 258, 355, 369–70. See also minority and low-income communities
industrial food animal production (IFAP) industry, 2, 11, 46, 47, 141–42; corporate consolidation, 143–50; defenders of, 336–37, 338–39, 340–41, 354; definition, 33, 142; history, structure, and trends,

1–15; origin and development, 1–13, 194–95; as percentage of all food animal production, 141–42; response to sustainable agriculture movement, 336–37, 338–39, 340–44, 348–49; suppression of IFAP-related research, xiv–xx. *See also* concentrated animal feeding operations (CAFOs); meatpacking industry

infectious diseases, IFAP-related. *See* zoonoses

influenza A viruses, 105, 121–22; avian, 122–23, 128; swine (H1N1), xvii, 105, 121, 124–25, 129

influenza B virus, 125

influenza C virus, 125

influenza D virus, 123–24, 125

integrator contracts, 80, 93–96

International Study of Asthma and Allergies in Childhood, 57

Invariant, 375–76

Investigate Midwest, 365

investigative journalism, xxi, 359–66, 367, 368, 371

Iowa: agriculture-related water pollution, 18, 29–33; right-to-farm law amendments, 227–32

Iowa, CAFOs, 18–19, 30, 32, 230; cattle CAFOs, 29; hog CAFOs, 18, 29, 169, 170, 172, 195, 196, 222, 294; in minority communities, 169, 170, 172; nuisance litigation against, 195, 217–18, 220, 222, 224, 227–32, 237; poultry CAFOs, 18, 29; regulations and regulatory failures, 212–13, 217–19, 237

*Iowa Concentrated Animal Feeding Operations Air Quality Study,* xv–xvi

Iowa Farm Bureau, xiv

Iowa State University, xv–xvi, xviii–xix, 13, 90–91

Izaak Walton League, 13

JBS, 142, 144, 145–46, 148–49, 257, 262–63, 268, 270–71, 273–74, 366; USA Food Company, 265, 267

Jewell, Jesse Dixon, 4–5, 6–7

Johns Hopkins University, 368; Bloomberg School of Public Health, x–xi, 367–68, 378; Press, xi

Jones, Christopher, xix–xx, 16–45

*Jungle, The* (Sinclair), 256, 360–63, 371–72

Keokuk County Rural Health Study (KCRHS), xvii, xviii, 57–58, 59, 61

Khanna, Ro, 376

Kilpatrick, John A., 97–98

Kindy, Kimberly, 365

Kline, J., 58

Koch Foods, 257, 270

lawsuits: for enforcement of environmental regulations, 70–71, 201, 202–3; by IFAP industry, 201; by meatpacking workers, 263, 274–75. *See also* nuisance lawsuits

Leath, Steven, xvi

legumes, 9–10, 16, 20, 31, 349, 379

*Leptospira,* 47

Lerner, Sid, 378

Licolli, Magaly, 370

*Life and Death of the American Worker, The* (Driver), 370

*Listeria monocytogenes*/listeriosis, 117

livestock, introduction into the Americas, 9

Livestock Marketing Association, 375

local government: air pollution regulatory oversight, 70–71, 210, 217–19; CAFO regulatory oversight, 197, 217–18; CAFOs regulatory oversight, 70–71, 217–19, 221, 225–26; community distrust of, 154–55; lack of IFAP oversight power, 177, 179; land-use decision-making power, 158; right-to-farm laws, 225–26; water pollution regulatory oversight, 210, 217

Lower Saxony Lung Study, 88

lung cancer, 66, 68

macronutrients, 16. *See also* fertilizers

Malin, Mike, 8

manure/animal waste treatment technologies, 8, 18–19, 46, 51, 67, 176, 239, 294–337; in agroecological farming systems, 352; antibiotic residue transmission in, 119, 172; background, 297–303; best available technology, 203–4; best management practices, 324; binders, scrubbers, and covers, 303–4; co-application with

Miller, René, 374
mink farms, 62–63, 65
Minnesota Environmental Quality Board, 90
minority and low-income communities, impact of IFAP on, 368; community advocacy for, 168, 182, 185, 370–71; disproportionate effects, 173–75, 178; environmental injustice, 166–93; health effects, 166–67, 173–75, 177, 182; investigative reports on, 364–65; nuisance litigation response, 233, 364, 368, 381; quality of life effects, 89, 93–96, 182, 368
Moran, Jerry, 379
Murphy, Wendell, 6–7, 93–96, 177–78
Murphy-Brown, LLC, 93–94; nuisance lawsuits against, 232–38, 374
Murphy Farms, 177–78

National Academy of Sciences, National Research Council, 91–92
National Antimicrobial Resistance Monitoring System, 115
National Association of Local Boards of Health, 92
National Beef Packing Company, 145–46, 257, 264–65, 366
National Cattleman's Beef Association, 375, 379
National Institute of Occupational Safety and Health, xvii, xviii, 259, 260, 275, 276–78; Health Hazards Evaluations, 262
National Pollutant Discharge Elimination System, 200, 202–6, 324
National Pork Producers Council, 159, 375–76, 377
Natural Resources Defense Council, 90, 324
Nature Conservancy, 12
Neighbors Opposing a Polluted Environment, 155
Neill-Reynolds Report, 361–62
neurotoxins, 80–81
Newcastle disease virus, 123
New York University, 367
NGOs. See nongovernmental organizations

Niman, Bill, 1–15
Niman, Nicolette Hahn, 1–15
NIOSH. See National Institute of Occupational Safety and Health
Nipah virus, 125
nitrate, as water pollutant, xix, 8, 19–21, 30, 32, 33, 55, 302
nitric acid, 300
nitric oxide, 19, 50–51
nitrogen/nitrogen fertilizers, 16; animal waste-produced, 8, 18–19, 21, 26–27, 30–32, 37, 301–2; biological fixation, 16, 18–19, 20; budgeting, 20; commercial formulations, 16, 17–18, 30, 35; denitrification technologies, 305–7, 312, 315–21, 323, 327, 328; inputs and flow paths, 20; in soil organic matter, 18–19, 20; volatilization, 19; as water pollutant, 8, 19–21, 23, 26–27, 28–29, 35, 302
nitrogen/nitrous oxides, 19, 47, 54, 55, 67, 82, 207, 301
noise pollution: CAFOs-related, 150–51, 153, 154, 195, 226; in meat processing plants, 260–61
nongovernmental organizations, advocacy against IFAP, 366–67, 370–71
nonprofit organizations, 365
North American Meat Institute, 271
North Carolina: Department of Environmental and Natural Resources, 180–81; right-to-farm law amendments, 232–36
North Carolina, hog CAFOs: in minority and low-income communities, 166, 169–70, 171, 179, 180–81, 364, 368, 371; nuisance litigation against, 195, 196–97, 232–35, 374–75, 381; regulations and regulatory failures, 18–19, 214–16, 218–19; Swine and Poultry Waste Management Center, 214–16, 239–40; Swine Farm Environmental Performance Act, 214; waste management technologies, 214–16, 239–40, 295–97, 298–99, 304–5, 307–23, 325–26
North Carolina Environmental Justice Network, 168, 182, 185, 370–71, 374
North Carolina Pork Council, xv
NPDES. See National Pollutant Discharge Elimination System

renewable fuel standards, 34–35
Resource Conservation and Recovery Act, 374–75
respiratory conditions, CAFO emissions-related, x, xvii, 12, 14, 46–78, 300–1; in CAFO workers, 47–48, 55–56; in children, xvii, 56–61, 63, 68, 87, 88; in minority and low-income communities, 174, 368; as mortality risk factor, 65–66, 68; in neighbors and rural communities, 61–64, 86–87, 174; odor/odorants-related, 81, 86–88. See also asthma
Rift Valley fever virus, 123, 127
right to farm, 173
right-to-farm laws, 70, 99, 354–55; federal jurisprudence of, 229, 231–32, 237; first-generation, 225; as protection against nuisance lawsuits, 152–53, 157, 158, 175, 209, 211, 220, 227–32; recommended reforms, 158; second-generation/amendments, 220, 226–37; state jurisprudence of, 225, 226–38
Rinsky, Jessica, 166–93
Roberts, John, 229
Rockefeller Foundation, 347
Rodale, J. I., 344
rodentiosis, 112
Roosevelt, Franklin D., 4, 9
Roosevelt, Theodore, 361–62
rotavirus, 126
rural communities: benefits of sustainable agriculture for, 347, 348, 353–54; community relationships, 348; human waste disposal practices, 198
rural communities, effects of IFAP on, 141–65, 347, 353–54; air pollution, 47, 50–54, 56–66, 67–68, 347; civic participation, 154–55, 158; community conflicts, 151, 157; COVID infections, 265–66; income inequality, 149, 157; odor/odorant exposures, 79–80, 81–93, 150–51; policy recommendations for, 157–59; socioeconomic conditions, 142–43, 147–49, 154, 157, 353–54; water pollution, 347; zoonotic disease exposures, 353. See also property rights and values, near CAFOs
Rural Residents for Responsible Agriculture, 155

Safe Drinking Water Act, 20
Salmon, David, 113
*Salmonella*/salmonellosis, 47, 109, 113–14
Salsbury, Joseph, 3
Sanders, Bernie, 376
Sanderson, Wayne T., 46–78
SARS-CoV-2, 65, 122, 124, 270. *See also* COVID-19 pandemic
Sauna, Amy van, 375
Scalia, Eugene, 376
Schiffman, 84
Schnoor, Jerald L., 46–78
segmentation, in agriculture, 2, 3, 4–5, 10–11
setback requirements, 51, 59, 70, 82, 91, 202, 216–17
sheep and lamb production, 8, 11, 62–63, 65, 107, 111, 257, 349; grazing requirements, 8–9; zoonotic diseases, 106, 112, 113, 114, 115, 126–28
Shiga toxin, 112
Short Form 12 Health Survey, 89
Showers, Bill, 8
Sigurdson, S., 58
*Silent Spring* (Carson), 337
slaughter and processing plant workers. *See* meatpacking and poultrypacking workers
*Smell of Money* documentary (Berger and Bannon), 371, 374
Smith, Tara C., 105–40
Smithfield Farms/Corporation, 1, 93–96, 99, 144, 257, 264–65, 267, 271, 366, 380, 374
soil: acidification, 301; CAFO-related pollution deposition in, 301; conservation, 12; erosion, 9, 12, 34, 35–36, 339, 341, 364; fertility, 344; organic matter, nitrogen cycling in, 18–19, 20–21
Soil Conservation Service, 9–10
solar energy, cycling in ecosystems, 350
Southern Environmental Law Center, 181
soybean production, 19; for animal feed, 17, 35, 144–45; fertilizer requirements, 29
specialization, in agriculture, 2, 3, 4–5, 10–11, 15n12, 132
*Staphylococcus aureus*, 109, 116–17; LA-MRSA, 117, 119–20

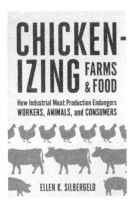

Milton Keynes UK
Ingram Content Group UK Ltd.
UKHW031451220824
447277UK00002B/2

9 781421 450407